RESOURCE NATIONALISM
AND ENERGY POLICY

CENTER ON GLOBAL ENERGY POLICY SERIES

CENTER ON GLOBAL ENERGY POLICY SERIES

Jason Bordoff, series editor

Making smart energy policy choices requires approaching energy as a complex and multifaceted system in which decision makers must balance economic, security, and environmental priorities. Too often, the public debate is dominated by platitudes and polarization. Columbia University's Center on Global Energy Policy at SIPA seeks to enrich the quality of energy dialogue and policy by providing an independent and nonpartisan platform for timely analysis and recommendations to address today's most pressing energy challenges. The Center on Global Energy Policy Series extends that mission by offering readers accessible, policy-relevant books that have as their foundation the academic rigor of one of the world's great research universities.

Robert McNally, *Crude Volatility: The History and the Future of Boom-Bust Oil Prices*

Daniel Raimi, *The Fracking Debate: The Risks, Benefits, and Uncertainties of the Shale Revolution*

Richard Nephew, *The Art of Sanctions: A View from the Field*

Jim Krane, *Energy Kingdoms: Oil and Political Survival in the Persian Gulf*

Amy Myers Jaffe, *Energy's Digital Future: Harnessing Innovation for American Resilience and National Security*

Ibrahim AlMuhanna, *Oil Leaders: An Insider's Account of Four Decades of Saudi Arabia and OPEC's Global Energy Policy*

Resource Nationalism and Energy Policy

VENEZUELA IN CONTEXT

David R. Mares

Columbia University Press
New York

Columbia University Press
Publishers Since 1893
New York   Chichester, West Sussex
cup.columbia.edu

Library of Congress Cataloging-in-Publication Data
Names: Mares, David R., author.
Title: Resource nationalism and energy policy : Venezuela in context / David R. Mares.
Description: New York : Columbia University Press, [2022] | Series: Center on Global
Energy Policy series | Includes bibliographical references and index.
Identifiers: LCCN 2022003660 (print) | LCCN 2022003661 (ebook) | ISBN 9780231202947
(hardback) | ISBN 9780231202954 (trade paperback) |
ISBN 9780231554794 (ebook)
Subjects: LCSH: Energy policy—Venezuela. | Energy industries—Political aspects—
Venezuela. | Nationalism—Venezuela.
Classification: LCC HD9502.V42 M26 2022 (print) | LCC HD9502.V42 (ebook) |
DDC 333.790987—dc23/eng/20220202
LC record available at https://lccn.loc.gov/2022003660
LC ebook record available at https://lccn.loc.gov/2022003661

Cover design: Noah Arlow
Cover image: Shutterstock

CONTENTS

Part II. Venezuela Case Study

ACKNOWLEDGMENTS

This book is the fruit of more than a decade working on distinct issues in the oil and gas industry and energy trade in Latin America. It is an extension of my work on Latin America's international relations. I am extremely grateful to Amy Meyers Jaffe for introducing me to the energy world and mentoring me through it at the James A. Baker III Institute for Public Policy at Rice University. I spent a sabbatical with her at the Baker Institute analyzing energy politics in Venezuela, Mexico, Bolivia, and Brazil, and we continued to collaborate after she moved on to the Council on Foreign Relations.

I am also the beneficiary of a close working relationship with Laurence Whitehead on the domestic politics of energy reform. His experience working on the politics of democracies proved a great help in thinking about how interest groups, institutions, and leaders interact around energy policy. Laurence hosted my sabbatical at Nuffield College and the Oxford Institute for Energy Studies. Anouk Honoré was generous with her time and helped me better understand the political economy of natural gas, while Kate Teasdale guided me through the accessing of the institute's valuable materials.

Sengen Zhang of the Chinese Academy of Social Sciences (Emeritus) facilitated many trips over a decade for me to interact with academics, analysts, and officials at the Institute for Latin American Studies, Chinese

Development Bank, China National Offshore Oil Company, and China Institutes of Contemporary International Relations regarding Venezuela and oil politics. My understanding of the Latin America–China energy relationship and its impact on energy policy making owes a great deal to these valuable interactions.

I was privileged to spend sabbaticals as a Visiting Research Fellow at the Oxford Institute for Energy Studies (2013), Visiting Fellow at the Inter-American Dialogue (2012), and Visiting Fellow in Energy Studies at the Baker Institute (2007). I also served as a member of the Energy Working Group, Inter-American Dialogue, funded by the Inter-American Development Bank during 2010–2014. I have been fortunate to continue my ties with the Center for Energy Studies at the Baker Institute as a Nonresident Scholar for Latin American Energy Studies and benefit from discussions with Peter Hartley, Francisco Monaldi, and Kenneth B. Medlock III.

The late Ramón Espinasa and Osmel Manzano of the Inter-American Development Bank, and others whom I have thanked privately because of their need to remain anonymous, helped me understand the oil and gas industries and the role of foreign investment, and to appreciate the legal frameworks within which energy policy is made.

I thank the following graduate students who served me well as research assistants: Addison Blair, Katherine Collins, Esteban Ferrero-Botero, Matthew Heiden, Remington Krueger, Sofia Lana, Jazmín Martínez, Ashley McWhorter, Aleister Montfort, Bryn Philibert, Amanda Singh, Nancy Turtletaub, and Weijun Yuan.

I benefited immensely from critiques received at seminars on early drafts of my project at the Buffett Center for International and Comparative Studies, Northwestern University; the Latin American Studies Center, University of Chicago; El Colegio de Mexico; the Center for Latin American Studies, Nankai University; China Foreign Affairs University; BRICS Study Center, Fudan University; the Council on Foreign Relations; China Development Bank; and China National Offshore Oil Company.

Useful comments were received on papers presented at workshops and conferences, including "The Legacy of Plenty: State Capacity and Institutional Legacies After the Resource Bonanza," King's College London; the Petroleum Forum cosponsored by the U.S. Embassy and the Ecuador Section of the Society of Petroleum Engineers (SPE), Quito, Ecuador; "The Governance of Unconventional Gas Development Outside the United States of

America," World Bank Institute, Washington, D.C.; "China's Green Energy Experience in Latin America," Shanghai Forum, Shanghai, China; "Mexico's Energy Reform," Nuffield College, Oxford University; "Resource Nationalism and National Oil Companies in Latin America," Geopolitics of Energy Project, John F. Kennedy School of Government, Harvard University; "Geopolitics of Gas," Rice University; "Geopolitics of Natural Gas," John F. Kennedy School of Government, Harvard University; "The Future of Oil in Mexico," Oxford University; and "The Changing Role of National Oil Companies in International Energy Markets," Japan Petroleum and Energy Council, Tokyo.

I also continue to benefit from the intellectual partnership with my wife, who for over forty years has served as a sounding board in the development of my projects.

As always, any errors of fact or interpretation are my responsibility. I look forward to ongoing dialogue with colleagues on the model and analyses presented here.

ACRONYMS AND ABBREVIATIONS

AA	association agreement
AD	Acción Democrática
ANH	Agencia Nacional de Hidrocarburos
ARI	Advanced Resources International
bcfd	billion cubic feet per day
bpd	barrels per day (alternatively, b/d)
BP	British Petroleum
CAPN	Control de la Administración del Petróleo Nacional
CEPE	Corporación Estatal Petrolera Ecuadoriano
CIF	cost, insurance, and freight
CNP	Conselho Nacional de Petróleo (National Petroleum Council)
CNOOC	China National Offshore Oil Company
CONAIE	Confederación de Nacionalidades Indígenas del Ecuador
COPEI	Comité de Organización Política Electoral Independiente
CORDIPLAN	Oficina Central de Coordinación y Planificación
CVP	Corporación Venezolano de Petróleo
CVT	Confederación de Trabajadores de Venezuela
Ecopetrol	Empresa Colombiana de Petróleos, S.A.
EIA	Energy Information Administration
ENARSA	Energía Argentina, Sociedad Anónima
EOR	enhanced oil recovery
E&P	exploration and production
EPF	Empresa Petrolífera Fiscal

ES	energy security
FDI	foreign direct investment
Fedecámaras	Federación de Cámaras y Asociaciones de Comercio y Producción de Venezuela
FIDES	Fondo Intergubernamental para la Descentralización
FIEM	Fondo de Inversión para la Estabilización Macroeconómica
Fonden	Fondo de Desarrollo Nacional
Fondespa	Fondo para el Desarrollo Económico y Social del País
ICBF	Instituto Colombiano de Bienestar Familiar
ICO	Interconnexión Centro Occidente
IEASA	Integración Energética, Sociedad Anónima
IESA	Instituto de Estudios Superiores de Administración
IFI	international financial institutions
IGO	intergovernmental organization
IMF	International Monetary Fund
INTEVEP	Instituto Tecnológico Venezolano del Petróleo
IOC	international oil company
IOSC	Integrated Oil Service Contract
IPC	International Petroleum Corporation
IRA	independent regulatory agent
ISI	import substitution industrialization
JV	joint venture
LNG	liquified natural gas
LPG	liquified petroleum gas
MAS	Movimiento al Socialismo
MBR 200	Movimiento Bolivariano Revolucionario 200
mbpd	million barrels per day (alternatively, mb/d)
MVR	Movimiento Quinta República
NOC	national oil company
NGO	nongovernmental organization
OBM	Obsolescing Bargain Model
OPEC	Organization of Petroleum Exporting Countries
OSA	operating services agreement
PDVSA	Petróleos de Venezuela, Sociedad Anónima
PEG	Participación del Estado en las ganancias
PRI	Partido Revolucionario Institucional
PSA	production sharing agreements

ACRONYMS AND ABBREVIATIONS

PSUV	Partido Socialista Unido de Venezuela
RC	resource curse
RE	risk exploration
RN	resource nationalism
R/P	reserves to production ratio
RRR	reserve replacement ratio
SDFI	state's direct financial interest
SELA	Sistema Económica de América Latina y del Caribe
SENA	Servicio Nacional de Aprendizaje
SENIAT	Servicio Nacional Integrado de Administración Tributaria
SOE	state-owned enterprise
TCF	trillion cubic feet
UNOCAL	Union Oil Company
USAID	United States Agency for International Development
VAT	value added tax
WGI	Worldwide Governance Indicators
XCONST	Constraints on the Executive
YABOG	Yacimientos Bolivianos Gulf
YPF	Yacimientos Petrolíferos Fiscales
YPFB	Yacimientos Petrolíferos Fiscales Bolivianos

INTRODUCTION

Resource Nationalism and the Political Economy of Energy Policy

Energy markets vary in response to constant shifts in supply. These shifts are often stimulated by extreme swings in the oil and gas policies of governments. Academic and business literatures usually explain and try to predict the policy changes by determining whether and to what extent a country displays the quality of *"resource nationalism"* (RN). Perusal of the arguments using RN, however, reveals an opaque concept that is used to describe government policies that hinder (for good or ill, depending on the perspective of the user) the exploitation of natural resources by private companies, rather than an analytically sharp tool to provide an explanation for policy choices. The purported causal variable (resource nationalism) thus becomes simply a descriptor.

But even as a description, "resource nationalism" hinders understanding because it is ill-defined and encumbered with political baggage. We encounter claims that policy X demonstrates that a government is becoming "more" or "less" resource nationalist; the implicit definition is that resource nationalism is state control over a natural resource, whether through state monopoly or strict controls on the private sector. Yet state monopoly has been on the decline for the past two decades, and there are few, if any, indications that governments are interested in returning to the days of state monopoly—even Hugo Chávez in Venezuela wanted partners. If RN is not state monopoly, however, how much "state control" constitutes RN? It is not unusual to see any change in government policy that increases government intervention in any country described as RN. But it is difficult to see the analytic utility of lumping a U.S. increase in offshore royalties,[1] a Norwegian requirement for domestic content in the development of an oil field,[2] a Brazilian constraint on which exploration and production (E&P) projects can be fully owned by foreign investors,[3] and an Argentine demand that foreign investors increase their investments into a concept of resource nationalism.[4]

A NEW POLITICAL ECONOMY MODEL FOR UNDERSTANDING CHOICES IN THE ENERGY SECTOR

If the concept of resource nationalism is to be analytically useful, it must be clearly defined and provide a basis, consistent with the characteristics of the definition, for understanding a wide variety of policies. The characteristic that best defines resource nationalism is, in fact, the ownership of subsoil and submarine layer resources: resource nationalism means that subsoil and submarine resources belong to the nation while they are in the ground/under water. Resource nationalism is thus a legal concept, not a mode of behavior, nor does it require specific policies. This simple definition is far more analytically useful than definitions that assume a certain behavior of the government of that resource-owning nation and therefore suffer from either ambiguity or tautology.

Consider a resource nationalism definition based on the abstract and apolitical concept of the *landlord state*, which is a subset of *rentier state*.[5] According to this perspective, the government as landlord regulates access to the resource and appropriation of the value of the resource.[6] This formulation gives the landlord agency but not purpose. Without some assumptions about what the landlord wants from its ownership of the resource, we cannot go beyond the mere fact that any access to the resource requires the acquiescence of the landlord, who will demand a fee (monetary or otherwise) for that access.

What the landlord desires in return for that acquiescence can vary across a wide range that spans enriching top office holders to saving it all for the benefit of future generations. Specifying landlord interest requires building a model about the landlord's preferences, whether that model remains at the level of an abstract state or incorporates domestic politics (which can be influenced by international actors and state bureaucracies).[7] A number of analysts use the fact of national ownership of subsoil resources and the concepts of "landlord" and "state" to justify or condemn government control over access to the resource or acquisition of some significant portion of the value of the resource. That behavior is thus alleged to constitute resource nationalism, with positive or negative connotations depending on how one judges the goals and behavior of the government. (See subsequent discussion.) Positive interpretations see appropriation for the "common good," while negative ones see the appropriation as rent seeking to reward itself and its constituencies at the expense of the common good.[8]

But if we define *resource nationalism* in accord with some definition of how those resources are used, we ground the concept in contested debates about those uses and the metrics for evaluating their implementation. Ultimately, we want to discuss use and metrics, but a number of factors determine government behavior, among which national ownership of the resource may not be the most important. Consequently, it is more analytically useful to separate the concept of ownership from that of policies and uses.

Defining RN simply as national ownership of subsoil and submarine resources puts the analysis of energy policy squarely in the court of politics. Because these resources belong to the nation, the nation has a legitimate call on some undefined share of the value of that resource. The value of the resource, however, is not inherent but determined by the market in which it is offered for exchange in the present with a discounted value for the future. The terms of that exchange will vary in line with the dynamics in that market. How much of a share of that value the owner of the subsoil resource receives will be determined by what that owner must do to bring the resources to market and her plan for how to use the wealth appropriated. Whoever helps the subsoil owner achieve that market value will demand a share in the realized value. These bargaining dynamics are discussed in chapter 1, but it is important to note here that mere ownership of the resource does not determine the conditions of a "legitimate" bargain. Hence resource nationalism as I have defined it is not the key driver in these bargains.

A new political economy model for understanding choices in the energy sector using the narrower definition of RN described earlier allows political goals to be included in the analysis and evaluated in their own right. A government that claims to represent the nation (as any democratic and many nondemocratic governments do) has a legitimate call on those resources and the revenue they generate only if it utilizes them for the benefit of the nation (i.e., public goods, particularly related to development and to the alleviation of poverty) rather than as private goods (e.g., patronage or corruption). Similarly, exploration and production of the resource in a manner consistent with resource nationalism would promote current production in a sustainable manner that maximizes the resource benefits to the nation across generations. These are normative parameters consistent with national ownership of a resource. RN can be legitimated only by recourse to some concept of responsibility, otherwise any "landlord" can do what it wants with the resource.

There is an economic literature on the most efficient depletion path for nonrenewable natural resources,[9] but this is not what I mean by sustainable development. The benefit to future generations of the nation of "efficient" depletion is to invest the resource wealth in creating alternative means of generating wealth after the nonrenewable resource has been effectively depleted.[10] In short, the benefit to the nation is not measured by the level of natural resource wealth appropriated by the government, but by how the government utilizes however much wealth is appropriated. Under conditions of resource nationalism, *appropriation of natural resource wealth is simply a means for attaining sustainable national development.*

Defined simply by legal ownership of the resource, there is no distinction between "legitimate" and "illegitimate" resource nationalism. Resource nationalism gives governments, as representatives of the nation, the responsibility to ensure that the nation profits directly from the exploitation of its resources, and not merely as a byproduct of the private wealth garnered by some of its citizens or foreigners operating in the country. That special responsibility deriving from the legal regime then interacts with geology, economics, and politics to determine public policy toward the resource sector. Resource nationalism thus neither describes nor determines policy but is a foundational factor in the development of natural resource policy. Those policies themselves may be classified as "legitimate" or "illegitimate" depending on their fidelity to the government's obligation to utilize resource wealth for the benefit of the nation.

Resource nationalism defined as national ownership of the resource is the dominant legal reality in the oil and gas world—only the United States and some Canadian provinces give surface property owners the rights to subsoil resources. But even in the United States, some subsoil and submarine resources are found on federal or state property, and thus the responsibility of the government to ensure that the people benefit from resource extraction is present. Consequently, the definition of resource nationalism offered here is globally relevant.

As one of several factors, resource nationalism's weight in determining policy varies across time and place. Geology, markets, politics, and the legal regime for natural resources (RN) combine to determine *the varied level of government intrusiveness into the marketplace to capture some of the value generated by the monetization of the resource.* That value can be captured in the form of taxes imposed on profits of producers (who could be domestic or foreign private companies, companies owned by foreign governments, or its own state-owned enterprises, or SOE); dividends earned by the resource-holding nation's own SOE; and taxes and royalties on "rents" or "excess profits" generated by market volatility and the characteristics of specific natural resource deposits that influence the costs of producing the resource.[11]

Governments may seek to capture more or less of that value than would be optimal from an economic perspective. That variation in policy preferences can be explained by focusing on the interaction among three political variables—the *inclusiveness* of the political system, the *competitiveness* of the policy-making body, and the *leader's characteristics* in terms of risk acceptance and policy innovation. These three political variables combine with geology and markets to produce national oil and gas policy.

LATIN AMERICAN OIL AND GAS POLICIES

Latin America provides excellent case material for elucidating the reasons for development and change of energy policy across the spectrum of state-market relations. The region has experienced extreme policy swings over more than a century of oil and more recently natural gas production. Those wide swings have not settled down in the past few decades. Venezuela has the largest oil reserves and seventh largest gas reserves in the world, and its oil and natural gas policies over the past two decades provide the empirical data to test the argument. Venezuela broke its national oil company's (NOC) oil monopoly in the upstream during the early 1990s, a few years later offered extremely favorable terms to private investors to entice them to invest in the high-risk/high-potential extra heavy oil deposits in the Orinoco Belt, then progressively altered the contracts and put the NOC back in control a decade later. Under Hugo Chávez's Bolivarian Revolution, Venezuelan policy changes generated a significant negative impact on the productive capacities of the NOC and the fields, but they stopped far short of eliminating private and foreign participation in the oil sector. In natural gas, in contrast, the reforms of the Bolivarian Revolution reversed prior law to permit 100 percent private and foreign ownership of projects.

Venezuela's is a dramatic experience, but its extreme policy swings and wildly fluctuating energy outcomes are far from unique in Latin America. In Argentina, Carlos Menem used his first presidency (1989–1994) to continue the deregulation of the Argentine natural gas sector begun by the military dictatorship in the late 1970s and to privatize the NOC, Yacimientos Petrolíferos Fiscales (YPF). Foreign investment poured in, large reserves of natural gas were discovered, and the country became a major regional gas exporter to Bolivia, Chile, Brazil, and Uruguay. By 2001 the economy had collapsed (GDP fell 12 percent), natural gas prices were fixed, and the country would cease gas exports the following year and thereafter become an importer of gas and liquefied natural gas (LNG). Presidents Nestor Kirchner (2003–2007) and Cristina Fernández de Kirchner (2007–2015) significantly reregulated the energy sector and renationalized YPF in 2012.[12] In Mexico, oil and gas reserves grew exponentially under government monopoly in the late 1970s. The country decided to limit gas exports in expectation of a growing domestic market but developed into a major oil exporter in the 1990s. The domestic gas market outgrew Mexican supplies, and in 1995 the government broke the national monopoly in the mid- and downstream in an attempt to make the market more efficient. By the early 2000s Mexican oil reserves were falling quickly, and the country now faces the prospect of depleting its reserves by 2028.[13] Mexico struggled through a marginal energy reform in 2008, whose chief goal was to maintain the national monopoly, and in 2013 passed a constitutional reform to end that monopoly as a means of increasing reserves and production.[14] The current administration of Andrés Manuel López Obrador is making significant efforts to roll back the reform.[15]

Outside of the largest producers, other Latin American countries also exhibited extreme swings. Bolivia sold 51 percent of its NOC, Yacimientos

Petrolíferos Fiscales Bolivianos (YPFB), in the 1990s and deregulated the natural gas sector, attracted foreign investment, and became a major supplier of gas to Brazil and Argentina.[16] After riots related to energy policy drove out two presidents (in 2003 and 2004), YPFB was renationalized in 2006 and the sector reregulated; reserves fell, and Bolivia has had trouble meeting its export commitments since, but supply at home has supported the development of a domestic gas market. Criticized by many for pursuing "neo-extractivism," the Morales government began courting international oil companies (IOC) in search of new reserves.[17] Brazil's bleak oil and gas outlook in the 1970s pushed the government into supporting costly ethanol innovations; by the 1990s the government broke the NOC monopoly, partially privatized the NOC, and in the next decade experienced major oil and gas discoveries in ultradeep waters ("pre-salt"). The government responded to the scale of the discoveries by first suspending auctions in the pre-salt areas under the Atlantic Ocean, then in 2010 legislating a controlling role for its NOC in the exploitation of newly discovered oil and gas fields in the pre-salt, but not in other hydrocarbon basins. In 2017, confronting corruption in its NOC Petrobras and a reticence of foreign investors, Brazil began to liberalize the pre-salt regime,[18] and the country is now expected to have the largest growth in non-OPEC oil production outside of the U.S. Permian shale basin.[19]

CURRENT EXPLANATIONS FOR ENERGY POLICY

The social science and business literatures offer three prime candidates to explain the extreme variations in oil and gas policy and the performance of these domestic and regional energy markets: a resource curse (RC) resulting from the geological endowment of hydrocarbons; volatility in the global oil market; and political ideology of the government.

The "resource curse" literature claims that increases in revenue lead governments to intervene in the resource value chain with a focus on maximizing short-term appropriation of the wealth. This reliance on a source of wealth generated by foreigners who exploit the resource permits a government to distribute the largesse without becoming beholden to the domestic recipients. The resulting lack of powerful domestic interest groups independent of the government not only diminishes government accountability and increases rent-seeking, it undermines the growth of economic activities not directly tied to the natural resource, and thus the economy underperforms as commodity prices fluctuate.[20] This rent-seeking behavior undermines the productive capacity in the resource sector, the absorptive capacity of the economy through the associated "Dutch Disease,"[21] and the capacity of the state to administer the wealth in a manner that promotes political stability and sustainable national development.[22]

The RC argument explains the adoption of policies that lead to instability and economic crisis by dynamics that derive from the government being in some way financially dependent (variously defined) on natural resource–derived revenues, in particular oil or gas revenues.[23] David Wiens argues that the RC can be avoided only by having strong and accountable institutions that control government before the country becomes dependent on resource wealth or by no longer being dependent on natural resource revenue.[24]

But, as the historical literature on Latin America's oil policies demonstrates, even countries that produced little oil or gas or had few geological prospects for producing adopted policies typically associated with the resource curse. This fact strengthens the institutionalists' argument that it is not geology but institutions that drive behavior consistent with an alleged curse. Institutionalists argue that rather than a "curse," the phenomenon is more a "trap," conditional on the character of economic, social, and political institutions. In this sense they disagree with Wiens and see the correct institutions as exogenous to the curse. Nevertheless, institutionalists disagree about which institutions matter, how they matter,[25] or even how to classify outcomes.[26]

The resource curse literature focuses on "oil-rich'" countries (utilizing varying definitions) and the policies they adopt. Again, however, even countries that do not qualify as oil rich may adopt the same policies and experience similar positive and negative outcomes. We therefore have adoption of similar policies but without the alleged geological drivers, suggesting that adoption of these policies is determined by factors other than geology. The relevant universe of cases for studying the implications of natural resource wealth could therefore be expanded to include almost a dozen Latin American countries and decades of experience with state interventions into the oil value chain.

Volatility in the global oil market is another common explanation for extreme policy variation and the performance of domestic and regional energy markets. Volatility in oil and gas markets, with their long and expensive lead times for exploration and production, is exacerbated by governments' attempts to manipulate supply to boost prices or to deal with budget shortfalls. One can certainly see these patterns of boom and bust in the market, but they are not determinant of how a nation's energy policy responds, or even of how it uses its NOC. Some countries adjust well to the fluctuations, drawing on responsible indebtedness, moderate austerity, and moderate countercyclical spending to weather the downturn (e.g., Colombia, Peru, and Brazil). Other countries avoid austerity through inflationary countercyclical spending and ever-increasing indebtedness, thereby creating a debt crisis and diminishing the resilience of the national economy and society to weather the downturn and take advantage of the resource market recovery when it comes.[27]

Even in the midst of a terrible oil market, policies can strengthen the sector, and, conversely, at the height of a boom, policies can weaken the sector. Brazil's oil and gas policies in the 1990s provide an example of the former. Its NOC Petrobras developed into a technologically sophisticated and internationally capable company, and reforms for conventional E&P were sustainable when the market recovered in 2003. In contrast, during the tight oil and gas markets of 2003–2014, Argentine, Mexican, and Bolivian policies could not attract the necessary investment to increase reserves.[28]

More generally, it's certainly not the case that government intervention and the presence of an NOC inevitably produce erratic policies and terrible results. Norway's Equinor (formerly Statoil) is a premier company, despite its government's policies requiring foreign investors to utilize domestically produced supplies as well as domestic capital, technology, and skilled labor.[29] Petrobras's recent corruption scandals are not likely to transform the company into an ineffective and marginal partner in the global search for oil and gas.[30] Malaysia's Petronas effectively expanded its international partnerships as domestic reserves were depleted and improved its efficiency while generating additional sources of revenue to meet its national responsibilities.[31] Venezuela's NOC Petróleos de Venezuela, Sociedad Anónima (PDVSA) used the context of a bust in the oil market to become a major oil company. California may have inefficient energy policies regarding oil and gas drilling and the location of LNG terminals because it prioritizes environmental and social issues, but these policies have been stable, and, apart from the power shortage of 2000–2001, the state's energy markets that fuel its powerhouse economy have not been crippled by these choices.[32]

Other analysts have argued that the political ideology of the government, leftist versus rightist or authoritarian versus democratic, largely determines policy choice, with energy policy simply a subset.[33] But there is a great deal of empirical and theoretical work that demonstrates that political institutions and processes produce significant divergence along a pro-market to statist continuum within Latin American left-wing governments' economic policies.[34] For example, leftist governments did not make laws requiring NOC majority control over oil projects retroactive in Brazil but did in Venezuela; did require majority control over gas projects in Bolivia but not in Venezuela; and did convert all E&P contracts into service contracts in Ecuador but not in Argentina. In addition, a rightist government in Mexico reaffirmed national monopoly in the oil sector, and a leftist government in Argentina reaffirmed open access to oil and gas. As the historical chapter will demonstrate, the alignment of ideology and energy policy choices diverges frequently.

An overview of the Latin American experience in general from roughly the mid-nineteenth century to 1990 allows us to see that there is a puzzle to be solved: What accounts for the wide variation in oil and gas policies both within countries and across the region, as well as within and across eras? The answer in in-depth study of four governments in Venezuela from 1989–2016 provides data for evaluating my political economy model. The variety of policy choices within and across those governments enables us to have confidence that the three political variables in my argument have a significant impact on oil and gas policies, and that these policies have consequences for national development as well as for the international market.

Explaining these policy variations requires that we look beyond the misleading rhetoric of "resource nationalism versus markets" or left versus right and refrain from positing an inherent relationship (positive or negative) between resource nationalism and energy security or resource nationalism and national development. The puzzle is not only of intellectual and scholarly interest. Governments across the globe, multinational energy companies, and citizens everywhere are confronting challenges in energy markets today that are conceptualized as a struggle among the resource nationalism of important exporting countries, the energy security concerns of consumers in both importing and exporting countries, and the profit demands of private firms. A better understanding of the dynamics of energy policy can promote broad-based national development and contribute to a more positive and sustainable relationship among consuming and producing nations.

In this book I seek to explain (1) the determinants of national oil and gas policies, as well as (2) whether the policies adopted are consistent with the expected contribution of the oil and gas sector to national development strategies, as required under the responsibilities of resource nationalism. My perspective is based on the observation that natural resource endowment and international constraints are significantly underdetermining of national energy policy. In addition, I assume that the domestic institutional context constrains choices except in revolutionary times, which are defined as the rebellion of significant parts of society against those institutions. Postrevolutionary societies, in consequence, are constrained by the new institutions they installed.[35] Thus we should understand institutional constraints in terms of the willingness of social groups to abide by them, rather than as exogenous variables themselves. I argue, consequently, that three key political variables are fundamental in understanding oil and gas policy: the *inclusiveness* of the political system, the *competitiveness* of the policy-making body, and the innovative and risk-averse *characteristics of individual leaders*. Whether the oil and gas policies contribute to national development strategies is determined by whether those policies produce sustained development of the energy sector and that national policies utilize the sector's wealth for public goods.

RESEARCH DESIGN

The study is informed by social science and business literatures because answering questions about causation requires a good understanding of the empirical phenomenon being studied, in our case, the oil and gas industry. I first define terms broadly utilized but differently understood to provide a coherent tool chest for rigorous analysis. I also highlight relevant characteristics of the oil and natural gas value chains and note the public policy challenges for an energy policy. A historical overview of the region from 1862 to the 2000s demonstrates the puzzle: a wide variation in oil and gas policy choices that do not correlate well with the three common factors purportedly driving policy, that is, geology, markets, and ideology. Drawing on literature regarding government provision of public goods, I then develop my hypothesis that oil and natural gas policy may best be understood as resulting from the variables of inclusiveness of the political system, competitiveness of the deliberative body, and leadership characteristics.

The political economy model of energy policy making is evaluated through a theoretically driven, structured, and focused comparison of Venezuelan oil and gas policies across four Venezuelan administrations from 1989 to 2016. These presidential administrations encompass two political systems, the Punto Fijo (1958–1999) and the Bolivarian Revolution (1999–present). I begin in 1989, when oil prices were still low following their collapse in the early 1980s, proceed through their historic peaks in 2008, and continue through 2016, when oil prices had fallen significantly once again. Each case examines how the three political variables as well as the geology and economics variables played out over time, including their interactions, and the variations in oil and gas policy are tracked against the hypotheses generated from the model. The model generates surprising hypotheses about common and contrasting policies among the four administrations that dispute many contemporary analyses of Venezuela since the election of Hugo Chávez in 1998.

Primary source materials include memoirs of relevant actors, company documents, and government documents. Secondary sources include biographies; published interviews with major industry and government leaders; literature from history, economics, sociology, political science, and business; and think-tank working papers. Research was carried out in Argentina, Bolivia, Brazil, Mexico, and Venezuela, as well as in Washington, D.C., Beijing, and Oxford.

PART I

Energy Policy and Resource Nationalism

Chapter One

THE PARAMETERS OF NATIONALISM
AND ENERGY POLICY

National energy policy regarding oil and natural gas determines two fundamental issues: the role of the market and the distribution of the revenue that is generated from the exploitation of these natural resources. Other topics associated with energy policy, such as social justice, development, environment, and even climate change, have at their core either or both of these issues. Discussing these other important matters inevitably throws us back into questions concerning how much of a role the market should play and the criteria for distributing natural resource wealth.

RESOURCE NATIONALISM

Controversy over the distribution of the wealth generated by oil and gas develops from the nature of property rights in the sector.[1] In most of the world (only the United States and three Canadian provinces differ), subsoil resources belong to the nation.[2] The government, given its role (elected or not) as the leader of the nation, thus has special responsibilities to ensure that the nation profits directly from the exploitation of its resources, and not merely as a byproduct of the private wealth garnered by some of its citizens or foreigners operating in the sector. Portions of the wealth generated in the sector can be captured in the form of taxes and royalties imposed on third-party producers; dividends earned by the resource-holding nation's own national oil company (NOC); and special taxes on "rents" (also known as excess profits) generated by market volatility and the characteristics of specific oil and gas fields. Given the high costs and high risks inherent in exploiting oil and gas, the owner of the resource may want to use some of those potential rents to exploit the resource; that may mean selling those property rights to or sharing some proportion of the rents with those who can more effectively exploit the resource.

In the United States and some areas of Canada, the owners of the surface also own subsoil resources, and they may sell, lease to others, or exploit the resources themselves, singly or in partnership. Thus the wealth created by the exploitation of those privately owned resources is distributed through contracts among private actors, as well as through government tax policy. Even in these two countries, however, federal and state governments own properties with oil and gas resources (particularly in offshore waters), and here they seek to use their legitimate authority to benefit the nation regarding the distribution of the wealth generated by the exploitation of these subsoil and submarine resources.

Whether property rights lie with the nation or surface owners, governments can give market forces a greater or lesser role in determining the supply of hydrocarbons as well as the demand for them. There is no one-to-one relationship between ownership characteristic and the role of the market. Even the U.S. federal government can seek to limit the role of the market in the oil and gas sectors for domestic purposes, as it did by forbidding the export of oil between 1973 and 2016,[3] or regulating natural gas pipeline services from 1938 to 1992 and the wellhead price (i.e., price at which gas was sold to the market) of natural gas from 1954 to 1993.[4] The Department of Energy must approve liquefied natural gas (LNG) exports, and it has only recently begun to look favorably on them.[5] At the opposite end of the spectrum, nations where the state owns the subsoil resources at the federal and provincial levels can let the market determine supply and demand, as Argentina did during most of the 1990s and the United Kingdom does today.

The pattern for distributing the wealth generated in the sector and the role of the market are public policy choices. It is common among analysts, industry specialists, and journalists to categorize these choices in terms of their alleged "resource nationalism," leading to claims that specific nations are "more" or "less" resource nationalist or going through bouts of resource nationalism. The concept of resource nationalism, however, is inconsistently and poorly defined.[6]

In this book, I argue that *resource nationalism* (RN) is most usefully defined as a perspective about public policy regarding natural resources that is based on four interrelated claims: (1) the natural resources in the ground or under the sea are a "national patrimony"; (2) the proper usage of national resources is for the generation of public goods; (3) the government determines how the wealth generated from natural resources is used; and (4) sometimes the government uses the wealth for the generation of public goods and sometimes it does not. *RN thus provides legitimacy for government to intervene in the market but does not render any action taken by the government in its name appropriate. Only when public goods are produced can we usefully argue that a government is acting in accordance with the principles of resource nationalism.* Otherwise, and despite a government's rhetorical claims, a government is appropriating national wealth for private gain and thus not in accordance with resource nationalism. Despite the term *nationalism*, RN is not about whether foreign or domestic companies exploit the resource since what matters is the use of the wealth for sustained national development. Foreign companies that pay high royalties to the national authorities who then use that revenue for the provision of public goods adhere to resource nationalism more than domestic companies that pay excessive wages, purchase domestically produced high-cost and low-quality inputs, and pay high taxes and royalties that are distributed by the government in patronage and corruption.

In my conceptualization, resource nationalism either exists or does not; policies adopted in its name are what vary across time and place. I seek to explain the way resource nationalism is manifested in oil and gas policy. That manifestation is produced through the domestic political process; it is not inherent in the characteristics of RN. *Note that appropriation of the wealth in the sector by a government simply on the basis of being in control of the nation is* not *an expression of resource nationalism.* Such an assertion lacks the legitimizing claim that the resource belongs to the nation and that its proceeds must benefit the nation.[7] I will also demonstrate that the particular manifestation, and not resource nationalism itself, is what accounts for successful or failed national development.

My reconceptualization of resource nationalism differs significantly from that of other analysts. Resource nationalism is often used as a rhetorical device to condemn or praise depending on the user's ideology or as a purported explanatory variable with ambiguous content. The phrase can be used without definition, apparently assuming that the reader knows,[8] or, as Pryke notes, "with descriptive value, but little analytic purchase."[9] For example, many analysts define resource nationalism as simply "government control" over the upstream (exploration and production) phases of the sector,[10] or efforts to limit private enterprise and assert more government control in the sector,[11] or "resource policies . . . designed to direct economic activity in the mining and energy sectors . . . towards politically defined national goals."[12] Stevens recognizes that there are many competing definitions of RN and offers one in line with his focus on the NOC-IOC relationship: RN consists of limiting operations of international oil companies (IOCs) and seeking greater national control over resource development. He also claims that RN has "self-feeding cycles" and that Canada and Australia are "often" used as examples of RN.[13]

Other scholars believe it is necessary to bring in some sense of national benefit: "the desire of the people of resource-rich countries to derive more economic benefit from their natural resources and the resolution of their governments to concomitantly exercise greater control of the country's natural resource sectors,"[14] or "the idea that natural resource wealth should be used for the benefit of the nation."[15] Interestingly, Cawood and Oshogoya see no need to include government in a definition that focuses on national benefit, arguing that what all definitions have in common is "a sovereign claim on resource assets by citizens of a mineral rich country, in which this claim must deliver maximum benefits to them."[16]

With such broad definitions, however, even the U.S. government could be categorized as a resource nationalist state since, in addition to what I already mentioned, it regulates private companies' exploitation of natural resources via environmental regulations, and in 2005 it effectively killed an effort by China National Offshore Oil Company (CNOOC) to acquire Union Oil Company (UNOCAL).[17] Actually, Bremmer and Johnston do reference "emerging" resource nationalism in the United States.[18]

Resource nationalism may also be defined with assumptions about providing public goods (e.g., "government actions to extract the maximum developmental impact and value from a country's natural resources for its people"[19]). Alternatively, a definition of resource nationalism can bring in all the elements found in the literature: "*the maximization of public revenues;*

the assertion of strategic state control (ability to set political or strategic direction to the development of the sector); and enhancement of developmental spillovers from extractive activity."[20] But these efforts to combine policies and goals in which authors believe lapse more into description or prescription than contribute to systematic analysis.

In the conclusion to their edited volume, Haslam and Heidrich propose classifications of limited-moderate-radical RN and provide metrics for evaluating the three levels.[21] But the argument does not hold together because they do not provide a systematic argument about the relative weights of the various components listed under each criterion nor an argument about the interactions among these criteria. Mexico is classified as "limited RN" despite the fact that its reform in 2013 reaffirmed state ownership of subsoil resources and only moves the country marginally away from the monopoly over the entire oil value chain that it maintained from 1958 to 2013. Pemex, the NOC, was given E&P rights to 85 percent of Mexico's known reserves, with the government entitled to provide it with more.[22] Although private investment was now permitted, no concession contracts were allowed, and the legal framework of the reform gives the president the ability to overturn many of its components at will.[23] The government's policy toward the sector discussed using oil as the basis of national development and continued its short-term revenue maximization for the public budget, thus starving the NOC of capital to perform its state-assigned functions; Pemex is the most indebted NOC in the world because of its subordination to Mexican governments.[24] Haslam and Heidrich classify the Morales government in Bolivia as radical RN, and though the government certainly was radical, it nonetheless negotiated a deal with foreign investors for access to the country's lithium reserves that provoked demonstrations against the low royalties and lack of domestic content, forcing the Morales government to rescind the deal.[25] In 2016 the government also began adjusting contracts and tax incentives to attract more foreign direct investment (FDI) into the declining gas sector.[26] One might wonder why this behavior does not fall into the "limited resource nationalism" category rather than the radical one. Venezuela's Bolivarian Revolution constitutes a radical government, but its hydrocarbon policy is radical only in oil since the Chávez Natural Gas Law, though claiming ownership of the resource, permits up to 100 percent private ownership of natural gas activities throughout the value chain, including the upstream.[27]

Nevertheless, granting Chevron the right to international arbitration to woo it into a joint venture with Petróleos de Venezuela, Sociedad Anónima (PDVSA, Venezuela's NOC) violates the usual view of sovereignty within radical critiques of FDI.[28] In addition, the left's critique of "neo-extractivism" and permitting any production sharing with private capital means that, from that perspective, the Bolivarian Revolution was left but *not* radical.[29] Consequently, there is no clarity on what constitutes limited, moderate or radical RN.

Bremmer and Johnston define RN as efforts to shift control of the energy sector to the government and its NOC.[30] But "control" is not well defined, since it includes any fiscal measures imposed by government. The definition led them to claim in 2009 that RN was "rampant" in Canada and Britain and "emerging" in the United States and Australia. The authors also claimed that there were at least four variants of RN (revolutionary, legacy, economic, and soft), with no systematic effort to distinguish them using common metrics nor to indicate where one might find "other" variants.

Definitions emphasizing the national benefit of these alleged resource nationalism policies encounter problems since "maximum appropriation" of value from the sector or maximum developmental impact is usually measured by short-term goals without analysis of the medium- or long-term outcome. The determination of a "strategic sector" is also simply left to government fiat; even within nationally owned hydrocarbons, natural gas and petroleum are often treated differently by the same government.

If efforts to promote national development are integral to the concept, governments that exert influence in the sector in the name of the citizenry but provide private goods (e.g., rewards for political partisans or domestic content regulations that benefit a few businesses and their unionized labor force at the expense of higher oil costs to the economy) should reasonably be excluded from the category of resource nationalism.

But analysts working within the "national benefit" perspective never undertake such an analysis. Ex post, many of these same cases of governments ostensibly promoting national development feed the "resource curse" literature about natural resource revenue and underdevelopment when their negative implications come to fruition and the country collapses into economic and political crisis. Since policies labeled "resource nationalism" sometimes promote and often undermine national development,[31] we should *take the outcome of resource nationalism as variable rather than making it an integral part of the definition.*

All this ambiguity naturally leads to a conclusion that there are many resource nationalisms and a proliferation of adjectives to describe them. In addition to the four offered by Bremmer and Johnston and the three by Haslam and Heidrich discussed earlier, we have "hybrid RN," "subnational resource nationalism," "people-based resource nationalism," and undoubtedly many others.[32] All these seem to be attempts to tailor definitions of who is a resource nationalist to particular situations but at the cost of analytical clarity for the concept.

In short, resource nationalism is usually defined tautologically—a policy outcome (e.g., an increase in royalties) or declared intent (e.g., to benefit the nation) is used to label a government "resource nationalist." Weak definition, however, muddles analysis of how resource nationalism affects energy policy. It is incumbent on analysts who seek to use the concept to provide conceptual clarity if it is to be analytically, rather than simply rhetorically or politically, useful. My definition provides a clear and coherent foundation for embarking on a systematic analysis of energy policy and understanding what role, if any, ownership of natural resources plays in that policy.

The manifestation of resource nationalism can be most fruitfully classified in terms of intervention in the oil and gas value chain discussed in the next section. That intervention can be direct, such as when an NOC explores and produces oil, or indirect, via regulation. Those regulations can be for inputs into production (capital, labor, equipment), valuation of the projects and companies involved in production, or intended to have a direct impact on demand (e.g., via price controls).

The rationale that national ownership of the resource implies and requires national benefit has a legitimizing foundation in property rights and national purpose. For example, *Norway Petroleum*, the information site run in cooperation by the Ministry of Petroleum and Energy and the Norwegian Petroleum Directorate, states that "revenues must accrue to the Norwegian state and thus benefit society as a whole. *Since these resources belong to society as a whole*, the Norwegian state secures a large share of the value creation through taxation and the system known as the State's Direct Financial Interest (SDFI) in the petroleum industry."[33]

Resource nationalism thus cannot be simply a means by which government leaders might enrich themselves and their cronies by selling the resource. Again, what distinguishes government appropriation of some portion of the natural resource wealth as resource nationalism rather than simply predatory rent-seeking behavior is their grounding in the legal fact of national ownership and the responsibility of governments to use those national resources for the benefit of the nation.[34]

This purpose is pursued through government setting the terms for exploration, production, transportation, and distribution of those resources. If the government fails to deliver on its task, its failure calls into question the government's commitments and skills, not the nation's property rights or the government's responsibilities with respect to those property rights. Thus development success or failure is not attributable to a resource nationalism perspective but rather to the manner in which that perspective has been translated into public policy and the conditions under which it has been implemented.

RESOURCE NATIONALISM, THE OIL AND GAS VALUE CHAIN, AND POLICY VARIATIONS

Variations in energy policy do not signal a departure from resource nationalism since the nation remains the owner of the resource. But variations in policy are fundamental determinants of whether government policy is utilizing the national resource for the benefit of the nation, irrespective of the geological situation of the country, the state of the international market, or the historical legacies of a particular country. To think analytically about those policy variations, we need to begin with the oil and gas value chain—that is, an understanding of how all the components of the industry come together, from initial exploration to final consumption. Figure 1.1 illustrates the three components of that value chain: the upstream (exploration, field development, and production), midstream (transportation, processing for gas, as well as storage and distribution for both), and the downstream (refining for crude oil and petrochemicals, wholesale and retail marketing for oil and gas).

Different parts of the value chain can prosper temporarily even if public policy negatively impacts other parts. The government's promotion of national wealth and national development built on the nation's ownership

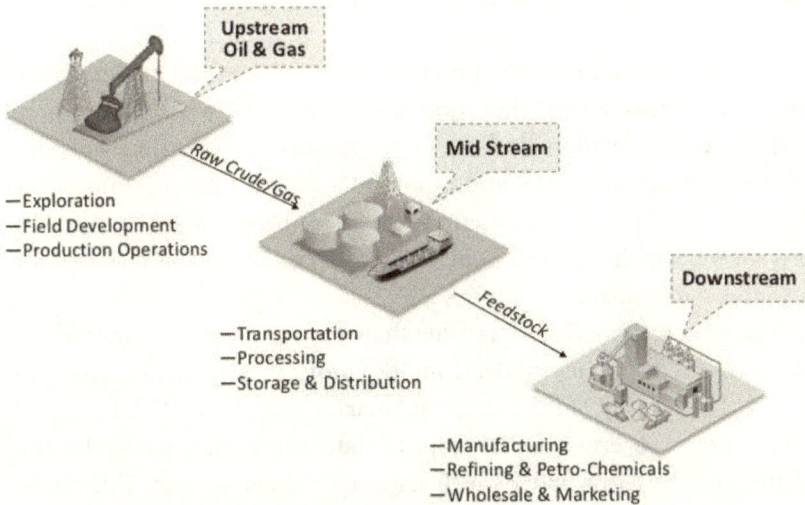

FIGURE 1.1. The global oil and gas value chain. Reprinted from Theo Acheampong, "The Global Oil & Gas Industry: Prospects & Challenges in the Next Decade," October 10, 2012, https://www.slideshare .net/theoacheampong/theo-acheampong-presentation.

of these subsoil resources, however, will depend on the government's ability to stimulate sustainable development of the oil and gas sector across the entire value chain. In addition, public policy must appropriate a level of wealth consistent with sustainable development of the sector and utilize the proceeds for public goods.

There is a continuum along which we can array the various means by which the government may take responsibility for creating value in the oil and gas sector in order to provide public goods for the nation. The range extends from total responsibility to minimal (but not total abdication), and in between we find various types of contractual arrangements between governments and private investors in the areas of production, transportation (pipelines and even tanker trucks), distribution, and secondary production (gasoline and other petroleum derivatives, petrochemicals, and power generation) and retail. *Total responsibility* means a state monopoly on the development of the sector and appropriation of the wealth for public goods; *minimal responsibility* reflects a decision to limit "government take" to the level of general corporate taxes outside the sector and merge those taxes into the general government budget that provides public (as well as private) goods. *Total abdication* of responsibility would mean either no appropriation of any wealth from nationally owned resources or total allocation of such revenues to private goods; the logic of resource nationalism does not recognize the legitimacy of either of these measures, so total abdication falls outside the range of resource nationalism. Note that, by definition, government policy dealing with private ownership of the resources is not relevant to the discussion of resource nationalism.

Table 1.1 uses the oil and gas value chain to summarize the range of variation in energy policy under conditions of resource nationalism (i.e., national ownership of subsoil and submarine resources). We can usefully group those concerns into the scope of state control (i.e., across the value chain) and the terms under which state and market interact. This classification permits us to distinguish among those who agree that the resource belongs to the nation but differ on whether the nation benefits most when market signals or state direction guides oil and gas policy. We can usefully label the former "pro-market resource nationalists" and the latter "statist resource nationalists."

Norway provides a good illustration of my argument about how energy policy under conditions of resource nationalism can be less rather than more intrusive in the sector but provide the basis for sustainable national development. The country is a resource nationalist country because it owns all its oil and gas deposits. It has a national oil company, has used its oil and gas wealth to develop the nation despite the hydrocarbons booms and busts of the past half century, and has used part of its oil wealth to develop

TABLE 1.1
Energy Policy Options Under Resource Nationalism

		Scope		
		Upstream	Midstream	Downstream
	Monopoly			
Terms	Direct state control			
	Tax and regulation			

the world's largest sovereign wealth fund, which itself has diversified away from hydrocarbon holdings.[35]

Using table 1.1, we can classify Norway in the upstream as choosing the option of tax and regulation, rather than a monopoly for a state entity or direct control over private actors. Norway's taxation policies focus on the companies rather than the oil and gas fields they operate because the government believes that the nation's resource wealth can be sustainably realized only if it is profitable for a company to produce. Total government revenue from the nation's oil and gas resources consists of (in order of importance since roughly 2003) taxes; the SDFI (a return on the state holdings in a number of oil and gas fields, pipelines, and onshore facilities); dividends from the NOC, Equinor (previously named Statoil); environmental taxes; and royalty and area fees.[36] "In 2017 the ordinary company tax rate is 24%, and the special tax rate (aka 'resource rent tax') is 54%."[37] This gives a marginal tax rate of 78 percent. "In 2016 the rates were 25% and 53% [and the government is concerned] to prevent the high tax rate from reducing the willingness of companies to invest on the Norwegian shelf."[38] Companies can carry forward losses on exploration or be reimbursed for them in the specific year in which they occur.[39] From this description we can see that the Norwegian government has designed its policy to take a direct and significant return on the nation's resources but in partnership with private partners whose need to earn competitive profits is taken into account.

Norway did not develop its industry with a focus on what private partners needed, but with a focus on how the country could maximize its participation in the energy bonanza. The country had domestic content requirements for sourcing and employment under its first two petroleum laws passed in 1972 and 1985. Section 54 of the Royal Decree of 1972 mandated that foreign companies give priority to Norwegian suppliers who were cost and quality competitive and made foreign companies responsible for ensuring that their foreign subcontractors complied with these terms as well. Technology transfer was pursued by requiring that at least 50 percent of research and development related to Norwegian fields was carried out in Norway with domestic partners. Companies were also required to train Norwegian workers and civil servants in their relevant areas of expertise.[40]

These domestic requirement regulations had been very successful. At the beginning of Norway's oil and gas boom in 1969, none of the goods and services in the industry were supplied by Norwegian companies, but by the 1980s, 60 percent of these products were sourced locally, with small and medium enterprises benefiting, and geographic dispersion of growth poles.[41] The long-term partnership between BP (British Petroleum) and Statoil helped the NOC learn to develop proprietary technology that it uses in its operations.[42] The domestic requirements began to ease only when Norway joined the European Economic Area in 1994 and the World Trade Organization in 1995,[43] and the Petroleum Act of 1996 finalized the transition.[44] Norwegian public and private companies are currently quite active in the export of oil and gas machinery and services and in the exploitation of oil and gas resources overseas.[45]

KEY CONCEPTS FOR THE STUDY OF THE OIL AND GAS INDUSTRY

Analyzing energy policy requires understanding a number of key terms and their implications: ownership of the resource, resource endowment, investment, rents, and the role of the market.

Ownership of the Resource

By historical tradition and political constitutions, all Latin American countries own the subsoil resources in their political jurisdiction (this includes offshore oil and gas). Although in the early to mid-twentieth century governments often transferred ownership of reserves to companies through oil concessions, the practice has been virtually eliminated in the region. Today ownership of these resources cannot be bartered or sold; depending on national laws, different legal structures (e.g., joint ventures, service contracts) might be permissible means through which parties other than the owner (the national or provincial government acting in the name of the country or province) may have access to the subsoil resources.[46] All countries in the world have similar ownership claims, except as noted previously, the United States and certain Canadian provinces.

Commercial Viability, Not the Mere Existence of a Resource, Is What Generates Wealth

There are rhetorical claims that the commodity itself has an intrinsic monetary value, not one determined by the market, and that this value belongs to the nation.[47] But although in the early days of the oil industry petroleum may have seeped from the ground or been found in easily tapped shallow reservoirs, the easy and high-quality oil has been depleted. Oil (and gas) is harder to find, of poorer quality, and harder to develop from difficult and costly reservoirs. The monetary value of that oil and gas, therefore, is dependent on its commercial viability.

Resource Endowment and Production Are Dependent on Investment

Reserves are divided into three categories: proved, probable, and potential.[48] *Proved* reserves (P1) are exploitable under current market conditions using current technologies; wildcat wells (drilling in areas where no oil or gas has been produced) are necessary to certify exploitation conditions. An oil reservoir does not yield all the oil in it due to geological conditions and technical limitations, so the *recovery factor* of a given field is a ratio of exploitable oil to total oil. *Probable* reserves (P2) are from known reserves that are not yet commercially viable but have at least a 50 percent chance of becoming so. *Potential* or *possible* reserves (P3) are from known reservoirs with less than a 50 but at least a 10 percent probability of becoming commercially viable. Governments and markets are also interested in a country's *reserves-to-production ratio* (R/P), which suggests how long the reserves would last if the country continued to produce at the same rate.[49]

From this description one should note that a country's resource endowment as well as its production depends on investment, which can be quite substantial. For example, Mexico calculated that it would cost US$38 billion dollars to fully develop its Chicontepec oil field, and the cost of just one well drilled in Brazil's pre-salt reservoirs can exceed US$200 million.[50] Investment could come from either public or private entities. Innovation and human skills are also key components in exploration and production, especially in technologically challenging situations (e.g., extra heavy oil in Venezuela in the 1990s, pre-salt reserves in Brazil, as well as shale oil and gas in Argentina today).

Investment Capital May Be Scarce and Always Has Opportunity Costs

Capital availability and price depend on the state of the international energy and financial markets, national budgetary priorities, and, to a lesser degree, the priorities of international development banks. The challenge of raising capital affects both IOCs and NOCs. Opportunity costs mean that projects are always competing with other uses for this capital, including buying back one's own stock or subsidizing domestic gasoline. For example, even as oil prices escalated to record highs from 2006 to 2008 (thus signaling the need to find additional energy sources), Exxon Mobil purchased its own stock to the tune of $32.6 billion in 2006 and $31.8 billion in 2007.[51] Opportunity costs affect governments as well. NOCs often find their E&P budgets slashed in favor of subsidizing domestic energy consumption, social programs, or patronage. Energy subsidies cost the Argentine government US$10 billion in 2011, even as private companies' investments in gas exploration dwindled because the subsidies were not sufficient to offset the low domestic price.[52]

Natural Resource Rents Are Economic, Their Distribution Political

Natural resource rents are theoretical constructs, best defined as "super" profits, that can only be realized by getting the resources to market. Market conditions determine the level of rents at any particular time, but distribution of rents falls in the political arena. Rents are calculated as "the payment to a factor of production over and above the sum necessary to induce it to do its work"—i.e., earnings above the costs of production plus a competitive rate of return to capital.[53] Prices are determined in a global market for oil and regionally or bilaterally for gas, but production costs per barrel of oil (including the cost of capital) vary widely by field and country; in Latin America they range from $1 to $15 a barrel for oil.[54] In these circumstances, the size of rents varies by field and can be quite high. But when the market is weak, no rents are produced—e.g., when oil prices fell to ~$10/barrel in the 1990s or in 2020.

Since rents are earnings beyond some determination of normal profit and ownership of the resource lies with the nation, the question of the distribution of those rents between the owner and the producer arises. Since the rent theoretically belongs to the owner of the resource, some analysts, politicians, and citizens argue that the nation should appropriate the entire rent. *But if the government needs a partner to bring the resource to market, that partner will bargain for access to a portion of the rents.* Thus, in practice, realized rents never belong 100 percent to the nation unless the government has a monopoly in the sector.

The distribution of rents is particularly conflicted when contracts have not been designed to deal with price volatility.[55] Rents are appropriated by the owner of the asset largely in five ways: fees, royalties, taxes, production sharing, and risk sharing; the combination comprises what is referred to as "government take."[56] (Other means of appropriating rents include dividends paid by NOCs, increasing a company's cost of business through redundant employment policies, domestic content requirements, responsibilities for social programs, bonuses, etc.) Utilizing the tax structure to capture rents is inefficient because of the information asymmetries concerning deductible expenses between the company and the government; the tax structure can also provide perverse incentives that lead a company to produce from higher-cost fields. While some analysts believe that the royalty is the key mechanism by which the owner of the resource can capture rents, since 2007 Norway has given up the royalty in favor of a special tax.[57]

Royalties nevertheless create their own problems when prices fluctuate significantly, as has been the case for oil since 1973. Consider the following simplified example, based on a 50 percent royalty. A price of $50/barrel with production costs of $15/barrel produces $25 for the government and $10 for the firm. When the price doubles to $100, the government gets $50 and the firm gets $35, meaning that the company has increased its profit by 250 percent, while the government has seen a substantially lower increase at 100 percent.[58] This disproportionate distribution of the additional rents produced by an increase in the market price will usually generate political demands from some sectors of society for the government to reconsider the contract, but not all governments will be amenable or vulnerable to those pressures.

How much rent a nation receives depends on many factors. The Obso-lescing Bargain Model (OBM), developed by Vernon and elaborated or modified by many others, tells us something about the process of nego-tiation between government and investor.[59] It accurately describes the advantages investors with capital, technology, marketing, and operational skills have when a nation initially seeks development of its natural resources. OBM also provides a framework for understanding the poten-tial modifications that can occur over time as those initial investor advan-tages dissipate and the nation's ownership advantage becomes more relevant, especially when prices rise.[60] The model's extension outside of natural resources into the product life cycle in manufacturing provided a basis for understanding cycles in oil bargains as the global market demanded more supply either to offset OPEC restrictions or to meet increasing demand. Thus "heavy" oil (higher sulfur content requiring special refining technol-ogy and equipment to meet increasing pollution restrictions), "deep" water production, tar sands, extra-heavy oil, and now shale oil and gas produc-tion all shifted the advantage back to investors, and the bargaining began anew. As evidenced by the extreme efforts of Saudi Arabia in the past few years to flood the market and depress prices to bankrupt U.S. shale pro-duction or Mommer's assertion in 2002 that there "cannot be any doubt that the country [U.S.] is running out of oil," many of these innovations are unforeseeable.[61]

But OBM neither provides an explanation of why some governments might prefer no deal if they cannot get their minimum terms nor explains why some pursue modification of the initial bargain and some do not, nor how much modification will be pursued. Answering those questions requires developing a model of the domestic drivers of policy. Ramamurti focuses on the role investor confidence plays in a government's development strategy and provides a long list of domestic and foreign interests that lead governments to adopt different development strategies. He makes an impor-tant point that bilateral bargaining between government and investor occurs in a context structured at the international level by negotiations involving states, international government organizations, and international financial institutions. But he leaves the domestic politics side of the resource nation out of his bargaining model.[62] Vivoda notes that the OBM does not just depend on prices but must incorporate the goals, resources, and constraints on both parties.[63] Nevertheless, his 2009 and 2016 analyses are dominated by prices because he offers no argument about the determinants of goals, resources, and constraints and how they come together to affect the bargain. He did offer the beginnings of a model in 2011 with a long list of actors and relationships that might potentially influence the decision to initiate rebargaining, the relative power of the dyadic actors, and the outcomes.[64] At the conclusion of this process, however, Vivoda can only call for the accumulation of rich empirical cases that might reveal sufficient data to inductively stipulate the key relationships and players. Rosales argues that state capacity is the key, and that some governments may face ideational and "structural" constraints on state capacity to enact policies that could shift the bargain in the government's favor.[65] His argument is rich in detail about the Correa government in Ecuador, but none of the propositions are developed in a manner that would facilitate examining them across the wide array of governments that have centralizing and authoritarian characteristics and underdeveloped state capacity.

This perusal of a wide literature adding factors to the basic OBM model is empirically rich but provides no testable propositions about which variables need to be added, when, and with what payoffs. My analysis in this book draws on the insights of the OBM regarding geology and price but is more systematic. I seek to bring analytic rigor to the argument of why a government would or would not adopt policies that shift the bargain with foreign or domestic investors in favor of the state. I present my causal model, develop hypotheses about government policy, and test it empirically.

The OBM focuses on state-foreign investor relations, but the distributional debate about sharing of rents also occurs with other states and within domestic society. Now that many NOCs are investing internationally, the distributional question can pit one government's interests against another's. For example, when Bolivia nationalized its gas fields in 2006, the company most affected was Petrobras, the Brazilian NOC. Even developed countries like the UK, Canada, and Norway forced private oil companies to renegotiate their production contracts when oil prices boomed.[66] Yet not all oil exporters did so, demonstrating that price is a factor but not the only one determining contract renegotiation.[67] The battle for rents is fought in still another arena, often overlooked by analysts focusing on international markets: within the producing country, between elite and poor, rural and urban, and a variety of other domestic distinctions that have political salience.

The distribution of rents also becomes an issue domestically when important sectors of society believe that they have not been getting their fair share or one commensurate with their development needs. When society questions the representativeness of their public agents, the question of appropriation of rents for private or public benefit can polarize politics and policymaking.

The issue of appropriation of oil and gas wealth, or who benefits from excess profits in the oil and gas sector, is of critical importance in resource nationalist polities. Oil nationalists generally comprise two groups, who battle between themselves to guide natural resource policy. There are statists, who believe in direct government control of the industry for purposes of distributing the resource to the citizenry in ways that maintain political support for the government. There are also pro-market oil nationalists who focus on making the sector and the NOC economically efficient in order to increase sustainable overall government take from the sector. Statists are concerned that some rents that could be funding national development or the political coalition in power are being appropriated by the private sector (foreign or national) for their own private gain. Alternatively, "pro-marketers" are more concerned that "excessive" government capture of rents will generate (more) corruption and undermine the long-term development of the sector to the detriment of the citizens. These are ceteris paribus descriptions; domestic politics will affect the manner in which statists and pro-marketers will seek to distribute that oil and gas wealth.[68]

It is worth highlighting that both pro-marketers and statists have proven quite willing to accept the appropriation of natural resource rents for private gain. When labor unions force producers (even if they are NOCs) to pay above labor market compensation, consumers demand the natural resource domestically at below market prices (e.g., gasoline, heating oil, electricity), or national politicians fund development projects with little public benefit, they, too are appropriating rents for private purpose. Some empirical examples are the Mexican oil workers union, middle-class automobile drivers in Venezuela, and gas-generated heating of Argentine middle-class homes. It would be far more efficient to provide public goods and target subsidies for helping the poor if the goal were to promote broad-based and sustainable national development.

Role of the Market

If we think about private and public determination of the terms of exchange (that is, market vs. government control) as arranged along a continuum, at one end is the total substitution of market forces by government control of production and distribution, while the total elimination of the state as an actor in the energy marketplace represents the other extreme. Note that, even in this latter situation, politics is not absent, since permitting the market such a wide latitude is a political decision. In between is a range of possibilities for the balance between market and government determination of the terms of exchange. For example, the market could set a general price for gas, and the government could provide targeted subsidies to people below a certain income level; in this instance the market plays a greater role in the domestic provision of gas than the government. Alternatively, the government could cap the price of gas and leave companies to scramble to drive down costs; companies that can do so remain in business, those that cannot close their doors. In the latter case, the role of the market is significantly subordinate to government policy.

When discussing Latin America, it makes sense to consider the role of the market in three arenas: the international, regional, and domestic markets. For the purposes of thinking about energy policy, such distinctions are important, although clearly each one of these markets is affected by events in the others. For example, in the 1980s Mexico and Venezuela exported oil on terms determined by the international market yet made a special arrangement to supply Central America with petroleum on politically negotiated terms and supplied their own domestic market at subsidized prices.[69] Thus while utilizing the price in the international market, both countries applied political considerations in setting prices in select regional and domestic markets.

KEY CONCEPTS FOR UNDERSTANDING
THE ROLE OF GOVERNMENT
Institutions of Government Matter

Government institutions (constitutions, laws, offices, and agencies) influence the content of legislation, the transparency of governmental behavior, the credibility of any commitments entered into by the government, and the incentives that lead people and firms to make the energy-related decisions they do.[70] Because countries vary in their institutions of government, the way in which the energy sector will be regulated also varies across countries.[71]

Government institutions similarly affect what resources constitute power and therefore which individuals and groups have influence. For example, before the new constitution in Bolivia gave indigenous communities veto over exploration in their geographic areas, the only way they could stop exploration and production was through physically blocking access; since the communities are small and dispersed, it was difficult for them to resist the police and the army. Evo Morales (2006–2019) is indigenous, supported a culturally sensitive agenda, and promoted a new constitution designed to empower indigenous communities. Nonetheless, he was often dismayed and forced to alter his development plans when small indigenous and rural communities protested against his government's efforts to implement neo-extractive policies.[72] Institutions also affect for whom government will make policy (their own private interests, those of partisans, or for the public good) through the incentives they provide politicians. In addition, institutions affect how much discretion governments have in implementing laws and abiding by contracts. An intertemporal commitment challenge arises when governments sign contracts that are binding on future governments, so ordinarily one would want minimal discretion permitted for overturning legal contracts.

The discretion issue, however, is more complex than a focus on the sanctity of contracts suggests. The individuals and companies that benefit from a particular interpretation want future governments to be constrained in reinterpreting those laws. But discretion can be a particularly contentious issue when reformists are elected by newly empowered groups in the expectation that they will use their discretion to alter the distribution of costs and benefits *under the law* (i.e., not rejecting or discarding the law) yet learn that they are far too constrained by institutions to do so. This situation can contribute to the development of new constitutions or major new legislation to force through changes that were theoretically possible under the prior institutional structure but were blocked by opposition groups, as occurred in Venezuela, Bolivia, and Ecuador in the past two decades. Since governments are "sovereign," international courts have minimal ability to sanction a state for changes in the fiscal terms of the contract; thus domestic institutions that make such changes more or less likely will have an impact on energy policy via this mechanism as well.[73]

Government Capacity Is Not Inherent but Needs to Be Developed

If the government is to carry out its roles effectively and efficiently in the energy sector, it must have the relevant capacity and skills. Geddes has defined these roles of government in a general sense, and they are relevant to energy policy: the ability to tax, coerce, shape the incentives facing private actors, and make effective bureaucratic decisions during implementation.[74]

Capacity doesn't imply having just the institutional right to the task, but also the skill and autonomy to carry it out effectively in the name of the public good. If government agencies depend on the agents whom they are supposed to regulate for the necessary information, their ability to carry out effective oversight will be diminished. By the same token, if government agencies are directly beholden to politicians for their positions or resources, they will be more likely to provide opportunities for patronage rather than public goods. This may be a particularly challenging task for a country seeking to exert more control over the oil sector because of, on the one hand, informational asymmetries favoring investors, but also because the government can be focused more on appropriating revenue quickly rather than building state capacity to effectively control the sector.[75]

In the context of energy markets, one of the key players from the public sector should be the Independent Regulatory Agent (IRA). To be effective, this agent should be independent so that it can constrain both the government and the private sector. Among the important tasks of the IRA should be to limit the ability of the government to starve the NOC of resources, use it for patronage purposes, or, if private actors participate in the market, use its powers to favor the NOC.[76] Consequently, institutional constraints on the discretionary scope of a regulatory agent are also important and will affect the credibility of contracts and therefore investment.

The importance of the IRA can be inferred from the varying performances of NOCs. A number of studies demonstrate that some NOCs have been efficient competitors with IOCs.[77] The studies highlight the importance of a proper institutional framework, viz, an independent regulator to insulate the NOC from rent-seeking politicians and ensure competition in exploration, production, and sales. Partial privatization of the NOC via the selling of stock (as Norway, Brazil, and Colombia have done, and Peru and Saudi Arabia authorized) or the opening up of exploratory blocs and productive fields without giving up managerial control (as Brazil in the pre-salt and Venezuela in all oil fields, though not in gas, undertook) will make the NOC more transparent, but, as the case of Petrobras demonstrated, it is not a guarantee against mismanagement and should not substitute for the independent regulator.

Public Goods, Public Services, and Private Goods

Public goods are characterized by two properties: nonrivalry and nonexcludability. Nonrivalry means that the consumption of the good by one person does not affect the ability of another to consume it, while nonexcludability means that it is very difficult, if not impossible, to keep someone from consuming the good even if they do not pay for its provision. Defense and clean air are examples of public goods. The power of such a classification comes from understanding that physical or technological characteristics significantly determine the provision and distribution of these goods.

Although most goods provided by government cannot meet the strict definitions of nonrivalry and nonexcludability, the basic idea that some goods are designed to benefit the country as a whole rather than specific groups is a powerful distinction by which to evaluate government behavior. Thus it is standard in political economy studies to distinguish between "pure public goods" and simply "public goods" or, alternatively, public services, which are provided by the government for the benefit of society as a whole.[78] Private goods, in the political economy sense, benefit specific groups (connected in some way to the government financing or allocating the goods) to the exclusion of others; hence they are also classified as "selective benefits." As Snidal notes, "the notion of exclusion is central to understanding the political aspects of public goods analysis."[79]

The identity of the national goal pursued (whether it be development, equality and social justice, or something else) is not key to the basic argument that the use of this wealth is legitimate to the extent that it provides public goods. Ranking of public goods demands varies by societies and will be affected by the national institutional structures that aggregate preferences within the political system. Which public goods are pursued with national wealth is thus not inherently fixed.[80] The implication of that fact for our purpose is that we cannot explain the rankings among public goods by reference to resource nationalism; we can only note whether or not they are pursued with the wealth generated by ownership of these resources.

Why isn't the correlation between natural resource wealth and the existence of national goals sufficient to claim resource nationalism? When the state budget is significantly dependent on mineral wealth (taxation and royalties) rather than on taxation of citizens, governments can determine the distribution of state-provided goods and services with a freer hand and less scrutiny.[81] Under some conditions, these revenues can underpin the political bargains that support democracy, which we can classify as a public good.[82] Yet often these conditions result in a distortion of the provision of public goods to cronies and clients, and to the detriment of the nation.

Government can therefore effectively privatize what should be a public good or service by providing it in ways that undermine its public goods characteristics—e.g., by funding public services not through a common budget and process that prioritizes need and contribution to national goals but through pork barrel log rolling.[83] Governments can also create private goods, such as when they assign rights and privileges to particular groups.

Governments in Latin America have often created private goods under the guise of generating public goods and services. During the 1950s–1970s Latin American governments and societies pursued import substitution industrialization (ISI) as a public good. It was believed at the time to contribute to the overall development of the economy, stimulate national technological and scientific innovation, improve trade imbalances, reduce wealth inequalities, and permit the government to increase funding for social services.[84] Government-sponsored ISI was thus theoretically a public good.

In support of ISI, governments legislated high tariffs on many manufactured products. The tariffs generated benefits for the owners of the firms and their labor force that produced these previously imported consumer goods. But the profits and wages in these ISI industries were subsidized by domestic consumers who paid higher prices for domestically produced (and usually lower-quality) goods. Primary product exporters in agriculture and mining faced increased taxation and an overvalued exchange rate to pay for necessary intermediate and capital goods for the industrial sector. When governments rationed foreign exchange, preferential rates to support ISI meant that the public purse contributed to subsidize ISI as well.

The situation for labor under ISI is particularly interesting from the perspectives of public goods in a labor surplus economy, a desire to reduce inequality, and promotion of social justice. Latin American governments advocated ISI partly through foreign exchange access and credit provision, which favored the import of labor-saving machinery. The labor unions in the protected industries (representing a minority of the labor sector) used their political influence to prolong import protection and public subsidies of the firms in which they were employed, hence creating a private good for these unions and their members.

In Latin America, these ISI firms overwhelmingly failed to become internationally competitive. ISI thus became a drag on rather than a stimulus to national development. Governments could not adjust ISI policies to meet the original goal because the political costs were too high.[85] Latin American economies crashed with the collapse of the 1970s commodity boom and 1980s international debt crisis, which had allowed them to sustain ISI policies.[86] So much for theoretical public goods.

ISI was not the only massive public goods program to go awry in Latin America. The commodity booms of the 1970s and early 2000s fueled another colossal failure. The international transfer of wealth from consumers to the producers of these primary commodities offered an opportunity for governments to significantly increase their provision of public goods. Government programs directed toward the poor to promote social justice and increase standards of living through improved health, education, and social welfare programs can benefit society and the economy as a whole if distributed efficiently, in a sustainable manner, and nondiscriminatorily within the poor. But nontransparent budgeting, minimal accountability for public and private operators and distributors of the services and products, and often political litmus tests to screen beneficiaries plague these government programs. For example, the provision and location of schools and health clinics may respond to partisan politics rather than their contribution to development or social justice, and the services themselves can be undermined through corruption. Public housing projects may be rife with graft and of such poor quality that their benefits lapse in the short to medium term. The public budget is often politically saddled with these programs even as they fail as public goods.[87] In these circumstances, what appear to be government investments in public goods are in actuality a means for private goods provision, which, once established, are politically difficult to terminate.

The Relevant Governance Structure for the Energy Sector

Governments seek to promote investment in the energy sector as well as further national development. In pursuit of these objectives, governments pass legislation, issue decrees, and sign contracts. The laws and agreements attempt to find common ground among competing interests: investors seek economic returns, and national development requires distributing a portion of those returns for public goods and generating linkages between enclave sectors and the larger economy.

Governance refers to a process by which actors beyond the government have a direct impact on the forms and rules guiding the specific arena under consideration, in our case, the oil and gas sector. Governance includes the public and private sectors, as well as civil society. It is operationalized through rules and institutions that are created by the interaction among these three categories of actors, though it can be effectively biased in favor of one actor. Governance is designed to conceptualize a rulemaking and rule-implementing context in which government does not impose its choice, but the relevant actors formally and informally negotiate the terms of the choice.[88]

Governance in the case of a natural resource is underpinned by the property rights associated with the resource. As noted, when subsoil resources belong to the nation rather than to the surface owner, the government has, in the eyes of its citizens, a legitimate responsibility to appropriate wealth associated with resource development. In a nondemocratic polity, the government claims the unique right to decide how the nation can best benefit from the use of its resources, while in a democracy the government has been elected by a broad electorate to make those decisions in its name.

Contrast the legitimacy of that governmental claim with those of a private firm or a civil society group. The private firm is relegated to contesting whether the fruits of its labor in getting the subsoil resource to the surface should convey ownership rights *at that point* and leveraging its financial and technological resources and operational skill to persuade the government to create the conditions that make it profitable to invest. This situation pits private profit against the national good, unless the firm can argue that production is difficult, if not impossible, in the absence of private initiative and that its profits will be "reasonable." Even a civil society actor or group finds it difficult to lay claim to the legitimate authority to decide how the national patrimony should be used, since it represents one interest group among many in the nation.

Given the special claim of a government in a resource nationalist state, governance structures will reflect the needs of the host government more than one would expect in a polity in which ownership of subsoil/submarine resources belong to the surface owner. But whether the governance structure in a national resource state produces public goods is not a foregone outcome. The democratic accountability of the government and the transparency of both its decision-making process and implementation of policy are prerequisites for governance to represent the priorities of the citizenry regarding the economic and environmental trade-offs inherent in the exploitation of its natural resources. Even democratic polities generate private goods and exclude some groups from the decision-making process.

Energy Security

Energy security (ES) embodies a claim for government action to protect national economic activity from shocks emanating from the international or domestic energy market. Adjustment to a price shock from the international market could be market based: decreased use of this resource via either increased efficiency or reduced activity and a search for alternative sources of energy. The time required for, and the difficulty of, increasing efficiency and developing alternatives creates adjustment costs that are not simply economic but also include social dislocation as jobs, consumption, and investment are affected; even political realignment or upheaval pursuant to a major social and economic adjustment process can occur. Therefore the usual response by governments to a significant external shock is not to let the market determine adjustment but to adopt public policies to mitigate at least some of those costs while market adjustment unfolds.

This defense of the domestic economy to an energy-related shock can be pursued via government regulation of private companies or consumers in national energy markets or through direct state provision of energy at subsidized prices. In either case, the policy goal of energy security implies subordination of other policy goals (e.g., production of food, environmental protection, or increased competitiveness of the national economy in world trade) to a more aggressive pursuit of domestic supplies, price controls, or trade restrictions. In the United States, for example, in the name of energy security the export of oil and natural gas was limited, domestic production of corn-based ethanol was subsidized, and there were high tariffs on the import of more efficient sugar cane–based ethanol. But even net oil and gas exporting governments can be concerned about energy security when they perceive competition between the domestic and international markets, as in Bolivia since 2006.

While the concept of energy security first came to the attention of publics in the United States and Western Europe after the Arab oil embargo of 1973, it is a longstanding concern in Latin America. Already in the 1920s the major countries in the region were concerned about it. As the international market began to shift into surplus in the late 1920s and the major oil companies colluded among themselves to protect market share, their production in high-cost Latin America (Venezuela was the only low-cost producer) declined.[89] These countries had to use scarce foreign exchange to meet domestic demand for crude or petroleum products at high oligopolistic prices, negatively affecting the domestic economy.

The argument about the opportunity costs of producing your own high-cost oil instead of importing it doesn't hold much sway with statists, particularly with respect to energy security. Producing oil at home is seen as a means of generating employment, subsidizing industrial development, and diminishing the threat of producer governments and their companies using access to oil to influence a country's policies.[90] Statists perceive that the defense of sovereignty and national development more than justifies the national economy paying higher costs for oil and petroleum products. In this sense, the energy security focus was one of the early harbingers of the import-substitution industrialization strategies that virtually all Latin American countries pursued to varying degrees from the 1930s through the 1970s.

In addition to these historical issues, today's ES concerns include, on the one hand, whether oil will be available in sufficient quantities in the future (known as "peak oil" debates) and, on the other hand, a growing concern for the environmental impact of hydrocarbons and a search for alternative sources of energy.

From the exporter's perspective, the ES issue is whether the demand for oil and gas, and hence national earnings, will be significantly reduced when a deep and global recession occurs, or if more environmentally friendly sources of fuel are embraced.[91] The loss in export revenue as oil and gas markets weaken can produce similar economic, social, and political adjustment issues for exporting countries, as described earlier for importers when those markets are tight. In major exporting countries, the specific route through which the impact is felt is often via a reduction in revenue that had permitted the government to subsidize consumption of energy goods or to absorb a great deal of low-skilled labor. For example, riots broke out in both Venezuela and Iran when governments attempted to raise extremely low gasoline prices because export revenues were no longer sufficient to cover the cost of the subsidies.[92]

The relationship between government appropriation of the value produced in the oil and gas sectors and energy security is variable. Under certain circumstances, a producing country pursuing energy security via cheap domestic energy can undermine optimal revenue capture by lowering the profitability of the industry to the point that reserves are depleted, no new exploration is undertaken by private firms, and the NOC becomes too inefficient and unskilled to pursue the requisite exploration and production (E&P) to increase reserves and maintain production. While one can see cheap domestic energy as a transfer to consumers of the value created in the sector, the point is that it is unsustainable, and thus the generation of future revenues will fall or be lower than would occur based on geological or market conditions. On the other hand, pursuing maximum revenue appropriation can undermine ES by diminishing private investment and giving more control to a less effective NOC, resulting in decreased productive capacity and ultimately supply shortages. At the international level, the pursuit of energy security by importing countries can fuel short-term strategies by producing countries to capture more revenue now before alternative sources of energy can be adopted on a large scale. And of course, high levels of revenue appropriation in exporting countries can fuel increased efforts at ES in importing countries if the latter perceive that investors will leave these countries, thereby threatening supply.

Producers and Consumers

In addition to the wealth distribution and role of the market issues already discussed, two subsidiary issues appear on the resource nationalism agenda: who should extract the resource (public or private firms), and to which markets (foreign or domestic) the resources should flow; in more radicalized versions, a distinction between domestic markets for the elites and the "people" is also made. These issues span the spectrum of natural resources, but in this book we will be concerned with their manifestation in the oil and gas sector.

The question of who should extract and market the resource has two variants. The dominant variant is the public-private divide, and the secondary is the foreign-national private investor/producer issue. Statists believe that only a state-owned enterprise (SOE) would be willing to exploit the country's natural resources with national interests in mind. These claims refer not only to the prices at which the commodities would be sold but also to their rate of exploitation. Today statists focus on not running down reserves too quickly in order to benefit foreign consumers, but in the middle of the twentieth century, statists' concerns were that the IOCs were not exploiting many Latin American oilfields because Middle Eastern production was cheaper, thus producing the problems for the government noted earlier.

Once a country has decided to open its oil and gas sector to private investment, some statists seek to favor national investors. Part of the reasoning in favor of national capital follows the preference for national capital in sectors deemed "strategic" under ISI development paradigms: by restricting foreign investment, the government was expected to help create a national industrial capitalist class. In recognition that few national capitalists had the capital, skills, or know-how to invest in these opportunities, governments might permit foreigners to invest; in these cases, it was usually only in partnership with private national companies. Nevertheless, the limitations of this path for promoting sustainable and broad-based national development have been well documented in the ISI literature and contributed to the backlash against privatization after 2001.[93]

But some statists fear creating a powerful domestic interest group if private national capital is given preference. Thus when Venezuela sought to reduce the influence of IOCs during the early 1960s, the government considered and rejected opening the sector to private national investment. Instead, it created a state company (Corporación Venezolana de Petróleo, CVP) to negotiate with the foreign privately owned IOCs.

Two efforts of note to broaden private capital participating in NOCs so as to benefit the "average" or poor citizen were developed in Bolivia and Mexico. In Bolivia the government of Gonzalo Sánchez de Lozada, while not an exponent of statist conceptions of the responsibilities inherent in resource nationalism, recognized that simply opening the oil and gas sector to private investment would not win popular approval. Consequently, when the government sold 51 percent of the shares of its NOC YPFB in 1996, as well as those of a number of other SOEs, it distributed shares to private pension funds to stimulate a national credit market, create adherents to the market, and convince average Bolivians that they would benefit directly once they reached retirement age.[94] In Mexico, the 2008 reforms of Felipe Calderón, who also would have preferred to reject statist approaches, limited private participation in Pemex to Mexican citizens who could purchase bonds. Though this strategy was never implemented, it was based on a hope that this ownership would convince average Mexicans that they should be more concerned about how Pemex was performing rather than by who owned it.[95] When the Cardoso administration in Brazil first offered shares in Petrobras they were limited to national citizens, but within two years, purchasing was opened to everyone.[96]

Statists can also be concerned about whether the domestic or international market has priority for consuming the natural resource. This can be a particularly relevant issue in countries with many poor who cannot pay the price demanded by the international market. Export controls have been used historically in Latin America for this purpose.

RESOURCE NATIONALISM, RESOURCE WEALTH, AND ENERGY POLICY

The concept of resource nationalism can help us understand energy policy. But we must define it nontautologically and systematically, following the logic of our definition where it leads. In this chapter I have argued that the most useful definition of resource nationalism places it at the center of a specific relationship that exists in most of the world, not just in developing countries: the nation is the rightful owner of the subsoil and submarine natural resources. The chapter then examined the issues that arise when one discusses the generation of natural resource wealth in the context of national ownership of the resource. I argued that only policies that generated sustainable public goods logically followed from this understanding of resource nationalism. I also offered examples of governments utilizing their legitimate role in appropriating natural resource wealth for private rather than public benefit and thus violating the legitimacy provided by a resource nationalism perspective.

Statists in resource nationalist polities articulate lofty goals, and that is their attraction to people who feel exploited by markets. Their underlying concern is how to use rents to quickly promote national development, and they focus on the absolute level of money appropriated by the government. Unfortunately, without ensuring efficient use of that money, it is possible that a government that appropriates a greater percentage of natural resource rents and spends it inefficiently promotes national development far less than a government that appropriates a lower share but invests it wisely. Just being "pro-market," however, does not mean that the resource is being used for the benefit of the nation rather than private interests. It is competitive markets, with well-functioning regulation to tax and deal with negative externalities, and investment in public goods that transform state ownership of natural resources into national benefit.

The focus on private goods, whether by statists or pro-marketers, produces what many have misleadingly called the "resource curse." As I discussed in the introduction, though theorizing causality is unsettled, the ability of a nation to avoid the negative economic and political manifestations associated with the resource curse depends on institutional factors. Those institutions generally make government's use of the wealth generated by the resource transparent and subject to evaluation, while holding the government accountable to the nation in whose name it collects that resource wealth.

The concept of resource nationalism that I propose recognizes both the importance of governments seeking to appropriate natural resource value for the sustainable provision of public goods and the inherent complementarity of national goals and private investor goals. This chapter has demonstrated the multiple options for implementing an energy policy based on the fact that subsoil and submarine resources belong to the nation and a recognition of the responsibility of government to utilize resulting revenues to advance national development. The analytic challenge thus becomes understanding the determinants of variations in energy policy adopted and implemented.

Chapter Two

THE PATHS TO DIVERSE PARTNERSHIPS IN THE CONTEXT OF RESOURCE NATIONALISM

Understanding the history of Latin American oil and gas policies matters for three key reasons. It enables us to recognize the puzzle of extreme policy swings that cannot be explained by geology, markets, or ideology; it demonstrates that Latin American countries have had the goal of increasing the benefits, including national development, of their oil and gas resources since the beginning of oil and gas exploration in the region; and it opens our eyes to false assumptions in analyses of how governments have implemented their RN responsibilities.

Starting in the mid-nineteenth to early twentieth century, depending on the country, the eight Latin American oil and gas producers sought to recover control over subsoil resources and establish a state role in determining how those resources were to be used. The timing, process, and scope of nationalization varied widely, oftentimes contrary to much of the literature concerning these events. Although the literature does recognize that initially *nationalization* meant monopoly control and today it spans the spectrum from monopoly to majority control, there is no explanation for where on that continuum a government would seek to place the country. This chapter will illustrate that the range is wide and steps are repeatedly retraced within and across countries

National control and energy security were promoted at times in the name of some abstract notion of sovereignty, but at other times for enhanced government revenues for public and private goods and a desire to stimu-late national industrialization via linkages to other sectors and the freeing up of foreign exchange to support those sectors. More recently, nationaliza-tion in partnership with the private sector offers the prospect of rents for export-led industrialization (part of the recent Brazilian debate) or for the expansion of a social welfare state (Venezuela, Bolivia, and Ecuador and their versions of "twenty-first-century socialism"). Although in other parts of the world nationalization may be undertaken in order to simply enrich leaders or gather resources to fight a civil war, fortunately, this has not been the case in Latin America.[1]

Many good histories have been written about the oil industry in Latin America and they are reflected in the notes to this chapter. I have also writ-ten a more detailed synthesis of that history, which is available on my personal website.[2] There I have added details that historians and economic historians may have felt were extraneous for their studies but which are important for understanding energy policy variation across place and time.[3] From those sources we can see that issues associated with ownership of the resource, the division of rents between government and investor, and the role of an NOC in national development are not new; the region has struggled with them since the early days of the industry in the nineteenth century. This chapter highlights energy policies that demonstrate the wide variation over time, across the region, and within countries in Latin American approaches to those issues, thus setting up the puzzle that drives this book: What explains energy policy? Though the chapter does not reca-pitulate the historical record, it presents sufficient detail to document the wide policy variations. The first section tackles the fundamental issue of who owns the resources, while the second explores the terms of access to those resources. The third section examines the multiple paths to and from nationalization, since countries differed on the reversibility as well as timing and scope of nationalization. The final section investigates the creation of national oil companies and their varying relationship to private capital.

ASSERTING OWNERSHIP

Exploration for oil in Latin America began in the mid-nineteenth century, just a few years after the discovery of oil in Pennsylvania, which heralded the modern petroleum era. If any regulations were operable, they were those set up for the centuries-old mining industry. It was not until the early twentieth century, however, that commercial activity became profitable and stimulated investment in Latin America. The oil and gas industry had greater uncertainty than the mining sector about the existence and size of deposits as well as the costs of production and their market value. In addition to a lack of infrastructure linking many of these resources to major cities or ports, investment was costly and risky, resulting in many early failures. But, if successful, private investors could potentially capture extremely large portions of the resource rents.[4] Traditional mining regulations were thus quite inadequate for promoting national interests in the new industry. The U.S. and European governments were actively asserting the "rights" of their investors in Latin America and defending them through diplomatic, economic, political, and military means.[5] Many Latin Americans were suspicious and concerned about the influence of the British and U.S. investors attracted by their oil, as well as of their own governments' dealings with the foreigners and use of the revenues generated.[6]

The patterns of ownership varied in the nineteenth century, when oil became of interest. In Brazil, Colombia, and Mexico, liberal economic reforms changed the Spanish colonial perspective, in which subsoil resources belonged to the Crown, to permit private ownership of subsoil deposits. Argentina, Bolivia, Ecuador, and Venezuela never made such changes, leaving subsoil resources in the hands of the state. Bolivia's first mining law in 1872 recognized the value of hydrocarbons and made coal and oil the property of the state, whether found on the surface or in the subsoil.[7] Peru never privatized ownership of subsoil resources except for one special case: the Liberator Simón Bolivar granted such ownership to the hacienda La Brea y Pariñas, belonging to a friend. This property was sold a few times, winding up in 1913 in the hands of a Standard Oil of New Jersey subsidiary, the Canadian-registered International Petroleum Corporation (IPC), and encompassing the country's largest oil field ever, La Brea. Each owner considered themselves to be governed by the original decree of Bolivar, rather than subsequent legislation.[8]

In Argentina, the dispute over ownership of subsoil resources was not between public and private, but between provincial and federal governments. The creation of the federal republic in 1853 recognized federal and provincial ownership of subsoil resources in each of their jurisdictions.[9] When oil was discovered in 1907 in Patagonia, the mining code of 1887 became the basis for provinces' rights to collect royalties from hydrocar-bon production in their territories.[10] In 1949 a new constitution was a deci-sive step in the federal-provincial oil rivalry, putting all oil reserves under federal jurisdiction. A military coup in 1955 returned the relevant hydro-carbon reserves to provincial governments. But in 1958 the military gov-ernment abolished the constitution, thereby reinstating federal jurisdiction over all oil fields.[11] A constitutional reform in 1994 transferred ownership back to the provinces for nonfederal property but left the power to legislate with the national congress. Legislation in 2007 transferred legislative pow-ers over hydrocarbons on provincial lands back to the provinces.[12] This transfer resulted in provinces creating their own oil companies and offer-ing better terms than the federal government for exploration and produc-tion; YPF protested this disloyal competition, and in 2014 Congress limited provincial incentives.[13]

The Brazilian Federal Constitution in 1891, the first after the dissolution of the Empire of Brazil in 1889, granted landowners full ownership of all subsurface resources. This regime remained in place until a new Federal Constitution in 1934 provided that the Federal Union had ownership over all subsoil minerals, oil, and gas.[14]

From 1858 until 1874, some Colombian departments (i.e., states) granted private ownership of subsoil resources on private lands. The Constitution of 1886 created a centralized republic, and the president issued a decree that all subsoil resources belonged to the nation. The Supreme Court, however ruled that Congress had the power to legislate on the matter.[15] Since Con-gress refused to act, the country had two subsoil ownership structures. This discrepancy was resolved when another president decreed a petroleum law on June 20, 1919, proclaiming all subsoil resources belonged to the nation. The Supreme Court again ruled that only Congress could legislate, and Congress passed legislation later that year that subsoil resources belonged to the nation. The legislation, however, was not retroactive for contracts signed before 1874.[16]

The Mexican government changed the mining laws in 1884, 1892, and 1909 to permit, among other incentives, private ownership of subsoil resources.[17] The Mexican Revolution of 1910–1917, however, enshrined national ownership of subsoil resources in article 27 of the Constitution of 1917.

CONTROLLING ACCESS TO THE
HYDROCARBON SECTOR

The search for oil in Latin America was quickly successful in a number of countries. Mexico became the number one exporter in the world for over a decade into the 1920s, and Venezuela took the mantel in 1928.[18] Argentina, Colombia, and Peru were moderate producers in that early period. Latin American governments did not perceive ownership of the resource and access to it for others as necessarily conflicting concepts. The issue became the terms for the access. Different types of contracts developed over time as the market changed, governments learned more about the business, and domestic politics evolved. The standard contract was the "concession" in which private contractors had total control over the physical area to develop it or not, could sell the concession to anyone, and were granted ownership of the resource once it was brought to the surface to sell at whatever price and to whomever they chose. In the 1960s the concession regime began to change, providing producer states with more control and revenue.[19]

Latin American governments (except Venezuela into the 1940s) did not simply hand out access but made revenue and production demands and imposed sanctions when investors failed to meet contracted terms. Even countries that had poor geology under the technological and market conditions of the day (Ecuador and Bolivia) or were led by nonradical governments (Colombia, Bolivia, Mexico) still legislated access aggressively. Governments and companies became increasingly aware of the experiences of the oil industry in other countries, but regulation was irregular, was inconsistent, and varied across countries. Contrary to postulated OBM cyclical dynamics, even as the oil market entered into a global oversupply stage in the late 1920s and the Depression submerged the global economy in the 1930s, around the region governments became more aggressive in asserting their rights to regulate the sector and demanding renegotiations of contracts.

Regarding claims already registered, most countries expected development right away. But some individuals and companies were merely speculating with leases, others had difficulty raising capital, and still others preferred to develop fields in accord with their overall business plans rather than a country's national development plans. A company's business strategy might mean not producing in a country and importing crude or refined products, but governments worried about revenue lost by not producing, the use of scarce foreign exchange to import a product that could be produced at home, or how to fuel national development. The question of access thus became intimately involved with that of developing the oil sector. As for tax policy, companies wanted to pay as little as possible to the myriad local and national authorities, while governments sought to tap into what was perceived as a lucrative business to increase the national budget for both private and public goods. And societies were anxious to see the benefits of oil production and sales.

Nationalization is a means of regulating access to ensure at least a formal sense of state control over the resource, and it can vary from monopoly control over the industry through majority control of either a specific or all firms in an industry.[20] Nationalization is usually associated with expropriation (involuntary forced divestment) and FDI,[21] but Latin America's experience demonstrates that even national firms can be expropriated, and that governments can legislate control over the oil industry or parts of it without expropriating any firms. Nationalizations have been a constant phenomenon in Latin America except in the 1980s and 1990s, but that exception was passing; in 1998 Mommer wrote that nationalization "has already been defeated, definitively, radically and irreversibly" just before the most recent burst of nationalizations.[22] At times the process is planned in advance, but achieved through small, progressive regulatory and fiscal acts until majority control is achieved or the firm sells its assets to the government in frustration (known as "creeping nationalization").[23]

All countries that perceived a potential to develop energy resources faced these issues, whether or not their geology supported those dreams. Their responses varied across time as the national political economic context changed, demonstrating that geography and markets alone do not determine energy policy. It is also notable that governments did not always just acquiesce to IOC demands. With an ahistorical view of the oil and gas industries and politics, one might criticize these governments for not demanding enough, but it is important to recognize that they did not simply give investors open and cheap access to the region's hydrocarbon resources.

The first Mexican Petroleum Law in 1901 did not refer to private property but was only concerned with concessions on federal lands.[24] Though the dictator Porfirio Díaz favored foreign investment, his government's regulations helped structure the industry through fiscal and licensing policies.[25] Once the revolution nationalized subsoil resources, government became involved in all access issues since the constitution did not prohibit private participation in hydrocarbon exploitation. Concessions prior to 1917 were the first contentious issue, with presidents and the Supreme Court disagreeing on the legality of retroactivity in 1922 and 1925 and Congress accepting all the concessions in 1928.[26]

Mexican oil legislation in the 1930s up to the nationalization in 1938 was not especially opposed to private capital, domestic or foreign, with new concessions and taxes in the works right up to expropriation.[27] In the face of a complete shut-down of the oil industry as labor and companies deadlocked in a strike, the Mexican government expropriated all the major companies (about 10 percent of production remained in the hands of small companies, including Mexican ones) in line with the stipulations of the Expropriation Law of 1936.[28] A law in 1939 forbade concessions and constitutional reform in 1940 enshrined the prohibition against contracts with private parties, yet the Petroleum Law of 1941 permitted risk contracts in which companies explored and produced oil, receiving total reimbursements of their expenses and investments and 50 percent of the value of the oil produced, and provided for Mexican capital to invest in exploration projects with Pemex.[29] It was not until 1958 that the Statutory Law of constitutional article 27 prohibited these types of contracts and limited private capital to service contracts with Pemex in which no petroleum was offered.[30]

Venezuela's first oil concessions were offered beginning in 1907 to friends of the dictators, speculating in the market. By 1913 virtually all concessions had been sold to Shell.[31] Venezuelan dictatorships into the 1940s were quite willing to grant effective control over vast territories to foreign investors.[32] An early effort to regulate the industry occurred in 1920 when a development minister drafted a petroleum law that reduced the size of concessions and increased royalties from 5 percent to 15 percent. But the government removed the minister, modified the proposed legislation, and in 1922 let the oil companies write the oil law. Not surprisingly, Venezuela's oil law was the most favorable to foreign investors in Latin America: Congress had no input into the law and only the president could grant concessions, contracts were extended to forty years, there was little pressure to develop fields, there was no limit on the size of holdings, and customs exemptions were granted for all imports for this vertically integrated industry.[33] The Supreme Court undercut efforts by a transition government to gain a greater share of the rents after the death of the dictator Gómez.[34]

The petroleum law of 1943 made a significant change in the relationship between the oil companies and the country. It applied retroactively to all contracts and sought to achieve a fifty-fifty split of net profits with the companies. Domestic refining was promoted through a requirement that set minimum levels of production. In return, new forty-year contracts were offered, investigations into disputed titles were terminated, and the government provided new fields for lease at a faster rate. The law also severely limited the participation of private national companies in the petroleum sector because government officials feared the political power of an alliance of international and national capital.[35] Extraordinary taxes on the companies were decreed in 1945, 1946, and 1947 to bring the government's take back up to 50 percent.[36] In the 1950s a military dictatorship favored the IOCs, in particular allocating them new concessions.[37] With the return of democracy in 1958, Venezuela stopped granting oil concessions and rejected the fifty-fifty split, increasing its share of the profits to close to 65 percent.[38] An NOC, Corporación Venezolana de Petróleo (CVP), was created in 1960 to build national capabilities in the sector.

The Reversion Law, enacted in 1971 during the conservative government of Rafael Caldera (1969–1974), reserved future exploitation (concessions were due to run out in 1983) for a wholly owned state corporation and subjected the contracts to immediate reversion if the leaseholders did not exploit them efficiently. Nationalization of the Venezuelan oil sector was legislated in 1975, becoming effective in 1976. Natural gas nationalization followed a quicker path. The Venezuela president began to consider entering the growing LNG business in 1969 and reached out to private companies. Congress, nevertheless, nationalized natural gas in 1971 and limited exports to associated gas, giving CVP an export monopoly. Nonassociated gas was reserved for the development of a domestic market.[39]

Argentina banned private companies from the most promising sections of the large Rivadavia field in 1907 and in other federal territories from 1924 to 1927; private companies could operate anywhere else in the country, subject to local laws.[40] Provincial ownership and fear of centralization in national politics and budget drove provinces to be more willing to offer concessions to investors than was the central government in the early twentieth century.[41] The federal government tried to push through Congress the expropriation of all private holdings and the establishment of a fully owned state monopoly in 1928 but failed because the upper house was opposed to nationalization, some advocates of nationalization were opposed to a wholly state-owned NOC, and provincial governments made deals with IOCs that allowed them to continue expanding production in provincial fields.[42] The federal government issued a decree in 1931, followed by the Oil Law of 1935 limiting private companies to existing concessions or fifty-fifty partnerships with the NOC Yacimientos Petrolíferos Federales, YPF, in federal territories; provinces followed suit in 1936.[43] Jersey Standard attempted to divest itself of this situation, but the Argentine Congress refused to purchase its Argentine assets. The private companies could neither expand nor leave and found themselves in a context controlled by the government.[44] The situation changed in the late 1940s and early 1950s when the nationalist government of Juan Perón (1944–1952, 1952–1955) sought to attract new investment in E&P, but the IOCs refused to enter under those conditions. When the Perón government signed a contract with Standard Oil in 1954, it contributed to his overthrow the following year and a repeal of the contract.[45] Continuing the erratic pattern, contracts were opened again with FDI in 1958 and most contracts were canceled in 1963, only to be restored in 1966.[46] A law in 1967 provided for multiple types of contracts that federal and provincial governments could offer private hydrocarbon companies, but until 1990 federal Argentine governments insisted on service contracts to YPF.[47]

In 1937 the Argentine government secretly divided the domestic market between foreigners (Shell and Jersey Standard with half) and Argentines (YPF and some small companies getting the other half). Although there was a public uproar when the agreement was exposed in 1938, it remained in effect until 1947 and thereafter settled in at 60–40 in favor of YPF.[48] In 1947 the government also tried to end the IOC's monopoly on oil imports, giving it instead to YPF, but the lack of marketing contacts meant it could not secure the oil, so the effort failed.[49] Governments regulated the domestic oil market, keeping national prices uniform and low into the 1950s. The country's refining and distribution sectors remained open to private companies, although plans in 1966 and 1971 to fully nationalize these operations were aborted by military coups (reasons for the coups were not concerned with oil).[50]

Domestic policies starved the Argentine gas sector of capital, and gas shortages were feared in the 1960s.[51] The 1972 Bolivian-Argentine pipeline

(Yacimientos—Bolivia Gulf, YABOG) to transport Bolivian gas proved contentious because the market in Argentina evolved in a manner unforeseen by either government. Neoliberal policies under a subsequent Argentine government attracted domestic and foreign investment, and by 1978 large gas reserves were being developed in Argentina.[52] Expansion of the Argentine natural gas transport and distribution system followed, increasing gas supplies and lowering internal prices below the rate negotiated with Bolivia.[53] In an example that demonstrates that rent issues divide Latin American countries as well, Argentina demanded that Bolivia renegotiate the agreement with reduced prices and was successful in 1987.[54]

Colombia offered its first concession (two million acres) in 1905 to a French speculator, Roberto de Mares; Standard Oil of New Jersey would wind up with the concession in 1920 by purchasing the Tropical Oil company. Another speculator, General Virgilio Barco, sold his concession in 1916, and Gulf Oil wound up with it in 1926. These would become the two biggest producing fields in Colombia and the center of state-IOC tensions until the expiration of the concessions in the 1950s.

Colombia's Congress split in 1917 and 1918 over the issue of state versus private control of the nascent industry but adopted a Petroleum Law in December 1919 requiring exploration and production to be registered with the government, limiting contracts to thirty years, and requiring exploration and production to begin within one year.[55] Colombia was interested in more than upstream production. In a contract with Tropical Oil, Colombia became the first Latin American government to mandate state takeover of the concession once the contract expired, and Colombians had to staff at least 25 percent of supervisory positions. Production taxes were set at 10 percent, operational disputes were under the jurisdiction of national courts, and Tropical Oil was required to build a refinery within three years to supply the domestic market.[56]

Colombia canceled the Barco concession (a five-thousand-acre area, of which about 90 percent was American owned, but in the process of being sold by Cities Service to Gulf Oil) for nonperformance in 1926 and confirmed the decision in 1928;[57] Gulf Oil turned to the Colombian courts, and the government worked out an agreement that overturned the revocation and permitted Gulf Oil subsidiary Colombian Petroleum Company to exploit 500,000 acres, set royalties at 10 percent on inland production and 6 percent on the coast, and required the company to build a refinery once daily production reached twenty-eight thousand barrels.[58] Under the right-wing government of Miguel Abadía Méndez (1926–1930), Colombia increased rent appropriation in 1927 by increasing taxes from 10 percent to 15 percent. When companies protested, Congress threatened nationalization in 1928 with an "Oil Emergency" law halting all new concessions, doubling production taxes on private land, and giving concessionaires six months to provide lease contracts or proof of landownership or face heavy fines and even forfeiture of their rights. Three months later the six-month deadline was reduced to thirty days by executive decree.[59]

U.S. advisors were contracted to write a new petroleum law in 1931, and the threat of nationalization receded. The resulting law considered the interests of both foreign investors and nationalists. Investors saw royalties decline, with ranges set from 2 percent to 11 percent on production from public lands and 1 percent to 8 percent on private lands. Export duties on all petroleum exports were eliminated for the first thirty years of any production. Though not negotiated by a left-wing government, the agreement required preferences for Colombian investors, proof of title was required for registration, concessions to a single person were limited to fifty thousand hectares, disagreements were required to be settled in Colombian courts, and transfer of concessions to "foreign governments" was prohibited—largely affecting Shell, partly owned by the British government at the time.[60]

The NOC Empresa Colombiana de Petróleos, S.A. (Ecopetrol) was created to take over the de Mares concession when it expired in 1951. A series of decrees and laws established the terms: Decree 2939 in 1956 permitted Ecopetrol to contract with others throughout the value chain;[61] Decree 3211 in 1959 provided the basis for the NOC to enter into joint ventures (JVs) in the mid- and downstream; Law 10 of 1961 reduced the period for the exploration phase and increased the government's share in production; and Law 20 of 1969 provided the government with the ability to declare any oil area a "national reserve" to be exploited by the NOC either by itself or in association with public or private capital.[62] Legislative Decree 2310 of 1974 ended the concessions system and required companies that wished to explore for oil and gas in any part of the country to associate with Ecopetrol under the terms of the 1969 law.[63] The government purchased the Cartagena refinery from Jersey Standard in 1974, providing the NOC with a monopoly over refining.[64] In 1978 the government gave Ecopetrol a monopoly over oil exports, requiring all domestic production to be sold to the NOC.[65] Although Colombia was willing to have partners with the NOC for natural gas production, Ecopetrol monopolized distribution (restricted to the domestic market).[66]

The Peruvian oil industry began in the 1860s, but regulations were not codified until the Mining Law of 1877. The legislation permitted indefinite control over any mineral deposit simply by registering a claim and payment of "surface taxes," whether the resources were exploited or not. From 1910 to 1922 the government suspended registration of claims because the inadequate records of property boundaries produced overlapping claims. The government regulated the domestic market and imposed an export embargo in 1918 when IPC cut supplies as a means of pressuring the government over taxes. By special agreement granted in 1922 after another financial deal, and approved by an international arbitration panel, IPC's La Brea holdings were exempted from the provisions of the Petroleum Law for fifty years, and its other concessions were extended for fifty years. Over time, the oil companies and some Peruvian presidents engaged in mutual threats concerning production, distribution, taxes, and forced loans. Both benefited at the expense of the country because presidents rewarded companies by permitting local prices to be high enough to generate huge profits.[67]

The Peruvian hacienda granted ownership rights by Bolivar was taxed as if it were merely the size of ten claims, though its extent was equal to 41,600 claims, and IPC benefited greatly from the special status of its property.[68] The first Petroleum Law in 1922 established a 10 percent royalty on crude oil production and provided that any claims abandoned became "state reserves," and those reserves could be opened to private investment only by a specific decree. A few claims reverted to state control in 1924 when their stakeholders abandoned them. IPC periodically paid for tax exemptions with cash for the government and by helping the government raise loans in New York.[69]

In 1927–1928 Peru contracted with Phillips Petroleum Co. to reexplore the area abandoned by Shell in 1924, but Phillips also failed to find oil. In 1937 the government passed legislation providing favorable terms for oil exploration in the Amazon, but after two companies received concessions, nationalist opposition terminated the efforts.[70] The governments of the 1940s controlled prices in the domestic market, producing an increase in demand that displaced half of the country's crude exports. With the Petroleum Law of 1952, the government tried to stimulate discoveries and production by granting concessions under very liberal terms, abolishing existing state reserves, providing companies some relief on domestic prices, and lowering depletion and export taxes. Yet the government was not simply turning the sector over to private interests; the law retained the right to declare new state reserves and gave Peruvians preferential access to the areas to be explored. The law also increased the percentage of an oil production project that the government had a right to purchase, from 25 percent to 30 percent. A limit on the length of an oil concession was also introduced, varying from forty to fifty years in the coast, sierra, and Amazon, with one-time extensions being twenty to twenty-five years, depending on the region. The government also adopted the Venezuelan policy of a fifty-fifty split on the profits generated by oil. Almost 1,200 concessions covering approximately sixteen million hectares were granted, but despite a large oil find in the neighboring Ecuadorian jungle in 1967, no important oil discoveries were found in Peru.[71]

In 1968 IPC agreed to hand over the largely exhausted La Brea field to the government in return for a new concession in the Amazon and expansion of its refinery for the domestic lubricants market. A military coup overthrew the government for largely nonoil reasons, and the agreement was annulled. In 1969 the left-wing military government expropriated all IPC holdings, endowing the Peruvian NOC (PetroPeru) with those properties. The government did not totally nationalize the industry, however, permitting other private companies to remain.[72]

Ecuador granted its first petroleum concession in 1878 and passed its first mining law in 1886. A lack of success, despite production in neighboring countries, made companies cautious about exploring their concessions. In 1909 Ecuador granted a concession to a British firm that gave the state 10 percent of profits; the enterprise does not appear to have prospered.[73] Once again contrary to OBM expectations, Congress was undeterred by poor geology and decreed in 1919 that companies develop their property within two years or forfeit their concessions; the decree also eliminated new lease purchases and the transfers of lands. The first Ecuadorian petroleum law in 1921 modified the congressional decree, gave companies five years to begin activities, and permitted the president to authorize the transfer of oil rights.[74]

Initial production began in 1925 along the coast, but it was minor and exhausted quickly.[75] Despite a small domestic market and no oil discoveries to exploit from the 1920s to the 1960s, Ecuador, under left-wing nondemocratic governments (Ecuadorian Radical Liberal Party, 1926–1934, 1938–1944, and Ecuadorian Socialist Party, 1935–1938) often took a hard line with companies, in contrast to OBM expectations. In 1931 the government renegotiated the Leonard concession with Standard Oil of New Jersey and canceled it in 1937 for unpaid debts and lack of production. The oil law in 1937 raised royalties, and a decree in 1938 confirmed state ownership of mineral deposits.[76]

Attention turned to the Amazon, where Shell obtained the first concession in 1947 but failed to find oil.[77] After a significant discovery in 1967, concessions proliferated, and by 1968 most of the available acreage in the Amazon was under contract. In 1969 the government renegotiated the Texaco-Gulf contract. Acreage was reduced; royalties were nearly doubled to 11.5 percent; and personnel were nationalized, reserving 95 percent of workers, 80 percent of administrative personnel, and half of technical positions for Ecuadorians. Texaco-Gulf was also required to develop roads and an oil pipeline from the coast over the Andes and into the Amazon to bring the petroleum to market.[78]

The Ecuadorian Law of Hydrocarbons in 1971 reaffirmed state ownership of subsoil deposits, increased royalties and taxes, and applied specific taxes for education and public works in the petroleum-producing areas. Decree No. 430 of 1972 made the 1971 oil law retroactive, thereby providing Ecuador's NOC Corporación Estatal Petrolera Ecuatoriana (CEPE) with a windfall of more than four million hectares in the booming Oriente. Concession periods were also halved, from forty to twenty years, royalties increased from 11.5 percent to 16 percent, natural gas production was nationalized, and the NOC was provided with an option to purchase up to a 25 percent share in any company doing oil and gas business in Ecuador. The decree also set up novel terms for contracts: an export tax on all exports (15 percent) and a government share in profits. Some firms chose to leave or suspend their operations in Ecuador, and one company refused to pay and had its concession canceled. Under this new law, the government forced Texaco-Gulf to renegotiate their contract and specifically required the companies to invest $60 million and increase production to 400,000 barrels per day. The aggressiveness of the Ecuadorian governments had its short-term payoffs:

Ecuador's tax structure produced greater rents than those in Venezuela or the Middle East in 1972.[79] By one calculation, government take reached 92 percent in the CEPE/Texaco consortium for the Amazon.[80]

In the face of collapsing production and low prices, Ecuador changed tactics. In 1982 risk contracts were permitted, and further reforms in 1993 created new contract structures, tax incentives, and reductions in government take.[81] Association contracts created in the 1970s were replaced with production-sharing contracts, with reductions in state participation from 89 percent to 26.4 percent.[82] In the midst of another commodity boom, however, in 2006 and 2007 fiscal terms were altered in the state's favor, and in 2010 the government legislated that all E&P contracts would be transformed into service contracts retroactively.[83]

In Bolivia speculators began registering claims in 1906, but little activity resulted. The government adopted an annual tax per hectare in 1916 to stimulate development. Despite having no production, Bolivia also legislated a 10 percent federal tax on the expected production. The stimulus proved inadequate in the face of minimal transportation infrastructure and uncertain geology. In 1920 lease terms were extended from fifty to sixty-six years to add a carrot to the stick. But this arrangement was still no giveaway to the companies, despite the governments of this period being tied to the tin-mining interests, seeking FDI, and pursuing good relations with the United States.[84] At expiration of the lease, the fields and production facilities became government property, 20 percent of net profits were to be paid to local governments, and the national government was given the right to expropriate an operation after twenty years if supply could not meet domestic demand.[85] In 1921 the size of leaseholdings was reduced. The government demonstrated a willingness to act against companies failing to develop their concessions: in 1924 Royal Dutch Shell's claims were confiscated for nonperformance. But the government was also amenable to negotiation, permitting Standard Oil of New Jersey (also known as Jersey Standard) to purchase two of the pre-1921 leases without subjecting them to the current petroleum legislation.[86]

Bolivia's energy policy spats have included its Latin American neighbors. Without access to the sea, Bolivia's crude had to pass through a neighboring country to reach world markets. The Argentine government, however, wanted oil companies to export Argentine crude and thus in 1927 refused to permit an oil pipeline linking Bolivia to the Parana River and placed a high tariff on Bolivian crude passing through its territory. Jersey Standard gave up on Bolivia—it stopped drilling in 1932 and in 1936 began shopping its assets. Bolivia sought to force the company to explore and produce by claiming back taxes owed for the 1920s. When the Chaco War (1932–1935) with Paraguay broke out, the Bolivian government wanted an increase in aviation gasoline and at lower prices than offered by Jersey Standard. The government initially seized the Jersey Standard refinery but returned it when they realized they could not operate it successfully.[87]

Brazil adopted a mining law in 1921 that was generally favorable to oil investors, generating some exploration activity. But by 1924 no oil had been discovered, and the discouraged investors abandoned the search for Brazilian oil.[88] In the 1930s the growing market for petroleum products and military interest in the national security implications of oil (Brazil was a rival of Argentina and participated in World War II) stimulated the search for energy security.[89] The constitution of the nationalist dictator Getúlio Vargas (1930–1945) in 1934 stipulated that only Brazilian citizens or corporations could receive exploration licenses, and that surface property owners had first priority for exploration and participation in profits generated.[90] In 1938 a National Petroleum Council was established, with authority to regulate oil exploration, production and imports, drilling concessions, as well as refinery ownership and location.[91] The Constitution of 1946 permitted the establishment of monopolies, but the government waited until 1953 to begin to establish a monopoly in the oil and gas sector (Federal Law no. 2004/1953), and the monopoly was not incorporated into the constitution until the new Constitution of 1967.[92]

THE CHARACTERISTICS AND IMPLICATIONS OF NATIONALIZATION

Table 2.1 summarizes the significant variation across and within the eight Latin American oil and gas producers regarding when nationalizations occurred as well as the provisions under which nationalization was carried out. There were twenty-four episodes of nationalization in these eight countries up to 2016.

The column on timing demonstrates that nationalizations across the value chain occurred in every decade once the industry got established, except in the 1980s and 1990s. The earliest nationalizers were Argentina (in

TABLE 2.1

Oil and Gas Nationalizations in Eight Latin American Countries

Country	Timing	Process*	Terms**	Scope***	Action Reversed
Argentina	1907	U[b]	M[b]	E,P	—
	1924–1927	U[b]	M[b]	E, P	1993
	1935 federal	U	P[b]	E, P, Tr, M	1954, 1958, 1967[f]
	1936 provinces	U[b]	P[b]	E, P	—
	2012	X	P	T	Reversed 1993 YPF privatization
Bolivia	1937	X	P[c]	T[c]	1955
	1969	X	P		1996
	2006	X	P		—
Brazil	1953	U	M	E, P	1975
	1964	X	M	I, R	1964
	2010	U	P	E, P in pre-salt	2016
Colombia	1948[d]	C	CR	E,P, Tr	—
	1974	NC	P	E, P (R de facto)	—
	1979	FCR	RET	E, P	2003
Ecuador[e]	1971	NC	P	P, R, Tr, M	~1986
	1972	FCR	P	M	2001 transport/marketing
	1976	FCR	M	M	~1986
	2010	FCR	M	T	—
Mexico	1938	X	SEL	T	—
	1958	NC	M	T	Partial for gas 1995, partial for petrochemicals 1996, 2008 services for oil, 2013 for entire sector
Peru	1968	FCR	P	T	1991–1993
Venezuela	1976	X[a]	M	T	1993, 1994, 1995 for different oil projects
	2007	X	P	E, P	—
	2009	X	M	P	—
	2010	X	M	M	—

Source: Data compiled from countries' histories on author's website, https://sites.google.com/ucsd.edu/david-mares/home. The historical record is incomplete, especially with respect to the "Action Reversed" column.

*Process of nationalization: (U)nexplored areas; (C)oncession expiration; e(X)propriation; FCR forced contract renegotiation; NC new contracts
**Terms of nationalization: (M)onopoly; (P)articipation; (CR) applicable only to concession reversions; (RET)roactive; (Sel)ective to companies
***Scope across value chain: (T)otal; (E)xploration; (P)roduction; (R)efining; (Tr)ansportation; (M)arketing; (I)mports
[a] Venezuelan concessions were set to expire in 1983
[b] Reserved most promising areas for the NOC.
[c] De facto monopoly since legislation did not prohibit partnerships with the NOC but terms were not attractive for investors.
[d] Decided to nationalize in 1948 but waited until concession ran out in 1951 to implement nationalization.
[e] The military government of 1972–1979 intended to nationalize after IOCs increased production but was forced out of office before production rose to desired levels.
[f] Argentine governments signed contracts with IOCs in 1954 and 1958, but subsequent governments rejected them; in 1967 law was changed to permit all types of contracts, but until 1990 governments refused to permit any contracts other than service contracts subordinate to YPF.

1907 and 1924–1927 they reserved the most promising federal lands to a government agency and YPF, respectively), Bolivia (1937), and, though it is often cited as first, Mexico (1938). The last to nationalize were Bolivia (2006), Venezuela (2007), Ecuador (2010), Brazil (2010), and Argentina (2012, Repsol's assets in YPF). In between there was one nationalization in the 1950s (Brazil E&P in 1953) and another five in the 1960s–1970s (Brazil 1964 for import and refining, Peru 1968, Bolivia 1969 monopoly for the entire sector but permitting E&P service contracts, Ecuador 1972, and Venezuela 1971 for gas and 1976 for oil). The fact that Venezuela didn't nationalize until decades after becoming a major oil exporter while Brazil nationalized before discovering oil means that one can't assume that the determinant of nationalization is the existence of large rents. The government of Lázaro Cárdenas (1934–1940) was very clear that Mexicans had to make "sacrifices" to support the nationalization and that he had to rein in his national strategy of radical transformation to make sure that the oil sector could prosper under nationalization.[93]

The timing column also reveals an interesting phenomenon that has not been adequately discussed—the internationalization of Latin American NOCs. As international oil companies themselves, these NOCs can become targets of nationalization. Petrobras has experienced this in both Bolivia when the Morales government nationalized the gas fields (2006) and Ecuador when the Correa government unilaterally turned all E&P contracts into service contracts (2010). In Bolivia, the Brazilian government pressured its NOC to remain as a minor partner,[94] but Petrobras left Ecuador.

The process by which nationalization was carried out also varied, as indicated in the relevant column of table 2.1. In a number of countries, existing private investments were expropriated (Bolivia in 1937 and 1969, Mexico 1938, Venezuela 1975, and Peru 1968), while in others, contracts were forcefully renegotiated to provide for or increase NOC participation in the operations (Argentina 1935, Colombia 1978,[95] Ecuador 1972, Venezuela 2007); in still another, there had been no important discoveries at the time nationalization was decreed (Brazil 1953). In the Venezuelan case, the fact that concessions were set to expire in seven years helped the IOCs come to terms with the nationalization decree in 1975.

The column regarding terms is of significant interest. Latin America's experience demonstrates that from the very beginning of the nationalizations in the 1920s, these were most often not designed to provide the state with a monopoly. But this is misleading, as many Latin American countries in the 1930s–1970s nationalized IOCs only after they failed to negotiate a greater take, the regulatory options they pursued were ineffectual, or they failed to generate more investment as lower-cost producers developed in Venezuela and then the Middle East. In addition, the evidence from Latin America across countries and over the sixty years during which governments sought to assert their control over the resources demonstrates that the strategy of nationalization under terms that permitted subordinate private participation was adopted long before the 1980s.

The terms of nationalization in Latin America ranged from monopoly (Mexico by 1958, Venezuela 1975) to required partnership with the state (Colombia 1974, Peru 1971, Ecuador 1972, Argentina 1935). Some governments nationalized only specific companies (Mexico 1938, Peru 1968, Argentina 2012) while others nationalized the entire sector (Mexico 1958, Venezuela 1975 and 2007). Some nationalizations were de facto monopolies, with government regulations making the sector so unattractive to private investors that the government was left to operate in the sector by itself (e.g., Bolivian E&P after 1937 and Colombian refining after 1974).

Latin American governments also varied regarding where in the oil and gas value chain they wished to assert control (column labeled "scope"). Some governments nationalized the downstream and midstream but not the upstream (Argentina at different times), while others did the opposite (Colombia in all three nationalization episodes, Brazil in 1953). A number monopolized the entire value chain. Mexico took the step in 1958–1995 for gas and 1958–2008 for oil. Venezuela had a monopoly across the value chain from 1976 to 1993 but permitted service contracts from the very beginning, much to the chagrin of statists.

Table 2.1 also demonstrates that the decision to nationalize the industry or sectors of it is neither irreversible nor unrepeatable (reversed column) but is an action that repeats erratically.

NATIONAL OIL COMPANIES

As summarized in table 2.2, Latin America's historical experience demonstrates that nationalization does not imply creating a NOC, nor does having a NOC imply nationalization. Once again, we see significant variations over time, and within and across countries.

TABLE 2.2
NOC and Nationalization Episodes

Country	NOC Created	Dates of Nationalizations*	No Nationalization Upstream with NOC
Argentina YPF	(1907**) 1922	1910, 1935, 2012	Multiple back and forth to 2012
Argentina ENARSA	2004	—	2004–2012
Bolivia	1936 (2006**)	1937, 1969, 2006	1955–1969; 1972–2018
Brazil	(1938**) 1953	1953	1975–1988; 1997–2018
Colombia	1948 Restructured 2003	1974	1951–1969; 2003–2018
Ecuador CEPE	1972	1976	1972–1976
Ecuador Petroecuador	1989	2006	1993–2006
Mexico Petromex	(1925**) 1934	—	1934–1937
Mexico Pemex	1938	1938/1958	2013
Peru EPF	(1934**) 1946	—	1934–2018
Peru PetroPeru	1968	1968	1991–2018
Venezuela CVP	1960	1976	1960–1976
Venezuela PDVSA	1976	2007	1994–2007

Source: Data compiled from countries' histories through 2018, compiled on author's website, https://sites.google.com/ucsd.edu/david-mares/home.
* At least one characteristic activity is nationalized.
** A government agency, staffed by the public bureaucracy, was created to carry out certain functions in the oil sector; while these agencies could compete with private companies, they were not national oil companies themselves.

As noted earlier, Argentina restricted part of Rivadavia for federal development in 1907, ran it with a small, underfunded, and understaffed company under the Ministry of Agriculture, created YPF in 1922, and thirteen years later gave the NOC privileged rights beyond Rivadavia. Gas del Estado was created in 1946 for the transmission and distribution of gas domestically; it was privatized in 1992.[96] Argentina created ENARSA in 2004 in order to have a state presence once again in the energy market that had been privatized in the 1990s; this NOC was reorganized as Integración Energética Sociedad Anónima (IEASA) in 2018 and is in the process of returning to its original name, with increased responsibilities in the power sector.[97] YPF, privatized in the 1993, was renationalized in 2012 by forcing Repsol to sell 51 percent of its shares to the government.[98]

Brazil waited fifteen years between asserting its right to regulate and operate throughout the oil value chain with the Conselho Nacional do Petróleo (CNP) and creating its NOC, Petrobras (1938–1953). In 1951

President Getulio Vargas (1951–1954; dictator 1930–1945) submitted a bill to Congress for the establishment of an NOC with 49 percent private ownership that would operate as a holding company for the development of the oil industry. Insisting on a national oil monopoly, Congress approved legislation in 1953 creating Petrobras as a fully state-owned company and giving it a monopoly over all exploration, development, and refining, except for the existing two small private refineries.[99]

Mexico delayed two decades to create Pemex (1938) after the constitutional prohibition on private ownership of subsoil resources in 1917 and a decade after the Oil Law of 1925 that provided a framework for private companies to legally operate their pre-1917 concessions; the government had failed in its efforts to create a joint state–Mexican private capital NOC in 1935. In 1937 the government replaced Petromex with a government agency, the Administración General del Petróleo, returning the assets to state control, then created Pemex after nationalization the following year.[100]

Venezuela waited almost twenty years after demanding a fifty-fifty split with IOCs to create its first NOC, CVP, in 1960, though it did create a new NOC, PDVSA, when it nationalized the entire industry in 1975.[101]

The creation of a national energy company in and of itself does not constitute nationalization of the sector. Colombia, Peru, and Ecuador all created their NOCs at the time of developing regulations to guide the industry. Ecopetrol came into being as a wholly state-owned company when the de Mares concession reverted to the state in 1951. The government offered Jersey Standard a continuing minority stake in the de Mares fields, but the IOC declined. In 1955 the Barco concession reverted to Ecopetrol.[102] Peru created a Petroleum Department in 1934 to explore for oil, which was reorganized into the country's first NOC, Establecimientos Petroleros Fiscales (EPF), in 1946. Peru expropriated all IPC holdings in 1968, reorganizing EPF as PetroPeru and endowing it with those properties. The government did not totally nationalize the industry, however, permitting other private companies to remain under production-sharing contracts.[103] Ecuador created CEPE in 1972, and all companies seeking new concessions were required to associate with it. Texaco-Gulf was forced to sell 25 percent of its Ecuadorian consortium to CEPE. The NOC assumed management of the mid- and downstream. As noted earlier, Petroecuador was created in 1989 as a holding company but did not have a monopoly until 2010, when the government forced all E&P contracts to become service contracts for the NOC.

Bolivia created its first NOC a year before nationalizing the industry. In December 1936 the Bolivian government created a NOC (Yacimientos Petrolíferos Fiscales Bolivianos, YPFB), to compete with Jersey Standard, and the law permitted the NOC to engage in joint ventures. Within a month the concessions that Jersey Standard was not actively pursuing were given to the NOC. Two months later YPFB was given a monopoly over imports, and then Jersey Standard was expropriated that same March 1937; it took four years to negotiate an agreement to compensate Jersey Standard.[104]

The timing for the creation of national energy companies varies. Worldwide, the 1970s were a particularly propitious time for the development of national oil companies, and seventy-eight were created worldwide, including one in Latin America (Ecuador).[105] But lest we think that high oil prices after 1973 propel NOC creation, consider the Latin American experience. Latin America underwent three periods of NOC creation when prices were low: the 1930s, the 1950s–1960s, and the late 1980s. Although Argentina created the second NOC in the world, YPF, in the boom year of 1922, Mexico (1936) and Bolivia (1937) made the move during the Depression. In the post–World War II period of softening prices, Colombia created Ecopetrol in 1948, followed by Brazil (1953), Venezuela (1960), and Peru (1968). Ecuador created a new NOC, Petroecuador, in 1989, in the midst of a collapsing international oil market.

Having an NOC and nationalizing various sectors of the industry have not been synonymous occurrences in the region. Mexico, Bolivia, Brazil, Ecuador, and Peru all nationalized the industry at the time, or within one (Bolivia) or two (Mexico) years of creating their NOCs. Venezuela (1960–1976) and Colombia (1948–1969) nationalized the industry long after creating their NOCs.[106] NOCs also exist in nonnationalized oil and gas industries today: Argentina (Energía Argentina, Sociedad Anónima [ENARSA], created in 2004), Brazil (Petrobras), Colombia (Ecopetrol), and Peru (PetroPeru). Bolivia's YPFB was converted from an NOC to a regulator and service company in 1997 with no exploration, production, or marketing responsibilities, and the 2006 nationalization also included these features. In Venezuela, four fields in the heavy oil Orinoco Belt were offered to private investors in the 1990s when this oil was not yet commercially viable. (They were subsequently nationalized in 2007.)

In 1934 Ecuador began exploration efforts under the jurisdiction of the "Petroleum Department," which was reorganized and became the NOC Empresa Petrolífera Fiscal (EPF) in 1946 after a few minor discoveries.[107]

It is also important to understand that having an NOC does not imply shutting out private investors from the company. The idea of a mixed private-state company is not new, as Mexico's Petromex in 1934 and Bolivia's YPFB in 1936 were chartered to have a split with private investors. The Argentine government considered chartering YPF with 51 percent state ownership,[108] Colombia's Congress debated creating an NOC with public and private (including foreign) shares,[109] and Mexico's energy reform of 2008 contemplated selling shares in Pemex to Mexican citizens, but the sale was never implemented.[110] Brazil's energy reform beginning in 1995 resulted in the sale of Petrobras stock to domestic and foreign investors in 1999–2000.[111] Table 2.3 indicates that six NOCs raised capital by selling some shares to investors, but the NOC remained under state control.

Tables 2.2 and 2.3 demonstrate that state ownership does not automatically mean high levels of statist nationalism. Rather than seeing NOCs as simply a means for appropriating rents for self-serving politicians, our comparative historical analysis demonstrates that in Latin America NOCs are created for a variety of other reasons as well. In pursuit of national development, governments have identified energy as a "strategic sector" that ought to be promoted; short of focusing on the entire sector, at times specific phases (e.g., refining) have been reserved for the state in order to ensure employment, cheap fuel, or other national priorities. Governments may

TABLE 2.3
Private Participation in NOCs

Country	NOC	Public Shares (%)	Nationals Only?
Argentina	YPF 1993–1999	41%	No
	2012	42%	No
Argentina	ENARSA	35% Class C	No
Bolivia	YPFB	1936 permitted but no takers	Yes
		51% 1999–2006	
Brazil	Petrobras 1999	68% / 46%*	No
Colombia	Ecopetrol post-2007	10.1% (20% authorized)	No
Mexico	Petromex	50% but no takers	Yes
Peru	PetroPeru	49% authorized; none sold	No

Source: Data compiled from countries histories compiled on author's website, https://sites.google.com/ucsd.edu/david-mares/home.

*Though the government only owned 32 percent of the shares up to 2010, it retained management control; in 2010 it increased its shares to 54 percent through purchases of new stock offered by the NOC.

even use NOCs to make markets function more effectively when they have been dominated by a monopoly or an oligopoly. Under the right conditions, NOCs can be market enhancing, not just market distorting, and thus an appropriate tool for promoting national development.[112]

This historical review of Latin America's experience provides substantial evidence that policy across the oil and gas value chain has varied significantly over time, across the region, and within countries. The traditional conceptualizations of resource nationalism discussed in chapter 1 are too imprecise and ambiguous to be a useful variable for analyzing such variations in natural resource policy. By the early 1970s, Latin American countries' energy policies were all situated at the higher end of statist-oriented nationalism and energy security continuums, but they took different routes to get there and diverged again by the 1990s.

The historical review makes clear that oil market economics, geology, and ideology are not determinant of energy policy. Brazil in the 1950s (even Chile in the 1950s, as note 7 indicates) and Mexico and Peru in the 1960s all could have argued for open markets based on low prices and what appeared to be poor national geology, but instead they pushed ahead with efforts to maximize national control. Conservative governments, even while seeking good relations with the United States and foreign investment (e.g., Díaz in Mexico, Liberal Party presidents in Bolivia), sought national control, raised taxes and fees, and attempted to use the oil and gas sector to promote industrialization. Such dramatic variation in policy making that fails to consistently line up with geology, market conditions, or ideology requires that we search elsewhere for the determinants of energy policy making.

The different policies used to increase government take are based on the fundamental notion that the resource belongs to the nation. This claim is not just government rent-seeking but has legitimacy within society and the law. We need to look at the politics of how the nationalist claim of ownership is translated into policy governing the sector, addressing energy security, and distributing the benefits of that ownership across society.

Chapter Three

EXPLAINING OIL AND GAS POLICY

The explanation for the characteristics of a particular energy policy emerges from analysis of the political interactions that occur within a structural context set by geology and economics, factors beyond political actors' immediate control. In this chapter I begin with the assumption that it is the political process of policy making that translates interests into the policy adopted. I discuss policy in terms of the levels of government intrusion in the market justified by an appeal to a resource nationalism perspective (see the discussion in chapter 1).

After an introduction to the model, the chapter moves to focused discussion of my explanation of energy policy, that is, inclusiveness, competitiveness, and leadership characteristics, specifically innovation and risk acceptance. In each of these three subsections, we discuss the logic for why the political variable matters in the context of the argument and operationalize it. In the concluding section, hypotheses are developed concerning the impact of these variables on oil and gas policy, individually and in concert. The causal dynamics of the model will guide the case studies examined in part 2.

A POLITICAL ECONOMY MODEL OF
ENERGY POLICY MAKING

In my analytic framework, three political variables combine with geology and the market to explain oil and gas policy: the inclusiveness of the political system, the competitiveness within the deliberative body that makes policy, and the leader's character in terms of innovativeness and risk acceptance. My geology variable is measured by proved reserves (P1). Though P1 is affected by investment and the state of the market, the geological characteristics of hydrocarbon areas (geophysical characteristics of the rock, e.g., resistance to fluid flow) and the physical properties of the hydrocarbons (e.g., viscosity) are the chief determinants of how much investment and at what market price a specific area needs to be commercially viable.[1] Consequently, for policy makers and the public, P1 is the way in which they conceive of their oil and gas wealth. The operationalization of the market variable is carried out by reference to international oil prices (Brent).

My historical review in the previous chapter demonstrated that geology and markets are significantly underdetermining of the oil and gas policies adopted by Latin American oil and gas producers. This is not to argue that they do not matter. My argument is that they matter in two ways: first, they set the context within which policy will be made, raising challenges and providing opportunities for policy makers; and second, geology and markets will have a fundamental impact on the success of the policies adopted and thus in the case of failure will be a spur to new oil and gas policy making. But the adoption of policy, I argue, is determined by the interaction among three political variables.

The first political variable, inclusiveness, determines whose interests are represented, as well as which interests pose a potential threat to the policy because they are outside of the system. This variable has an impact on the degree of intrusiveness of government policy in the market and the push toward provision of private or public goods. Our second variable, competitiveness of the policy-making body, explains whether the policy pursued will be oriented toward providing public or private goods. Finally, political leadership, as exemplified by the leader's degree of innovation and risk acceptance, helps determine how the various interests will be incorporated into policy and whether the leader will seek to challenge or accept the institutional constraints that threaten to limit her impact on policy. In short, the way natural resource wealth is captured is the result of a political process, and how the state uses that wealth is a political decision; therefore capture and use will vary in accordance with the incentives faced by the politicians who make those decisions. I argue that it is the interaction among these three variables (inclusiveness, competitiveness, and leadership characteristics), in the context of geology and markets, that determines the specific content of a country's oil and gas policy.

Inclusiveness

Public policy is often explained by reference to the fact that the government has to meet the demands of its constituencies rather than simply adopt the "best" policy. This claim is insufficient and misleading. All governments have constituencies—these are the groups and individuals who support the people in office. In the case of democracies, we can speak of voters and interest groups, but even dictatorships need the support of some people and groups. The point about a constituency is that it wants the people it supports in government to make public policy in that constituency's specific interest; if public goods are produced along the way, fine, but businesspeople and homeowners want tax breaks, unions want benefits for unionized workers, and so forth. The natural constituency for public goods is rare and limited; think of a philanthropist. We should not, therefore, simply blame politicians if public policy fails to provide public goods. Investing the nation's wealth in physical and human infrastructure may be beneficial to society as a whole, but a politician's constituency may very well demand private goods.[2]

Democracies may be less prone to such situations because the size of the electorate makes it difficult for everyone to get a private good; thus voters tend to favor the provision of public goods. But as agricultural subsidies in the European Union and the United States demonstrate, democracies are not immune to providing key groups with private goods.[3] It should not surprise us, then, that in Latin America the newly incorporated groups want private goods in the name of justice and local development. The specific characteristics of these groups will vary by a country's social, economic, and political history, but what they have in common is a sense of long-term and systematic exclusion from the benefits of their nation's wealth at the hands of foreign and domestic elites. When the newly included groups constitute the vast majority of citizens in a country with large natural resources, it is difficult for leaders (even if they so desire) to argue that reforming public policy in a manner that is sustainable over the medium to long term is better than simply redistributing today's wealth.

The privatization policies adopted by Bolivia in the 1990s can help us understand the challenges facing reformers. A coalition of parties undertook the privatization effort in the name of the country's welfare, but the wealth generated went overwhelmingly to private firms while the country suffered (energy was not the only sector poorly managed), and people at the bottom of the social structure (mainly poor and indigenous) suffered even more than other groups. In this context, leaders from outside the party system rode a wave of citizen outrage to office and then confronted demands for immediate redistribution of rents to meet the needs of the poor. Of course, when the new reformers run out of rents to distribute (gas reserves are on the decline given lack of investment),[4] they too will confront the wrath of those who suffer because the populist reforms proved unsustainable. The capacity to turn natural resource wealth into public benefit is thus fundamental to the sustainability of reform.[5]

Inclusiveness is defined not in terms of whom the system claims to represent, but in terms of who can influence the selection of a government and its policies. Groups that are included are "empowered."[6] But I want to capture the difference between being empowered inside the system and being empowered because one is able to exercise power in the streets against the system. In the contemporary era, many different groups have been empowered in many countries, demanding participation as independent actors and not just as symbolic beneficiaries. Large-scale public demonstrations brought down presidents in Ecuador in 1997, (bringing together trade unions, social movements, upper middle-class, and indigenous affiliated with the Confederación de Nacionalidades Indígenas del Ecuador, CONAIE), 2000 (CONAIE and middle-rank military officers), and 2005 (middle class in the capital, Quito);[7] in Bolivia in 2003 (some coca growers, miners, urban poor, indigenous in both cases, and middle-class residents of the capital, La Paz) and 2005 (radical left, indigenous, and the Movimiento al Socialismo [MAS] Party);[8] and in Argentina in 2001 (fairly broad representation of society).[9] Despite this appearance of success in enforcing their will, the rioters' impact on policy adopted afterward depends on their having access to the institutions where policy is made.

My inclusiveness variable means that the group is politically relevant as an independent agent, not simply because someone claims to make policy in its name.[10] Voting alone is insufficient to demonstrate inclusiveness[11]— the 1990s saw many presidents elected in Latin America on antiliberal platforms, and once in office they adopted policies against which they had campaigned.[12] Being excluded ranges from total nonparticipation in the political system to the perception by policy makers that actors require placating, but simply as an object of policy determined by others. Whether a group is totally excluded or merely an object of policy makes a difference for the prospects of mobilization, and thus will impact the stability of a policy adopted on the basis of exclusion.[13] But for explaining the adoption of the policy itself, the distinction within the "excluded" category makes no difference, since by definition a member of this category cannot affect policy adoption.

When a leader claims to act in the name of certain constituencies but by her actions disregards their disagreements when they make use of the institutional paths for expressing that disagreement and pays insignificant political costs, there is representation without accountability. For example, Latin American populism has traditionally claimed to act in the interests of the working class, peasants, and the poor. Populist policies, nevertheless, have largely favored politicians, middle classes, and a small unionized labor force at the expense of the general working class, peasants, and poor.[14] Thus populist governments may deliver goods to some groups without being accountable to them when they disagree with government policy.

Even politicians who favor a market approach may turn to populism when adopting policies that impose large costs on the lower classes.[15] The ability to implement the liberalization projects of the 1980s and 1990s in some countries was partly based on the votes of sectors that had been marginalized in prior periods. For example, Bolivian presidents Gonzalo Sánchez de Lozada (1993–1997 and 2002–2003) and Hugo Banzer (1997–2001) talked of empowering local communities but then ignored these groups' opposition to the privatization of water and the export of natural gas through Chile in 2001 and 2003, respectively.[16] Contrasting with this paternalistic representation is actual policy change occurring in response to opposition. In the Brazilian energy reform of 1997, for example, President Fernando Henrique Cardoso (1995–2003) moderated his privatization policies in the energy sector in response to opposition from members of

Congress and their constituencies. The general lesson is that policies must deliver for empowered groups or they will withdraw their support for those policies.[17]

To have inclusiveness of the political system as a causal variable consequently means not only that one is represented in the system, but also that leaders are institutionally accountable to these groups. Accountability doesn't just happen at election time but requires that the behavior of elected officials be influenced by constraints that result from included groups making use of their rights as codified in the rules governing the political system, generally the constitution. Newly included groups may demand a new constitution if they believe the current one has sufficient ambiguity and loopholes that politicians can effectively ignore demands from these new actors. The pressures for direct democracy that we see today represent efforts for inclusion in the policy-making process by citizens who have historically perceived themselves as marginalized and benefiting less, despite their exercise of a right to vote in elections.[18]

Unfortunately, the marginalized sectors of Latin American societies have become a focus of government in many contemporary Latin American nations in a manner that continues the regional legacy of exclusive, opaque, and unaccountable institutions.[19] This result is particularly detrimental (and paradoxical) because the marginalized have few resources with which to influence political elites and should therefore be most in favor of transparency and accountability. But interest representation is a dynamic process, and along the way, many actors will be tempted to create enclaves in which they can monopolize rents or even divert the process into new forms of elite rule over those who voted for them in the interest of positive change. In short, one cannot have inclusiveness without transparency and credibility.

The dynamics of governing are best understood if we examine the domestic political coalitions that underpin a political system, rather than focusing on the party system itself. Parties are mechanisms of representation, but a party system that appears stable may be unable to gain support for its policies from sectors of the population critical for successful policy implementation. This situation can occur if a society has de jure or de facto limited the ability of significant groups to participate effectively in politics, that is, evolved a party system from which significant groups feel alienated.[20] Illustrative of this fact is the recent sudden and dramatic demise in Latin America of what were thought to be stable party systems and of traditional parties even where the system continued.[21] Thus it is important to look beyond the party system to the domestic political coalition for understanding policy.

The importance of inclusiveness in the political system is illustrated by the efforts of international actors to help countries heavily dependent on natural resources improve their policy making. The World Bank, Catholic Relief Services, and many academics point to three characteristics of government institutions that determine the quality of government policy: transparency, accountability, and fairness.[22] The experience of the World Bank in Chad demonstrates the importance of citizen empowerment for attaining these changes, which would not have occurred simply through the efforts of private investors and intergovernmental organizations (IGOs).[23]

A consortium of ExxonMobil, Petronas (the Malaysian NOC), and ChevronTexaco needed World Bank participation to develop the oil fields in Chad and to build a pipeline to transport the oil to a Cameroonian port on the Atlantic Ocean; the bank sought to ensure that the project promoted development and alleviated poverty. Transparency in expenditures was increased by depositing many of the funds generated by the oil exports in a London escrow account monitored by a newly created Chadian government agency and whose deposits from the consortium were publicized monthly. Chadian legislation explicitly earmarked the vast amount of revenues for poverty alleviation and a development fund. In theory, the accountability of government policy increased. It was, nevertheless, accountability to the multilaterals, not to the citizenry. Once oil and infrastructure were developed, neither the government nor the companies needed the World Bank, and the scheme for accountability and targeted expenditures on public goods was marginalized.

The interests of the citizenry and the multilaterals overlapped but were not identical. The World Bank continued to promote the oil development project even as the government increasingly reneged on its commitments. This case indicates that good projects and expert advice are not sufficient to achieve economic development and social justice, especially if governing elites believe that third parties (e.g., the IOCs) could help them outmaneuver the reform advocates. Chad's experience suggests that to achieve long-term change, the specifics of reform must be embedded in an overall context that makes it difficult for government to marginalize or undermine the reformers. Since the market demands oil and gas without concern for how that supply is developed, one can't expect private profit-making actors to impose effective sanctions on governments that use their natural resource wealth for private gain.[24] Therefore we must continue to depend on inclusiveness of the domestic political system for long-term change.

The operationalization of inclusiveness has both subjective and objective indicators. I measure the perception of Latin American citizens regarding whether they are represented in the political system by drawing on the World Bank Worldwide Governance Indicators (WGI), specifically its voice and accountability measure.[25] It is based on a list of indicators developed by other surveys to measure a variety of governance aspects that reflect on Voice and Accountability. The World Bank analysts rescaled these different measures and developed a statistical procedure to weight them for inclusion in the WGI Voice and Accountability measure.

While subjective indicators help us determine whether citizens perceive that they are included in the political system, this is not sufficient for our purposes. Citizens may not be aware of the subtle ways in which institutions structure their participation into channels through which their voice is significantly distorted or underrepresented. I thus add an institutional measure of inclusiveness. The objective measure of inclusiveness draws from Polity IV's variables regarding regulation of political participation ("parreg"; scale of 1–5) and restriction on competition ("parcomp"; scale of 1–5)—or, as the Polity IV manual puts it, the "operational question is the extent to which the political system enables non-elites to influence political elites in regular ways."[26] The polcomp variable is a composite of parreg and parcomp, providing a general measure of broad experience of voice on a scale from 1 to 10.

Ceteris paribus, we can offer the following hypotheses concerning the impact of the inclusiveness of the political system variable on energy policy. A cautionary note to the reader is important here: inclusiveness, while desirable morally and politically, does not necessarily generate good energy policy unless enhanced by the competitive and leadership variables.

Political systems that have low levels of inclusiveness will be focused on private goods

- Low inclusiveness based on the exclusion of the popular sectors pulls in the direction of *less intrusive government* because the private business sector can appropriate wealth from the energy sector without the government. The private sector will favor enough intrusiveness to appropriate wealth for distribution as private goods for those in the government coalition, but it prefers to self-regulate the sector and minimize government intervention beyond this low level of government intrusiveness, thereby privatizing management and access to the resources.

- Low inclusiveness based on the exclusion of national business pulls in the direction of *more intrusive government* because the popular sectors need the government to appropriate wealth from the energy sector for distribution as private goods to the popular sector.

Political systems that are highly inclusive will have governing coalitions that are correspondingly larger and thus generate pressures for greater control of resource wealth to generate funds with which to reward members. The size of the coalition provides incentives to generate public goods.

- Inclusiveness pulls in the direction of more intrusive government policy in the energy sector
- Inclusiveness pulls in the direction of more public goods.

Competitiveness

Despite the fact that constituencies are self-centered, and all governments have constituencies, some governments work with markets in ways that promote efficiency and effectiveness and public goods, while others largely promote the private gain of their constituencies. Thus we need to examine the political incentives that push politicians to act in one way or the other. In the case of energy policy, governments might seek to capture rents through fiscal policies (royalties and taxes) or to take all the natural resource wealth through ownership of production itself via a national oil company. Once captured, however, there is a temptation for government to utilize wealth for the personal benefit of politicians or to reward important constituencies through corruption or patronage, all of which divert the use of this wealth away from social and economic development. The question is thus whether investing those rents and NOC dividends in public goods furthers politicians' career interests, which is what Barry Ames calls "political survival."[27]

Geddes has labeled this need to manage public policy effectively and yet reward leaders' constituencies the "politician's dilemma"; although she is referring to the management of state-owned enterprises, the logic holds for public policy in general.[28] The coalition that supports the government faces a collective action problem: all members of the coalition would be well off if the government managed public policy effectively because they would continue winning elections. If one member, however, were able to use public policy for patronage, the government would still succeed, and that member would get an extra benefit. All members realize this situation, and if they act in a manner that is rational for their specific group (seek the extra benefit), they would all seek patronage. The result would deprive the government of the human and financial resources to produce the level of public and private goods to retain the allegiance of voters. The failure of government policy would, in a democracy, result in losses in the next election for the governing party.

The problem of forgoing patronage if rivals have access to it is not just a concern of policy makers in a democracy. Nondemocratic governments contain political cleavages within themselves, and if these constituent groups compete for rents, the authoritarian government's ability to generate growth and important infrastructure projects (which are public goods) to sustain that growth will be undermined. Latin America's experience with failed authoritarian governments proves that they are not immune to the political costs of policy failure.[29]

In the energy arena, government capacity to work effectively with markets affects its ability to use natural resource wealth to generate public goods or to create the conditions for the domestic market to have sufficient energy at adequate prices to promote sustainable growth. The key to the development of state capacity is that it must be in the specific interests of the politicians that design and enable the agencies of government to operate; this is not a matter of "political will" but of career interest.

Guided by the works of Ames, Geddes, Bueno de Mesquita et al., and Spiller et al.,[30] but extending the logic to nondemocratic systems as well, I argue that political competition within the deliberative body that designs policy (e.g., the legislature in a democracy) is the key to getting politicians to view the delivery of public goods as in their career interests. The importance of competition is that it constrains people from doing exactly what they want; constituencies will feel that constraint as they seek to form coalitions behind a specific politician. In addition, competitive deliberative bodies are more likely to develop independent legal systems to protect what is broadly known as "property rights"—which include not only physical property but contractual obligations and civil rights—because everyone knows that at some point their groups will not be running the government, and thus they want protection from those in office.

Legislators will respond to the same constraints as they compete with potential challengers for the support of the relevant constituencies. Presidents and even dictators will also operate under some of these constraints as they seek to maintain the support of key constituencies. (This point is elaborated on in the next subsection on leadership.)

So how does competition promote effective public policy?[31] When different political groups are evenly balanced within the body that deliberates and designs policy, they will have equal access to patronage. There is no incentive to forgo patronage unless at least one group perceives that it can gain favor with the voters or dictator by supporting the development of state capacity and the provision of public goods. Even in a deliberative body with a dominant party, if a groundswell of opposition is developing against the use of public resources for patronage, the leaders of the dominant party will have an incentive to forgo patronage and build state capacity.[32]

Every political system has an arena in which competing groups interact to determine policy. In a democratic polity, this locus is found in the relationship between the legislature and the executive; political parties are usually the key interlocutors in this policy-making process, and access to this group is formally institutionalized in electoral procedures and the rules for lobbying. Because oil revenues and expenditures can be opaque, competitive politics will be more likely to shed light on how much revenue is collected from the sector and how it is spent.

Although nondemocratic governments do not have an influential legislature, one can still find the deliberative body that interacts with the leader to determine policy. If deliberative bodies can constrain authoritarian leaders to abide by their policy commitments, then they must be able to impose costs on the leader for violating the policy.[33] In these polities, the size of the body is significantly smaller than in a democracy, reflecting the limited access society has to the government, whether as voters or through lobbying. The size of an authoritarian deliberative body can vary from minimal (e.g., limited to the personal confidantes of the supreme leader, a Security Council of the commanders of the armed forces, or a Central Committee of the authoritarian party) to a larger but still limited body (a caucus of colonels or ad hoc meetings of notables from constituency groups). Given limited resources, even with oil revenues, the larger the group represented from these deliberative bodies, the greater the likelihood that some public goods will need to be delivered alongside the corruption and patronage.

For a measure of legislative competition in a democracy, I use two variables. The first variable is whether the governing party has a *majority in the legislature*, because for some legislation a simple majority may be sufficient. If the governing party has a majority, the level of competition will be lower than if it needs to build a coalition with other parties to pass legislation, because those other parties will have their own views and will demand some form of benefits to support the policy. A second variable is drawn from Polity IV and measures the constraints from the legislature and society on the executive (XCONST). This variable captures the ability of the legislature and society to affect policy; if the executive can largely declare and adopt policy without legislative or societal input, competitiveness will be low.

The following hypotheses about the impact of competitiveness on energy policy are based on the argument that the greater the competition among those responsible for public policy, the more likely it is that politicians and their constituencies cannot count on controlling government for a long period and using that discretionary scope to secure private benefits.

A deliberative body with low levels of competitiveness will develop an energy
policy that produces private goods for distribution to the dominant
coalition's constituency

- If the dominant coalition favors the private sector, energy policy will have low levels of government intrusion, but there will be little effective regulation, and private-sector monopolies will characterize the energy sector.
- If the dominant coalition favors the lower socioeconomic sectors of society, energy policy will have high levels of government intrusion, but with little

effective regulation to prevent state institutions in the sector from essentially serving as a mechanism for the distribution of private goods to the coalition's constituency.

The more competitive the deliberative body, the lower levels of government intrusion will be

- If the competitiveness occurs within the national business sector, there will be low levels of intrusion into the operational side of the energy sector because business wants neither to be regulated nor to be replaced by government. But in this scenario, we expect to see moderate fiscal regulation of the sector to reduce the ability to use wealth from the sector to consolidate political dominance.
- If the competitiveness occurs within the popular sectors, there will be high levels of intrusion into the energy sector to both control it and maximize government take. But there will also be high levels of oversight of the resource revenues accruing to the government to reduce the ability to use wealth from the sector to consolidate political dominance.

The more competitive the deliberative body, the greater the likelihood that natural resource wealth will be used for public goods

- Competitors seek to prevent the coalition in power from using government revenue and policy to consolidate their control over government. Competitors need to demonstrate that they promote policies that benefit citizens beyond their own constituency in order to win elections in the future.

The relationship between inclusiveness and competitiveness is important for explaining the level of state intrusion into the oil and gas sector and the level of public goods provided. The inclusiveness variable tells us about the number and heterogeneity of the relevant actors in the governing coalition and the bias toward government intrusiveness into the oil and gas sector, as well as the government's provision of public and private goods. The competitiveness variable tells us about the incentives facing decision makers when they are making choices about policy. The inclusiveness variable has three variants: low with national business favored, low with the popular sectors favored, and high, which includes business and the popular sectors. The competitiveness variable also has three variants: low with national business in control, low with the popular sectors in control, and high, in which control of the decision-making body is fluid. Numerically, this makes for nine combinations, but low inclusiveness favoring national business cannot combine with low competitiveness favoring the popular sector, nor can low inclusiveness favoring the popular sector combine with low competitiveness favoring national business. Thus there are only seven possible combinations.

The low-low combinations mean that the included group can behave according to expectations generated simply by examining the inclusiveness variable. From the discussion on inclusiveness, when national business is favored we expect a low level of state intrusion as well as a low level of public goods provisions. The low-low combination favoring the popular sectors generates a high level of state intrusion to provide benefits for the popular sectors. Those benefits are distributed in ways that focus on popular-sector consumption, thereby effectively creating private goods for the sector (e.g., education budgets that starve established and selective universities in favor of proliferating and populating new universities that are poorly staffed but open to everyone).

When low inclusiveness favors national business, we expect less intrusiveness. But high competitiveness among national business groups means that they compete to control the government. They thus worry that a group currently dominating government might be able to use its position to consolidate control, thereby reducing competitiveness. I therefore expect the level of intrusion to increase moderately in order to generate funds to produce a moderate level of public goods (only those that national business sees as indispensable). Because these public goods will benefit all the business sector, the business group in office will not benefit disproportionately, and competition will remain high. Since inclusiveness is low and favors national business, the intrusion will be focused on generating a moderate fiscal take by government and less on the operations side. Because government take will be moderate and public goods need to be produced, this combination generates oversight of government behavior by the deliberative body to stimulate more efficient use of the wealth to allow for the provision of public goods.

When low inclusiveness favors the popular sectors, we expect high intrusiveness. But high competitiveness within the popular sector means that popular-sector parties will be trying to keep the party in power from using the oil and gas sector to consolidate its rule. Nevertheless, the level of intrusiveness will be high because the popular sectors have few ways to generate funds to finance the vast expansion of benefits they seek. Competitiveness will generate legislative oversight of government use of SOEs and regulatory agencies. The level of public goods provision will be high because oversight makes it difficult to provide many private goods to segments of the popular sector.

The combination of high inclusiveness, low competitiveness, which favors national business, is expected to produce a low level of intrusion as well as a low level of public goods provision, though more than in the low-low combination favoring business. Low competitiveness in which business dominates means that the business party in control of government distributes private goods to those subsections of the popular sector that help it to remain in power. When high inclusiveness, low competitiveness favors the popular sectors, we expect a high level of intrusion to maximize government returns from the oil and gas sector. Yet this wealth produces only a moderate level of public goods because the government will need to provide private goods to keep national business in a coalition dominated by the popular sector.

In the high-high combination, high inclusiveness pushes toward more government intrusion, but high competitiveness drives the level of intrusion down. The result is expected to be a moderate level of intrusion and a high level of public goods provision. To accomplish this, government must be more efficient in its production of public goods or it will lose the next election.

Table 3.1 summarizes how the two variables inclusiveness and competitiveness come together in the hypotheses presented in this section.

Leadership: Innovation and Risk Acceptance

Leaders are not just a sounding board for their constituencies; political leaders vary in the constraints within which they function and may retain important discretionary capacities and therefore have an ability to make a

TABLE 3.1

Impact of Inclusiveness and Competitiveness on Level of State Intrusion and Provision of Public Goods

	Low Inclusiveness; Favors National Business	Low Inclusiveness; Favors Popular Sectors	High Inclusiveness
Low Competitiveness; Favors National Business	Low level of state intrusion; private goods favored	— —	Low level of state intrusion; private goods favored
Low Competitiveness; Favors Popular Sector	— —	High level of state intrusion; private goods favored	High level of state intrusion; moderate level of public goods
High Competitiveness	Moderate level of state intrusion; moderate level of public goods	High level of state intrusion; moderate level of public goods	Moderate level of state intrusion; high level of public goods

fundamental difference in policy.[34] Whether leaders can promote policies only within their formal constraints or push beyond them depends on their level of innovation and their risk acceptance. This subsection develops the argument about leader characteristics, then relates them to the institutional constraints that leaders face to produce hypotheses about how leaders are expected to influence energy policy.

The leadership qualities hypothesized to matter can be usefully summarized as the ability to innovate and the willingness to take risks. Innovation in policy is the development of a new vision or strategy, not just the offering of an alternative idea. Innovation is important because when a crisis occurs, it means that the current policy has proven inadequate to the challenges. The absence of new ideas on how to think about or distribute the benefits at stake suggests a continuation of failure and opens the door to the possibility of mobilization of previously excluded groups and even the restructuring of the political system to move beyond the failed policies. With respect to energy policy, creating an independent regulatory agency (IRA) is innovative in the national context because it dramatically upsets existing patterns of natural resource wealth appropriation and distribution. The risk is a political one of losing support and losing office; it is not simply the economic risk of whether the policy is successful in economic terms. A policy that is an economic failure does not mean that the leader will lose political support—her constituencies may not blame her or feel that the alternative leader would be worse for their interest. Alternatively, the policy could be an economic success but alter the distribution of benefits to the cost of key constituencies, and thus the leader loses their support.

Risk acceptance is important for two reasons. If a leader has new ideas but is timid about putting them on the agenda, the institutional constraints will determine whether he does. Only under very loose constraints will a risk-averse leader propose new ideas that do not have the possibility of immediate support. In contrast, a leader who is risk acceptant and has new ideas will be quite willing to seek to create the political conditions that mitigate the institutional constraints. The combination of risk acceptance and lack of innovation is dangerous; it suggests a leader who is willing to push ahead on poorly conceived new ideas or recycle failed ones. The leader who is both innovative and risk acceptant fits the category others have labeled either "reform monger" or "norm entrepreneur."[35]

It is important to determine whether a leader is innovative or risk acceptant through nontautological means (i.e., avoiding the following claim: "important changes are only carried out by innovative and risk acceptant leaders, and since energy policy changed dramatically, the leader was innovative and risk acceptant"). We can do so by drawing on studies of leaders' behavior in crises on matters other than energy policy. Specifically, we can look to the following. *Innovativeness* is defined in the national context; we can usefully assume that ideas that have been around in other political systems but not discussed in the country under study confront too many disincentives for anyone of influence to promote them. That means we need to ascertain whether anyone in a similar position of power previously pushed these ideas. Regarding *risk acceptance*, two questions help us gauge this. Is the leader going against the perspectives of his own party or constituency? Is the leader challenging government actors who could cause his overthrow or significantly limit his government's program (Congress, judiciary, the military)?

Table 3.2 brings institutional constraints and leader characteristics together. When leaders are not innovative and fear risk, the level of institutional constraints has determining influence, and policy will emulate what was done in the past. When institutional constraints vary, leader characteristics gain importance. A leader who is risk averse but innovative will push new ideas only when the institutional constraint

TABLE 3.2
Hypotheses Relating Leader Characteristics and Institutional Constraints

	Risk Taker: Yes	Risk Taker: No
Innovator: Yes	Pushes new ideas while seeking to alter institutional constraints	If institutional context is permissive, pushes new ideas
Innovator: No	Pushes old ideas while seeking to alter institutional constraints	Reacts to events by sticking to traditional policy positions; strong hand of history

is permissive, that is, moderate or weak. The leader who is a risk taker but not innovative will bring forward problems to address but will offer ideas that have been tried in the past. Institutional constraints are directly challenged by risk-acceptant leaders, but the innovator will use that opportunity to pursue new policy options, while the leader who is not innovative will propose policies that have been tried in the past.

Political entrepreneurs who face looser constraints should be expected to quickly use their administrative powers to undertake dramatic policy changes. In the short term, these measures cause political grumbling among the beneficiaries of the old policies, but the new leader's popularity may allow him to survive until the presumed benefits of change begin to kick in and generate benefits for the constituency after all.

HYPOTHESES ABOUT LEVEL OF GOVERNMENT INTRUSIVENESS IN ENERGY POLICY

Each of the three variables—inclusiveness, competitiveness, and leader characteristics—has a hypothesized impact on the variations in level of government intrusiveness in a country's energy policy. Four hypotheses about that interaction in democratic polities are particularly interesting for considering energy policy in Latin America.

- Hypothesis 1: Low Inclusiveness + Low Competitiveness + Innovative and Risk Acceptant Leader low levels of government intrusiveness and moderately low provision of public goods. This situation may characterize right-wing authoritarian populist regimes with a dominant party, such as Menem's Argentina in the 1990s. In this case, the innovative and risk-acceptant leader is willing to push for some public goods despite pressure from her constituency and the deliberative body for immediate private goods.

- Hypothesis 2: High Inclusiveness + High Competitiveness + Innovative and Risk Acceptant Leader moderate levels of government intrusiveness and moderately high levels of public goods. This situation may be found in a liberal democracy, such as Brazil under Cardoso (1994–2002) or Lula (2002–2010). The innovative and risk-acceptant leader will push for ways to get around the deliberative body's constraints to administratively intervene in markets and divert resources to provide private goods for his constituency.
- Hypothesis 3: High Inclusiveness + High Competitiveness + Innovative and Risk Averse Leader low levels of government intrusion and high levels of public goods provision. This situation may be found in a liberal democracy, such as that of Raúl Alfonsín (1983–1989) in Argentina. The innovative but risk-averse leader will accept the demands from a competitive deliberative body for the provision of public goods to meet the demands from a highly inclusive constituency. The president will be a key advocate of innovation in energy policy, especially as regards an independent regulator, but will follow the lead of the legislature.
- Hypothesis 4: High Inclusiveness + Low Competitiveness + Innovative and Risk Acceptant Leader high levels of government intrusiveness and moderate level of public goods provision. This situation may represent a left populist government with a dominant party, such as that of Evo Morales (2006–2019) in Bolivia. The innovative and risk-acceptant leader will push for ways to get around the deliberative body's emphasis on high levels of government intrusiveness for private goods provision to a broad constituency. The leader is innovative because she sees the need for longer-term investments in public goods and is willing to confront the legislature and electorate. But the dominance of a single party representing an inclusive electorate limits the ability of the leader to provide public goods for national development.

In summary, I argue that three political variables significantly determine the character of energy policy that is developed within the context set by geology and markets. The hypotheses suggest that there are two combinations corresponding to right and left governments that are most likely to generate broad distribution of public goods and sustainable national development. A country in which ownership of subsoil and submarine resources lies with the nation is most likely to develop an energy sector with high levels of state intrusion and higher levels of public goods provision when the political system is *inclusive*, political competition is *unbalanced*, and political leaders are *innovative and risk acceptant*. On the other hand, a country in which ownership of subsoil and submarine resources lies with the nation is most likely to develop an energy sector with lower levels of state intrusion and higher levels of public goods provision when the political system is *inclusive*, political competition is *competitive*, and political leaders are *innovative and risk averse*.

PART II
Venezuela Case Study

Chapter Four

VENEZUELA'S POLITICAL ECONOMY, 1989–2016

This chapter presents a historical narrative of the political economy of Venezuelan politics during our study period, 1989–2016. It consists of four sections, one for each of the presidential administrations: Pérez, Caldera, Chávez, and Maduro. The chapter neither discusses nor analyzes energy policy but provides the empirical context to situate our five variables in the next chapter and to understand the energy policies analyzed in chapters 8 and 9.

Venezuela entered the 1990s in a structural economic and political crisis. By the late 1980s the economic crisis resulting from becoming too dependent on declining oil prices deepened. The fear of running out of oil that contributed to nationalist sentiments in the 1960s had been masked by the oil price boom in the 1970s. But once prices fell, the concern over the level of petroleum reserves became paramount once again, and now with a fear of declining production. The nationalization in 1975 created a government monopoly across the oil and gas value chains, except under very limited and specific conditions for the upstream and subject to review and approval by the National Assembly (article 5). In natural gas, the upstream had been nationalized in 1971, and in 1973 the Ley que Reserva al Estado la Explotación del Mercado Interno de los Productos de Hidrocarburos set the goal of establishing a monopoly in the mid- and downstream.

The hero of the first oil boom and now president again, Carlos Andrés Pérez (1974–1979; 1989–1992), attempted to impose fiscal discipline and structural economic change across the economy. Pérez's *Gran Viraje* (Great Turnaround) meant dismantling the import substitution industrialization strategy that had used oil wealth to spawn a proliferation of inefficient SOEs, private businesses that supplied those SOEs, and the labor unions that worked in both.[1] Pérez selected a group of independent economic advisors in the planning agency (Oficina Central de Coordinación y Planificación, CORDIPLAN; Miguel Rodriguez and Ricardo Hausmann), Ministry of Development (Moisés Naím and Imelda Cisneros), and the Central Bank (Pedro R. Tinoco and Ruth Osterreicher de Krivoy) to develop the path for the Great Turnaround.[2]

The VIII Plan de la Nación was developed in 1989 and presented to Congress at the beginning of January 1990.[3] The plan declared the end of the import substitution industrialization era, the arrival of globalization, and the need for Venezuela to be competitive in this new international economic context. Pérez's Gran Virage envisioned a significantly reduced role for the state in his new development model, and the plan uses the word *apertura* (opening) throughout to refer to the role for private domestic and foreign investment in Venezuela's future development. State enterprises were to be privatized and the few remaining ones made efficient, subsidies for consumption cut and those for productive enterprises rationalized and audited, and the private sector encouraged to invest and become an important driver for economic growth. To reduce the misuses and inefficiencies of the oil wealth revenue as it passed through the budgetary process ostensibly to fund national development, the hydrocarbon sector projects in oil, natural gas, petrochemicals, and coal were to be used as development poles themselves rather than simply as revenue sources.

These dramatic structural changes were proposed as state capacity was declining because of the ongoing financial and economic crisis. Nevertheless, and unlike in his first term, President Pérez lacked support in Congress for his policies. As the Punto Fijo political system weakened under the weight of corruption and domination by two political parties, policy making grew more contentious and partisan. Pérez attempted to implement his economic restructuring by maneuvering around Congress as much as possible. This approach demonstrated that he was attempting not only fundamental economic changes but also important changes in the political process of policy.[4]

Reforms were also targeting the oil sector because, in Pérez's view, financing economic and social adjustment and dealing with the large foreign debt required increasing Venezuela's proved resources and exports to compensate for low oil prices with increased volume. Despite some opposition from within their own parties, this "supply strategy" for the oil sector would be a constant for the three administrations (Pérez 1989–1993, a transitional government led by Ramón J. Velázquez in 1993, and Rafael Caldera 1994–1998), which governed Venezuela from 1989 until the election of Hugo Chávez in 1998.

There were, however, significant voices in the opposition across Congress, the military, and civil society opposing the dismantling of the interventionist state. They desired a national oil strategy that would strengthen OPEC's capacity to reduce supply, drive up prices, and fund the old development program. Not everyone who opposed the VIII Plan was a statist—many were just political rivals of Pérez—but statists were consistently opposed to these ideas, even when presented by Caldera after 1996. Many of these statists would become important players in the Chávez administrations of 1999–2012.

New political, economic, and financial tensions developed as the Venezuelan political economy shifted in favor of the Bolivarian Revolution after 1998. The economy became increasingly dependent on oil exports, high prices, foreign investment in the oil sector, and foreign loans explicitly backed by oil exports. Taking over from Chávez and winning his own term in the controversial elections of 2013, Nicolás Maduro enjoyed a year of near record high prices, but his legitimacy was contested, and when oil prices collapsed, the Bolivarian model was on the ropes. The opposition finally won control of the National Assembly in 2015, and splits began to develop within *chavismo* as Maduro struggled to respond to the political and economic crisis as our period of study closed in 2016.

Although oil continued to be at the center of Venezuela's political economy in these two historical periods (1989–1998 and 1999–2016) the dominant terms and players changed significantly. The political economy of Venezuela in each of the four presidencies (Pérez, Caldera, Chávez, and Maduro) is briefly presented in this chapter to provide context for the next chapter, in which the values of the variables used to explain energy policy are presented.

CARLOS ANDRÉS PÉREZ, 1989-1993

Pérez's Gran Viraje quickly hit a roadblock when it became apparent that he intended to dramatically reduce the role of the state in the economy and thereby reform the patronage system on which Punto Fijo had been constructed and maintained in the decades since its founding in 1958. The decision to subject the economy to a "shock treatment" also promised to have significant social costs. His own party opposed most of the reforms, and he had to look for independent collaborators to staff his cabinet and adopt policies by decree. The heterogeneity of a cabinet comprised of technocrats and key political allies meant obstruction in the implementation of policy as well. With Decree 727 in 1990, Pérez eliminated many restrictions discouraging foreign investors. These included permitting foreign investors to remit profits to parent companies without first obtaining official permission, opening the domestic capital market to foreign investors, opening some sectors of the economy previously closed to foreign investment, and reducing government discretion and interference with foreign investment.[5]

The elimination of multiple exchange rates, an opening of the economy to trade, liberalization of domestic prices, increased rates for public services, and a major devaluation significantly decreased purchasing power across society. Though the government was able to restructure foreign debt and increase targeted (though still insufficient) subsidies to those at the bottom, intense opposition developed from the beneficiaries of the old system as well as previously excluded people who still believed that the country was rich because of its oil. In Pérez's first year, personal disposable income fell by 14 percent and real salaries by 11 percent.[6] Riots erupted as fuel prices increased (known as the *Caracazo*, in which hundreds were killed as the government tried to regain control of the streets), and Pérez responded by declaring a state of emergency.[7]

Though the economy grew by 6.5 percent and 10.4 percent in 1990 and 1991, respectively, the economic and political damage was so severe that few could see the end of austerity in sight. Social dissatisfaction and crime increased, and there were major protests during 1991–1992.[8] A national opinion poll at the end of 1991 revealed only 12.3 percent support for Acción Democrática (AD) and President Pérez. Social protests revealed significant discontent among the populace, particularly the poor, not only with the IMF economic reform package but also with the two-party political system dominated by AD and COPEI. An increasing number of citizens blamed the economic crisis on a political system known to be corrupt and the foreign oil companies and governments who wished to fuel their own development and consumption with cheap oil.[9]

There were two failed military coups in 1992 that sought to end the Punto Fijo system and replace it with a transitional civil-military government. The February attempt was led by four lieutenant colonels, including Hugo Chávez and Francisco Arias Cárdenas, who for years had been planning an uprising in conjunction with remnants of the 1960s rebellion (Movimiento Bolivariano Revolucionario 200, MBR-200).[10] It failed, but Pérez was convinced to permit Chávez to address the public by radio to convince everyone to lay down their arms. His speech was unrepentant and condemned the system, earning Chávez some sympathy among frustrated Venezuelans. Senator Caldera also gave a speech condemning the coup but blaming the Pérez government for creating the conditions for it.[11] An attempted coup in November by officers from the navy and air force with links to MBR-200 also failed.[12] All participating military leaders were arrested and jailed.

Pérez, however, continued to lose support. Congress was caught up in discussions over whether the constitution should be reformed or replaced, and the left conditioned its support on holding a national referendum to revoke Pérez's tenure (the constitution did not provide for such a referendum). He was impeached in May 1993 after the Supreme Court ruled that there was enough evidence for a trial on misuse of funds (in 1996 the Court found him guilty of minor misuse of funds). Congress appointed Octavio Lepage to administer the office while it selected Ramón J. Velázquez to finish out the term. Congress provided Velázquez with sufficient support to pass some legislation stymied under Pérez.[13]

RAFAEL CALDERA, 1994-1998

In 1994 Caldera, a founding father of COPEI, ran as a political outsider with a new party, Convergencia. Caldera announced during his campaign that he would pardon the military officers who rose up in rebellion against the political system, including Chávez. His victory signaled the effective end of the Punto Fijo political system, though the final nail in the coffin would wait until a new constitution was adopted in 1999.[14]

Caldera had two distinct national development strategies. His first national strategy upon taking office in 1994 was a traditional adjustment policy pursued by statists seeking to stay on the path of import substitution industrialization. The strategy depended on financing adjustment through income from exports since the country could not increase foreign debt by significant amounts and the domestic economy was not attractive to private investors, given structural problems, administered pricing, and foreign exchange controls. Without a governing coalition behind him to effectively address the economic and political crisis, Caldera fought with Congress, threatening it with a constitutional convention that would replace them, and managed to get short-term fixes approved. But the lack of a significant tax reform and increased social spending meant that he would be rapidly facing a fiscal crisis. The Caldera administration's task was further complicated by a banking failure that began just before he assumed office and ballooned into crises by the middle of his first year.[15] The currency collapsed amid government takeover of the failed banks and payouts to depositors. The government suspended constitutional rights while it dealt with the crisis. One estimate is that the banking crisis cost at least $7.3 billion.[16] Consequently, Caldera would quickly need a major influx of foreign funds; in Venezuela, that meant a greater volume of oil exports.

In his first year, 1994, and using decree powers granted by the legislature,[17] he lowered the regressive value added tax (VAT) but kept the budget for funding state government infrastructure projects (Fondo Intergubernamental para la Descentralización, FIDES) at the same level, thereby creating conditions that would increase fiscal deficits. The political decentralization reform of the later 1980s further constrained Caldera since the federal government had lost much of its political hold over governors and municipalities.[18]

By September 1995 the failure of this development strategy was clear, and Caldera changed course. The finance minister announced that economic policy would gradually free the economy and the government would seek IMF assistance the following year. But at the end of 1995 foreign reserves fell to US$9 billion and the Caldera administration devalued the currency by 41 percent. In April 1996 Caldera announced an economic structural reform that was more "shock" than gradual adjustment (the Agenda Venezuela).[19] The administration gained IMF approval by lifting price controls on all goods except medicines, ending foreign exchange controls, freeing interest rates, and intending to reduce public spending, strengthen the financial sector, and sell SOEs in telecommunications, aluminum, steel, petrochemical, and power sectors.[20]

Caldera's administration was therefore very dependent in both national plans on the oil sector generating funds through increased exports or an increase in foreign investment flows. But state governments were also looking for protection from the revenue cuts. In 1998 Congress required that oil royalties had to be shared between the federal and state governments, further limiting federal revenue just as oil prices were collapsing to their lowest point in our study period (US$19.12 in 2017 dollars).

The structural adjustment program undertaken produced an erratic recovery, partly because the economy was so dependent on oil exports and partly because no government could hold together a coalition behind a policy long enough for it to have an impact.[21] Oil prices recovered a bit during 1995–1997, but GDP growth remained problematic. And even when GDP growth recovered, its benefits did not filter down to the middle and lower classes:[22]

- 1998 real wages were less than 40 percent of 1980 level.
- Purchasing power of the minimum wage in 1994 was one-third that of 1978.
- Percentage of the population below the poverty line was 36 percent in 1984 and 66 percent in 1995.
- Percentage of the population living in extreme poverty was 11 percent in 1984 and 36 percent in 1995.
- Per capita social spending by the government in 1993 was only 60 percent of its level in 1980.[23]

Relying on the country's traditional strength, the Caldera administration's plan was to generate revenue by dramatically increasing oil production and promoting natural gas production. The administration opened the oil sector further than article 5 contemplated. PDVSA contracted with IOCs to develop new conventional oil fields and enhanced oil recovery in declining wells. But as oil prices fell in 1998 and the Venezuelan political and economic crisis continued, opposition to this supply strategy, to the partnerships with IOCs that it entailed, and to the political system itself increased dramatically.

HUGO CHÁVEZ, 1998-2013

In 1998 Chávez achieved a landslide victory, receiving 56.2 percent of the votes (in Venezuelan democratic history only Jaime Lusinchi in 1983 received a greater share at 58.4 percent), with a turnout of 63.4 percent of eligible voters. The first two years of the Chávez government were largely spent developing the institutional structure that would permit the implementation of a new political economy for Venezuela. Many voices in the 1990s called for a new constitution, and Chávez immediately supported a referendum for a Constituent Assembly (approved by 92.4 percent in April 1999 but with only a 37 percent turnout). Chávez and his supporters stacked the electoral process for the Assembly to ensure they would dominate it—with 65.8 percent of the votes, they controlled 94 percent of the seats (46.3 percent turnout). The Assembly ignored the limitations decreed by the Supreme Court in reviewing the call for a referendum and made itself the sovereign power the moment it was seated. The new constitution was approved by an overwhelming majority of voters—71.8 percent voted yes, but turnout was only 44.4 percent, which represented a decline of a third compared to the presidential election just a year earlier.

The Constituent Assembly declared itself the supreme political institution, closed Congress, fired scores of judges, and proceeded to write a constitution that centralized power in the executive and called for new presidential elections for 2000. The new constitution changed the name of the country to the Bolivarian Republic of Venezuela, increased the presidential term from five to six years, and replaced the bicameral legislature with a unicameral National Assembly with 165 seats, 110 of which are elected on a first-past-the-post system, 52 on a party list system and 3 reserved for indigenous peoples, with separate electoral rules. The new constitution affirmed national ownership of subsoil resources but permitted foreign investment in the oil sector without requiring a special review as in article 5 of the prior constitution, demonstrating a degree of pragmatism toward the sector (in contrast, Mexico did not permit any private investment until the constitutional amendment of 2013).[24]

The new constitution was not a wholesale rejection of the liberal frame-work under which the prior democratic governments had operated. Take, for example, the issue of international arbitration in cases where parties did not have confidence in the ability of national courts to adjudicate a case fairly. Many of the nationalist supporters of Chávez opposed this clause as a violation of sovereignty. For example, Alí Rodríguez, a former guerrilla, leader of the left in Congress since the 1970s, and key advisor to Chávez on oil issues who would become minister of energy and mines and then presi-dent of the NOC, led the unsuccessful appeal to the Supreme Court in 1998 against the inclusion of such clauses in the contracts. Yet the Constituent Assembly adopted article 127 of the 1961 Constitution that permitted inter-national arbitration for contracts of public interest on a case-by-case basis and with the approval of the National Legislature (article 151).[25]

Pragmatism was not limited to the Constitutional Assembly. During the first years of the Chávez government, academic and business analysts char-acterized government behavior as pragmatic, despite the rhetoric.[26] The electoral coalition that brought Chávez to power in 1998 was heterogeneous and not yet ready to support radical change.[27] Between 1999 and 2001 Chávez wanted to create poverty-reduction programs using funds from reserves building up from oil revenues as prices began to recover. He appealed to his planning minister, Jorge Giordani, to agree with these plans, but in the face of Giordani's insistence that financial reserves needed to increase first, Chávez relented and waited until the political challenges of 2002–2004, along with increased revenues from continued price rises and tax reforms, to create his various *Misiones* social programs.[28] Another example of Chávez's flexible pragmatism is the government response to pro-tests in January 2001 against the educational reforms and use of textbooks with a strong Bolivarian bias through the proposed Resolution 259 and Decree 1.011. The protest movement was led by middle-class parents whose children went to privately run schools. Chávez denounced the protesters and called them "selfish and individualistic," but the government retracted the proposed changes.[29]

Similarly in the labor sector, efforts to tame the labor movement in 1999 after an oil worker's strike were unsuccessful. First, Congress did not adopt the toughest language that radical *chavistas* proposed for the national ref-erendum on terminating all union leaders' tenure and holding new union elections under government supervision within 180 days. And second, when those new elections were held, the old union leadership group emerged largely victorious despite Chávez's support for the alternative slates, depriving the chavistas of the opportunity to create a labor movement controlled by the Chávez administration at that time.[30]

Many who had benefited from the Punto Fijo political system, however, worried about the growing centralization of power. The political Right perceived the Bolivarian Revolution as a radical experiment or an effort to convert Venezuela into a vassal of the Cuban Revolution. A radical right-wing opposition sought to lead this opposition, drawing support from the U.S. administration of George W. Bush and the Miami community of Latin American anticommunists.[31]

Chávez won the presidential election in 2000. Neither AD nor COPEI carried much weight in the new political system. Chávez's main opponent was Francisco Arias Cárdenas, one of the four lieutenant colonels (including Chávez) who organized the 1992 coup attempt and ran under the Causa R banner (the main radical party threatening Punto Fijo in 1993), with which he had won the governorship of Zulia state in 1995.

The coalition behind Chávez consolidated its control of the courts and legislature and passed more authority to the president. Rather than undertake the internal negotiating and public discussions involved in legislating, in November 2000 the Assembly provided Chávez with decree powers for one year.[32] Chávez waited until the last day, November 13, 2001, and, without public consultation, decreed forty-nine laws to further government control over the economy and polity.

As Chávez sought more direct influence over the PDVSA Board of Directors, NOC leadership called a strike in April 2002 to defend "meritocracy" within the company and keep it focused on the oil business, not politics. The political opposition to Chávez quickly joined, seeking an opportunity to discredit, if not replace, the government.[33] President Chávez withstood the challenge. The first protests attracted 500,000 people. After clashes between the government and protesters killed more than fifteen people, the Venezuelan military briefly took control of the government. The coup was poorly handled, with its leaders and the new pretenders to the government behaving as if they intended to force a return to the discredited ancien régime. Pedro Carmona, president of the Venezuelan Federation of Chambers of Commerce (Fedecámaras) was declared president, and the National

Assembly and the Supreme Court were ordered shuttered. Latin American governments protested the coup, but the U.S. government quickly recognized the new government. Support for the coup even among anti-chavistas began to dissipate. Chávez supporters took to the streets, and the military backtracked rather than risk escalation to violent repression. Chávez made a triumphant return to office after two days, with renewed public support.[34]

Chávez was initially conciliatory toward PDVSA. Alí Rodríguez was recalled from his post at OPEC, where he was secretary general, to become PDVSA president and establish order within the company. The political opposition to President Chávez supported Rodríguez's appointment to PDVSA, substantiating his high standing as knowledgeable and pragmatic.[35] Rodríguez was, nevertheless, a statist when it came to oil and a foe of the "old" PDVSA. He announced that he was "not neutral" regarding the role of PDVSA in the government's national policies and expected PDVSA employees to toe the line.[36]

In December 2002 the political opposition began a sixty-nine-day strike, which PDVSA joined; according to Oil Minister Rafael Ramírez, the strike cost PDVSA U.S. $12.8bn in losses and damages.[37] President Chávez defeated the opposition/PDVSA strategy because U.S. support for the strike tainted it among many Venezuelans, Chávez had purged the military of most opponents, and his constituency firmly rejected a return to the elite-dominated Punto Fijo system.

Surviving the 2002–2003 popular revolts, however, did not mean that the Chávez coalition was now in complete control of the country's political economy. As part of the resolution to the strike a recall referendum, heretofore opposed by the Chávez administration, was allowed to go ahead. The fact that his own constitution sanctioned the process limited Chávez's ability to resist domestic and international pressure. The Chávez government used the Electoral Commission, the Constitutional Court, and implied threats against those who signed the petition calling for the recall to thwart, if possible, or delay the referendum until the massive strikes forced his hand. Social spending by the government, now that it controlled the finances of the NOC, increased dramatically between 2003 and 2004, up by 20 percent.[38] The message conveyed by the government's spending and the opposition's derision of Chávez and his movement was clear—the opposition intended to roll back all the social benefits and investments that the

Bolivarian Revolution was just now significantly increasing. In the polarized political environment of the time and with a significant majority of Venezuelans still trying to recover from the economic debacle of the 1980s and 1990s, Chávez won the August 2004 recall with 58 percent voting no; turnout was 70 percent, up more than 10 percent over the 1998 election that first brought Chávez to power. International observers could find no credible reason to dispute the outcome and certified its results.[39]

Dismayed by the results of the recall election, the opposition faced internal disagreements over how to confront the Bolivarian Revolution—should they engage in wholesale rejection and demonization of the Revolution's leader or accept many of its social and political reforms and focus on its authoritarian nature? To complicate matters, the government was growing increasingly powerful as its oil revenues increased and popular as its distribution of benefits proliferated. The government was now openly harassing and repressing opposition leaders. The opposition decided to boycott the legislative elections of 2005 and to appeal for international recognition of Venezuela as a failed democracy.

The strategy that brought Chávez's victory in the 2004 recall—taking advantage of high oil prices to fund social programs directly linked to President Chávez—became a defining characteristic of the Bolivarian Revolution. It merged the chavistas' interest in delivering social services to the public with a political rationale for enhancing their ability to win semicompetitive elections. The government ensured that the electoral field was not level: though the elections were openly contested and voting occurred without direct intimidation and obstacles on election day, opposition candidates were harassed and, in some cases, arrested on questionable charges, the opposition press was attacked, and people working in the public sector were pressured to vote for Chávez. Most infamously, PDVSA president Rafael Ramírez warned an assembly of the NOC's middle and upper managers just before the December 2006 elections that opposition candidates could not campaign at PDVSA. He also threatened, "Our pulse is not racing. From this company, we have removed nineteen thousand five hundred enemies of this country, and we are willing to continue to do so, to guarantee that this company is in line and matches the love that our people has for our president."[40]

The opposition's boycott strategy proved disastrous in 2005: no new international aid for their cause was raised, and the government now had a free hand in the legislature, controlling 96.4 percent of its membership. In the presidential elections of 2006 the opposition regrouped around a single candidate, Manuel Rosales, governor of the oil state of Zulia, who ran on a platform that recognized the need for some social reform. Chávez, nevertheless, won a resounding victory.

The constraints on the Bolivarian Revolution, both external and internal, loosened considerably. In addition, oil prices seemed now to be in a sustained upward trajectory, enabling the Chávez government to fund programs to benefit his supporters at home and abroad. Within four months of winning reelection, Chávez announced the creation of a new party, Partido Socialista Unido de Venezuela (PSUV), that would absorb the various political parties that supported Chávez and that he would lead. When confronted by a reluctance of parties on the left to be absorbed, Chávez denounced them as unreliable. The eleven parties that merged into the PSUV in 2008 represented 45.99 percent of the presidential vote in 2006, while the twelve parties that did not join but supported Chávez accounted for 14.60 percent of the vote. The implication was clear: Chávez preferred a hegemonic party that he controlled and not a coalition of political forces, each of whom might disagree over a particular path to be taken by the Bolivarian Revolution.

Elections continued to be important for the Bolivarian Revolution even after Chávez's victory in 2006. For example, in 2007 the executive branch sent a constitutional amendment proposal to the National Assembly that would reform thirty-four provisions to facilitate the path to socialism. The reforms included permitting the continuous reelection of the president (but not of any other public official). The National Assembly added thirty-six other constitutional reforms to the package before approving it for a national vote. The electorate rejected it 51 percent to 49 percent. Chávez waited until late into the night to accept the result, saying "for now, we couldn't," but the facts that the National Assembly complicated the proposal and that Chávez had to accept the outcome illustrate that at the margins there were still important constraints on executive power.[41]

Chávez and his radical allies did not trust even chavistas to move the revolution forward. In January 2007 the National Assembly, though it had a supermajority of chavistas and thus could virtually legislate at will, provided the president with another enabling law permitting him to decree legislation, this time for eighteen months. A total of sixty-seven laws were decreed, including twenty-six on the last day of his decree authority. The laws spanned the economy, bureaucracy, and armed forces, nationalizing ownership and centralizing control.[42]

Political turmoil continued as the country polarized around the ambiguously defined Bolivarian Revolution and its "Socialism of the 21st Century." The government attempted to deflate the opposition by closing the popular television station RCTV in May 2007, and university students took to the streets in protest. As campaigns got underway for the 2008 legislative elections, some three hundred candidates were banned by the Venezuelan General Comptroller on accusations of corruption, and the Supreme Tribunal ratified their expulsion from the electoral process. Although the opposition won five state governments and the municipality of Caracas, Chávez's PSUV won seventeen state governments.[43]

Despite the continuing turmoil, support for the chavistas grew as the economy recovered strongly from the political strife of 2002–2003. Oil prices were spiking, and government expenditures were spreading the rapidly growing wealth; GDP grew 10 percent in 2006, 8 percent in 2007, and almost 5 percent in 2008. But the vulnerability of the economy was evident since growth rates were slowing significantly even in the face of high oil prices. When the U.S. financial crisis hit in 2008, oil prices fell and so did the Venezuelan economy: by over 3.2 percent in 2009 and a further 1.5 percent in 2010.[44]

To preserve the Bolivarian Revolution, the Chávez administration was locked into promoting a sense of well-being and reinforcing perceptions of a threat from the old elite and their international allies. Minimum wages, government spending, and domestic credit continued to grow, and inflation hit 32 percent in 2008 while only slowing to 30 percent in 2010, despite two years of recession. Inflation was blamed on hoarding and unwillingness to invest by the elite, supported by the U.S. government. Nationalizations spread across the economy (agribusiness, finance, construction, oil services, and steel), ostensibly to bring productive resources into the hands of those who would support the revolution, but effectively reducing output as skilled labor and capital left the enterprises. Price controls were instituted and tightened for food and medicines. But political polarization, economic mismanagement, supply bottlenecks, and rising crime rates made it impossible for the economy to generate any source of growth outside of the oil sector.

The government turned to various foreign-exchange control schemes, devaluations, and foreign debt in a vain effort to control the hemorrhaging until oil prices could boom once again. In 2011 oil prices recovered dramatically.[45] But rather than providing relief to the economy and supporting policies to decrease its vulnerability, the new revenues were used to facilitate increased expenditures (both legal and corrupt). In addition, the government floated some $17 billion in government and PDVSA bonds as well as negotiating up to $10 billion more in Chinese loans to be paid in oil shipments,[46] putting the economy further into a hole.

The Bolivarian Revolution suddenly encountered another significant challenge: Chávez's cancer. Diagnosed in June 2011, the cancer worsened as the 2012 elections for president, governors, and mayors approached. Though the economy briefly recovered via oil prices and debt, there was growing concern and speculation (his actual condition was kept secret) that Chávez would die. The opposition finally came together around a credible candidate, Henrique Capriles, and there was an expectation on all sides that he could attract significant votes. The Chávez administration was suspected of using up to $12 billion from the unaudited development fund (Fonden), bond sales, and PDVSA contributions to support social programs during the electoral campaign.[47] Chávez won a decisive victory, 55 to 44 percent, only to die five months later. As Chávez succumbed to cancer in early 2013, the economy and government remained heavily dependent on high oil prices.

NICOLÁS MADURO

Nicolás Maduro was an important labor union leader who spearheaded the drive to replace the Confederación de Trabajadores de Venezuela (CVT) with a pro-Chávez union movement in 1999–2000; he became foreign minister and subsequently vice president. After having been elected to a new term in October 2012, Chávez announced in December, as he suspected that he would not survive, that he wished Vice President Maduro to succeed him, thus avoiding a fight within *chavismo* as to a successor. Ignoring procedures outlined in the chavista constitution (article 233), Maduro acted as president during Chávez's incapacitation and death, then in the lead-up to elections in April 2013. Capriles again ran as the opposition candidate, and although polling suggested an easy victory for Maduro, he received 670,000 votes fewer than Chávez just five months earlier, with Capriles gaining 772,676 votes. Maduro was declared the winner, 50.1 percent to 49.9 percent.[48] For the next year and a half there were massive demonstrations in the streets as the opposition refused to accept the results. Violence erupted as opposition protests were fanned by the rhetoric of the extreme right and confronted by chavista paramilitaries as well as the police. Opposition leaders were arrested and stripped of their political rights, but the Maduro government could not stabilize itself.

As oil prices began a new and deeper decline in 2013, debt repayment burdens rose, the productive apparatus of the country collapsed, and crime increased. Inflation began to rise significantly from the already high levels of the Chávez period, rising to 62.2 percent in 2014, 121.7 percent in 2015, and 254.9 percent in 2016.[49] The government was incapable of stabilizing, much less reversing, the crisis. Government controls increased, and rhetoric about elite and foreign conspiracies suggested to radical chavistas that the revolution was about to take its next step to socialism. But the once beneficiaries of Chávez's largesse were increasingly experiencing the economic crisis and their allegiance waivered. In addition, democratically oriented chavistas were increasingly worried about the overtly antidemocratic measures taken by Maduro's government.[50]

Although Maduro began governing by mimicking Chávez's bluster and efforts to bias the electoral playing field, the collapsing economy contributed to shocking electoral losses in the 2015 legislative elections. The opposition not only won a national election for the first time since 1998 but gained a supermajority in the legislature. Maduro initially responded as Chávez had to prior, though lesser, advances by the opposition: by using institutional mechanisms to take power away from the legislature (as Chávez had done with governorships) and arresting leading opposition leaders on questionable criminal charges. Maduro thus eliminated the legislature and replaced it with one dominated by his supporters. First, Maduro called for the elevation of an alternative institution, the People's Communal Legislature, to be the rightful legislative branch of government and refused to recognize legislation passed by the National Assembly (though it had been created by Chávez's constitution). The judicial branch supported the president, going so far as decreeing a closing of the Assembly in 2016. In the face of international pressure, Maduro backtracked on the Supreme Court decision, thereby demonstrating the lack of a division of power, but without recognizing the authority of the Assembly.[51]

But with a continuing economic decline, these measures were not sufficient to head off growing expressions of discontent. In 2016, at the end of our period of study, Venezuela was peppered with food and political riots and the Supreme Court issued numerous rulings blocking every piece of legislation passed by the Assembly. In the summer Maduro threatened to close Congress.[52] Amid an economic crisis of horrendous dimensions, the Maduro government would respond in 2017 by adopting a measure that Chávez had not seen necessary, though perhaps he saw it as the end goal: the institutionalization of a one-party state.

Chapter Five

SCORING THE VARIABLES

In this chapter we place the five variables in the model in their Venezuelan context; the chapter neither offers explanations of events nor describes their complexity. Each of the variables is addressed in a section, with the metrics calculated for each presidential administration. Once the values for each variable are calculated, hypotheses are developed from the model regarding the characteristics of energy policy for each government. Since Chávez experienced two significantly distinct institutional periods (1998–2004 and 2005–2013), I calculate the variables for each of those subperiods. These hypotheses will be evaluated in the two subsequent empirical chapters, where the nuances, complexities, and evolution of energy policy from 1989–2016 are examined.

VARIABLES IN THE MODEL
Geology

Oil. The geology variable is measured by proved reserves (P1).[1] Venezuelan proved reserves of oil (see figure 5.1) fell significantly to 19.5 billion barrels in 1980, and PDVSA invested in increasing those reserves. Within two years, proved reserves increased to 25 billion barrels, and they doubled by 1985, but the rate of increase leveled off.[2] During

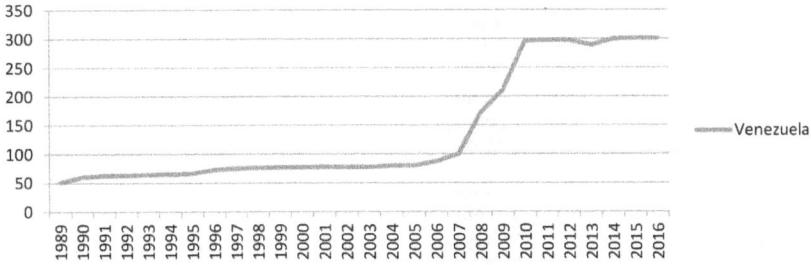

FIGURE 5.1. Venezuela, proved reserves of oil.

Pérez's second administration (1989–1993), they hardly grew, going from 59 billion to 64.4 billion barrels. Literature on Venezuela's oil situation in the early 1990s continued to see the possibility of running out of conventional oil; the upward revision of reserves in 1986 was seen as risky and costly enough that the possibility of their *not* being developed drove much of policy.[3] There was a greater increase under Caldera, from 64.9 to 76.1 billion barrels (1994–1998), as *Apertura* investments began to pay off. By 1998 the idea that Venezuela would experience a dramatic jump in proved reserves began to look credible as the first oil began to be produced (though not yet commercially viable) out of the heavy oils in the Orinoco Belt.[4]

A slower growth in discoveries, the falling price of oil (which makes it harder for some reservoirs to meet the "commercially viable" criterion for classification as "proved"), and an increase in production (see table 5.1) meant that the country's reserves-to-production (R/P) ratio had fallen by a third to the end of 2001, with a ratio of 63.5 years.[5] Yet concern about "running out of oil" did not reappear. In the first six years of Chávez's administration, proved reserves hardly improved, with increases from 72.6 to 80 billion barrels (1999–2005).[6] Nevertheless, production fell over time to 2005, even excluding the decline due to the oil strikes in 2002 and 2003, so the R/P ratio was not a concern to the government. The success of the Orinoco upgrading projects, one of which began commercial production in 2001, led the ministry to seek certification of the existence of enormous petroleum deposits in the area. There was a significant increase in proved reserves in 2007, to 100 billion barrels, then again to 172.3 billion barrels in 2008, and

TABLE 5.1
Venezuela Oil Production by Presidential Administration, 1989-2015

President	Year	Production (thousands of barrels per day)
Pérez	1989	2,010
	1990	2,245
	1991	2,500
	1992	2,500
	1993	2,590
Caldera	1994	2,750
	1995	2,960
	1996	3,137
	1997	3,321
	1998	3,480
Chávez	1999	3,126
	2000	3,239
	2001	3,142
	2002	2,895
	2003	2,554
	2004	2,907
	2005	2,937
	2006	2,824
	2007	3,237
	2008	3,228
	2009	3,038
	2010	2,842
	2011	2,755
	2012	2,704
Maduro	2013	2,680
	2014	2,692
	2015	2,631
	2016	2,387

Sources: BP Amoco, *Statistical Review of World Energy*, 2000, p. 6; *BP Statistical Review of World Energy*, June 2007, 8: *BP Statistical Review of World Energy*, June 2018, 14. There is a very slight difference in data for 1996–1999 between the 2000 and 2007 editions, and I use the 2007 numbers for those years.

Note: Includes crude oil, shale oil, oil sands, and natural gas liquids (NGLs)—the liquid content of natural gas where this is recovered separately. Excludes liquid fuels from other sources, such as biomass and derivatives of coal and natural gas.

jumping to the world's largest proved reserves, just under 300 billion barrels, in 2010, where they have remained.[7]

Natural Gas Reserves. In addition to its first-in-the-world ranking in oil reserves, Venezuela has significant proved reserves of conventional natural gas (see table 5.2). Approximately 90 percent of the gas is associated gas—when Venezuela produces petroleum, natural gas is often a byproduct.[8] There were major nonassociated gas discoveries offshore in 1978 and again in 2009, but in areas lacking infrastructure for bringing the gas to market.

TABLE 5.2
Natural Gas Proved Reserves

Year	Trillion cubic feet (tcf)	R/P (number of years)
1989	101	*
1998	142.6	*
2001	147.6	*
2010	192.7	*
2011	195.2	*
2015	198.4	173.2
2016	201.3	166.3

Sources: BP Amoco, *Statistical Review of World Energy*, 2000, 20, tcf converted from tcm; *BP Statistical Review of World Energy*, June 2002, 20; *BP Statistical Review of World Energy*, June 2011, 20; *BP Statistical Review of World Energy*, June 2012, 20; *BP Statistical Review of World Energy*, June 2016, 20; *BP Statistical Review of World Energy*, June 2017, 26.

* At the time, BP did not calculate the ratio if it was above one hundred years.

At the end of 1996 the country was the seventh largest holder of proved natural gas reserves, while in 2016 its 201 trillion cubic feet (tcf) put it fifth. The lack of domestic and international markets for Venezuelan natural gas has resulted in a ratio for reserves to production of over a hundred years.

Market

In the model, market influence is determined by reference to international oil prices. In 1980 oil prices hit historic highs of $36.83 in current dollars ($109.56 in 2017 dollars), but the market collapsed in 1986 to $14.43 current dollars, and in 1988 the price was still only $14.92. A recovery began in 1989, just as Pérez was taking office for his second term. Table 5.3, however, demonstrates that after 1990, prices moved down consistently (with small recoveries in 1996 and 1997), bottoming out at the end of Caldera's term in 1998 at $12.72 current dollars. The price variable thus went from bad to worse during the Pérez and Caldera administrations, even as reserves were growing. Revenues needed to increase, and that meant either prices or volume had to rise. Statists were drawn to rejuvenating OPEC to restrict supply, but Caldera's team saw little prospect for significant supply restrictions in the face of weak global demand.

Prices began to recover just as Chávez took office in 1999. Two factors beginning in 2003 proved favorable for prices: rising demand for oil from developing economies like China and India, and, during the Iraq War, reduced supply from a sanctioned Iraq and increased fears that supplies from the Middle East could be disrupted. Oil prices surged to levels far higher than those targeted by OPEC during the preceding period. In addition to these events, the Venezuelan national strike of December 2002–February 2003, which resulted in a loss of almost 3 million barrels per day (mbpd) of crude oil production, contributed to a sharp increase in world prices.

Nevertheless, in real terms the price scenario experienced by the Chávez administration in 2000–2002 was like that faced by Pérez. In 2003, however, Chávez began to experience the oil boom as prices reached historic

TABLE 5.3
Crude Oil Prices 1989-2017 by Presidential Administration (U.S. dollars per barrel)

President	Year	Current Prices	In 2017 Prices
Pérez	1989	$18.23	$36.03
	1990	23.73	44.50
	1991	20.00	36.00
	1992	19.32	33.76
	1993 (through May)	16.97	28.79
Caldera	1994	15.82	26.16
	1995	17.02	27.37
	1996	20.67	32.29
	1997	19.09	29.16
	1998	12.72	19.12
Chávez	1999	17.97	26.44
	2000	28.50	40.56
	2001	24.44	33.83
	2002	25.02	34.10
	2003	28.83	38.41
	2004	38.27	49.65
	2005	54.52	68.43
	2006	65.14	79.21
	2007	72.39	85.58
	2008	97.26	110.72
	2009	61.67	70.46
	2010	79.50	89.36
	2011	111.26	121.24
	2012	111.67	119.22
Maduro	2013	108.66	114.33
	2014	98.95	102.45
	2015	52.39	54.18
	2016	43.73	44.67

Source: Elaborated from BP Statistical Review of World Energy, June 2017.
Notes: 1980–1983 Arabian Light posted at Ras Tanura, 1984–2017 Brent dated. ($2017 deflated using U.S. Consumer Price Index.)

highs in 2008 and 2011, with 2012 just slightly off the high. The Maduro administration continued to experience high prices during the first two years, but prices collapsed in 2015 by almost half, then continued down in 2016. Prices for Maduro's term during our study, 2012–2016, nevertheless, were higher in real terms than for Pérez, Caldera, and the first five years of the Chávez administration, 1999–2003.

Regarding natural gas, there was no international market for Venezuelan gas in our period of study. Prices in the small domestic gas market were set by the government and not the market. Hence natural gas prices have not been an autonomous factor in Venezuelan natural gas policy.

Inclusiveness of the Political System

As noted in chapter 2, an indicator from the World Bank's Worldwide Governance Indicators measures subjective inclusiveness. A composite measure from Polity IV ranking is used for objective inclusiveness. Elections played important roles in the demise of the Punto Fijo regime and its replacement by the Bolivarian Revolution system, so in the case of Venezuela (where voting is voluntary), I add voter turnout data (table 5.4) to help interpret the subjective measures regarding inclusion. Venezuela ended compulsory voting in 1993, so the turnout in the 1988 election that brought Pérez to office is not comparable to later elections and is included simply for reporting purposes. Turnout on its own cannot be used for determining whether citizens vote because of clientelistic reasons or because they feel inclusively empowered. But turnout can be used in conjunction with subjective measures to determine whether satisfaction with democracy is the result of a sense of empowerment regarding how government behaves or preference because the largesse of politicians is being directed their way.

Subjective Indicator. The "Voice and Accountability" indicator from the World Bank's World Governance Indicators begins with 1996 and is based on a variety of distinct surveys, ranging from eight for 1996 and 1998 to nineteen for 2011 and 2012. The Governance Score for Voice and Accountability ranges from +2.5 to −2.5, and we can break our inclusiveness variable at 0.0.

The Voice and Accountability score for 1996 reflects the declining support of citizens for the Punto Fijo political system as it is slightly below our breakpoint at −0.09. For 1998 the Voice & Accountability indicator rises to just above our breakpoint at +0.11, reflecting the interest in the 1998

TABLE 5.4
Voter Turnout

Election Year	Issue	Turnout (%)	Spoiled Ballots (%)	Abstention (%)
1988*	Presidential	81.9	2.79	18.08
1988*	Congressional	81.7	0	18.03
1993	Presidential	60.2	3.65	39.84
1993	Senate	46.3	0	53.7
1993	Deputies	60.3	0	39.8
1998	Senate	54.5	—	—
1998	Deputies	52.7	—	—
1998	Presidential	63.76	6.45	36.55
1999	Constitutional referendum	37.8	<0	62.2
1999	Constituent Assembly	46.2	~13	53.8
1999	Constitution approval	44.4	<0	55.6
1999	Union leadership	23.5	—	76.5
2000	Presidential	56.38	5.28	43.62
2000	Parliamentary	56.05	32.04	43.95
2004	Presidential recall	70	0.26	40
2005	Parliamentary	25.26	5.72	74.74
2006	Presidential	74.60	1.35	25.31
2007	Constitutional reform	55.89	1.32	44.11
2009	Constitutional reform	70.33	1.76	29.67
2010	Parliamentary	66.45	—	33.55
2012	Presidential	80.48	1.89	19.52
2013	Presidential	79.68	0.44	20.32
2015	Parliamentary	74.17	—	25.83

Source: Consejo Supremo Electoral, *Elecciones Presidenciales Cuadro Comparativo 1958–2000 (voto grande)*, 4–5, http://www.cne.gob.ve/web/documentos/estadisticas/e006.pdf. For other elections, see the list provided at "Elections in Venezuela," Wikipedia.org, https://en.wikipedia.org/wiki/Elections_in_Venezuela.
*Venezuela ended compulsory voting in 1993.

elections scheduled for governors, the legislature, and the presidency. The lead in the presidential polls changed hands over the course of the year, with Chávez emerging in the lead only in August. Even so, Chávez' political party, Movimiento V República (MVR), did not do especially well in the legislative elections on November 8 of that year. MVR won 8 of 54 Senate seats, far behind AD's 21 and just ahead of COPEI's 6. In the Chamber of Deputies, MVR won 35 of 207 seats, again behind AD's 61 and with COPEI coming in third with 26 seats. Consequently, Venezuelan voters felt significantly empowered to split their vote at the presidential and legislative levels. The fall in voter turnout in the key elections of 1999 regarding a new constitution and a reform of the union labor movement, as well as in the 2000 presidential election, however, suggest that the electorate may have been getting frustrated at the polarization of politics. The high level of support for Chávez in 1998 in terms of both turnout and votes won, as well as

TABLE 5.5
Venezuela: Voice and Accountability

Year	Number of Sources	Governance Score (−25 to +25)	Percentile Rank (0 to 100)	Standard Error
1996	8	−0.09	48.00	0.20
1998	8	0.11	54.23	0.20
2000	9	−0.07	49.75	0.19
2002	11	−0.46	35.32	0.16
2003	12	−0.44	35.82	0.15
2004	13	−0.60	29.33	0.15
2005	16	−0.64	27.88	0.15
2006	16	−0.62	30.29	0.12
2007	17	−0.75	26.44	0.12
2008	17	−0.75	26.44	0.11
2009	18	−0.85	24.64	0.11
2010	18	−0.87	24.17	0.11
2011	19	−0.93	20.66	0.11
2012	19	−0.91	22.07	0.11
2013	18	−0.95	22.07	0.11
2014	15	−1.08	19.70	0.13
2015	15	−1.09	19.70	0.13
2016	15	−1.13	18.23	0.12

Source: Worldwide Governance Indicators, updated October 4, 2018, https://databank.worldbank.org/reports .aspx?source=worldwide-governance-indicators#.

the subsequent fall in voter turnout, indicate high levels of frustration with the old elite and their Punto Fijo political system, but also a level of uncertainty about the alternatives being offered by the new coalition in power. Voice & Accountability scores again drop just below our breakpoint (−0.07, based on nine surveys) in 2000 (see table 5.5).

As the constitutional and administrative changes of 1999–2003 began to consolidate the Bolivarian Revolution, the perception of citizen voice and accountability began its own downward spiral through to the end of our study period, 2016. Clearly the opposition would feel that they had no voice and that the government was not accountable, but there are indications that supporters of the Bolivarian Revolution were becoming content to depend on Chávez's will to benefit them rather than their own empowerment to create the redistribution framework. The fact that the chavista-dominated legislature in both 2000 and 2007 gave Chávez decree powers for 1 and 1.5 years, respectively, supports the interpretation that voters perceived that benefits depended on Chávez's good will rather than institutional accountability. Since voter turnout jumped for the recall in 2004 and again for the presidential election in 2006 but fell dramatically for the parliamentary election in 2005, the interpretation of voters' expectations that Chávez would provide benefits because of his beliefs rather than because of constituent pressure is reinforced. (Part of the collapse in 2005 turnout is explained by the opposition's decision to abstain, but the turnout rate of 25 percent indicates that even supporters of Chávez did not vote.)[9] But once the politicization of the opposition to Chávez and the distribution of patronage by the Chávez administration became established, voter turnout shot up to historic records: 2000 presidential election 56.31 percent; 2004 recall election 70 percent; 2006 presidential election 74.69 percent; 2012 presidential election 80.52 percent; and 2013 special presidential election after Chávez's death 79.68 percent (table 5.4).

Objective Indicator. The objective measure of inclusiveness draws from Polity IV's variables regarding regulating of political participation (termed "parreg," scale of 1–5) and restriction on competition ("parcomp," scale of 1–5)—as the Polity IV manual puts it, the "operational question is the extent to which the political system enables non-elites to influence political elites in regular ways."[10] The polcomp variable is a composite of parreg and parcomp, providing a general level of political competitiveness. The polcomp variable is not simply a sum of the values for parreg and parcomp but rather is based on their interaction.[11] Table 5.6 provides the scores on these variables for Venezuela from 1989 through 2016.

Polity IV classifies Venezuela as an Institutionalized Open Electoral Participation polity (5, 5, and 10 across the variables) during the beginning of our study period, 1989 to 1991. The legitimacy of the AD and COPEI parties and the Punto Fijo system as a liberal democracy facilitated the clientelistic relationship between parties and citizens and thus meant the dominant parties had neither need nor ability to regulate citizen participation (1989–1991). As the system weakened (1992–1998), the liberal democratic system had no ability to keep the minor parties from gaining or new parties from being created. The stress developing within the system in 1992, however, produced a relatively peaceful transition away from that institutionalized competitive system. Polity classifies Venezuela as in "democratic retrenchment," with limited overt coercion and its parreg variable now representing a citizenry with multiple political identities, creating numerous political parties (parreg = 2), all of which have access to the electoral system without many state-imposed constraints (parcomp = 4).

TABLE 5.6
Regulating of Political Participation and Restriction on Competition

Venezuela Polity IV Scores			
Year	parreg	parcomp	polcomp
1989	5	5	10
1990	5	5	10
1991	5	5	10
1992	2	4	9
1993	2	4	9
1994	2	4	9
1995	2	4	9
1996	2	4	9
1997	2	4	9
1998	2	4	9
1999	2	4	9
2000	2	4	9
2001	2	3	7
2002	2	3	7
2003	2	3	7
2004	2	3	7
2005	2	3	7
2006	2	3	7
2007	2	3	7
2008	2	3	7
2009	3	3	6
2010	3	3	6
2011	3	3	6
2012	3	3	6
2013	2	3	7
2014	2	3	7
2015	2	3	7
2016	2	3	7

Source: INSCR Data Page, Center for Systemic Peace, https://www.systemic peace.org/inscrdata.html.

The Bolivarian Revolution articulated a greater inclusiveness of those at the bottom of the socioeconomic strata, but as we saw in chapter 4, Chávez began his administration without making an overt break with business and the middle class. From 1999 to 2008 the parreg variable continued to register at the same levels as 1992 to 1998 (2), indicating the continuing fluidity of political identities and parties. The parcomp and polcomp variables also remained the same from 1992 to 2000, meaning that the first years of the Bolivarian Revolution were objectively as inclusive as the liberal Punto Fijo at its end.

However, the objective inclusiveness of the Venezuelan political system fell during 2001 to 2008 because even though parreg remained at 2, the parcomp variable moved from 4 in the preceding years to 3. Polity consequently reclassified Venezuela as a system of Factional Competition (polcomp = 7). For our purposes, Venezuela fell into the Non-Inclusive categorization because in this type of polity,

> national elections for both executive and legislative branches of government are deemed to be "free" but not "fair" by domestic and international observers. The electoral process is often rife with partisan-based political violence. The government consistently uses its institutional powers to interfere with, and/or unduly influence the outcome of, the electoral process. A polity is coded here if democratic elections are held in an environment of persistent and widespread civil unrest (rebellion, revolution, and/or ethnic conflict). . . . Factional competition is often associated with societies deeply divided by "class consciousness"—societies in which rival classes actively struggle with each other for control of the state apparatus.

Venezuela's objective inclusiveness drops even further in 2009–2012 because the parreg variable shifted to a level of 3, which, combined with a parcomp level of 3, resulted in a Polity IV classification as Factional/Restricted Competition (6). The Bolivarian Revolution had now consolidated control, and with the constitutional reforms in 2009 Chávez achieved the ability to be reelected for as long as he lived. Polarization was driving political identities into divisions based on class rather than a multitude of cleavages. The group in power (chavistas) was also now effectively using "central authority to exclude substantial groups from access to resources and restrict the identity/interest mobilization of groups that may, potentially, seek greater access."[12]

The death of Chávez in 2012 opened political space for more ways of identifying one's political identity through the end of our study period, 2016 (parreg = 2). Within the opposition, debates developed over how to identify the new political opportunities, and within *chavismo* there were disagreements about the definition of the Bolivarian Revolution, the path to follow to get there, and who would lead them.[13] Since the parcomp variable remained at 3 from 2012 to 2016, as *chavismo* sought to retain power, the Bolivarian system under Maduro up through 2016 became no more

TABLE 5.7
Inclusiveness of the Venezuelan Political System

Period	Inclusiveness
1989–1991	Inclusive
1992–2000	Inclusive
2001–2008	Exclusive
2009–2012	Exclusive
2013–2016	Exclusive

Source: Author's calculations per text.

inclusive than it had been during 2001–2008 (polcomp = 7). Though I disagree with the Polity scoring for 2016, for our purposes it makes no difference as Venezuela would remain exclusive anyway.[14]

The two inclusiveness indicators are roughly in agreement about whether citizens' views are taken into consideration in the two political systems governing Venezuela in the period 1995–2016, disagreeing only slightly about 1996 and 2000. Given the openness and fluidity of politics in those two years, I believe we can follow Polity. Table 5.7 gives the scoring for the inclusiveness variable.

Competitiveness in the Decision-Making Unit

To gauge the level of competitiveness in the decision-making unit, I use two variables: governing coalitions in the legislature and Polity IV's constraints on the executive (XCONST).

Governing Coalitions. Tables 5.8a and 5.8b provide the governing coalitions in the Congress for each of the presidential administrations.

The legislature Pérez had to deal with was quite competitive in 1988. Outgoing president Jaime Lusinchi had supported someone else in AD for the nomination, so although AD was close to a majority in both houses, it was internally split. Once Pérez abandoned his campaign rhetoric and adopted the Gran Viraje, he further alienated members of AD in both houses.

Caldera also faced a very competitive legislature, as the party he founded to run for the presidency only won 13 percent of House seats and 11 percent of Senate seats. The two Punto Fijo parties, AD and Caldera's former party COPEI, were the major parties in Congress. Neither party had a majority, though together they could have constituted a majority.

TABLE 5.8A
Governing Coalitions, National Congress

1988			1993			1998		
Party	House	Senate	Party	House	Senate	Party	House	Senate
Acción Democrática (AD)	48.25%	47.82%	AD	27.09%	30.18%	AD	29.10%	39.58%
Partido Socialcristiano (COPEI)	33.33%	43.47%	COPEI	26.10%	26.41%	Movimiento V República (MVR)	25.92%	25%
Movimiento al Socialismo (MAS)—Movimiento Izquierdista Revolucionario (MIR)	8.95%	6.52%	Causa Radical (Causa R)	19.7%	16.98%	COPEI	14.28%	14.58%
New Democratic Generation	2.98%	2.17%	National Convergence (CN)	12.80%	11.32%	Proyecto Venezuela (PRYZL)	12.69%	0%
Others (6)	6.43%	—	MAS	11.82%	9.43%	MAS	8.99%	10.41%
			Others	2.46%	5.66%	Others	8.97%	10.41%

Source: Information for elections taken from Inter-Parliamentary Union, http://www.ipu.org/parline-e/reports/2347_arc.htm.

TABLE 5.8B
Governing Coalitions, National Assembly, 2000–2015

2000		2005		2010		2015	
Party	Seats in National Assembly (%)	Party	Seats in National Assembly (%)	Party	Seats in National Assembly (%)	Party	Seats in National Assembly (%)
Polo Patriótico (MVR + MAS)	60%	Movimiento V República (MVR) & allies	96.40%	Partido Socialista Unida de Venezuela (PSUV)	59.39%	Mesa de la Unidad Democrático (MUD) + indigenous representatives	67%
Acción Democrática (AD)	19.39%	Others	3.50%	MUD	39.20%	PSUV	31.13%
Proyecto Venezuela (PRYZL)	4.24%					Partido Comunista Venezolana (PCV)	1.19%
Partido Socialcristiano (COPEI)	2.42%					Vanguardia Bicentenaria Republicana (VBR)	0.59%
Others	13.93%						

Source: Information for elections taken from Inter-Parliamentary Union, http://www.ipu.org/parline-e/reports/2347_arc.htm.

But though Punto Fijo was on the ropes, the two parties could not cooperate to save the system.

Chávez confronted a similar situation when he was elected in 1998: AD was the major party in the House and Senate, with Chávez' party MVR controlling only 26 percent of the House and 25 percent of the Senate, and COPEI the third largest party. In the Senate the Punto Fijo parties had 54 percent of the seats. The Congress in 1998 thus looked to potentially be an important constraint on Chávez.

Chávez did not have to deal with that Congress, however. In July 1999 the Constituent Assembly for a new constitution (in which Chávez supporters held 90 percent of the seats despite winning only 52 percent of the vote) declared itself the supreme political institution and closed Congress. The new constitution centralized a great deal of power and significantly decreased legislative and judicial constraints over the president. The unicameral legislature created by the new constitution gave the Chávez governing coalition a significant majority in 2000, with MVR winning 56 percent of the seats and, together with its ally Movimiento al Socialismo (MAS), holding 60 percent of the seats.

In 2005 the opposition boycotted the elections and the Chávez coalition received 96.4 percent of the seats, giving it the possibility of adopting significant changes with its supermajority. The opposition participated in 2010 and Chávez's new party, PSUV, gained a 59 percent majority but would need to ally with others to generate supermajority votes. In short, institutional changes, popularity of Chávez, and selective repression of the opposition vote by disqualifying candidates and pressuring voters who had government jobs (see chapter 4) generated a pro-Chávez legislature, but supermajority votes in 2000 and 2010 legislatures depended on Chávez's party's coalition with other parties.

Maduro had almost two years with a majority in Congress (2013–2015), but the legislative elections in 2015 produced an overwhelming majority for the opposition (a supermajority was only avoided by the Supreme Court disqualifying three opposition candidates after the vote). Since the opposition was quite heterogeneous, competition within the opposition and between the legislature and the executive should both have been high. But, as noted in chapter 6, Maduro, with the help of the Supreme Court and the police power of the state against demonstrators, eliminated the legislature from the policy-making process.

The variable for competitiveness in the legislative unit thus breaks down into the following:

- Competitive 1989–1998
- Not competitive 1999–2016

Constraints on the Chief Executive. Polity IV's constraints on the executive measure runs on a scale of 1–7. The scoring for Venezuela indicates that in the Punto Fijo system, the executive (Pérez and Caldera) was significantly constrained by a variety of accountability groups, including the legislature (1989–1998 scores of 6, see figure 5.2).[15] Polity's classification of 1999–2012 reflects the increasing centralization of power under Chávez, though the process was not fast, unilateral, or absolute. Chávez faced "substantial" institutional constraints early in his regime (1999–2005 = 5), and it was not until 2006 that those levels dropped (2006–2008 = 4). The height of executive authority in our study period is reached in 2009–2012 with a score of 3, indicating real but limited constraints on the executive. With Chávez's death, the Maduro government faced a slight increase in constraints (2013–2016 scores rise to 4) that reflects tensions within *chavismo* regarding how to pursue Chávez's legacy, the resurgence of the opposition after Chávez's death, and the growing economic crisis.

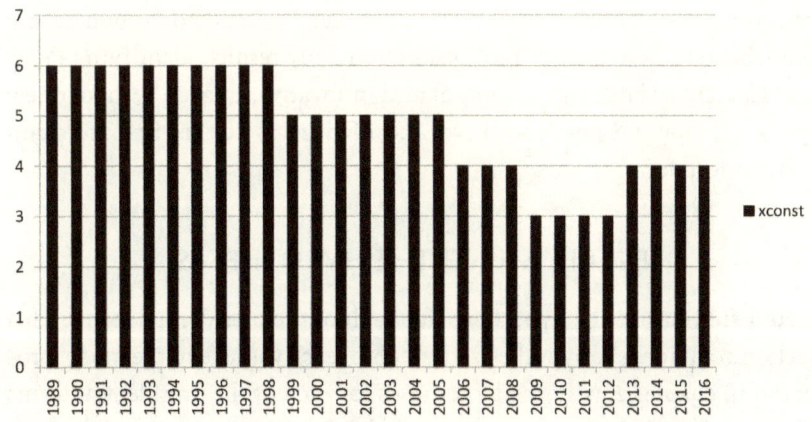

FIGURE 5.2. Venezuela, constraints on the executive (XCONST).

Polity IV's XCONST variable produces the following classifications:

- 1989–1998 high
- 1999–2005 important constraints
- 2006–08 limited constraints
- 2009–2012 very limited
- 2013–2016 limited constraints

Combining the two measures produces a classification for Competitiveness in the Decision-making Unit for 1999–2005 as "moderate" because, although the legislature was not competitive, Polity IV found "substantial" institutional constraints on the executive outside of the legislature. This produces the following classification for our study period:

- 1989–1998 high competition
- 1999–2005 moderate competition
- 2006–2016 low competition

LEADERSHIP CHARACTERISTICS

As noted in chapter 2, I have identified six nonenergy-related crises in the political lives of presidents in this period and evaluated each president's response in terms of willingness to accept the risk of opposition by his supporters and whether that response was different from responses in the country's past. Discussions of the individual crises and responses are available on my website.[16] Table 5.9 presents my results, identifying Pérez and Caldera as both risk-acceptant and innovative, Chávez as moderately risk acceptant and not innovative, and Maduro as neither risk acceptant nor innovative.

ESTABLISHING THE HYPOTHESES

Here I summarize the hypotheses for each of the presidential terms. This section combines the hypothesized effects of each variable in the model proposed in chapter 2, with the hypotheses for each of the presidential terms based on the political economic context and the characterization of the variables presented earlier.

TABLE 5.9
Leadership Characteristics and Key Policies in Crisis Times

Activities	Risk-Acceptant?	Innovative?
Carlos Andrés Pérez (1974–1979, 1989–1993)	**YES**	**YES**
Action 1 1974 Reform of the state	Yes	Yes
Action 2 1989 Cabinet	Yes	Yes
Action 3 1989 Gran Viraje	Yes	Yes
Action 4 1989 Direct elections governors & mayors	Yes	Yes
Action 5 1990 Labor Law not vetoed	No	Yes
Action 6 1998 New party for Senate campaign	Yes	No
Rafael Caldera (1969–1974, 1994–1999)	**YES**	**YES**
Founded UNE and COPEI	Yes	Yes
Pacification policy—amnesty	Yes	No
Attempted to move COPEI to the center-left	Yes	Yes
Banking crisis 1994	Yes	Yes
Founded Convergencia Nacional 1993	Yes	Yes
Pardoned coup members	No	Yes
Hugo Chávez (1999–2013)	**MODERATELY**	**NO**
Plan Bolívar 2000	Yes	Yes
Pragmatic policy 1999–2001	Yes	No
Educational reform	No	Yes
Constitutional reform proposal 2007	No	No
Launched ALBA	No	No
Attacks on the opposition	Yes	No
Nicolás Maduro (2013–2016)	**NO**	**NO**
"Safe Homeland" program	No	No
Emergency powers to confront shock to economy	No	No
Reached out to allies for economic assistance	No	Yes
Broke diplomatic ties with Panama	No	No
Fair Price Law	No	No
2017 Constituent Assembly	Yes	No

Source: See author's website, https://sites.google.com/ucsd.edu/david-mares/home.

Pérez

During Pérez's second term, the geologic outlook was improving for the long term, though it remained negative in the short term since the country was depleting its conventional oil reserves and the technology to convert heavy and extra-heavy Orinoco Belt reserves into valuable commodities had not yet been developed. Oil prices were unstable around a moderate recovery, and LNG markets were largely speculative. Based simply on the geologic and market variables, one would expect a government with a four-year term and no reelection possibility to adopt a pro-market oil and gas policy. The political variables in the model allow us to narrow the range of policies that are adopted and explain outliers.

The Punto Fijo political system was characterized by low inclusiveness because the lower classes were incorporated as clients of the two major parties; this variable means that I expect the government not to have to respond to the needs of the lower classes but rather to the needs of the elites. The first variable consequently puts pressure on the government to be less intrusive in the hydrocarbon sector (as discussed in chapter 3). The second variable, competitiveness in the legislature and between the legislative and executive branches, is scored competitive. Although Pérez's party was close to a majority within the legislature, AD's members opposed the Gran Viraje, and Pérez was forced to adopt key policies via presidential decree. This variable should thus pull in the direction of less government intervention in the oil sector and greater provision of public goods with the revenues collected. Pérez was risk acceptant and innovative, so, combined with a possible ability to rule by decree to implement policy, he would be relatively unconstrained in following the policies he believed served his government best.

The values for the political variables during the Pérez administration, 1989–1993, therefore, are:

Inclusiveness LOW + Competitiveness HIGH +
Leadership RISK ACCEPTANT + INNOVATIVE

These lead to the following hypotheses about energy policy in Venezuela during the Pérez administration:

- Since the popular sector experiences low inclusiveness, there will be an incentive for government to be less intrusive in the oil and gas value chain and provide private goods for the elite.
- Since the deliberative body is competitive, energy policy will be characterized by low levels of government intrusion in the oil and gas value chain.
- Since the deliberative body is competitive, natural resource wealth will be used for public as well as private goods.
- Pérez, as a risk acceptant and innovative leader, will push new ideas while seeking to alter the institutional constraints on his leadership.

Caldera

During Caldera's second term, the medium-term geologic outlook improved, though it was still technologically challenging, with attendant high cost. The short-term geologic picture was still daunting at the beginning of his term, with conventional reserves continuing to decline as production increased significantly throughout his term. Oil prices were unstable around a lower price in the first four years of his presidency, collapsing in his final year, 1998. LNG markets continued to be underdeveloped. Based simply on these two variables of geology and markets, one would expect a greater tendency than under Pérez to market friendly oil and gas policy.

The Punto Fijo political system was in its dying days. The two major parties were minor players, their old clientelist networks dismantled by new parties that promised to be more accountable to their voters. The Voice and Accountability of the system, nevertheless, was under severe stress. Turnout for the election in 1993 that brought Caldera to office for a second time, but this time at the head of a new party, was the first in which voting was not compulsory and recorded a post–World War II low of 60.2 percent. Caldera won with only 30.5 percent of the vote, or just under 20 percent of the electorate, indicating that the system was exclusive in favor of the elite-affiliated voters. Congress was extremely competitive during Caldera's tenure. Caldera's party was a distant fourth in Congress, and the two traditional parties that he bucked by creating a new party had a combined majority. Congressional constraints on Caldera were high because, lacking a majority, he could not count on getting Congress to provide him with decree powers and it would be difficult to get his policies through Congress. But Caldera was both risk acceptant and innovative, so he could be counted on to push his preferred policies in new ways.

The values for the political variables during the Caldera administration, 1994–1998, are:

Inclusiveness LOW + Competitiveness HIGH +
Leadership RISK ACCEPTANT + INNOVATIVE

These lead to the following hypotheses about energy policy in Venezuela during the Caldera administration:

- Since the popular sector experiences low inclusiveness, there will be an incentive for government to be less intrusive in the oil and gas value chain and provide private goods for the elite.

- Since the deliberative body is competitive, energy policy will be characterized by low levels of government intrusion in the oil and gas value chain.
- Since the deliberative body is competitive, natural resource wealth will be used for public as well as private goods.
- Caldera, as a risk acceptant and innovative leader, will push new ideas while seeking to alter the institutional constraints on his leadership.

Chávez

SUBPERIOD 1, 1999–2004

Though the geological picture hadn't yet improved substantially, expectations were high based on the upgraded technologies proving themselves. Current prices were rising steadily, but real prices were not significantly higher than during Pérez's second term. LNG markets were now developing regionally. Geology and markets did not portend an economic boom during this first subperiod of Chávez's tenure but did herald a significant loosening of constraints. The impact of these two variables is ambiguous: on the one hand, they could demonstrate the benefits of a pro-market policy, but they could also suggest that the time had come for greater government intervention to rebalance the distribution of benefits produced during the recovery of the hydrocarbon sector.

With respect to the political variables, regarding inclusiveness, 1998 was the end of Punto Fijo and the beginning of the Bolivarian Revolution. During 1999–2000 the political system was in transition and broadly inclusive, pulling in the direction of high levels of government intervention and provision of public goods. But after 2000 the chavistas became more focused on promoting the revolution and exclusive of those who disagreed with them. The inclusiveness variable consequently puts pressure on the government to be more intrusive in the hydrocarbon sector in 2001–2004 to distribute private benefits to the lower classes in the name of the revolution. Competition in the decision-making apparatus (Congress and legislative-executive relations) was moderate from 1999 to 2005. This variable also pulls in the direction of more intervention in the oil sector and greater provision of private goods to supporters of the revolution. Chávez was moderately risk acceptant and not innovative, so when confronted by opposition from supporters of his early victories, we expect him to back down and respond with policies traditionally used by statists—continue distributing benefits even as the economy weakens.

The values for the political variables during the 1999–2004 subperiod of the Chávez administration produce two equations because the inclusiveness variable shifts from high to low after 2000. These calculations lead to the following hypotheses about energy policy in Venezuela during this subperiod of the Chávez administration:

1999-2000

Inclusiveness (HIGH) + Competitiveness MODERATE +
Leadership MODERATELY RISK ACCEPTANT + NONINNOVATIVE

- Since inclusiveness is high, there will be an incentive for government to be more intrusive in the oil and gas value chain in order to finance public goods.
- Since the deliberative body is moderately competitive, however, energy policy will be characterized by moderate levels of government intrusion in the oil and gas value chain. There will be significant underlying pressure to assume an even greater intrusive stance.
- Since the deliberative body is moderately competitive, natural resource wealth will be distributed for both private and public goods.
- Chávez, as a moderately risk acceptant and noninnovative leader, will seek to alter institutional constraints without generating too much opposition. Because he is not innovative, Chávez will advocate old ideas, but not to their extreme points.

2001-2004

Inclusiveness (LOW) + Competitiveness MODERATE +
Leadership MODERATELY RISK ACCEPTANT + NONINNOVATIVE

- Since inclusiveness is low but favors the poor, there will be an incentive for government to be more intrusive in the oil and gas value chain and provide private goods to the poor.

- Since the deliberative body is moderately competitive, energy policy will be characterized by moderate levels of government intrusion in the oil and gas value chain, but with significant underlying pressure to assume a more intrusive stance. Since the political system is moving to be less competitive, pressures for more intrusiveness will be greater than in 1999–2000.
- Since the deliberative body is moderately competitive, natural resource wealth will be distributed for both private and public goods. Since the political system is moving to be less competitive, pressures for more private goods will be greater than in 1999–2000.
- Chávez, as a moderately risk acceptant and noninnovative leader, will seek to alter institutional constraints without generating too much opposition. Because he is not innovative, Chávez will advocate old ideas, but not to their extreme points.

SUBPERIOD 2, 2005–2012

The promise of geology was now commercial: huge reserves of both oil and gas that could be produced and sold. Oil prices fluctuated wildly, but with a dramatic overall increase. LNG prices were still set by long-term contracts, making government credibility key for production; unfortunately, the credibility of the Chávez administration regarding contracts was low. The geology and market variables lead us to expect increased government intervention and high government take and the ability to wait out fluctuations without significant adjustments to government policy along the way.

With respect to political variables, the Bolivarian political system was now consolidated, even as it faced opposition and was subject to further fine tuning. The system was exclusive, governed in the name of the lower classes, but without their having influence over policy. The decision-making apparatus was noncompetitive, and decisions referenced the needs of the lower classes. Constraints on the executive were low but not nonexistent. At this point Chávez would be confronted with few opposition voices within his support group, but when they surfaced, his moderate risk acceptance characteristic would lead him to modify his stance and respond with measures that had been adopted in the past.

The values for the political variables during the 2005–2012 subperiod of the Chávez administration are:

Inclusiveness LOW + Competitiveness LOW +
Leadership MODERATELY RISK ACCEPTANT + NONINNOVATIVE

These lead to the following hypotheses about energy policy in Venezuela during this subperiod of the Chávez administration:

- Exclusiveness pulls in the direction of more intrusive government because Chávez's constituency is the popular sector, and it needs the government to appropriate wealth from the energy sector more than the business sector would. Wealth will be distributed via private goods targeted to the lower classes.
- Low competitiveness in the deliberative body means that Chavez's government will develop an energy policy that produces private goods for distribution to its constituency. Since the Chávez coalition favors the poor, energy policy will have high levels of government intrusion, but with little effective regulation to prevent the NOC from essentially serving as a mechanism for the distribution of private goods to chavistas as well as the poor.
- As a moderately risk acceptant leader, Chávez will seek to alter institutional constraints without generating too much opposition, but since there is low competitiveness, he will not be very constrained and will have little need for such measures. Because he is not innovative, he will advocate old ideas, but not to their extreme points.

Maduro, 2013–2016

Geology continued to favor Venezuelan oil and natural gas. Oil prices fluctuated wildly, hitting historic highs at the beginning of Maduro's term, but with a dramatic collapse through 2016, the end of our study period. LNG prices were still set by long-term contracts, making government credibility key for production; unfortunately, the credibility of the Maduro administration regarding contracts was low. The geology and market variables lead us to expect increased government intervention and high government take initially but with significant adjustments to decrease government intervention and stimulate private investment as the price collapse lingers.

The Bolivarian political system was now consolidated, even as it faced opposition from within, and was on the path to a single party state. The system continued to be exclusive, governed now not in the name of the lower classes, but of the Bolivarian Revolution. This variable pulls in favor of government intervention in the oil and gas sector for the provision of private goods to save the Bolivarian Revolution, even at the expense of the lower classes. The decision-making apparatus was uncompetitive, with opposition within *chavismo* leading to expulsion and arrest. Decisions should promote greater government intervention and reference the needs of the Bolivarian Revolution. Constraints on the executive were low. Government policy in the energy sector should reflect Maduro's views of what is necessary to save his government. When Maduro is confronted by opposition voices within "official *chavismo*" (those who support Maduro's government), his low risk acceptance characteristic should lead him to back off his stance, and his low innovative characteristic should make him respond with measures that had been adopted in the past, especially by Chávez.

The values for the political variables during the Maduro administration from 2013 to 2016 are:

Inclusiveness LOW + Competitiveness LOW +
Leadership LOW RISK ACCEPTANT + NONINNOVATIVE

These lead to the following hypotheses about energy policy in Venezuela during the Maduro administration of 2013–2016:

- Exclusiveness pulls in the direction of more intrusive government because the Bolivarian Revolution's constituency is the popular sector and it needs the government to appropriate wealth from the energy sector more than the business sector would. Wealth will be distributed via private goods targeted to the lower classes.
- Low competitiveness in the deliberative body means that Maduro's government will develop an energy policy that produces private goods for distribution to its constituency. Since the Bolivarian Revolution favors the poor but is in danger of collapsing, energy policy will have high levels of government intrusion, but with little effective regulation to prevent the NOC from essentially serving as a mechanism for the distribution of private goods to chavistas, poor or not.
- As a low risk acceptant leader seeking to save the Bolivarian Revolution, Maduro will not seek to alter institutional constraints. Because he is not innovative, he will advocate old ideas but not to their extreme points.

This section has combined the hypothesized effect of each variable in the model proposed in chapter 3 with the hypotheses for each of the presidential periods based on the historical experience. The next two chapters evaluate the usefulness of the hypotheses for explaining the adoption and shifts of the major Venezuelan oil and gas policies in the period 1989–2016.

Chapter Six

EXPLAINING ENERGY POLICY UNDER
A COLLAPSING PUNTO FIJO

As noted in chapter 5, from 1989 to 1998 Venezuela was confronting a challenging, though promising, geological situation, the oil market was in crisis, and the Punto Fijo political system was collapsing. The administrations of Pérez and Caldera developed their energy policies within this context, and this chapter tests the hypotheses about the impact of politics on those energy policies.[1] It focuses on four key issues: the role of the NOC in energy policy making, commercialization, access to the resource, and fiscal and contractual matters. In each section we see the limits of what geology or the market would suggest as the rational policy response and why an incorporation of our three political variables of inclusiveness of the political system, competitiveness in the decision-making unit, and specific personal characteristics of the president are necessary to understand policy choice.

Neither geology nor market forces predict the creation of a government agency, nor its policy-making role once created. Analysts and policy makers have strong and varying views about how a NOC should behave. Because PDVSA has found itself at both the pinnacle and the nadir of oil company status, these debates about the role of the NOC have been particularly salient in the Venezuelan case, with an oft-repeated accusation that PDVSA behaved as a "state in a state." In the first section of this chapter, I demonstrate empirically that during the Pérez and Caldera administrations the NOC never legislated reforms, and when it did propose them, they had to fit in with executive and congressional views to become anything other than business plans. PDVSA was clearly an important actor providing information, but it did not adopt policy. Nor can one simply assert that PDVSA "convinced" the government to follow plans that the NOC autonomously developed and would implement as it saw appropriate. The section clearly demonstrates that the government's national development policy and the political economy behind it determined where oil policy fit and the government's willingness to accept, modify, or reject NOC proposals.

Commercialization is about production and marketing, and in Venezuela at this time those issues arose in the context of OPEC quotas on production, internationalization of NOC operations downstream, and the development of a natural gas sector. Geology doesn't give us any insights into whether an NOC will produce in line with externally determined quotas, internationalize its operations, or develop its natural gas reserves. Geology can endow a nation with significant natural gas, but the development of domestic and international natural gas markets lagged endowments virtually everywhere across the globe. A market perspective would expect autonomous NOC leaders to internationalize as a means of protecting company assets from rent-seeking politicians, but both the Pérez and Caldera administrations saw the benefits of internationalization. While Pérez wanted to rein in internationalization, he did not push to roll it back because having an attractive NOC was important for his plans to bring foreign investment into the Venezuelan oil sector. A market perspective would also expect government officials to stop the process when their own needs to access NOC resources was threatened, but the Pérez and Caldera governments did not force the sale of PDVSA's international assets even when the economic crisis worsened. To understand the continuation of the internationalization process of the NOC even while the government was short on revenue and dealing with political and economic crises, we need to see how internationalization contributed to presidential visions for addressing those challenges and the politics of policy making.

The third section of this chapter examines the question of access to the natural resource. The literature on Venezuela generally treats the opening of the oil sector as either an NOC policy foisted on a naïve or corrupt political class or an inevitable outcome of the collapse of the oil market. Certainly the dramatic fall in oil prices in the 1980s and the Venezuelan government's need to divert funds from PDVSA to repay foreign debt and provide benefits to key domestic constituencies meant that the NOC was short of capital to explore all promising areas, develop and implement enhanced oil recovery (EOR) for mature wells, and develop the financial and technological expertise and skilled personnel to commercialize the significant reserves of heavy oil in the Orinoco Belt. But that could have resulted in the full privatization of the industry, including the selling of the NOC, as was done in Argentina and Bolivia in the 1990s. Alternatively, Venezuela could have sold shares in its NOC to raise capital, as was done in Colombia and Brazil at this time. Or it could have passed a very narrow reform limited to service contracts designed to strengthen the NOC, as Mexico did in 2008.

Important PDVSA leaders wanted an opening that would include NOC privatization, but government officials rejected that possibility.[2] There were opponents of the policies favored by the government and its NOC, and they argued that these options effectively "privatized" the national resources. Some on the left wanted an opening for the private sector; the debate was over the terms under which such an opening would occur. Statists lost the political debate from 1989 through 1998 to pro-market nationalists, but not because PDVSA was a "state within a state," as statists charged.[3]

Once the decision was made to open the sector to others, questions arose regarding how much to open and on what terms. Access to Venezuelan oil and gas began slowly, first with mature fields that had been virtually exhausted or even abandoned by the IOCs before nationalization or by PDVSA afterward. Next up were the costly and technically challenging heavy oils in the Orinoco Belt and nonassociated natural gas, both of which also faced market uncertainty. The opening process was completed with the auction of light and medium crude blocs, areas in which PDVSA's units had done well, though at shallower depths. Again, geology can reveal these potential reserves but not determine when or whether they will be exploited. A market focus can suggest that the search for optimal economic returns will lead governments to break monopoly control over these hydrocarbons when a market for the developed product is profitable, the opportunity costs for capital and labor are favorable, and technology is available at remunerative rates for seller and purchaser. A market approach does well at explaining access to mature fields and the heavy oils, but not for natural gas, where the market was so speculative that private investors did not pursue development even when offered contracts, or for light and medium oil where PDVSA could have further developed what it already did well.

The fourth issue concerns the fiscal and contract terms negotiated with investors. Geology, on the one hand, gave Venezuela an advantage because the country was well-endowed with oil and natural gas. But in the 1990s the markets for these products were dismal, so investors had to think more seriously about the long term. Here markets might have helped Venezuela, but no serious analyst in the 1990s saw a boom in the oil and gas markets. Instead, the perception was that hydrocarbon markets would remain weak as world demand grew slowly and new discoveries of oil and gas deposits continued. In this context, Venezuela was in a weak bargaining position. That position was even weaker given the country's nationalization of private oil companies fifteen years earlier, deep economic crisis, and rapidly fraying political stability.

The chapter's final section examines how the hypotheses generated in chapter 5 performed in explaining the oil and gas policies of the Pérez and Caldera administrations.

THE ROLE OF THE NOC

Presidential appointment of the NOC president created a direct relationship between the president of Venezuela and PDVSA. The potential for the NOC president to bypass control of the Oil Ministry undermined the hierarchical command structure. In particular, when Venezuelan presidents perceived the need to have business-focused leaders at the head of the NOC, the PDVSA president could compete with the minister (his formal superior and often a person from outside the oil sector) in advocating policies to the president. This institutional situation and PDVSA leadership's focus on its commercial needs led to accusations by statists that the NOC was acting like a "state within a state" in advancing its own rather than national policies. This section, however, demonstrates that only if the commercial needs of the NOC did not clash with the president's national policies and offered revenue that could advance his national agenda did Pérez or Caldera adopt policies consonant with NOC preferences.

In the election campaign of 1988, a year before business journalist Arrioja begins his story of PDVSA plans to open the hydrocarbon sector to private investment,[4] Pérez called for a domestic side to the international-ization policy of the 1980s, which he called "internalization." The man who had forced the congressional adoption of article 5 in 1975 now said he wanted foreign capital to help increase production, refine more products to increase the value-added of exports, transfer technology, train more Venezuelans in the new skills required, and develop the Orinoco.[5]

Signaling his seriousness about refocusing the NOC's attention inward, Pérez appointed as his oil minister Celestino Armas, who had opposed PDVSA's internationalization strategy when it was developing.[6] Retir-ing PDVSA president Juan Chacín criticized Pérez for "punishment" and "ending meritocracy" in the company when he appointed Andrés Sosa Pietri president and two people not associated with the oil industry to the NOC Board of Directors.[7] Sosa Pietri had been active in leftist politics in the 1970s, served on congressional oil committees, was involved in the petro-chemical industry, and owned a company that produced valves for PDVSA, but he was criticized for not coming from within the company. In addi-tion, PDVSA had focused on oil, but Pérez's intention to raise the NOC's interest in petrochemical development and local content acquisition is reflected in the VIII Plan de la Nación as well as in his choice for PDVSA president.[8]

Although many claim that the NOC was able to drive national economic policy because of a paucity of expertise in the public bureaucracy, the aca-demic and economic credentials of Pérez's team of economic advisors were impressive.[9] The qualifications of the heads of planning (CORDIPLAN, Miguel Rodríguez, who would later become Central Bank president, and Ricardo Hausmann), ministers of development (Moisés Naím and Imelda Cisneros), and the presidents of the Central Bank (Pedro R. Tinoco, who had been minister of finance 1969–1972, and Ruth Osterreicher de Krivoy, who was president of a major financial consulting firm) belie claims that they needed to depend on PDVSA economists to develop policy.[10] These leaders of the economic cabinet had no professional ties to the NOC, com-ing instead out of academia (Universidad Central de Venezuela and the Instituto de Estudios Superiores de Administración, IESA) or international organizations (Inter-American Development Bank, Sistema Económico de América Latina y del Caribe, SELA).

The national development plan developed by CORDIPLAN during Pérez's first year in office included a section on the hydrocarbon sector.

That section presents a comprehensive overview of the tasks for the ministry and the NOC to bring the hydrocarbon sector into the Gran Viraje restructuring of Venezuela's economy and increase export revenue to support the national plan. It began by claiming that OPEC agreements would have a major impact on oil prices and demand could spike in the short to medium term. It noted that large producers and refiners carried more weight in OPEC and that for Venezuela to continue as a major producer and exporter, a significant investment in the oil sector would be necessary from 1990 to 1993 (the period for the plan). It called for an improvement in the export basket, which required investment in optimizing production processes in refineries; minimizing the risk of commercializing crudes and lower-quality products (e.g., Orimulsion); and using appropriate commercialization strategies (e.g., internationalization) to deal with supply excesses in unstable markets. CORDIPLAN also called for significant investments from the private sector to help the development of other parts of the hydrocarbon sector that would permit a diversification of the sources of export revenue: petrochemical, fertilizers, coal, Orimulsion, LNG, nonconventional heavy crudes, maritime transportation, and technology.[11]

The document was clear about the need to open the sector to foreign investment. But while it advocated privatizing many SOEs, and though several PDVSA leaders would speak of the need to privatize the NOC, the Pérez administration expressed no interest in turning the oil sector over to private investors. The plan cautioned that public investment could not be dedicated to the oil sector, given needs elsewhere. Although it called for a larger role for private capital, the plan stipulated that PDVSA could not lose strategic control of the sector. A role for private investment was identified in specialty crudes, chemical products, and the domestic market. CORDIPLAN argued that domestic and foreign investors could be majority shareholders (*participación mayoritaria de accionistas*) in some of these projects, thereby permitting NOC capital to concentrate in the strategic sectors of the oil business. The plan also called for raising internal prices of oil products to levels that, while still below international prices, would rationalize domestic consumption and free up supply for export. PDVSA projects in nonconventional areas, expanding refineries, coal (Orimulsion was considered a bitumen coal), and petrochemicals, were expected to generate forward and backward linkages using Venezuelan products and labor, thereby contributing to diversifying the sources of growth.[12]

Subordination of the NOC to political authorities is best illustrated in the clash between PDVSA's expansion plans and the Pérez' administration's structural adjustment plans with the IMF that called for austerity. PDVSA President Sosa Pietri clashed with the Central Bank over the liquidity implications of these investments and Pérez replaced the NOC President with Gustavo Roosen, an outsider to the industry, with orders to rationalize and limit the NOC's plans for expansion.[13] The limits on expansion plans were particularly irksome to PDVSA because Venezuela had received a windfall in 1990 as oil prices rose in expectation of a conflict in the Persian Gulf. But the Pérez administration had collaborated with the IMF to create a Fund for Macroeconomic Stabilization to sterilize the extra money while structural adjustments continued. The administration, however, had spent the money and found itself short to meet IMF targets, so it turned to the NOC for funds. The government promised to return the funds after January 1992, lower taxes on the NOC, and compensate it for subsidies provided to the domestic economy—but none of this materialized.[14]

PDVSA's innovative product for heavy oil, Orimulsion, presents another example of subordination of NOC plans to government policy. The NOC sought to expand production and the market for Orimulsion in the early 1990s. But the ministry and others believed that it was a low-value product relative to crude oil and insisted that NOC investments give it low priority. Venezuela's rough adherence to OPEC quotas also raised challenges PDVSA wanted to eliminate. Orimulsion was classified by Venezuela as a noncrude (bituminous) competitor with coal, and OPEC was concerned about Orimulsion displacing high-sulfur fuel oil. The possibility that OPEC could require that Orimulsion constitute part of Venezuela's production quota reinforced PDVSA's desire for the country to abandon OPEC. Nevertheless, the Pérez administration would not leave OPEC and required the NOC to scale back its Orimulsion plans. To add salt to the wounds, these government decisions raised fears in PDVSA that other countries would develop their bituminous areas to compete with Orimulsion, and thus Venezuela would lose its first-mover advantage.[15]

Sosa Pietri lamented at the beginning of his presidency of PDVSA that the Oil Ministry subordinated the NOC. Sosa Pietri, like many in the NOC, considered oil policy a business issue, not a political one. Sosa Pietri's report that the audience at the annual Venezuela National Oil Congress in 1990 was shocked by his declaration that the NOC should contribute to the making of oil policy indicates that leaders in the oil sector did not perceive that PDVSA was determining oil policy. Writing in 1993 after he had been relieved of his presidency for clashing with the Oil Ministry, Sosa Pietri concluded that to become an efficient oil company, PDVSA should be global, privatized (not just some of its subsidiaries), and forced to compete within Venezuela.[16] Once the evidence during Pérez's second term is analyzed in detail, it is hard to disagree with Sosa Pietri, Baena, and Boué that the NOC might have won some battles (mainly on purchasing some international assets), but the ministry was definitely in charge.[17]

In the next administration, Caldera initially opposed Pérez's economic reforms and any negotiations with the IMF. As noted in chapter 4, Caldera had two distinct national plans: a first one that reflected traditional statist thinking (1994–1995), and a second one that adopted liberal views (1996–1998). Both plans rendered Caldera's administration very dependent on the oil sector generating funds through increased exports or an increase in foreign investment flows. Our question is whether such dependence led him to permit PDVSA to develop oil and gas policy as its leadership determined, or whether he required their development plans to fit within his national policies for the country.

Caldera favored one of PDVSA's senior officials, Julius Trinkunas, for the NOC presidency, indicating his general satisfaction with how PDVSA was operating. Another alternative was to leave Roosen in the presidency; he wanted to stay and had supporters on the NOC Board of Directors. But Caldera's oil minister, Erwin Arrieta, as well as a close confidant and oil minister in Caldera's first presidency, Hugo Pérez La Silvia, and one of his planning advisors (Teodoro Petkoff, whom Caldera would later name planning minister when he negotiated an IMF agreement) wanted the NOC to play a more active role in promoting a liberal oil policy and lobbied for the appointment of Luis Giusti, coordinator of strategic planning under Sosa Pietri.[18] Giusti had similar visions to Sosa Pietri regarding the NOC, including privatizing PDVSA. But Giusti believed it was necessary for the NOC to become involved in politics because the national political economy set the context, and therefore limits, of what the oil and gas sector could do. Giusti's views about a significant opening to foreign investment were known, which indicates that these key Caldera advisors felt that the administration's economic program, which would depend heavily on revenue generated by the oil sector, would fare best with Giusti's approach, and they convinced Caldera to appoint him, but not until Caldera had twice rejected their recommendation.[19] Since Giusti was not a senior NOC official, some analysts accuse Minister Arrieta and Caldera of undermining "meritocracy" and politicizing the NOC by appointing him to the NOC presidency, an accusation that further supports the view that the government is leading the NOC rather than vice-versa.[20]

Giusti and many of his supporters and opponents claim that he fathered the strategy of opening the oil and gas sector and increased the NOC's influence to the point that he effectively made energy policy.[21] But Pérez had already argued for opening the domestic side of the oil industry in 1988, and many people in Caldera's cabinet, Congress, academia, the private sector as well as within the NOC were interested in opening the sector to foreign capital. In August 1993 one of Caldera's advisors on oil issues, Asdrúbal Baptista, a professor at IESA and coauthor of many statist papers with PDVSA dissident and intellectual Bernard Mommer, published a piece that argued that the sector should be opened, that legislative changes were necessary, and that terms for investors had to be attractive.[22] In addition, a number of politicians within COPEI favored opening the oil sector to private investment and went to Giusti for advice on how to accomplish it, not whether to do it.[23] Giusti stands out as the leading advocate of getting the NOC involved in politics to accomplish a specific type of opening; other pro-market advocates preferred to advocate opening without bringing politics into the business, while statists wanted a limited opening that would maintain state control over all operations and offer few, if any, financial incentives to investors.

Opening the oil and gas sector beyond what had been achieved in Pérez's term was not straightforward. Before Caldera became president, PDVSA had been working on a proposal to open medium and light fields and raising the issue with members of the different political parties. In April 1993 they had concluded that private investors would demand equity oil if they were to participate. The NOC also selected sixteen areas that could be put out to bid. In September 1993 PDVSA's business plan included these speculations about the future of light and medium oil exploration and production. But the combative political climate of the December 1993 presidential election, followed by the contentious congressional activity devoted to passing the Colón natural gas and the first two Orinoco heavy oil contracts, diverted attention from these light and medium oil fields, and the project was put on hold.[24]

In August 1994 it was announced that deep drilling requirements in light and medium oil fields warranted opening these fields to private investment. Minister Arrieta and new NOC president Giusti expected to fast-track the proposal through Caldera and Congress, sending negotiated contracts to Congress the following month.[25] But Caldera consulted with the Left in Congress and had the proposal discussed in his cabinet before sending it to Congress. Congress then debated the proposal and did not consider final approval of contracts until almost a year and a half after Arrieta and Giusti had expected.

The strategy envisioned by Giusti, his PDVSA collaborators, and Minister Arrieta had to fit within the plans of the Caldera administration and Congress or they could not be pursued. The debates and results of the contract terms will be discussed shortly; here it is sufficient to note that the role of the NOC was to work together with the ministry to provide options to the president and the Congress; it was the latter who determined, in line with their specific interests, the options that would be accepted and their details. This hardly constitutes the role of a "state within a state."

Dealing with the level of reserves and falling production was understood by both the Pérez and Caldera governments during 1989–1998 to require breaking the government monopoly at least in the upstream. The last governments of the Punto Fijo political system used the article 5 framework to open space for foreign investors, but that space had to be attractive to investors, so other policies needed to change as well. Those changes will be discussed in the upcoming sections on access to the resource and tax and fiscal policy. What is important to note here is that Pérez himself (the man who nationalized the oil industry in 1975) used the existence of article 5 (which he had rammed through the Congress) as the vehicle by which he could implement a reversal in Venezuelan oil policy that would mirror the reversal of his own state-led development project in the 1970s and bring private investment in as major players in the industry. PDVSA's corporate leadership had also been moving in the direction of recognizing the need for foreign partners, and so the NOC found itself on the same side of the issue with the president. Under Pérez the NOC was a collaborator, not the leader of the policy to open the hydrocarbon sector to investment and competition. Caldera was aware of Giusti's views when his economic and energy advisors convinced him to appoint Giusti to head the NOC over others he had been considering. During Caldera's efforts to roll back Pérez's liberal development model he hesitated, but as the banking crisis advanced, his alternatives to an IMF agreement narrowed. In December 1995 Caldera decided to move in the direction of market reforms. In this context, Giusti's views on attracting more FDI to develop the country's oil sector fit into Caldera's political needs.

COMMERCIALIZATION

In this section we examine the three components related to production and marketing which constituted the key determinants of commercial policy in the Pérez and Caldera administrations: OPEC issues, internationalization and the mid- and downstream phases of the global oil and gas value chain.

OPEC Quotas and Prices

NOC management promoted a policy of producing and exporting as much petroleum as possible rather than attempting to increase revenue by withholding supply, as OPEC and some ministers favored.[26] PDVSA chafed against OPEC production quotas, perceiving that these limited the ability of the company to perform in line with company business plans. But the national development plan in 1990 made it clear that the Pérez administration believed in the power of OPEC to influence international oil markets and intended to remain in the organization. Even in the face of increased prices during the Gulf War in 1991, Pérez would not overrule Minister Armas's decision to respect the quotas. It was not until the Paris meeting of major consuming and producing countries, co-organized by Pérez himself and which produced OPEC revisions upward, that Pérez would permit PDVSA to officially increase production.

NOC leadership also unsuccessfully complained that the ministry set the prices on which PDVSA would be taxed as OPEC declared reference prices rather than reflecting the lower market price that the NOC actually received for its exports.[27] OPEC quotas also limited the Venezuelan crude that could be supplied to PDVSA refineries abroad, thus increasing the amount of crude PDVSA had to purchase in the market for these refineries.[28] To increase the incentives for investment in the challenging extra-heavy oils of the Orinoco Belt, however, the government decided to consider the oil produced by the Orinoco extra-heavy oil projects as synthetic crude and thus, like Orimulsion, not subject to OPEC quotas on oil production.[29]

Baena notes that PDVSA was unable to determine export levels in the 1990s, despite the increase in productive capacity that resulted from the Apertura.[30] Venezuela cheated on its OPEC quota, but cheating is not specifically an NOC desire; governments short on cash or seeking to preserve market share push their NOCs to produce more if they can. Even Saudi Arabia produced more than its quota in the 1990s, and Qatar was the greatest violator.[31] PDVSA would have had Venezuela cheat even more, but the government would not give up its ability to decide how much to export. PDVSA wanted Venezuela to leave OPEC, as Ecuador and Gabon did in the 1990s, but the government would not take that step.

Internationalization

Though Pérez wanted "internalization" to replace internationalization, he was also concerned about commercializing heavy crude and Orimulsion, and this is indicated in the 1990 Plan de la Nación. But when PDVSA announced in 1989 that it would purchase the remaining half of CITGO, the government was caught off guard. Pérez and his minister quickly declared that the NOC would sell half of CITGO at an appropriate time.[32] PDVSA then chose to expand CITGO in 1990 with the purchase of 50 percent of Seaview Petroleum Company's asphalt refinery (asphalt is a primary use for heavy crude) and marine terminal and a few months later purchased the other 50 percent.

The Seaview purchase increased the value of CITGO and thus was not necessarily in contravention of the idea that CITGO would be sold at a profitable moment. But PDVSA had not sought approval from the ministry for this operation, seeing it as a business, rather than policy, decision. PDVSA also began to accumulate foreign debt to finance its business plans in 1990.[33] Pérez was not, however, willing to permit the NOC such wide latitude in its business decisions. In August 1991 he instructed Minister Armas to issue an order requiring that further indebtedness, modification of assets, and leadership appointments and compensation obtain prior approval from the ministry.[34]

Though the ministry could have stopped further internationalization, it did not. In June 1992 Citgo purchased AMOCO asphalt refinery and marketing assets, probably to keep the business open and thus as a purchaser for Venezuelan heavy crude. In August 1992 another PDVSA subsidiary, AB Nynas, acquired two UK refineries (50 percent of the second) and became the second largest asphalt refiner in Europe. Also in 1992 Citgo began negotiations to purchase 50 percent of Lyondell Petrochemical refinery.[35] PDVSA's international expansion was focused on maintaining markets for its heavy crude. The acquired companies were either purchasers of Venezuelan heavy crude, which was competing with Mexican and Saudi heavy crudes, or on the verge of closing. When its joint venture with Union Oil of California, UNO-VEN, was underperforming, PDVSA attempted to reduce its costs of maintaining the operation by selling its shares to Kuwait.[36]

Pérez's national development plan in 1990 had been concerned about disruptions in demand for Venezuelan lower-quality products, so it is not surprising that his government accepted these internationalization efforts.[37] And these purchases did not divert the NOC's attention from pursuing the internalization that was at the heart of Pérez's oil strategy.

The process of internationalizing PDVSA investments and operations slowed but continued under Caldera. In 1997 PDVSA became the sole owner of the UNO-VEN refinery and joined with Mobil to purchase half of a refinery in Louisiana. The following year the NOC attained a 50 percent share in the Amarada Hess refinery in the Virgin Islands.[38]

Midstream and Downstream

Pérez's national development plan advocated for private investment in the mid- and downstream, but his administration was unable to advance on this before it was terminated early. Neither did Caldera's administration prioritize opening the mid- and downstream. At the end of his administration, Caldera and Congress opened the downstream in fuel via the Organic Law of Opening of the Internal Market for Fuels and Other Hydrocarbon Derivative Fuels for Use in Automobiles of September 11, 1998. The administration also looked to natural gas. While the government did not have the support in Congress to pass a new natural gas law, it could make administrative changes that could have significant impact. Gas prices were reformed to be more attractive for producers. The ministry determined that since methane and ethane were processed from the associated natural gas coming from the wellhead, they qualified as "refined products." This qualification permitted the ministry to argue that the midstream and downstream gas business should be regulated by the Law on the Internal Market (1973) rather than the Hydrocarbon Nationalization Law (1975). Under the authority of the 1973 legislation, the ministry enacted two measures (Decree 2532 of May 20, 1998, and Resolution 323 of November 13, 1998) that permitted private investors into most areas of the business.[39]

ACCESS TO THE RESOURCE: APERTURA PETROLERA

Pérez encouraged the ministry and NOC to bring foreign investors and technology into Venezuela's oil and gas sector in both the upstream and downstream. The controversial article 5 of the nationalization legislation provided a means to bring foreign investors back into the hydrocarbon sector without requiring a revision of the oil nationalization, which would have been highly contentious politically. That didn't mean that the process would be easy; there were challenges at home and with foreign investors. Bringing in foreign investment was also of interest to the NOC, though there were disagreements within PDVSA concerning contract terms (see the following section).

The Pérez administration's solution to this challenge was the Apertura Petrolera (called simply Apertura), an extension of the *apertura* approach to the entire economy from the VIII National Plan to the hydrocarbon sector. In the section on promoting private investment, CORDIPLAN stipulated that government policy could make investment opportunities more profitable by revising fiscal burdens, more attractive by opening reserved areas to private investment, and less risky by reforming domestic legislation and becoming members of international agreements.[40] The Apertura Petrolera would make extensive use of that reasoning.

A first effort was to increase production in abandoned or mature fields. PDVSA was short of investment capital, and enhanced oil recovery (EOR) in mature fields requires special skills and technology that the NOC had not developed. Service contracts were well established mechanisms in

Venezuela's nationalized and monopolized oil sector. The new NOC did not have established commercialization contracts after the nationalization, and article 5 enabled it to employ Shell and Exxon to market its oil and provide oilfield services; as the NOC expanded its competencies, the need for such services declined.[41] The innovation regarding EOR was for service companies to produce the oil and be reimbursed for their cost plus a profit. All the oil would be transferred to PDVSA's control and the NOC would market the crude. Expectations were that in ten years the contracted areas would be producing 350,000 bpd after an investment of U.S. $3.4 billion.[42]

Minister Armas declared in July 1991 that operating services agreements (OSAs) negotiations were part of government policy to stimulate private investment in the oil sector. He also announced that the ministry was giving PDVSA's subsidiaries Corpoven, Lagoven, and Maraven rights over the exploitation of those marginal fields,[43] thereby demonstrating that the ministry and not the NOC was in ultimate control of the nation's oil reserves.

Pérez was annoyed that Congress, which was blocking many of his Apertura initiatives throughout the economy, accused the administration of secret negotiations and wanted to rule on these operating agreements. He argued that public announcements had been made and the contracts clearly fit under the article 5 service designation. Though Congress accepted Pérez's position on the OSAs, it continued debating whether article 5 needed to be reformed to deal with the new Apertura context being promoted by the Pérez administration.[44]

In 1992 and 1993 PDVSA held the first and second rounds of bidding for operating agreements to reactivate fourteen production fields. The first round of auctions produced poor results (only five of nine fields received bids). The only major oil company to bid on the nine fields in the first round, Shell, turned back the field for which it had won rights because it could not get international arbitration included in its contract.[45] PDVSA knew that major foreign partners wanted this protection in their contracts but did not push for it because Congress was already raising havoc over whether these OSAs fell under the "service" as opposed to "association" norms of article 5 (this debate would instead be raised in the LNG contracts, to be discussed shortly).[46] To sweeten the pot in second round offerings, PDVSA included the possibility of drilling deeper rather than equity oil as preferred by IOCs.[47] Equity oil would have transferred ownership of the resource to the companies and was clearly not acceptable to Congress. To offer contracts with deeper drilling rights in the same field might have been considered opening new opportunities and thus requiring an association rather than a service contract. But the Pérez administration and not just PDVSA were unwilling to raise the issue with Congress.

The opening to foreign investment was not limited to oil. A major field of nonassociated gas had been discovered in 1978, a growing domestic gas market emerged in the 1980s, and developing the gas sector was important for Pérez's national development plan. Associated gas was linked to oil production and therefore a risky source of supply, given the concerns over the commercial viability of much of the country's proven oil reserves. The VIII Plan recognized the need for foreign capital and expertise and linked the development of nonassociated natural gas to both exports and more efficient domestic industrial products such as steel and petrochemicals, the latter of which could also be exported.[48]

Permitting private investment in natural gas was an issue because this hydrocarbon had been nationalized in 1971 with exclusive rights to the state. Pérez and CORDIPLAN had their eye on natural gas exports in 1989. PDVSA was ordered by the Pérez administration in 1990 to increase E&P for nonassociated gas and to begin contract negotiations with potential investors for the Cristobal Colón natural gas project.[49]

In 1990 the Council of Ministers approved development of the Cristóbal Colón LNG project to export to the U.S. market. At the end of 1990 PDV-SA's subsidiary Lagoven, whose jurisdiction covered the area, petitioned the Supreme Court for a decision on whether nonassociated natural gas had to be under exclusive control of PDVSA as a hydrocarbon stipulated by the nationalization legislation. In March 1991 the Court ruled that nonassociated natural gas was not subject to state monopoly, thereby opening the legal door for private investment. PDVSA selected Shell, Mitsubishi, and Exxon as international partners with which to undertake feasibility studies and negotiate contracts, which would have to be approved by the Congress. The proposal suggested that ownership of the gas produced by the joint venture would lie with it rather than the ministry.[50]

By March 1991 a preliminary agreement had been reached between PDVSA and its proposed partners, but specific terms were still up for negotiation. Congress was aware of the negotiations with potential investors and would need to approve the terms of access under article 5's association category. The conditions for association included issues of state control over the project, dispute resolution mechanisms that were extraordinary in the Venezuelan context, and fiscal terms and will be discussed in the next section.

In August 1993, after Pérez's impeachment, an alliance in Congress including AD and COPEI passed the LNG contract. Congress was skeptical about its commercial viability but saw its value as the first major partnership between Venezuela's NOC and major international oil companies. PDVSA president Chacín had told investors precisely that as early as June 1990.[51] In his January 1998 interviews with Arrioja, Ali Rodríguez said that he never thought Colón was commercially viable. He believed that the project was being used to open exploitation of a hydrocarbon in which the state would have minority partnership, the NOC would compensate investors for a state fiscal action, and international arbitration would be accepted.[52] The commercial constraints proved too great, and in 1996 the project was put on hold.[53]

Another Apertura issue was developing the Orinoco heavy and extra-heavy crudes. PDVSA wanted to move forward with major development of Orimulsion and now recognized the need for foreign partners. The ministry under Armas, however, was not supportive of investing in Orimulsion, and cuts in the NOC's budget meant that expansion of the Orimulsion business would be slow.[54]

Heavy crudes could also be blended with lighter crudes, but Venezuela was running out of lighter crudes, and such blends were thus both a suboptimal use of high-value oil and not sustainable. Pérez in 1988 and COR-DIPLAN when it prepared the VIII Plan de la Nación in 1989 articulated this need for foreign capital and technology to develop the heavy oil projects, and the plan noted that offers would need to be attractive enough to entice investors. A year after the plan was issued, PDVSA discussions with potential IOC partners for Orinoco development projects dangled the carrot of a possible opening of high-risk medium and light crude fields to foreign investment. The PDVSA business plan of 1992 specifically said that heavy oil projects might be linked with medium and light crude ones.[55]

The extra-heavy oil projects in the Orinoco Belt presented questions about access to the resource and to the midstream. The oil was so heavy that it required processing in upgraders before it could begin its journey to the refiners. The upgraders were the most expensive and technologically challenging components of these projects, so foreign partners were needed here as well as in the extraction phase of the heavy crudes. These projects had been identified in the 1990 Plan de la Nación. Four contracts were negotiated by PDVSA and approved by the National Assembly; contract details are covered in the next section. The contracts brought in a total investment of over U.S. $15 billion in their decade of existence and reached a production level of 650,000 bpd by 2006.[56]

The final major issue regarding access to the resource under Pérez concerns light and medium crude. Traditional production of these high-quality crudes in Venezuela had been in decline for years despite some exploration by PDVSA. Geological studies indicated that Venezuela likely had more of these crudes, but they were deeper than the fields that PDVSA developed, and all exploration is risky with respect to whether commercially viable reservoirs of petroleum can be found. With a reduced budget for E&P, these areas ranked low on the NOC's priority list. Yet their production was attractive for the Pérez (and subsequently Caldera) government because of export revenue and the possibility that the new projects could generate regional development poles as anticipated in the VIII Plan de la Nación.

The political problem was that these crudes were the traditional ones produced by PDVSA. Article 5 was designed for exceptions that were important to the national interest. Statists in particular, but even pro-market nationalists, were skeptical that these new light and medium crude areas posed exceptional challenges for exploration and production that PDVSA could not handle. Even some members of the PDVSA Board of Directors questioned whether producing that oil now rather than waiting for the NOC to raise the capital and develop its deep drilling expertise was in the national interest rather than just in the political interest of the Pérez administration's Gran Viraje. The ministry and PDVSA made multiple presentations to Congress regarding the "high-risk" argument for opening light and medium crude areas to foreign investment.[57] Congress, however, was busy with the service agreements and the LNG and the Orinoco proposals, as well as fighting the dying Pérez administration on other fronts, and these projects were left for the next administration.

Most of the heavy lifting for the Apertura in hydrocarbons was accomplished by the Pérez administration. Though Caldera had been a critic of the process during Pérez's term, he took full advantage of its approval and early investments during his second administration, 1994–1998. The goal of the Apertura under the Caldera administration was to double the country's crude oil production from approximately two million bpd to more than four million bpd within ten years (thereby returning to the production levels achieved prior to nationalization).[58] During Caldera's first national plan, 1994–1995, upstream efforts at bringing foreign capital to the Orinoco Belt continued, with an additional two association agreements negotiated. In the midstream, all areas of the petrochemical industry were open for private investment by 1995.[59]

To gain approval of association agreements for light and medium crude fields, a majority in Congress would need to be convinced that the alternative to no agreement would be no development rather than that PDVSA would develop the projects on its own. The Caldera administration and Congress, not PDVSA, would determine which option would now be pursued.

Minister Arrieta and NOC president Giusti worked on a proposal to present to Caldera in August 1994 for permitting FDI in light and medium crude fields. Given the economic context facing the government and the weak oil market, the proposal was based on the assumptions that the NOC would have no budget to quickly bring these fields online and that exploration was always risky and could lead to large financial losses for the NOC and country if PDVSA were forced to explore and develop these fields on its own. These are market-based explanations and thus were countered by statists' assertions that, with enough political will, the money would be found and the skills developed.

Caldera would not simply let the minister and NOC president determine oil policy. In his first few months of office, Caldera had been asked by Ali Rodríguez, president of the Energy and Mining Commission of the Chamber of Deputies (and member of the opposition Causa R Party), to clarify some aspects of light and medium crude projects. Caldera ignored the request, but before receiving Arrieta and Giusti to discuss policy recommendations, he met with congressional representatives of the left-wing MAS Party, which allied with his government periodically. Caldera knew MAS had been critical of many aspects of the opening during Pérez's term and had been in conversation with Mommer.[60]

When Arrieta and Giusti met with Caldera, they encountered his reticence to simply accept their proposal and his insistence that it be debated in the Council of Ministers. Not until December 7 did the council approve the proposal. Congress did not begin debating the model contract until

March 1995. In July Congress passed legislation allowing PDVSA to offer E&P rights to private companies for ten potentially rich light and medium oil tracts; none of these were from the original list of sixteen in the NOC's 1993 draft.[61]

Once Caldera changed course and adopted the liberal and IMF-approved Agenda Venezuela in early 1996, the Apertura progressed further. Though in 1975 Caldera had opposed article 5 and in 1990–1991 had promoted the idea that OSAs needed congressional approval, he now pushed the OSA exception to its maximum. In 1997 the third round of bidding for operating service contracts was held. These were the most successful, partly because they no longer offered mature fields, but rather ones with more potential and therefore akin to profit-sharing contracts rather than operating service ones.[62] But these same characteristics suggest that it was not credible to claim a need for FDI to develop them, and thus the contracts' relevance to the exception to state monopoly under article 5 was questionable. Progress was also made in the mid- and downstream. That same year Congress approved the sale of stock in PDVSA's petrochemical subsidiary, PEQUIVEN.[63] And in early 1998, the final year of Caldera's presidency, Congress approved the opening of distribution to the private sector.[64]

From the perspective of increasing oil production and government revenue, the Apertura was a success: production rose from 1.907 mbpd in 1989 to 3.167 in 1998, while public-sector petroleum revenues increased from $1.1 billion in 1993 to 9.648 billion in 1997.[65] By 2004, private oil companies were operating almost half of the country's oil production, and these contracts were producing over a million bpd by 2006, before the nationalizations.[66]

FISCAL AND CONTRACTUAL ISSUES

The financial terms of the Apertura contracts were influenced by both the general fiscal reform being advanced under the VIII Plan de la Nación to stimulate investment and specific terms for distinct hydrocarbon deposits. In 1990 the Pérez administration said it would reduce the tax on PDVSA (at the time 82 percent) by cutting the reference price on which it was taxed from 20 percent to 15 percent above real prices on exports. But in August 1991, when Congress approved the tax cut, it did so only for the joint venture projects; PDVSA projects would still pay the full tax of over 80 percent.[67] The government also promised to return to PDVSA the funds confiscated to replenish the IMF macroeconomic fund after January 1992, lower taxes on the NOC, and compensate it for subsidies provided to the domestic economy—but none of this materialized.[68]

The fiscal and contract terms under which private investments were made in Venezuela's hydrocarbon sector were influenced by a number of factors, none of which in the 1990s were favorable to the country.[69] Unfortunately, not only was the market for oil investments extremely competitive, the government had a credibility problem with private investors, who just fifteen years earlier had been nationalized. The oil market context was extremely poor, the technology to process EHCO was still in the development stage, and the IOCs were furthest along in this development process. As a result, Venezuela had very little bargaining leverage vis-à-vis the IOCs that it was seeking to convince to invest billions of dollars in the country.

Venezuela offered favorable terms in four distinct types of contracts, three in oil (OSAs, association agreements [AAs], and risk exploration [RE]), and one in LNG, to induce the participation of foreign investors. Under the operating service agreements, companies were considered to be providing a service rather than exploiting oil, so they were taxed at the general business rate of 34 percent rather than the hydrocarbon rate of 67 percent. But when PDVSA paid the service fee to the operating company and took possession of the oil, the NOC was considered to have exploited the oil and thus was subject to both the hydrocarbon tax rate and the royalty of 16.67 percent. The contracts were further enhanced for the private investor when, in the third round of contracts (1991, 1992, and 1997), fields that were not marginal were offered under the OSA scheme.[70]

The LNG projects, unlike EOR, required significantly greater investments and long-term supply contracts. In the expensive LNG projects, international arbitration became fundamental. International arbitration, based on Venezuelan law, was incorporated into contracts beginning in 1993, despite Venezuela's historic rejection of the right of foreigners to interpret the legality of contracts entered into by the country.[71] Opposition was not to international arbitration per se, but to its extension to the sovereign. Carmelo Lauría, a member of AD and president of the Chamber of Deputies, promoted Mommer's position that there should be two contracts, one between the foreign investors and the government and another between the investors and the NOC, to keep the access to fields issue separate from the production one and keep state sovereignty from being subject to international arbitration. But statists did not have the votes to modify the Caldera administration's position on international arbitration, and it was approved by AD, COPEI, MAS, and Convergencia votes, with La Causa R and the Communist Party opposing.[72]

The extra-heavy oil JVs benefited from a special tax category created by Congress for the companies participating in these contracts: income taxes were set at the general business rate of 34 percent rather than the hydrocarbon rate of 67.7 percent, and royalties were set at 1 percent rather than 16.67 percent for the first twenty years. International arbitration was incorporated, and the NOC also became a guarantor of the contracts by assuming liability should a future Venezuelan government decide to exercise its sovereign powers to alter the fiscal terms.[73] In doing so, PDVSA committed itself in the contracts to lobby its government for the continuation of the terms on which the joint venture was based and to be liable for damages suffered by its partners should the government revise the terms.

Congress approved risk exploration agreements to explore and extract oil in light and medium crude areas in 1995, and eight blocks were auctioned in 1996. Bidding terms required that companies assume all exploration risk and that the NOC had a right to buy in at 1–35 percent, included a government share of up to 50 percent of profits through a special tax (*participación del estado en las ganancias*, PEG), and the income tax was set at the hydrocarbon rate of 67 percent, but both levies could be subtracted from profits for tax and royalty purposes. Royalties were modified, with a variable system of 1–16.67 percent calculated by profit levels; since profit levels can be effectively reduced by a variety of mechanisms that use company-generated information, this change contributed to a lower royalty payment. In these contracts, the marginal government take began at 67 percent and rose to 86 percent after certain levels of profit were achieved.[74] Congress inserted the special PEG tax for up to thirty-nine years, with municipalities and states sharing in this revenue (they never did).[75] It also approved an international arbitration clause and accepted PDVSA's proposal that the national "control" of JV production, as required by article 5, could be instituted via a Control Committee, rather than with majority shares. Although statists in the Congress opposed the committee idea, the majority accepted it but modified the composition of the committee by insisting that the ministry rather than the NOC appoint its chair and thus hold the veto power.[76] Since PDVSA had to create this Control Committee because Congress would not have approved of the opening otherwise, its existence and composition further indicate that the NOC was not simply telling the government what to do.

Mommer, representing the statists' view, denounced these fiscal terms in 2003. "In 1981, gross income from hydrocarbon production, including refining, peaked at $19.7 billion. In 2000, a new peak was reached of $29.3 billion. Nevertheless, in 1981 PDVSA paid $13.9 billion in fiscal revenues, but only $11.3 billion in 2000. In other words, for every *dollar* of gross income, PDVSA paid 71 *cents* to the government in rents, royalties and taxes in 1981, but only 39 *cents* in 2000."[77] But statists miss the key point that if government insisted on a traditionally high government take, private companies would not have invested and production volume would not have increased; consequently, government revenue would not have increased.[78] The Apertura produced more government revenue because private investors were producing so much more even as prices fluctuated at low levels. The OSA contracts did not get the fiscal break offered for AA contracts, demonstrating that the government could distinguish between the types of incentives needed to attract capital and was not simply giving away the nation's patrimony.

PERFORMANCE OF MODEL IN EXPLAINING PUNTO FIJO POLICIES

Our model for explaining energy policy assumes that geology and prices do not sufficiently account for variations in oil and gas policy. In this chapter we examined the oil and gas policies of the last two Punto Fijo governments regarding the role of the NOC, commercialization, access to the resource, and fiscal and contractual matters. Here we evaluate how well the hypotheses derived from the model performed in helping to explain those policies.

Our four hypotheses from chapter 5 for the impact of our model's political variables on energy policy in Venezuela during the Pérez administration lead us to expect the following. First, government intervention in the oil and gas value chain would decrease (the prediction was that it would be low, but since it was high before 1989, that implies intervention would decrease). Second, energy policy will target revenues to provide public and private goods. Third, Pérez would seek to overcome institutional barriers to the adoption of his innovative energy policies. This means that Pérez would use innovative measures and risk confrontation with his own supporters (AD and the voters who elected him in 1988) to modify the expected levels of intrusion and the distribution between private and public goods. Market and geology would predict the first behavior but not the second and third.

Pérez had overseen a massive expansion in state presence in the economy during his first term. Contrary to a market and geology explanation, the subsequent governments of Luis Herrera Campins and Lusinchi did not significantly diminish that presence, despite the economic crises that developed in the wake of the crashing oil market and the fear of declining reserves (see chapter 4). Contrary to expectations at the time but in conformity with our model (and a lagged market/geology explanation), the Pérez administration's VIII Plan de la Nación articulated a reduced role for the government in the energy sector (actually, across the economy), and Congress approved the Apertura efforts of the Pérez administration.

Regarding energy policy and public goods, Congress supported ISI policies financed by oil revenues, but the ISI policies benefited specific industries and their workers rather than the economy as a whole and thus are private goods. Pérez came out against those policies with his VIII Plan de la Nación. Rather than using oil revenues to finance inefficient nonenergy development projects, the plan proposed that energy projects themselves could become development poles. With the opening of the sector to FDI, these energy projects were expected to benefit the national economy and national budget through sustainable growth. The expected increase in government revenues could be used for public goods rather than the ISI private goods.

Provision of public goods in the Pérez administration meant getting macroeconomic policy under control and moving the energy sector into sustainable development to handle the commodity cycle and still provide support for a diversification of growth. Managing the foreign and domestic debt and bringing inflation under control were necessary steps on the road to a sustainable recovery. PDVSA's budget requests were made considering its needs, not the economic crisis facing the nation; Pérez's subordination of those requests to the need for macroeconomic stability illustrates well his willingness to emphasize public over private goods. Piñeda and Rodríguez calculated that public nonoil capital stock per worker increased during the Pérez administration.[79]

While it is true that people at the bottom of the socioeconomic scale were not feeling better off, no one was since the structural adjustments to the economy were only beginning. The Gini Index calculated by the World Bank (table 6.1) indicates that under Pérez's reforms wealth was distributed significantly more broadly, meaning that the wealthier segment of the population was suffering relatively more. The Gini Index fell from 45.3 in Pérez's first year in office (1989) to 42.5 in 1992, a few months before he was removed from office. That is a level that was not achieved even by the Chávez administration through 2006.[80]

Pérez attempted to decrease gasoline subsidies, but subsidies like these that are not specifically targeted to the poor wind up disproportionately benefiting the middle and upper classes at the expense of the public purse and should be considered private rather than public goods.[81] Congress wanted to maintain gasoline subsidies, but Pérez used administrative measures to modify them. Congress was initially skeptical about permitting OSAs without the ability to review contracts to ensure that the state was maintaining national control over the operations and tried to assert itself. But modifying the OSA contracts negotiated during the Pérez administration would have reduced their attractiveness to foreign investors, with the result either that production would not increase or that PDVSA's budget would have to increase to finance the development of the necessary skills and technology within the NOC to increase production in these wells. In

TABLE 6.1
Gini Index, Venezuela 1987–2006

Year	Index
1987	53.4
1989	45.3
1992	42.5
1995	47.8
1998	49.8
1999	48.3
2001	48.2
2002	50.6
2003	50.4
2004	49.8
2005	52.4
2006	46.9

Source: World Bank, "Gini Index (World Bank Estimates)," https://data.worldbank.org/indicator/SI.POV.GINI?end=2006&locations=VE&start=1981&view=chart.
Note: Gini statistics after 2006 were not available for Venezuela.

the context of Venezuela's structural economic crisis, diverting scarce government funds to PDVSA would have meant providing a private good. Since Article 5 clearly permitted the OSAs to be executive-branch decisions, the Pérez administration did not yield despite Congress's continued discussion of impeachment.

Pérez pushed new ideas while seeking to alter the institutional constraints on his leadership. He selected an economic advisory group that was independent of his party and confronted his own party, Congress, and PDVSA over policy. His Gran Viraje strategy rejected ISI, pushed for privatization, and opened up the energy sector to foreign investment at home, while maintaining the NOC as the key player in the sector. He kept leadership over oil policy in the ministry and presidency, promoting an "internalization" strategy, but at a pace that corresponded to his needs, not PDVSA corporate strategy. There were high political costs to pay for this strategy, with respect to both the citizenry and Congress. Congress openly and continually discussed impeachment after the 1989 riots at the beginning of his term. But Pérez did not moderate his policies to curry favor with Congress, and his ultimate impeachment in 1993 on minor misuse of funds demonstrates that he was willing to risk the ultimate penalty for confronting Congress.

With respect to the Caldera administration, which followed Pérez, the hypotheses derived from our model lead us to expect the following. First, government intervention in the oil and gas value chain would be low (Pérez had already decreased it significantly). Second, energy policy and revenue would seek to provide public and private goods. Third, Caldera would seek to overcome institutional barriers to the adoption of his innovative energy policies but use innovative measures and risk confrontation with his own supporters (the voters who elected him in 1993 and the diverse coalition in Congress that he needed to pass legislation) to modify the expected levels of intrusion and the distribution between private and public goods. As in the Pérez case, market and geology would predict the first behavior, but not the second and third.

Caldera had been a statist nationalist in his first administration (1969–1974), and in the first year of his second term he was still supporting government monopoly over light and medium oil fields. In addition, he was reticent to appoint Giusti as president of PDVSA, not yet convinced that major changes in the oil sector were required. His rejection of Pérez's Gran Viraje led Caldera to adopt a traditional ISI-focused national strategy.

Outside of the energy sector, his handling of the banking crisis favored financiers over the public.[82] Thus, in contradiction to my hypotheses, Caldera began his second term demonstrating neither his innovative nature nor risk acceptance and seeking very much to work within his constraints.

But when the old statist policies failed to produce a recovery and the banking sector collapse exceeded the state's capacity to deal with it, Caldera performed an about-face and adopted the neoliberal policies that inspired Pérez's adjustment policies, though without the grand vision of his predecessor. Since Caldera could not constitutionally be reelected for another decade and in any case would be in his nineties by then, and his political party was weak and unlikely to prosper, the electoral constraints on him were weak. But Congress was wedded to the old statist development model and confronted Caldera. In line with the model's expectations, he pushed hard against the constraints from Congress, threatening to call a Constitutional Convention to replace it. He could not get legislative support for a new natural gas law but used administrative powers to reform natural gas prices and reclassify methane and ethane in ways that permitted the administration to open the natural gas midstream and downstream to private investment. The Caldera administration approved a number of operating service agreements without informing Congress of all the relevant terms, and the OSA contracts would later be found in violation of the law.

Once the Agenda Venezuela project was adopted, Caldera pushed to decrease government intervention in the oil and gas chain below where Pérez had brought it. Though he opposed article 5 in 1975 and promoted the idea that OSAs needed congressional approval in 1990–1991, Caldera now pushed the OSA exception to its maximum with the third round in 1997. His administration also pushed Congress to permit risk contracts in light and medium oil fields. The administration decreased state intervention in the mid- and downstream by pushing for the opening of refined petroleum products distribution and most areas of the natural gas value chain to the private sector, as well as the sale of stock in PEQUIVEN.

Regarding public goods, the Caldera administration did not conform to the hypotheses, despite success in the oil sector. In 1998 government revenue from oil, despite continued low oil prices, had increased significantly. The light and medium crude fields were producing at rates not seen since before the nationalization, and the heavy and extra-heavy oils of the

Orinoco were on their way to commercial viability. But the growth in the oil sector was not linked to the rest of the economy in a way to provide either macroeconomic improvement or social welfare. GDP growth rates were much lower than under Pérez and erratic, and inflation spiraled upward dramatically, hitting 100 percent in 1996, before dropping back down to a still punishing 36 percent in 1998 when GDP growth fell to 0.3 percent.[83] Piñeda and Rodríguez document the precipitous drop (~1/3) in public nonoil capital stock per worker during the Caldera administration.[84] But there was much more private goods provision in the Caldera administration than expected by the model. Unlike the Pérez administration, under Caldera the Gini Index worsened substantially, rising to 47.8 in 1995, Caldera's second year in office, and 49.8 in his final year, 1998 (see table 6.1).

Overall, the model performed well in understanding energy policy in the final two Punto Fijo governments. The Pérez government behaved very much in line with the expectations for a pro-market nationalist administration led by a risk-acceptant and innovative president. Caldera was consistent with the model regarding a tendency to be less intrusive in the market and a willingness to try to alter the institutional constraints on his leadership. Nevertheless, his administration presented some anomalies for the model. The lag in his movement toward less intervention in the oil and gas value chain was unforeseen, though his actions also defy a market-based explanation. In addition, the model does not account for Caldera's limited provision of public goods that would enhance the wellbeing of those at the bottom as government revenue increased and wealth concentrated.

Chapter Seven

ENERGY POLICY IN THE BOLIVARIAN REVOLUTION

The oil market did not look promising when Chávez took office in 1999, but his team's goal for the energy sector was to alter the market constraints it faced via a rejuvenation of OPEC and subordinate the NOC to a political program that prioritized political control over revenue. This was not the first time that PDVSA's business operations were subordinated to national policy, but under Pérez and especially under Caldera, increasing production was the route to increasing revenue. The Bolivarian Revolution prioritized political control of the energy sector, even when it resulted in massive declines in revenue (i.e., 2002–2003 and post-2014). The Bolivarian strategy for generating revenue was twofold: work with OPEC to decrease supply, thereby raising prices, and increase government take from the NOC and its private investor partners.

Market-oriented nationalists, including the NOC's professional management, were unable to blunt the thrust of statist nationalist energy policy. The collapse of Punto Fijo indicated the lack of legitimacy of the elite political class. Ironically, the commercial success of PDVSA in the 1990s undermined NOC management's standing since it came while living standards in Venezuela suffered a dramatic decline. The rhetoric and accusations hurled by the Chávez's political coalition identifying this NOC management as the enemy of the people facilitated popular acceptance of Bolivarian energy policy even once its negative consequences for production became evident. Targeting the NOC and pro-market energy policies thus helped the chavistas' rise to power and persistence in power at least until 2016, after which they were forced to became openly authoritarian in order to hold on to power.

With oil prices low, Orinoco production still a few years off, and the ability of OPEC to regroup and work with non-OPEC producers to influence the market still unclear, the market would have predicted that the new Venezuelan government would not be interested in upsetting investors. The political variables pushed in the same direction as the market ones in the first subperiod of the Chávez administration. By the second subperiod, however, market and political signals were beginning to diverge. Chávez and Maduro would squeeze capital more, borrow, and become increasingly authoritarian as the political needs of the Bolivarian Revolution overrode the market.

This chapter is structured similarly to the chapter on Punto Fijo in order to facilitate comparison. The four sections thus deal with the role of the NOC, commercial policy, access to the resource, and fiscal and contract terms. The conclusion evaluates how well the hypotheses generated from the model fare in helping us understand the variations in Bolivarian energy policy under Chávez and Maduro.

THE ROLE OF THE NOC

Analysts agree that after 2003 PDVSA became significantly subordinated to the executive branch. Chavistas see the outcome as a public good, and everyone else perceives it as rent-seeking by the Bolivarian Revolution. This subordination was not diminished by the calamitous drop in oil prices and subsequent collapse of the national economy in 2014–2016. A focus on the impact of markets on government control of NOCs would suggest that as the market booms, government control increases, but it could not explain the failure of the Bolivarian governments to loosen the reins on PDVSA when the market turned down significantly. Thus we turn to politics.

President Chávez and his oil team rejected the notion that PDVSA should enjoy any autonomy from the government, even regarding local-level management and operations. The ideological and political weight of the oil team had been forged in the congressional debates regarding nationalization in the 1960s and 1970s. Ali Rodríguez had been a guerrilla fighter in the 1960s, was elected to Congress after the amnesty, and opposed the Apertura from the beginning of the Pérez administration. He became Chávez's first oil minister in 1999–2000, was secretary general of OPEC in 2001–2002, and would become president of PDVSA in 2002–2004. Alvaro Silva Calderón, one of the authors of the nationalization legislation in 1975, was oil minister in 2001–2002 and secretary general of OPEC in 2002–2003. Both Rodríguez and Silva Calderón had been important figures in left-wing parties in Congress and were statists.[1]

Despite the strength of Chávez's oil team, his administration had a difficult time securing PDVSA's subordination. PDVSA had seven presidents between 1999 and 2005. Chávez's first appointment, Roberto Mandini (at the time president of CITGO), faced suspicion from within PDVSA even as he defended the company vis-à-vis the ministry. He resigned after only six months, citing policy disagreements and conflicts with factions within the NOC, including his director of planning, Héctor Ciavaldini. Ciavaldini had vocally supported the failed coup by Chávez in 1992 and in the 1990s was an inner member of Chávez's group of oil advisors. Mandini had asked Chávez to fire Ciavaldini, but instead Chávez requested Mandini's resignation and replaced him with Ciavaldini. PDVSA management, in turn, accused Ciavaldini of incompetence and suspected corruption. Ciavaldini also had disagreements with Chávez over how to run the sector, provoked a strike when he attempted to get a pro-Chavez union, and resigned after a year. Brig. General Guaicaipuro Lameda, an old military school classmate of Chávez and director of the Office of the Budget (Oficina Central de Presupuesto), took over. The general was progressively won over by PDVSA management's opposition to the new strategy for the company. Lameda resigned after a year and a half of clashing with Oil Minister Silva Calderón. Gastón Parra Luzardo then came over from the Central Bank to become president, and Chávez appointed a Board of Directors with loyal managers from within PDVSA, but who were far too junior to have ascended to the board in the past. Parra had opposed the Apertura and now, as president of the NOC, publicly attacked its management in the National Assembly.[2]

PDVSA's professional management considered options for opposing this political interference. When Chávez fired several PDVSA employees on live television on his weekly *Aló Presidente* TV show on April 7, 2002, PDVSA management called a strike in the name of defending meritocracy within the company and keeping it focused on the oil business, not politics. The

April strike was quickly joined by the political opposition to Chávez, which perceived an opportunity to discredit, if not replace, the government.[3] After the coup failed, Rodríguez took control of the NOC, demanding allegiance but offering conciliation.

Resistance of the "old" PDVSA to the new policies continued. PDVSA joined the December 2002 strike called by the political opposition. Rodríquez convinced Chávez to deal with the NOC with a heavy hand this time, although a number of his ministers were concerned over the impact on oil production and thus government revenue.[4] Eighteen thousand PDVSA employees were fired, including "close to four out of five of the successful company's exploration and well engineers; about an equal share of staff was sacked from [the] human resources and planning departments, and an even higher share was fired from the finance department. Lesser but nonetheless significant firings occurred in the maintenance, marketing, procurement, and operations departments."[5]

The Chávez administration created the "new" PDVSA (as they referred to it) in 2003, after the two major strikes. As later characterized by Oil Minister and PDVSA president Ramírez, "It was not possible to move forward with dismantling the petroleum opening without having control of our national petroleum company, without having PDVSA." The guiding principles of this "new" PDVSA included commitment to the people of Venezuela, subordination to the state, and high consciousness of national sovereignty.[6]

Chávez appointed Rafael Ramírez in 2004 to head both the ministry and PDVSA. Ramírez was a close friend of Chávez, an engineer and first head of the agency created by the Gas Law of 1999 to develop the natural gas sector, ENEGAS. The new dual appointment was the first time the two positions were unified under one person and indicates that the Chávez administration was not confident that it could run the NOC as a political rather than business enterprise, even with a loyalist at the helm. PDVSA would henceforth be run by statists who cared mainly about the distribution of oil rents and little about the NOC's ability to function as an oil company.

The new management of PDVSA had industry experience and articulated their view of the proper relationship between a NOC and the government. Those views reflected the intellectual, ideological, and political arguments of the political groups that lost out in the 1960s–1990s in determining how nationalization would proceed and government control over the industry would develop. But despite professional qualifications, supporting the Bolivarian Revolution in the short term, even at the expense of the NOC's ability to operate effectively, won out. Ramírez threatened to fire PDVSA employees who did not support Chávez in the 2006 elections.[7] After the major strikes in 2002 and 2003, Alí Rodríguez as PDVSA president proclaimed that "we need to reduce the costs, we need to increase the performance, and we need to enhance our productivity to increase the fiscal contribution [PDVSA makes to the government]."[8] Nonetheless, he oversaw the dramatic diversion of finances, skilled personnel, and effort into social programs rather than commercial tasks, thus putting the NOC on the path to its destruction as an effective oil company. Bernard Mommer, the intellectual mentor on oil issues for many of the leading statist nationalists in Venezuela, had written in his Oxford papers about the importance of maintaining operational independence of an NOC from the political direction of the ministry and the importance of a national private sector in the industry.[9] Yet as vice minister in the Oil Ministry and an external member of the PDVSA Board of Directors, Mommer ensured that the NOC followed the political strategy designed for it, even at the cost of weakening its operational capabilities.

The most fundamental change that the Chávez administration imposed on PDVSA concerned its social role. PDVSA previously had social responsibilities, with its subsidiary Palmaven supporting agroindustrial, social, and cultural programs. In 1997 the NOC spent $77.4 million on these programs. The Chávez administration, however, imposed much greater and more direct social responsibilities on PDVSA. PDVSA president Rodriguez discussed this realignment of tasks on Chávez's *Aló Presidente* program: "PDVSA has now broken away from its former policies and has decided to take an approach directed to the population and the sectors most in need."[10]

Because of the NOC's organizational and professional skills, the Chávez government also used it to plug holes in its national development strategy as the private sector disinvested, nationalized industries failed, and ever-expanding products and services were promised to the people. During 2008–2009 PDVSA created seven subsidiaries across a broad spectrum that included the agricultural sector, the service industry, the industrial sector, naval construction, communal gas development, engineering and construction, and urban development.[11] In brief, PDVSA was becoming the professional state bureaucracy.

We can see further evidence of the subordination of the NOC to the political needs of the government in the company's business plans. The "Plan Siembra Petrolera 2005–2030" (Sow the Petroleum) was developed by the new PDVSA board and stated that PDVSA would contribute to "a new model of economic development, one that is more just, equal and sustainable for combatting poverty and social exclusion. . . . Serve as a geopolitical instrument to support the creation of a pluri-polar system that benefits developing countries and at the same time, constitutes a counterweight to the current unipolar system."[12] This was the first time that PDVSA explicitly incorporated the political objective of the current national administration.

In addition to funding new social and development programs, PDVSA bore the significant costs associated with promoting the government's foreign policies. Venezuela's export structure could reasonably seek to reduce dependence on one single market. However, the "new PDVSA" did not pursue a commercially driven search for new markets to increase the return on export value. PDVSA's export volumes to the United States and Europe decreased in spite of the huge refining expansion there between 1996 and 1999. Exports were diverted to Central America and the Caribbean; though the firm used to have its largest profit margins here, these margins disappeared because of preferential contracts with low prices and generous credit conditions. PDVSA offered discounted oil sales, oil donations, and other support to a variety of countries, including Cuba, Bolivia, Argentina, and Uruguay. The total cost of these programs for 2006 was approximately US$1.73 billion. In addition, using the company to build inefficient projects, provide skilled consultancies for high-cost ventures by foreign partners, and supply allies with subsidized oil and gas increased demands on the NOC's already significantly diminished resources.

Chávez himself publicly recognized that the Bolivarian Revolution laid out the general parameters of a national development plan, but it was PDVSA that conceptualized and elaborated the Plan Estratégico 2005–2012. In presenting the plan, he said that "the plan was born in PDVSA, it was developed in PDVSA, but it is a national plan with which we are committed."[13]

The transformation of PDVSA under the Bolivarian Revolution repro-
duced the functional role that the NOC had in the 1990s under at least Pérez
and the early Caldera administrations. The similarity to PDVSA's contributions to the development of the Apertura Petrolera, whose guidelines
were laid out in Pérez's VIII Plan de la Nación, is striking—as we saw
there, the NOC elaborated oil plans in line with overall national development plans created by Perez's cabinet (see discussion in chapter 6). PDVSA
also not only funded Chávez's social programs, it also provided skilled personnel to implement them, just as it had provided technical staff to the
ministries and agencies before. In addition, the Chávez administration continued the practice of having PDVSA pay Ministry of Energy and Mines
employees working on hydrocarbon issues a monthly bonus that doubled
their official salaries.[14] The Chávez administration clearly subordinated the
NOC to a greater degree than Pérez had, but it hinders our understanding
of oil and gas politics to claim that the differences were not in many important cases ones of degree.

The characteristics of PDVSA's payments to the government should be
understood within the context of how the Chávez administration ran
PDVSA and delivered social programs. Taxes and royalties are payments
that went to the treasury and then to the official government budget. In the
budget process, state governments, the National Assembly, and the constituencies of each ministry had some influence over how resources were to be
allocated. Chávez, however, preferred a funding mechanism for his multiple social initiatives that was both the shortest route to the poor and more
directly under his control. Making PDVSA subsidize domestic consumption and assume social programs within its own budget met both of those
criteria. In addition, the government used this direct line to PDVSA-
generated money to help finance Chávez's presidential election in 2012.[15]

We can see the tension inherent in this structure for the NOC's contributions to government through two programs. Fondespa (Fondo para el
Desarrollo Económico y Social del País) was a social fund created by PDVSA
to promote infrastructure and other large projects coordinated by PDVSA's
Lagoven and the Ministry of Energy and Petroleum. PDVSA committed $4
billion to it during its two years of existence, 2004–2005. Fondespa was
replaced by another development fund (Fonden, Fondo de Desarrollo
Nacional), financed by foreign exchange generated from oil exports and
administered by the Central Bank.

PDVSA also contributed $23 billion to social programs from 2003 to 2008.[16] Although revenue increased as oil prices rose, the government appropriated a steadily increasing share of it, leaving the NOC short on investment funds (table 7.1). PDVSA, through its local subsidiaries Palmaven and CVP, now contributed management as well as financial resources to support social programs related to education, health care, job creation, and subsidized food distribution. Thus PDVSA was no longer funding its own small budget social programs but was now a major contributor to the extensive programs of a populist government. As a result, financial autonomy was eliminated.

By the time Maduro took office, PDVSA was a shadow of an oil company. Operating costs were high—e.g., payroll increased 350 percent from 1998 to 2012—almost tripling the cost of producing a barrel of oil. PDVSA's financial debt increased 150 percent from 2007 to 2012 to US$40 billion.[17] Although its business plan "Siembra Petrolera 2005–2012" had forecast a nearly 100 percent increase in oil production by the end of 2012, when Maduro took office in March 2013 production had instead fallen by at least 11 percent.[18]

There was an initial attempt in 2013 to lessen some of the burden on the NOC and increase its resources for exploration and production (see next section). But faced with growing political opposition and a collapsing economy after 2013, the Maduro government did not provide the budgetary relief and depoliticization that the company would need to become an important producer once again.

TABLE 7.1
PDVSA Extrabudgetary Social Revenues: Total, Relative to Pretax Profits and to Royalties and Taxes (US$ billions)

	2001	2002	2003	2004	2005	2006
Total extrabudgetary social revenues	0	0	0.249	1.242	6.909	13.784
Ratio of social revenues to pretax profits	0	0	5.4	11.5	57.0	113.7
Ratio of social revenues to royalties and taxes	0	0	3.2	8.5	27.0	50.2

Source: PDVSA, "Memoria y cuenta de Petróleos de Venezuela, S.A.," 2007, 5; and PDVSA, "Gestión y resultados" 2007, as cited in David Hults, "Petróleos de Venezuela, S.A.: The Right-Hand Man of the Government" (working paper no. 70, Program on Energy and Sustainable Development, Stanford University, November 2007), 25–26. For 2005 and 2006, Hults relied on updated figures from PDVSA "Gestión y resultados," 2007.

Instead Maduro intensified a statist strategy of using the NOC for polit-ical ends. There was concern now even among chavistas over the produc-tion crisis and the state of PDVSA. But the government's response this time was not just to continue using the NOC for social programs but also for political vendettas and rewards. In 2015 PDVSA president Eulogio Del Pino complained that he did not have the budget to reform and rejuvenate the NOC, but to no avail.[19]

COMMERCIALIZATION

Once the Chávez administration took office, it rejected the supply-side strat-egy for the oil, though not for the gas, sector.

OPEC Quotas

Alí Rodríguez and Chávez coordinated with Saudi Arabia to revive OPEC quotas and hosted the September 2000 OPEC summit in Venezuela after discussing production cuts with Mexico and Russia, non-OPEC mem-bers.[20] Venezuelan production, nevertheless, appears to have increased in 2000 and 2001.[21] After 2002 and to the end of our study period, Venezuelan production declined as a result not of OPEC quotas but of the political and financial instability that overtook the country. The two major strikes in 2002–2003 and the firing of eighteen thousand skilled PDVSA employees took its toll, as did the steady increase in government fiscal take (even from PDVSA), the inability of the NOC to pay its contractors and suppliers, and nationalizations across the value chain (see upcoming discussion)

Syncrude, though not Orimulsion, was reclassified and brought under OPEC oil quotas.[22] The Chávez administration also articulated a desire to diversify its markets away from the United States and into a South-South market, especially with the Chinese.

Internationalization

The Chávez administration had its own version of "internationalization." Despite early announcements intending to sell CITGO and other refin-eries outside Venezuela, the government kept many of them. The rhetoric continued to be to sell CITGO, but the reality was that Venezuela needed refineries that would use heavy crude and the U.S. market had turned toward lighter crudes given the shale oil revolution.[23] Even apart from CITGO and its subsidiaries, PDVSA owns shares in a number of international ventures created during the 1980s and 1990s, with 50 percent of the German RUHR OEL GMBH and 50 percent of the Finnish AB Nynäs Petroleum, with refineries in Sweden, Belgium, and the UK.[24]

PDVSA also became involved in partnering with foreign refinery projects in Brazil and Ecuador. In Argentina, it entered into a deal with ENARSA (the Argentine NOC) to purchase a refinery and distribution company with the intent of securing 12 percent of the Argentine market with six hundred PDVSA service stations.[25]

On top of these international goals, the Petrocaribe, Petrosur, and Petroandina initiatives were political and commercial facilitators to promote regional cooperation mechanisms among NOCs, supply crude oil at preferential rates, and construct gas pipelines. Fifteen countries in the Caribbean were part of Petrocaribe and received in total 200,000 bpd.[26] The preferential conditions when international prices exceeded $40 per barrel called for a financing of 40 percent of the sale to be paid in twenty-five years at 1 percent interest and a two-year grace period. Countries paid with bank notes, governmental guarantees, or commodities at special prices. In South America, Petrosur was created by a presidential agreement among Chávez, Brazil's Luiz Ignacio Lula da Silva, and Argentina's Nestor Kirchner in May 2005 and expanded to incorporate Uruguay and Bolivia at year's end.

The chavistas did not perceive this internationalization strategy antinational since it promoted the Bolivarian Revolution and supported a new international order. There were some domestic complaints from popular sectors about whether that money might be better spent at home,[27] but they had no voice in the matter because these were executive decisions, not issues to be debated in Congress.

Maduro's government maintained this international commercial policy. As prices collapsed in 2014, Venezuela verbalized respect for OPEC's new quota. But there was no possibility of cheating on it even if the government had desired. Though outside our period of study, it's worthwhile to note that despite an economic crisis that produced food and medicine shortages in Venezuela, the government continued to support Petrocaribe and make PDVSA subsidize gasoline stations in Argentina until 2018.[28] Even after those policies ceased, it continued to buy oil on the international market and sell it to Cuba at subsidized prices.[29]

Natural Gas

Chávez's electoral campaign in 1988 promoted the idea that natural gas could become another pillar of the economy, promoting industry and employment, as had Pérez back in 1989. PDVSA's business plan for 2000–2009, developed under Minister Rodríguez, forecast more than a doubling of Venezuelan gas production from 6 bcfd (billion cubic feet per day) in 2000 to 14.5 bcfd in 2010. In early 2000 the first auctions for exploration and production licenses to supply a yet-to-be developed domestic market were announced, postponed twice, and then held in 2001 for eleven onshore blocks. Only six blocks received bids, with just one attracting more than one bid. The initial interest of twenty-two foreign and eleven domestic companies and consortiums that prequalified for the auctions proved fleeting, as only seven submitted bids.[30] A new round of auctions for 2004 was postponed, and in 2006 gas production was essentially the same as it had been at the beginning of the gas opening, 6 bcfd.[31]

The muted response is partially attributable to the increase in political risk as the Bolivarian Revolution confronted challenges in 2002–2003 and responded partly by increasing control over the economy. In addition, the country lacked the necessary infrastructure and services to explore, process, and distribute the gas to the expanded domestic market that was expected to develop with subsidized prices.

Progress was made regarding infrastructure. The ICO gas pipeline connecting the eastern and western domestic markets was begun in 2004 and completed in 2006. PDVSA financed the Antonio Ricaurte gas pipeline built in 2006–2007 between Venezuela and Colombia. While Colombia is not a gas powerhouse, a Chevron-Ecopetrol project had excess gas in Guajira that could temporarily supply Venezuela. The expectation of both governments was that the Guajira fields would soon decline, and Colombia could import from its neighbor.[32] The expected date for the flow to reverse was 2012, but as of 2019 Venezuelan gas was not yet available to Colombia.

To stimulate progress, President Chávez declared a "Natural Gas Revolution" on his weekly radio program, *Aló Presidente*, in 2007, this time with international markets included as well. The goals of this program were to complete a gas infrastructure of pipelines, interconnections, and transportation networks that would link twenty-three states to expanded or new onshore and offshore gas fields. There were also foreign policy goals of becoming the major supplier of natural gas to South America via a $25 billion gas pipeline from Venezuela to Argentina, the Caribbean, and the Atlantic basin. These foreign markets would be supplied by new offshore projects, including LNG, with exports expected to begin in 2016. The PDVSA affiliate, PDVSA Ingeniería y Construcción, S.A., was charged with developing the CIGMA LNG Complex to feed two trains, with a third train shortly thereafter. A new PDVSA affiliate, PDVSA Gas Comunal, S.A., would operate in the mid- and downstream of the liquified petroleum gas (LPG) market. It had ambitious plans to construct refilling plants, fabricate LPG cylinders and tanks, and create a fleet of distribution vehicles and distribution centers to provide sufficient supply to cover the domestic as well as export markets.[33]

Great expectations concerning natural gas possibilities were renewed in the period 2007–2009. Not only were there investments in the upstream, the LNG projects seemed on the fast track. In 2008 Venezuela, though expecting to negotiate an agreement for only the first LNG train, encountered sufficient interest among investors to sign agreements for all three trains. The government announced that $19.6 billion would be invested in the offshore gas field and the trains, with firms from Japan, Russia, and Malaysia joining the project.[34] In 2009 the La Perla field in the Cardón IV block in the shallow waters of the Gulf of Venezuela was discovered; exploratory drilling led to estimates of 17 tcf in 2011. The block was licensed to Italy's ENI and Spain's Repsol, fifty-fifty, and PDVSA expected to buy in with its option of 35 percent. The three companies signed a Gas Sales Agreement for the development of the field to 2036.[35] (See table 7.2.)

Unfortunately, the Gas Revolution suffered from the disincentives generated by the economic and political collapse of the Bolivarian Revolution. Governments of the Bolivarian Revolution authorized eighteen natural gas exploration and production licenses, but only five of those were operating as of 2017. PDVSA Gas served as a minority partner in three of those.[36] Though La Perla began commercial production in 2015, as of 2018 PDVSA had not yet exercised its 35 percent option because it lacked the funds.[37] In 2010 Reuters reported that the administration intended to force gas license holders who had not yet begun exploration to turn their

TABLE 7.2
Venezuela's Natural Gas Projects with Foreign Partners

Joint Venture/Project Name	Estimated Production 2017 (Mcf/d)	Participating Companies and Their Shares (%)
Bielovenezolana (Zamaca West)	Unknown	Belarusneft (40), PDVSA Gas (60)
Cardon IV (Perla)	490	ENI (50), Repsol (50)
Ypergas (Yucal-Placer)	150	Total (69.5), Repsol (15), Inepetrol (10.2), Otepi (5.3)
Quiriquire Gas	128	Repsol (60), PDVSA Gas (40)
Gas Guarico	80	INPEX (70), PDVSA Gas (30)

Source: U.S. Energy Information Administration, based on information reported by PDVSA and its JV partners IPD Latin America, NewsBase Latin America Oil & Gas Monitor, BN Americas, and Rystad Energy. Accessed via EIA, "Country Analysis Brief: Venezuela," June 2018.

licenses in for a minority position in a new PDVSA-controlled joint venture.[38] Between 2004 and 2017 over 40 percent of total gas consumption was used to enhance production from Venezuela's declining mature oil fields as oil production increasingly became the sole driver of the country's economy. In 2016 domestic consumption continued to exceed domestic production. The ENI-Repsol La Perla field (with no participation by PDVSA) produces more than half of Venezuela's nonassociated gas, and the only two joint ventures with PDVSA participation (the NOC holds a minority position in both) produced less than 25 percent of the country's total in 2017.

ACCESS TO THE NATURAL RESOURCE

Constitution of 1999

Hydrocarbons are governed by articles 12 and 302.[39] The first establishes that the nation owns the subsoil mineral and hydrocarbons—"whatever their nature"—which conforms to nearly universal practice. Article 302 stipulates that "the State reserves for itself, through the relevant organic law and by reason of national expedience, the petroleum industry and other industries, exploitations, services and goods that are in the public interest and of a strategic nature." These two articles are of a broad character and provide great latitude to a government in deciding how to implement the legal fact of resource nationalism through organic laws.

Article 303 provides further evidence of this latitude. The article stipulates that in the interest of economic and political sovereignty and national strategy the shares of the NOC, whether PDVSA or a successor, can never be privatized. But the article does provide that the NOC's subsidiaries, strategic associations, or any other business enterprises that PDVSA finds it necessary to develop in the course of its business are exempt from this restriction. In 2012 Minister Ramírez discussed with the Chinese government the listing of an unnamed PDVSA subsidiary on the Hong Kong Stock Exchange as a means of raising capital.[40] Though a $10 billion deal with China seems to have obviated the need for such an offering,[41] the episode is another illustration of the Chávez administration's pragmatic approach to implementing national control within the context of resource nationalism, that is, national ownership of the resource. Despite denouncing the access of private capital in the 1980s and 1990s, the chavistas' intent from the beginning of their mandate was to restructure the opening, not close it down. In fact, given the diversion of the NOC's resources and the underinvestment in its productive capacities, the state came to rely on foreign companies, not PDVSA, for new E&P.[42]

Gaseous Hydrocarbons Law 1999

The Gas Law of 1999 was designed by a team appointed by President Chávez that analyzed natural gas laws in various countries.[43] The law was promulgated under decree powers granted to President Chávez by the National Assembly and is very generous to investors. Despite claiming ownership of all hydrocarbons, the law separated nonassociated natural gas from the 1975 and 1999 constitutional requirements that hydrocarbon activities be reserved to the state, except under specific conditions.[44] Since associated natural gas is produced in oil wells, that activity falls under the oil law. But the Bolivarian gas law went far beyond the Supreme Court decision in 1991 that permitted PDVSA to partner with private investors (see chapter 6). Private Venezuelan and foreign investors were now permitted under a system of licenses and permits to carry out activities across the entire value chain of nonassociated natural gas. Private investment was permitted to own up to 100 percent of a natural gas project. In addition, for associated gas reservoirs in which the crude oil or condensates could not be commercially viable under the Oil Law regulations, the ministry could apply the nonassociated gas rules.[45]

The generosity of the Gaseous Hydrocarbons Law was not based on ideology but on pragmatism. Chávez's energy team was astute enough to recognize that PDVSA had neither the capital nor skills to develop natural gas on the scale desired and that the country was in a weak bargaining position in natural gas. Here the international market was segmented and underdeveloped, while the domestic market was virtually nonexistent and likely to be subsidized when it developed.[46] Thus attractive terms beyond what had been achieved by the hated Apertura policies would need to be offered to bring foreign investment into the natural gas sector.

Organic Hydrocarbon Law of 2001

The law was drafted by Álvaro Silva Calderón.[47] The ministry appears to have consulted with IOCs regarding the new oil law, though we don't know what was modified as a result, and the companies were not entirely in conformity with the law.[48]

The Organic Hydrocarbon Law of 2001 supplanted all previous laws relating to oil and associated gas, including the Hydrocarbons Law (1943) and the Nationalization Law (1975), relating to oil and formed the basis for regaining the sovereignty over oil that the statists believed had been lost in the prior decade. The law reserved to the state a controlling interest (51 percent) in any venture engaged in the exploration and production of nongaseous hydrocarbons (article 22). The ministry was given the responsibility for overseeing the development of the sector and carrying out market research and analyses of prices (article 8). International arbitration of contract disputes was restricted (article 34(3)(b)) but not prohibited; royalties, with certain exceptions, were raised to 30 percent (article 44); and taxes were raised (article 48). The law also provided the government with important discretion relating to "increases of royalties, contributions and other compensations foreseen under this Decree-Law" (article 36). The law itself was silent on whether it was retroactive. Government officials tried to assuage investors by noting that the new law was not retroactive.[49]

The law was ready to sign in November, but the Chávez government was not yet ready to sign an Orimulsion contract with China. After approving the new law and a few weeks before it came into force, President Chávez signed an agreement creating a joint venture in the oil sector, in which Chinese capital would hold majority ownership in the Orimulsion Project, in partnership with a PDVSA affiliate—an arrangement that was clearly inconsistent with the framework established by the 2001 law.[50] Since the Sinovensa contract was signed before the law came into force, it was not subject to the new terms for the sector. The timing strongly suggests that the Chinese would not have accepted the terms of the new law and the project would have failed or needed to provide other terms to entice the Chinese to subject themselves to the new law.

Nationalizations

The Constitution of 1999 and the Oil Law of 2001 stipulated that oil exploration and production projects needed to be controlled by the country via PDVSA majority participation, but, as noted earlier, the government assured investors that the law did not apply retroactively. Yet, after unilaterally altering the fiscal terms under which the Apertura projects were created, the Chávez administration embarked on a path to nationalization.

Nationalizations began with the OSA contracts, when the ministry denounced them as illegal in April 2005 and the companies were ordered to migrate to Mixed Companies (Empresas Mixtas).[51] The National Assembly created a Special Commission to investigate the alleged irregularities in the Apertura-era contracts; the Special Commission held hearings in June 2005 with former ministers and PDVSA presidents from the era and under the Chávez government.[52] On May 25, 2005, Minister Ramírez delivered a scathing denunciation of the Apertura-era contracts to the National Assembly, claiming they were illegitimate, had legal problems, and contained unacceptable clauses, including limiting PDVSA to a minority partnership.[53] Subsequently, the National Assembly requested that "the National Executive, via the Ministry of Energy and Petroleum, elaborate a legal instrument that will permit this and future generations of Venezuelans full guaranty of the sovereign and rational exploitation of the Orinoco Oil Belt. In the same manner, the National Assembly insists that the National Executive revoke any agreement that prohibits the Bolivarian Republic of Venezuela from controlling the operations in the Orinoco Belt." The National Assembly also offered to "collaborate with the National

Executive in the juridical and political arenas to guarantee a majority participation of Venezuelans in the business of the Orinoco Belt."[54]

Companies with OSA contracts were required to form new JVs with PDVSA holding 60–80 percent of the shares. By 2006 most companies accepted the migration, though Exxon sold its minority stake in an original OSA to Repsol, while Total and ENI agreed to a buyout from the government. In 2007 the Orinoco projects were nationalized ("forced migration"). PetroCanada left rather than migrate, and Conoco and Exxon took their claims to international arbitration. These new JVs faced the same fiscal requirements as the migrated OSAs.[55] Although private and foreign investors were partners in these JVs, Minister Ramírez prohibited them from booking any oil reserves for accounting purposes.[56]

The Orinoco projects had been progressively targeted since Ramírez's May 2005 denunciation to the National Assembly and its Special Committee Report. In August 2005 Chávez announced on his *Aló Presidente* program that Venezuela could apply the Hydrocarbons Law retroactively to the associations but he hoped the companies would voluntarily negotiate the transition to mixed companies.[57] In April 2006 Del Pino (then head of CVP and later minister and president of the NOC) declared that PDVSA "would like all associations to migrate to *empresas mixtas*" and the "State's participation must be 51%." Del Pino stated that "in order for this to happen, he would need the support of both the National Assembly and President Hugo Chávez."[58] Vice Minister Mommer and IOCs discussed fiscal, legal (e.g., arbitration), and ownership terms with the companies.[59] But the government had the National Assembly's report demanding nationalization, the projects were now producing, oil prices were high, and the government was in discussion with international lawyers about potential outcomes if some IOCs chose to file suits against the state and the NOC.[60] In this situation there was no "negotiation"—Mommer announced to Congress on August 30, 2006, that all the companies had been "informed" ("ya se le informó a todas") that the migration to 51 percent state ownership would occur.[61] In this context, there was no agreement for what the government hoped would be a friendly "migration" to the new JV structure.

Finally, in December 2006, after Chávez won the presidential election, the decision was made to unilaterally nationalize these contracts with not 51 percent but 60 percent state ownership. The next month, January 2007, the National Assembly gave Chávez wide-ranging decree powers. As required by the constitution, Oil Minister Ramírez presented the draft nationalization decree to the cabinet and it was approved. President Chávez signed Decree 5,200, which gave companies four months to negotiate the terms of their participation in a mixed enterprise in which PDVSA would hold majority shares.[62] The majority partners in three of the projects (ConocoPhillips in Petrozuata and Ameriven, and Exxon in Cerro Negro) responded by filing suit and leaving Venezuela, but their minority partners (Chevron in Ameriven and BP in Cerro Negro) chose to migrate to the new ownership structure and remain minority partners. In the fourth Orinoco project, Total and Statoil reduced their shares in order for PDVSA to achieve majority ownership with 60 percent. As a result of the nationalizations, PDVSA's ownership share rose from 40 percent to 78.3 percent, and it now became the operator of all of them as well.[63] The Chávez government, nevertheless, did not return to the dreams of the original critics of the Apertura and settled for majority control of the projects rather than a state monopoly. Del Pino noted that the nationalization of the Orinoco Association contracts "represented savings of 3 billion U.S. dollars, and these significant annual savings will make it possible to finance social work."[64]

At the end of 2008 the government nationalized private gasoline stations, ending the opening that had been accomplished in 1998. Over the course of the decade, private companies had come to supply 54 percent of the internal market for hydrocarbon fuel. Three foreign companies (BP, Texaco, and Mobil) supplied 17 percent of the market, and six Venezuelan companies (Trebol Gas, Llanopetrol, CCM, Petrocanarias, La Petrolea, and Betapetrol) provided for the other 37 percent.[65]

FISCAL AND CONTRACTUAL ISSUES

Given campaign rhetoric and the statist backgrounds of key energy advisors and administrators, investors in the energy sector were concerned when Chávez won the election in 1998. The Chávez administration moved quickly to address investors' fiscal and contractual concerns. Decree 356 in 1999 provided the basis for the government to include a provision in a contract that would guarantee a stable tax rate for up to ten years. Congress would need to approve the contract (similar to the stipulation in the much-maligned article 5) rather than leaving it to the discretion of the Oil Ministry or president.[66] In 2001 the income tax for hydrocarbon companies was reduced from 67.7 percent to 50 percent.[67]

This situation changed beginning in 2002 for a combination of economic and political reasons. After a short-lived rise in 1999–2000, oil prices fell almost 20 percent in 2002 but then boomed from 2003 to 2008, rising over 300 percent in constant dollars. Manzano and Monaldi argue that a major reason government take rose in this period is that the contracts had not been designed to be progressive when prices rose.[68] But not all oil producers raised government take to the level that Venezuela did, nor was Venezuela the country with the highest take. Norway, not usually a country accused of "resource nationalism," had a similar government take at the time, while Mexico, with one of the most closed oil industries in the world, had an overall fiscal take of 70 percent, and Brazil used a sliding scale for adjusting government take.[69]

Because taxation is a sovereign attribute, moving forward on the fiscal side was a convenient first step that would be unlikely to generate full-scale revolt by the international investors and firms. The Chávez government thus increasingly perceived itself to be in the driver's seat and revised fiscal terms and ultimately the contracts themselves with virtually no negotiations with the affected firms.

Between 2004 and 2008 many fiscal changes were implemented to increase government revenues in the name of "resource nationalism" but actually for short-term private goods. Royalty rates were the first target in October 2004, unilaterally rising for the Orinoco projects from 1 percent to 16.67 percent.[70] In 2005 OSAs were assessed for three years of back taxes and had their income tax rates raised from 34 percent to 50 percent, as stipulated in the Hydrocarbon Law of 2001. Payments for services provided by OSAs were now to be made in local currency rather than U.S. dollars. An exploitation tax of 33 1/3 percent was promulgated in May 2006, applicable to all oil projects, thereby equalizing the rate across projects.[71] In August 2006, just before the nationalizations in 2007, Congress approved the Oil Ministry's proposal to raise the income taxes for the Orinoco projects from 34 percent to 50 percent. Although the tax authority Servicio Nacional Integrado de Administración Tributaria (SENIAT) proposed rules to limit carryforward losses to reduce tax liability and limit debt-to-capital ratios, Congress demurred, insisting that the ministry needed to make the proposals.[72] The ministry never did propose such fiscal limitations; ex post, one can surmise that the government was content to reduce the NOC's tax liability and indebt it to free up more money for its social and political agendas.

With prices rising dramatically, the Chávez government implemented a series of windfall taxes varying by oil price. The government initially set the threshold price at Brent despite the fact that heavy and extra-heavy Venezuelan crude is discounted; this price would have effectively increased the windfall tax for producers. But when the measure was announced, the price was set by the Venezuelan basket of crude, thereby revealing a concern not to cross a threshold beyond what the companies could accept.[73]

Further evidence of caution even in a context of hypernationalism and political polarization is found in the National Assembly. Despite a 90+ percent legislative majority for the chavistas, in 2006 the National Assembly adopted a reform to the 2001 Oil Law, stipulating that if a 30 percent tax was deemed an obstacle to commercializing mature fields or extra-heavy oil from the Orinoco, the executive could lower it without the need for congressional approval, to 20 percent until the time when 30 percent was appropriate.[74] Once again, this action demonstrates the desire of the Chávez administration for a free hand, but with institutional blessing.

A preliminary analysis in 2011 of the cap on the royalty and export tax suggested that the reform decreased the revenues paid by the IOCs that would be transferred to the national budget controlled by the legislature and increased the NOC's contributions to Fonden.[75] As noted, the fund is off-budget and under exclusive control of the president, rendering an accounting of how this appropriation of national wealth was spent in benefit of the nation impossible. Outright corruption and political patronage to sustain the Bolivarian Revolution, rather than provision of public goods, is the most likely explanation of this end-run around a Congress committed to that same revolution.

Manzano and Monaldi calculate that the fiscal measures, the subsequent nationalizations, and the increased oil prices created a marginal take for the government in 2008 of 90 percent to 92.7 percent for the three Apertura contracts that were not service contracts, up from original takes of 35 percent to 67 percent.[76] Despite its dramatically increasing take from the oil wealth, there never seemed to be enough revenue for the government, and new means of revenue appropriation were pursued. In 2012 Minister

Ramírez announced that PDVSA had negotiated a deal with China's CITIC for a 10 percent share in the Petropiar joint venture the NOC had with Chevron. This was the first time since the oil nationalizations of 2007 that PDVSA reduced its share in a project rather than forcing a foreign company to decrease theirs.[77] CITIC declined, so the effort did not generate more revenue.[78]

ENI, which had its Cación oil field nationalized in 2006 and accepted below book value as compensation, and Chinese and Russian national oil companies became partners with PDVSA in January 2010 in the JV to develop the Junin 5 block in the Orinoco Belt. A month later, Chevron and Repsol took minority stakes in two $15 billion projects in the Orinoco's Carabobo block.[79] These opportunities were utilized as carrots to persuade nationalized firms to accept reduced compensation or forgo international arbitration. Because of the boom in oil prices, Venezuela appears to have calculated that it could afford negative judgements and paid all judgments in the oil sector through Chávez's term.[80]

The increase in fiscal take and nationalizations plus the significant drop in oil prices in 2009 (more than 30 percent) combined to worry the Chávez administration that the new investment it needed to further develop the Orinoco would not materialize. The government once again demonstrated its flexibility in implementing its fiscal regime. Temporary reductions for royalties and extraction taxes were offered, varying by contract and apparently reflecting the distinct factors that affect profitability; the goal was to ensure investors' profits within a seven-year period for the six new Orinoco projects that were negotiated. While the income tax could not be lowered, the base on which it is calculated could be altered, thereby permitting an effective reduction without drawing the public attention that a tax decrease might attract. The PetroCarabobo and PetroIndependencia projects benefited from provisions regarding accelerated depreciation and carrying losses forward, while the PetroJunin and PetroBicentenario projects were permitted to form horizontally rather than vertically integrated business models and thus have the upgraders subject to the lower income tax for nonoil businesses. Participation bonuses paid to the state also vary in their timing across the new contracts.[81]

Natural gas was in a distinct regulatory and market situation from oil. The Chávez administration provided very generous fiscal and contractual incentives compared to oil in the Gas Law of 1999. The incentives for nonassociated gas hydrocarbons rivaled those of the Apertura, which the chavistas so criticized. Royalties and income taxes were lower than those for associated gas projects: royalties were set at 20 percent rather than 30 percent, and the income tax was 34 percent instead of 67 percent. Gas projects authorized under this law could be 100 percent nonstate owned. Although the Gas Law did provide for the NOC to purchase a 35 percent stake after a project reached commercial status, if the NOC exercised the option, the project could still legally be up to 65 percent non-state ownership.[82] The structure of the bidding for natural gas blocks in 2001 was designed to be attractive—licenses would be for an initial thirty-five years with the possibility of extension for another thirty years, an early requirement for every bid to include a Venezuelan company was dropped for nine of the blocks, and rather than competing on the basis of signing bonuses, which required up-front money, the auction used highest royalty offers over the minimum of 20 percent.[83] Nevertheless, the reputation of the Chávez administration regarding fiscal and contractual commitments was extremely compromised, and investors with alternatives globally (e.g., Chevron) or domestically (e.g., PDVSA itself through requirements imposed on it by the government) invested minimally in natural gas despite the incentives.

Fiscal measures were not just designed to capture more of the booming prices in oil. Despite a failure to get the "Gas Revolution" off the ground, fiscal measures increased government take here as well, pointing to the importance of statist interpretations of resource nationalism over market explanations. In 2005 Shell lost its license in the Mariscal Sucre gas project (which was the old Colón project) over the dispute regarding new taxes. PDVSA had a difficult time finding a new partner and the project stalled, demonstrating the willingness of the Chávez administration to forgo potential revenue and economic development in the short to medium term to signal its control. In 2009 Venezuela auctioned the project, but despite the interest of eleven firms, including from Japan, Qatar, and Brasil's NOC, Petrobras, the auction was unsuccessful. PDVSA attempted to run the project by itself, but in 2010 its solo exploration suffered a major setback when the submersible exploration platform it leased sank.[84]

Because PDVSA had become simply a "cash cow" for the government rather than an effective oil company, the NOC's ability to meet the ideological needs of the Bolivarian Revolution was also at risk. PDVSA had severe cash flow problems and was finding it difficult to keep up with its obligations as majority owner of all the oil projects. Oil service companies at first gave the NOC time to catch up with payments, but PDVSA soon demanded a renegotiation of the $13+ billion debt. The companies refused, and in 2009 the government responded by nationalizing sixty oil service companies—demonstrating that nationalization was about both controlling access to the resource (discussed earlier) and limiting liability. Minister Ramírez justified the nationalizations as bringing the oil service sector into line with article 302 of Venezuela's constitution, which reserved primary activities in hydrocarbons for the state. He thereby expanded the definition of primary activities to include services contracted by the NOC.[85] There was also some speculation that a charge against Chevron for contract irregularities was a pressure tactic to get the IOC to accept reduced payments for PDVSA debt.[86]

Venezuela's weakening economy even before the oil market collapse meant that Maduro needed to raise capital to continue subsidizing the national economy and address growing international debt. But oil production decreases and difficulties in developing gas meant that simply taxing or nationalizing more of the oil sector was not likely to help. The Bolivarian Revolution thus moderated its stance once again.

In February 2013 the National Assembly decreased the windfall profits tax for the oil sector and redirected to the national budget some of the fiscal contribution that used to go directly to Fonden. The impact of the modification in the windfall profits tax varied by the price of oil; IESA calculated in 2012 that at a price of US$100 per barrel, the change effectively reduced total government take from 83.4 percent to 81 percent. The fall in government revenue was expected to be offset by a devaluation (more bolivares would be available per dollar), a reduction in the cost of production for enterprises using oil and thus an expectation of increased production, and an improvement in the financial situation of PDVSA that could lead to more production.[87] Despite chavistas' previous denunciation of international arbitration, the Maduro administration included a clause for it in a contract under which Chevron would lend PDVSA $2 billion to permit the NOC to pay for its share of a joint venture.[88] PDVSA also negotiated contracts with CNPC and Rosneft for $4 billion and $1.5 billion, respectively, to increase production in their JVs with the NOC.[89] In the process, PDVSA turned over control of the fields to at least these U.S. and

Chinese companies.[90] After PDVSA suffered from decreased production rather than achieve a 500,000 bpd increase in production for 2012, the NOC negotiated a revolving credit line with Schlumberger for $1 billion, which was expected to contribute to an increase in production of 400,000 bpd for 2013.[91] Nevertheless, these changes were dwarfed by the economic and political uncertainties and disequilibria dominating the country, and the expected payoffs did not materialize.

In 2016 the Maduro government created new fiscal and contractual terms to attract companies and halt the declining production capacity of PDVSA. Faced with unpaid bills adding up to over US$1 billion and nationalizations, oil service companies pulled resources out of Venezuela, contributing to the dramatic decline in Venezuelan production. In May 2016 PDVSA began issuing US$1.366 bn of three-year credit notes with an interest rate of 6.5 percent to resolve debts with its primary service providers. Catching up on debt was not sufficient to bring in new investment, and in September 2016 a new structure of integrated oil service contracts (IOSCs) was implemented to entice private service companies to develop 576 oil wells at the Orinoco Belt Basin. The key obstacles were the problem of the credibility of payment and getting their money in dollars rather than bolivares. Under the new contracts, service contractors would get paid directly by the buyer of the crude or through the structure of a trust fund for the services executed, into which the buyer of the crude would pay.[92]

PERFORMANCE OF MODEL IN EXPLAINING BOLIVARIAN POLICIES

The Chávez and Maduro administrations experienced wide variations in their oil and gas policies. The commercial policies of the Punto Fijo and Bolivarian Revolution governments had some surprising similarities, while they differed in important ways. For the Bolivarian regime, internationalization was driven by international politics and responded to government rather than company needs. Rather than reversing the much-critiqued Apertura, Chávez initially broadened it across the oil and gas value chains, providing more access to the resource and the mid- and downstreams but with greater government control and fiscal terms that were more beneficial to the government. A greater difference was the willingness of the Chávez government to unilaterally change commercial policy, access to the resource, and contract and fiscal terms. Geology and the state of the market could not account for these variations. In this section I will evaluate how well the hypotheses derived from the model performed in helping to explain those policies.

In the first Chávez period 1999–2004, the political system was inclusive in the years 1999–2000, shifting to exclusive in 2001. We therefore have two sets of hypotheses. For 1999–2000 we expected the government to be less intrusive in the oil and gas value chain. Since the decision-making unit was moderately competitive, energy policy should have been characterized by low levels of government intrusion. The model also predicted that public goods would be provided. Since Chávez was moderately risk acceptant and not innovative, we expected him to push back only mildly against any institutional constraints (party and Congress) to policy making and adopt policies that had been debated before for Venezuela.

Chávez had denounced the internationalization strategy and the Apertura, but his Constituent Assembly wrote a constitution that permitted foreign investment in the sector far beyond what article 5 had permitted when it was adopted in 1975. The Natural Gas Law of 1999 was extremely conservative in providing foreign investors with up to 100 percent control over the development of the nonassociated gas fields, even though Punto Fijo governments in the 1970s legislated monopoly control. In addition, Silva Calderón and Rodríguez wrote an Oil Law that was not retroactive for the Apertura contracts. The first two policies reduced government intrusiveness in the oil and gas value chains, and the third committed the government to respecting the ownership shares negotiated by the Punto Fijo governments despite the legal requirement for increased state control in future contracts. These policies are well in line with the model's predictions.

Regarding provision of public goods, again we see the model performing well. The Chávez government provided the public good of macroeconomic stability, bringing inflation down, and prioritized the building of foreign exchange reserves over expanding social programs.[93] The provision of public goods also demonstrates the moderate risk aversion of Chávez. He had wanted to expend funds from the Fund for Macroeconomic Stabilization (FIEM, in Spanish), but Planning Minister Giordani opposed withdrawing funds, so Chávez demurred.[94] He was willing to accept rising inequality while wooing the private sector to get macroeconomics in order. The Gini

Index stayed higher in the first years of the administration than during Pérez's second presidency and even rose to levels higher than those in Caldera's second term, peaking at 52.4 in 2005 (see table 6.1).

As a moderately risk-acceptant leader, Chávez refrained from excluding foreign investors from "strategic sectors" of the economy. This was not an obvious choice since Chávez's leftist advisors had argued for excluding foreign investors when they opposed article 5 of the Nationalization Law of 1975 and the PSAs in the 1990s. There were also regional precedents: Mexico would reaffirm national monopoly in its oil-sector reforms of 2008, and Correa would relegate foreign firms to "service providers" in Ecuador. Chávez's noninnovative character could have resulted in a government monopoly, as occurred with the 1971 gas and 1975 oil laws. However, consistent with the primacy of risk acceptance (i.e., retaining office) over innovation, as noted in chapter 3, his moderate risk acceptance meant he would not break with the private sector or Venezuelans in his coalition who wanted to begin enjoying the fruits of the Apertura policies of Pérez and Caldera.

After 2000 the political system reverted to being exclusive, but this time favoring the poor. This situation from 2001–2004 provides an incentive for policy to be more intrusive in the oil and gas value chain and provide private goods to the poor. Since the decision-making unit remains moderately competitive, our hypotheses expected the provision of public and private goods. And again, we expect Chávez to be noninnovative and moderately risk averse.

It is precisely in 2001 that we begin to see an increase in government intrusiveness in the sector, with the Oil Law and the growing disputes over control of PDVSA. In 2004 royalty rates were increased for the Orinoco projects as well. These policies are in line with model expectations. The missions programs created by Chávez beginning in 2003 for the provision of health, education, and welfare services are private rather than public goods. During the boom years access was reported to be quite nondiscriminatory regarding whether one supported the government or not, although it became discriminatory when the economic crisis hit under Maduro. What makes the missions programs a private good, however, are the opaque way in which sites were chosen since there are not enough missions to meet demand, the lack of transparency regarding the budget or the supply chain for these programs, and no evaluation of either staffing of the programs or the product they ostensibly produce.[95]

In this first period Chávez expanded on the use of emergency decree powers delegated to the president by the Congress to legislate policy changes. Various Punto Fijo presidents used this measure, but Chávez did so more often and for longer periods. Even though his party held a majority in Congress, he wanted to avoid the potential for deputies to alter or question his policies, as well as to avoid public debate about them. Using decree powers was a noninnovative means for minimizing the risk of conflict with his congressional allies or civic partisans and is thus supportive of our hypotheses.

For the second period of the Chávez administration, 2005–2012, the first two hypotheses, concerning low levels of inclusion in the political system and low competitiveness in the decision-making unit, point to high levels of government intrusion in the oil and gas value chain and the provision of private over public goods. The constituency of the Bolivarian Revolution is the popular sector, though the leadership was only indirectly accountable to them from 2005 to 2016, given the unequal playing field for elections. Unlike the business sector, the popular sector needs the government to appropriate wealth from the energy sector if goods and services are to be directed toward the poor. The institutional constraints on Chávez loosened significantly after 2006, so his authoritarian tendencies were able to manifest more clearly, but he was still moderately risk averse and did not either fully break with his own constitution (e.g., the referendum debacle in 2007) or impose a one-party state. In the energy sector, the counterpart was a willingness to negotiate with the private sector when the unilateral measures undertaken by the government were unsuccessful.

The wave of nationalizations across the oil and gas value chain beginning in 2007 mark a clear distinction between the level of intrusion into the energy market in Chávez's first and second periods. The creation of a direct flow of resources from PDVSA to a proliferation of missions programs distributing goods and services that were under Chávez's direct control and whose fiduciary and performance accounts were opaque rather than to the treasury and legislatively determined budget priorities illustrates the private over public goods provision behavior.

But even in increasing government take and operational control, the Chávez administration began cautiously, with fiscal measures that would be difficult for IOCs to contest in international arbitration before moving on to partial nationalizations to ensure majority shares in a project for

PDVSA. Though oil contracts were unilaterally altered to provide PDVSA with at least 60 percent of a JV, the Chávez administration offered companies that were willing to accept the nationalizations opportunities on other projects. Some companies availed themselves of these offers, indicating their expectations that Chávez would be averse to again unilaterally alter contract terms. The model thus does well in explaining the Chávez administration's policies in 2005–2012.

Turning to Maduro, 2013–2016, the political system was exclusive, the decision-making structure was noncompetitive, and he is neither an innovator nor a risk taker. The hypotheses expect policies that are significantly intrusive in the oil and gas value chain and provision of private goods. We expect Maduro's response to opposition to government policy not to be innovative, but to mimic that of Chávez. We also expect Maduro to avoid confrontation with energy companies by negotiating his policies with various companies rather than setting policies unilaterally and demanding acceptance.

As the economy weakened, oil projects and exports became the only source of legal revenue for the government (without credible evidence. one can only speculate about corrupt sources of revenue). Maduro's energy policies continued to deprive the NOC of resources and discourage private investment even as production plummeted. Deteriorating budgets were dedicated to paying foreign debt without making domestic adjustments to begin an economic recovery. Nontransparent monetary transfers from a dwindling national budget, plus giving high-ranking military officers more roles in the civilian economy, kept the military loyal. The missions programs were used to distribute more goods and services as the economy veered toward collapse and hyperinflation. The short-term survival of the Bolivarian Revolution required a proliferation of private goods at the expense of public goods.

Maduro faced no significant institutional constraints from his coalition in his first three years. Chavista control of the electoral process provided him with a victory in the 2013 elections, and the legislative, judicial, and military authorities supported the repression of protests in the years after. He did alter formal institutional constraints when the opposition won the National Assembly in December 2016, but the Bolivarian Revolution had control of the National Assembly during the transition to seating the new Assembly, the Supreme Court, and the military, and they could be counted on to support his decisions. The decision to strip the National Assembly of its powers was not risky vis-à-vis his constituency or those who could push him out of power. The Venezuelan political opposition and many international actors cried foul, but they could not pose a significant threat to Maduro's continued rule.

Because Maduro is not innovative, he advocated the same ideas that Chávez did even as the political crisis and PDVSA's operational crisis worsened to 2016. Maduro's energy policy first sought to increase government take to the maximum, using traditional means of government intervention and producing private goods for his constituency. When that strategy failed to increase production, Maduro's government attempted to negotiate with foreign investors. With Venezuelans, however, like Chávez, he found scapegoats, who were then accused of corruption and/or attempting to undermine the Bolivarian Revolution. Again, like Chávez, Maduro interpreted the laws liberally to permit himself greater freedom of action and fiddled with contract and fiscal terms when necessary to attract capital to the oil sector. Like his mentor, Maduro refused to consider the operational needs of the NOC and drove it further into incompetency as an oil company.

The hypotheses generated from the model performed well in understanding the differences between the first and second periods of Chávez's government and the debacle under Maduro. Venezuela's geologic situation continued to be exceptional, and although the market took a dramatic tumble in 2009, it recovered to historic highs in 2011–2014 and then crashed in 2015. The problems that generated the crisis in the domestic oil and gas value chain had already begun and could have been managed from a purely economic perspective.[96] But the Bolivarian Revolution's exclusionary politics, noncompetitive decision making, and Maduro's leadership characteristics made the adjustments that would have been required impossible.

CONCLUSIONS

Resource Nationalism and Energy Policy

A key contribution of this book is the reconceptualization of resource nationalism, removing it as a rhetorical tool of political factions and defining it in an analytically useful fashion. The core idea behind a resource nationalism perspective is that the natural resources in the ground or under the sea are a "national patrimony" and consequently should be used for the benefit of the nation rather than for private gain. RN is thus not simply government take, or merely the distribution of resource wealth for alleviation of poverty in the short term, nor a means by which government leaders might enrich themselves and their cronies by selling the resource. Instead, the concept of resource nationalism creates a legitimate space for government intervention in the business of natural resource exploitation beyond that present in any other economic activity within its borders or carried out by the businesses of its citizens, taxation, and regulation.

The goal of RN is to maximize medium- to long-term wealth appropriation for the benefit of sustainable national development, thus benefiting current and future generations of the citizens of the country, who are the rightful owners of the resource. In the case of oil and gas, the means for pursuing this goal is by the central government setting the terms for their exploration, production, transportation, and distribution, including as energy. If the terms set by the government do not contribute to the achievement of the goal, they are contradictory to resource nationalism, and their adoption/implementation must be explained by something other than RN.

The underlying concern for resource nationalists, whether they are statists (e.g., Giordani) or pro-marketers (e.g., Pérez in his second administration), is how to use wealth generated by the oil and gas value chain, including but not limited to natural resource rents, to promote sustainable national development. In pursuing that agenda, a focus on the absolute level of money appropriated by the government and the level of government expenditure on infrastructure and social welfare is not sufficient and may be highly misleading. Without ensuring efficient use of that money on efficient and effective programs, it is possible that a government that appropriates a greater percentage of natural resource rents and spends it inefficiently promotes sustainable national development far less than a government that appropriates a lower share but invests it wisely. In that sense, the collapse of the Venezuelan economy evident after 2014 had its roots not in the commodity boom of 2003–2012 but in the way in which that windfall was utilized by the Bolivarian Revolution.

Venezuela during the Bolivarian Revolution demonstrates that pursuit of maximizing revenue capture in the short run can undermine both energy security and national development. The case also illustrates that revenue capture simply for distribution can create circumstances in which a radically nationalist government finds itself forced to offer very attractive terms for resource exploitation and marketing to foreign companies and governments to generate short-term cash flows.[1] Though those terms will likely be forcibly renegotiated when the domestic economy recovers, the erratic nature of energy policy and the low credibility of government policy that it generates will produce lower medium- to long-term returns to the country from their natural resources, ironically creating a parallel situation to the disparaged Apertura policies of the 1990s. The welfare of future generations is also undermined by the environmental damage caused by overconsumption of the resource by current generations—though because the country has so much oil reserves, future generations will unlikely soon be affected by depletion of those reserves. Such results can hardly permit one to argue that the government/political regime responsible for this pattern was acting in the "national interest," as demanded by the most analytically useful conceptualization of resource nationalism.

An analytically useful definition of RN is only a starting point for thinking about energy policy; it is not in itself the determinant of energy policy. The question that really should be driving resource nationalists is how best to translate the wealth appropriated into effective and sustainable benefits for the nation. Answering that question requires incorporating a model of natural resource policy making.

A second key contribution of the book, therefore, is elaboration of my political model, within the context of geology and market factors, in order to understand the formulation of energy policy. Inclusiveness of the political system, competitiveness of the decision-making unit, and the risk-acceptant and innovative characteristics of the leader allow the development of hypotheses predictive of energy policy formulation. In my model, who is represented, how they are represented, and the constraints under which policy makers ostensibly make policy in their interest are fundamental factors in understanding policy choice.

The hypotheses generated by the interaction among the three political variables in the model elaborated in chapter 3 facilitate an understanding of the degree of intrusion into the market by government policy and whether or not the provision of public goods will result from whatever appropriation of oil and gas wealth those policies achieve. The four case studies analyzed in chapters 6 and 7 provide support for the hypotheses as applied to Venezuelan oil and gas policies from 1989 to 2016.

The inclusion of political factors is essential because, as demonstrated in chapter 3, geology, market, and ideology have not historically been reliable predictors of energy policy. Being endowed with oil and/or gas has not determined the characteristics of oil and gas policies, not even the direction of such policy toward more or less government efforts to "control" or extract wealth from oil and gas. And though the market does have a fundamental impact on the outcome of energy policy, it doesn't determine how a government responds to market signals. Ideology, whether defined in left-right or "sovereignty over oil" terms, also fails to help us understand energy policy variation.

With respect to geology as a determinant, though Brazil's geological characteristics in the technological era of the 1950s were not remotely as promising as Mexico's, their energy policies were strikingly similar. And, as the market was moving away from Latin American oil producers other than Venezuela to the Middle East, Colombia increased government control and take in ways inconsistent with this market signal, while Bolivian policy was erratic, at times pushing toward monopoly for the NOC and at other times providing incentives to private investment. In addition, while some have argued that, as prices increased, Chávez became less practical in his oil policy, as demonstrated in part 2, examination of market fluctuations and different logical policy responses demonstrates that markets were significantly underdetermining of policy in the Chávez administration. Regarding ideology, we can look to the Pink Tide governments for confirmation of variation. Lula's government in 2010 did not make legislation either retroactive or applicable outside of the expected bonanza in the presalt; the Chávez government responded to the emerging Orinoco Belt bonanza by applying its new oil law retroactively and across the sector. The Bolivian and Ecuadorian Pink Tide governments were more intrusive in the oil and gas area than Chávez when the market boomed. Empirics, therefore, demonstrate the need for an argument more focused on politics.

Even if we limit ourselves to a subset of energy policy of great interest in the contemporary era, NOC behavior, market explanations are not privileged over political explanations either. Philips and Hults both argued that low oil prices lead governments to increase NOC autonomy.[2] However, part 2 demonstrates that NOC "autonomy" needs to be understood, first and foremost, in a political context. Thus the Pérez and Chávez governments in the weak markets of 1989–1991 and 1999–2000 sought to increase subordination of the NOC to national development strategy, and the Maduro government increasingly exploited (and continued to do so post-2016) the NOC to ensure the government's survival in the face of a market collapse.

The Venezuela case study that concludes the book allows us to test the effectiveness of the political model proposed here for explaining policy choice across two distinctly different political systems. Interestingly, and despite arguments by both the Left and Right, oil and gas policies had many important similarities in the Punto Fijo and Bolivarian Revolution eras, with some significant differences. For example, though the Left criticized the internationalization and Apertura strategies of the Punto Fijo era, the Chávez administration left most of the internationalization model intact and added to it in ways that promoted political goals of the administration rather than sustaining national development. Regarding the much-maligned Apertura, the Chávez administration did change the contractual terms, but by broadening the opening far beyond the statists' criticisms of article 5. Since Mexico was still emphasizing the need for a Pemex monopoly even with a conservative government in 2008, it's not self-evident that the chavistas would not go back to the dreams of the left in 1975 and boot out foreign investors. Even if one were to argue that the upgraded technologies necessary for the Orinoco projects required the continued presence of foreign investors, there could have been two parallel oil regimes: one for conventional oil projects and the other for the Orinoco projects. The Bolivarian Revolution had no problem having distinct regimes for oil and gas, and Brazil did decide in 2010 to distinguish legal and financial regimes for pre-salt and conventional hydrocarbon projects.

My model of energy policy making can help us think about how to generate energy policy that reflects resource nationalism: using the people's ownership of natural resources to generate sustainable national development. There are relevant lessons from the Latin American experience for envisioning the reform of energy policy within the contours of resource nationalism. The experience of Colombia during the commodity boom demonstrates the possibility of making progress toward national development consistent with RN, despite many of the ills that characterize Latin America: an exclusive political system, significant levels of political violence and human rights abuses, and a populist, semiauthoritarian leader. A brief review of that experience, while not definitive on the scale of the Venezuela cases, provides evidence of the promise of application of the argument to other oil-producing countries.

With investment, reserves, and production plummeting, the administration of President Alvaro Uribe (2002–2010) embarked on a major reform of Colombia's oil and gas sector. In Law 790 of December 27, 2002 the Congress granted the executive special legislative powers to reform the administration of government. The reforms of 2003 ended the legal monopoly held by Ecopetrol across the energy value chain, but particularly with regard to upstream oil and gas E&P in Colombia and in postexploration commercialization. Since that time there have been further legal reforms to improve the competitive situation in the oil and gas sector.

By comparing Colombia's situation with that of Mexico at roughly the same time (Mexico had an energy reform in 2008), we illustrate only a modest importance of the impact of geology and markets on energy policy choices. Mexico was still a major oil producer and governed by two pro-market nationalist governments (Vicente Fox, 2000–2006, and Felipe Calderon, 2006–2012); its reform was prompted by expectations that it would become an importer of oil in just over a decade if new E&P did not occur. Mexico's answer in 2008 was to seek ways to revitalize Pemex's monopoly position, unlike Colombia's response. My model of energy policy should provide insights into Colombia's choices.[3]

Uribe broke from the Liberal Party and ran in the March 2002 elections with his own party, Primero Colombia (Colombia First), denouncing the failed peace process and political corruption and promising to make structural changes. Turnout in Colombian national elections ranks quite low in Latin America, given a tradition of political violence and in the 1990s the increasing legitimacy crises of the two historical parties, Social Conservative and Liberal.[4] Turnout in Uribe's first election in 2002 was at the upper level of the norm with 46.5 percent, but he won the first round with 53 percent to the runner-up's share of 31.8 percent, and in 2006 he won reelection again in the first round with 62 percent of the vote, the runner-up coming in at 11.8 percent, and turnout at 45.1 percent.[5]

Legislative elections experienced smaller turnouts than presidential, with 44.2 percent and 44.4 percent for the Chamber and Senate, respectively, in 2002. In that election, those who did vote confirmed their antisystem sentiment by seconding their support for the independent Uribe, with an increase of seventy-five representatives and thirty-six senators elected from parties other than the traditional Conservative and Liberal Parties.[6] In 2006, twenty parties were represented in the chamber, and turnout fell to 39.8 percent, while in the Senate there were ten parties, and turnout was 40.5 percent.[7]

Gallup polling indicates that Uribe's popularity remained over 70 percent during each of the eight years of his administrations, and he left with an 80 percent approval rate for his government.[8] Nevertheless, the data indicate that Colombians do not feel empowered to select their national-level politicians, including the president. Voters expected that Uribe would provide benefits because of his beliefs rather than because of constituent pressure.

Our other subjective indicator of inclusiveness is the WGI Voice and Accountability; as noted in chapter 3, the Governance Score for Voice and Accountability ranges from +2.5 to −2.5, and we can break our inclusiveness variable at 0.0. The WGI Voice and Accountability measure for Colombia demonstrates an improvement over the eight years of Uribe's

TABLE C.1
Colombia: Voice and Accountability

Year	Number of Scores	Governance Score (−25 to +25)	Percentile Rank (0 to 100)	Standard Error
1996	8	−0.5	35	0.2
1998	8	−0.3	40.3	0.2
2000	9	−0.4	34.8	0.2
2002	11	−0.4	37.8	0.2
2003	11	−0.4	36.3	0.2
2004	14	−0.3	38.9	0.1
2005	15	−0.3	38.5	0.1
2006	17	−0.2	40.9	0.1
2007	18	−0.2	42.3	0.1
2008	18	−0.2	42.8	0.1
2009	18	−0.1	42.7	0.1
2010	18	−0.1	42.7	0.1

Source: Worldwide Governance Indicators, updated October 4, 2018, https://databank.worldbank.org/reports.aspx?source=worldwide-governance-indicators#.

two terms, but still falling just below the cutoff distinguishing inclusive and noninclusive (see table C.1).

The objective indicator, Polity IV's Polcomp measure, puts Colombia at 7 in the Uribe years, the same level as Venezuela. Colombia is thus classified as factional competition.[9] The combination of turnout, Voice and Accountability, and Polcomp leads to a classification of Colombia as an exclusive political system during the Uribe years, 2002–2010.

Our measure for competitiveness of the decision-making unit is based on whether the president's party controls a majority in the legislature and the Polity IV XCONST score measuring the constraints on the executive from the legislature and society.

Uribe achieved landslide victories, but his new party, Primero Colombia, was a personal vehicle and did not have a presence in either chamber of the legislature. He did have "coattails" as congressional candidates sought to identify themselves with him in the face of a collapsing party system. By one account, he was supported by 143 of 165 representatives and 86 of 102 senators, but that did not mean he controlled them.[10] For example, the constitutional referendum on reforming Congress on which he campaigned was significantly altered by supporters of Uribe in Congress and obstructed by the opposition parties and failed.[11]

Polity IV scores executive constraints at 6, Near Parity, for the entire Uribe period. Congress did not have the popular support that Uribe enjoyed, but it continued to exercise considerable influence over Colombian politics. The leaders of the Conservative and Liberal Parties, though not as powerful as in the past, had made it difficult to dismantle controls over state largesse and power. Polity IV also classified the judiciary as "inefficient, severely overburdened by a large case backlog, and undermined by intimidation from non-state actors (guerillas, paramilitaries, drug traffickers) and the prevailing climate of impunity."[12]

My analysis of Uribe's behavior in nonenergy-related political challenges during his career leads me to classify him as an innovative and moderately risk acceptant leader.[13] The values for the political variables during the Uribe administration, 2002–2010, are:

Inclusiveness LOW + Competitiveness HIGH +
Leadership MODERATELY RISK ACCEPTANT + INNOVATIVE

These lead to the following hypotheses about energy policy in Colombia during that administration:

- Since the popular sector experiences low inclusiveness, there will be an incentive for government to be less intrusive in the oil and gas value chain.
- Since the decision-making unit is competitive, energy policy will be characterized by low levels of government intrusion in the oil and gas value chain.
- Since the decision-making unit is competitive, natural resource wealth will be used for public goods.
- Uribe, as a moderately risk-acceptant and innovative leader, will push new ideas while seeking to alter the institutional constraints on his leadership but will retreat from an open confrontation with those institutional constraints.

To evaluate these hypotheses, I will briefly examine the four fundamental policy issues of chapters 6 and 7 that are characteristic of an oil and gas policy: the role of the national oil company, commercialization policy, access to the resources, and the fiscal and contract terms offered to investors. I will also examine provision of public goods under the Uribe government to judge its adherence to resource nationalism, as I have defined the concept in this book.

Role of the NOC. The reforms of 2003 and 2006 transformed Ecopetrol from a wholly state-owned company primarily responsible for administering the nation's hydrocarbon wealth to a publicly traded company with an independent board of directors and fiscal autonomy. Under the reforms, the company's focus moved squarely onto its core business of commercializing hydrocarbons with no policy-making role within the government of Colombia. The shift removed the government's role in setting operational directions for the company and transformed Ecopetrol into a commercially oriented entity operating at arm's length from the government to maximize profits and provide the optimum return to shareholders (including the government, its largest shareholder). Since the reforms, the company is treated under the same regulatory framework as other privately held firms operating in the country and does not perform uniquely institutionalized, noncommercial activities for the state.

Ecopetrol is a shareholding company, governed by the same statutes that govern private corporations in Colombia (Sociedades Anónimas), and with some modifications, rules established by the U.S. Securities and Exchange Commission for corporations listing their stock in the United States. The structure and operation of Ecopetrol under the reforms of 2003 and 2006 permit us to define it as autonomous to a degree far exceeding that of PDVSA in the pre-Chávez era.

Law 1118, promulgated by the Congress of the Republic of Colombia on December 27, 2006, formally amended the legal nature of Ecopetrol, stating that it should operate as a private firm.[14] Article 1 spells out the change of the company to that of a "Mixed Economy Company." Law 1118 further details that the nation retains a minimum 80 percent of the outstanding voting shares, as discussed in article 2, Capitalization of Ecopetrol S.A.[15] As of this writing, the government of Colombia owns 88.5 percent of the company's total capital, with plans to reduce that number in the future to the aforementioned minimum 80 percent ownership stake.

Access to the resource. As noted in chapter 1, the creation of an IRA to separate the NOC from the functions of setting the conditions of the market in which it operates is an important mechanism for increasing the efficiency of a NOC's capture of rents. An NOC that determines the conditions within which companies can operate will have the power to set terms that favor itself and thus not have an incentive to seek greater efficiency. Colombia created the Agencia Nacional de Hidrocarburos (ANH, National Hydrocarbon Agency) in 2003 to perform this function.

After Decree Law 1760 of 2003, Ecopetrol must bid along with other competing private firms for exploration blocks offered by the ANH. For Ecopetrol's international exploratory activities in Brazil, Peru, and the U.S. Gulf of Mexico, the firm receives no subsidy from the government. Ecopetrol is thus not vested with nor does it exercise exclusive or controlling power in oil and gas exploration.

Decree Law 1760 did not apply retroactively and thus did not change Ecopetrol's access to oil fields granted before the opening of the oil and gas sector to private investment. The ANH has no influence over joint-venture contracts between Ecopetrol and third parties in those blocks. As a result of this legacy, Ecopetrol has had an advantage if one were to simply consider which companies held exploration and production rights over Colombian fields. In 2014 Ecopetrol held such rights to 40 percent of Colombian fields, but this was down from 100 percent in 2003 and will continue to decline as new fields are auctioned and old fields are retired.

Commercialization. The company maintains no business monopolies and must compete equally against foreign and private firms for access to exploration and development rights for oil and gas and to downstream markets and infrastructure. Ecopetrol's role as a state monopoly fuel provider ended, and the company has no special role in meeting the state's social responsibilities. The Colombian government uses its own federal resources to reimburse all importers, including Ecopetrol, for losses that might result from government-controlled domestic fuel prices.

Fiscal and contract terms. Ecopetrol pays royalties as stipulated by law that applies to all oil companies in Colombia; the firm receives no special treatment on this matter. Under Colombian law, the government is the sole owner of the country's hydrocarbons and has full authority to determine rights, royalties, or compensation to be paid by public or private investors, including Ecopetrol. All companies with operations in the country are obliged to pay a percentage of their production to the ANH in the form of royalties. Changes to royalty schemes apply only to new discoveries and do not alter fields already in production. Furthermore, producing fields pay royalties in accordance with the applicable royalty program at the time of the discovery. Since 2002 the royalty scheme has ranged from 8 percent for fields producing up to 5,000 barrels per day (Mb/d) and up to 25 percent for fields producing in excess of 600 Mb/d. Royalties for gas production are also subject to a sliding scale scheme, depending on whether the field is onshore or offshore, and range between 8 percent and 25 percent.

Public goods. Under Uribe, social spending quickly experienced a significant increase through institutionalized channels. Within two years, 5 million people had been added to the subsidized health system, 2 million more Colombians received meals and care through the Institute of Family Welfare (Instituto Colombiano de Bienestar Familiar, ICBF), there was an increase of 1.7 million education slots in the National Service of Learning (Servicio Nacional de Aprendizaje, SENA), microcredit for small entrepreneurs rose 157 percent, unemployment fell from 15.6 percent in December 2002 to 12.1 percent by December 2004, and the budget for returning people displaced by the violence to their homes increased 800 percent.[16] These were not short-term efforts, designed simply to provide patronage, but investments in public goods. The payoff can be seen in a more than decade-long improvement in poverty rates and inequality, despite the collapse of the oil market.

At the end of Uribe's term, Colombia's Gini Index was lower than the year he took office (54.73 compared to 57.2), and it sustained improvement to the latest year available, 2017, at 49.72. Though the index bounced around below those levels over the course of his two administrations,[17] the economic reforms he implemented and that his successor Juan Manuel Santos (2010–2018) largely followed paid off for society. Poverty rates also experienced a significant and sustainable decline, from 19.67 percent in the year prior to Uribe taking office to 7.72 percent in 2010 and continued to drop substantially to 3.92 percent in 2017.[18]

As closing food for thought, I turn to General Lázaro Cárdenas, the president who stabilized a new Mexican political system and nationalized the oil industry in 1938. We forget that Cárdenas was a pragmatist above all: he made the political bargains that kept his party together, even supporting the moderate Manuel Avila Camacho for president in 1940 because he knew the country needed time to digest his reforms and that immediately pushing further ahead could undermine them. Despite the national distrust of its neighbor to the north, he helped ally Mexico with the United States in World War II because he saw the greater danger in fascism than in the Colossus of the North. In the oil sector, Cárdenas first tried to collaborate with the IOCs and private capital, but Mexican capitalists would not subscribe to Petromex, and the IOCs would not cut a fair deal with Mexico and its workers. Cárdenas (like the leaders in Peru, Ecuador, and even Argentina in 2012) did not demand a monopoly when he nationalized the major foreign companies.[19] It may be time to go back to Cárdenas's original vision: a balance between national control and the need to provide energy security to benefit the nation.

NOTES

INTRODUCTION

1. "Oil and Gas Royalty," Statement of C. Stephen Allred, Assistant Secretary, Land and Minerals Management, United States Department of the Interior, Before the Committee on Energy and Natural Resources, United States Senate, January 18, 2007, https://www.doi.gov/ocl/hearings/110/OilAndGasRoyaltyManagement11806. In justifying the increase in royalty from 12.5 percent to 16.7 percent, Allred said, "The American people own these resources and are entitled to receive a fair return.... In FY 2006 ... royalties totaling about $12.6 billion ... compliance and enforcement program has generated an annual average of more than $125 million for each of the last 24 years."
2. Farouk Al-Kasim, *Managing Petroleum Resources: The "Norwegian Model" in a Broad Perspective* (Oxford: Oxford Institute for Energy Studies, 2006).
3. Paulo Valois Pires, "Oil and Gas Regulation in Brazil: Overview," law stated as of July 1, 2019, Westlaw, https://content.next.westlaw.com/2-524-2451.
4. Hugh Bronstein, "Argentina Nationalizes Oil Company YPF," *Reuters*, May 3, 2012.
5. H. Mahdavy, "The Patterns and Problems of Economic Development in Rentier States: The Case of Iran," in *Studies in the Economic History of the Middle East*, ed. M. A. Cook (London: Oxford University Press, 1970), 428–67.
6. Merrie Gilbert Klapp, "The State—Landlord or Entrepreneur?," *International Organization* 36, no. 3 (Summer 1982); Klapp, *The Sovereign Entrepreneur: Oil Policies in Advanced and Less Developed Capitalist Countries* (Ithaca, N.Y.: Cornell University Press, 1987); and Bernard Mommer, *Global Oil and the Nation State* (Oxford: Oxford University Press, 2002). Terry Lynn Karl, *The Paradox of Plenty: Oil Booms and Petro-States* (Berkeley: University of California Press, 1997), 49, sees petro-states as a subcategory of landlord states.

7. On the abstract level, Revi Ramamurti, "The Obsolescing 'Bargaining Model'? MNC-Host Developing Country Relations Revisited," *Journal of International Business Studies* 32, no. 1 (2001): 23–39, sees a context in which MNC–developing country bargaining occurs within rules set by developed countries. On domestic politics issues, Klapp's "The State—Landlord or Entrepreneur?" and *The Sovereign Entrepreneur* build on a model of state bureaucratic autonomy; Karl's *The Paradox of Plenty* examines domestic institutions and rent-seeking; and Mommer's *Global Oil and the Nation State* assume an international context exploitive of developing countries and a class-based analysis of domestic social and economic dynamics that influence who controls "the state."

8. For a positive interpretation, see Dag Harold Claes, *The Politics of Oil: Controlling Resources, Governing Markets and Creating Political Conflicts* (London: Edward Elgar, 2018); for a negative one, see Karl, *Paradox of Plenty.*

9. Cf. Anthony A. Sampson, "A Model of Optimal Depletion of Renewable Resources," *Journal of Economic Theory* 12 (1976): 315–24; N. V. Quyen, "The Optimal Depletion and Exploration of a Nonrenewable Resource," *Econometrica* 56, no. 6 (November 1988): 1467–71; Hassan Benchekroun and Cees Withagen, "The Optimal Depletion of Exhaustible Resources: A Complete Characterization," *Resource and Energy Economics* 33, no. 3 (September 2011): 612–36.

10. William Ascher lists "extracting the right amount of wealth from resource exploiters, setting output prices to encourage economic efficiency, using resource wealth wisely, borrowing off the resource endowment and using the loans efficiently for long-term economic growth, finding the best means of taxing (which may or may not involve taxing natural-resource outputs)." William Ascher, *Why Governments Waste Natural Resources: Policy Failures in Developing Countries* (Baltimore: Johns Hopkins University Press, 1999), 20.

11. The theoretical concept of "rents" and the issues that arise as they are generated are discussed in chapter 1.

12. David R. Mares, "Natural Gas Pipelines in the Southern Cone," in *Natural Gas and Geopolitics from 1970–2030*, ed. David G. Victor, Amy M. Jaffe, and Mark H. Hayes (Cambridge: Cambridge University Press, 2006), 169–201; Mares, "The Governance of Shale Gas in Argentina" *Oil, Gas & Energy Law Intelligence* 12, no. 3 (June 2014).

13. BP, *Statistical Review of World Energy*, June 2019, 14, based on reserves to production ratio.

14. Duncan Wood, ed., *Mexico's New Energy Reform* (Washington, D.C.: Mexico Institute, Woodrow Wilson International Center for Scholars, 2018).

15. Francisco Monaldi, "Making Pemex Great Again?" *Americas Quarterly*, August 21, 2019.

16. In this book the term *gas* refers to natural gas and *gasoline* refers to the refined fuel derived from petroleum. For two different evaluations and explanations of these reforms, see Derrick Hindery, *From Enron to Evo: Pipeline Politics, Global Environmentalism, and Indigenous Rights in Bolivia* (Tucson: University of Arizona Press, 2013); and Vicente Fretes-Cibils, Marcelo Glugale, and Connie Luff, eds., *Bolivia: Public Policy Options for the Well-Being of All* (Washington, D.C.: World Bank, 2006).

17. Hindery, *From Enron to Evo*, 148–63; Nancy Postero, *The Indigenous State: Race, Politics, and Performance in Plurinational Bolivia* (Berkeley: University of California Press, 2017); "Bolivia Reaches Preliminary $2.5 Billion Oil, Gas Investment Deal," *Reuters*, February 26, 2018, https://www.reuters.com/article/bolivia-energy /bolivia-reaches-preliminary-2-5-billion-oil-gas-investment-deal-idUSL2N1Q G1DT.

18. Giorgio Romano Schutte, "Brazil: New Developmentalism and the Management of Offshore Oil Wealth," *European Review of Latin American and Caribbean Studies* 95 (October 2013): 49–70; Justin Jacobs, "Brazil's Pre-salt Promise," *Petroleum Economist*, November 2, 2017, https://www.petroleum-economist.com/articles /upstream/exploration-production/2017/brazils-pre-salt-promise.

19. Daniel Rodriguez, "Petrobras Expects Brazil's Deepwater Pre-salt Play to Remain Competitive to Shale," *SPGlobal*, May 6, 2019, https://www.spglobal.com/platts/en /market-insights/latest-news/oil/050619-petrobras-expects-brazils-deepwater -pre-salt-play-to-remain-competitive-to-shale.

20. The rentier state concept that underlies the resource curse was developed in Mahdavy, "Patterns and Problems of Economic Development in Rentier States"; Karl, *Paradox of Plenty*; Michael L. Ross, "The Political Economy of the Resource Curse," *World Politics* 51, no. 2 (1999): 297–322; Richard Auty, *Sustaining Development in Mineral Economies: The Resource Curse Thesis* (London: Routledge, 1993; Macartan Humphreys, Jeffrey D. Sachs, and Joseph E. Stiglitz, eds., *Escaping the Resource Curse* (New York: Columbia University Press, 2007). The journalist Thomas Friedman makes dependence on oil wealth a guarantee that democracy and, by extension, national development will fail, in "The First Law of Petropolitics," *Foreign Policy*, October 16, 2009.

21. Auty, *Sustaining Development*; Jeffrey D. Sachs, "How to Handle the Macroeconomics of Oil Wealth," in *Escaping the Resource Curse*, ed. Macartan Humphreys, Jeffrey D. Sachs, and Joseph E. Stiglitz (New York: Columbia University Press, 2007), 173–93.

22. Jeffrey D. Sachs and Andrew M. Warner, "The Curse of Natural Resources," *European Economic Review* 45 (May 2001): 827–38.

23. See Ross, "The Resource Curse"; Auty, *Sustaining Development in Mineral Economies*.

24. David Wiens, "Natural Resources and Institutional Development," *Journal of Theoretical Politics* 26, no. 2 (2014): 197–221, doi:10.1177/0951629813493835.

25. These vary broadly, from the general "weak state" thesis (see the review by Victor Menaldo, "The New Political Economy of Natural Resources in Latin America," *Latin American Politics and Society* 57, no. 1 [Spring 2015]: 163–73), to a focus on economic institutions (see Jeffrey Frankel, "The Natural Resource Curse: A Survey," in *Beyond the Resource Curse*, ed. Brenda Shaffer and Taleh Ziyadov [Philadelphia: University of Pennsylvania Press, 2012]).

26. Thad Dunning, in *Crude Democracy: Natural Resource Wealth and Political Regimes* (Cambridge: Cambridge University Press, 2008), used Venezuela as an example of oil facilitating the creation and stability of democracy, while Karl, in *Paradox of Plenty*, saw its democracy as already in crisis in 1997. Oksan Bayulgen disagrees that Azerbaijan and Kazakhstan have in fact averted "many of the

pathologies associated with the mineral curse." See Bayulgen, "Review, 'Oil Is Not a Curse: Ownership Structure and Institutions in Soviet Successor States by Pauline Jones Luong and Erika Weinthal,'" *Political Science Quarterly* 127, no. 1 (Spring 2012): 178–79.

27. See the cases analyzed in Ascher, *Why Governments Waste Natural Resources*; Humphreys, Sachs, and Stiglitz, *Escaping the Resource Curse*.

28. BP, *Statistical Review of World Energy*, oil and gas tables, June 2007 and June 2018; Business News Americas, *Oil & Gas Survey 2014: Opportunities Abound*, Intelligence Series, February 2014.

29. Al-Kasim, *Managing Petroleum Resources*; Andrew Cumbers, "North Sea Oil, the State and Divergent Development in the United Kingdom and Norway," in *Flammable Societies: Studies on the Socio-economics of Oil and Gas*, ed. John-Andrew McNeish and Owen Logan (London: Pluto Press, 2012), 221–42; Klapp, "The State—Landlord or Entrepreneur?"

30. Business News Americas, *Brazil's Oil and Gas Revamp: A New Dawn?*, Intelligence Series, 2017.

31. Klapp, "The State—Landlord or Entrepreneur?"; Silvana Tordo, Brandon S. Tracy, and Noora Arfaa, *National Oil Companies and Value Creation*, Working paper no. 128 (Washington, D.C.: World Bank, 2011), 62.

32. Katy Grimes, "Legislation Would End Oil and Gas Production in Most of California," *California Globe*, April 22, 2019, https://californiaglobe.com/legislature /legislation-would-end-oil-and-gas-production-in-most-of-california/; Christopher Weare, *The California Electricity Crisis: Causes and Policy Options* (San Francisco: Public Policy Institute of California, 2003).

33. Allan R. Brewer-Carías, *Dismantling Democracy in Venezuela: The Chávez Authoritarian Experiment* (New York: Cambridge University Press, 2010); Nikolas Kozloff, *Hugo Chávez: Oil, Politics, and the Challenge to the U.S.* (New York: Palgrave, 2006); George Ciccariello-Maher, *We Created Chávez: A People's History of the Venezuelan Revolution* (Durham, N.C.: Duke University Press, 2013).

34. Cf. Gustavo A. Flores-Macías, *After Neoliberalism? The Left and Economic Reform in Latin America* (New York: Oxford University Press, 2012); Kurt Weyland, Wendy Hunter, and Raúl L. Madrid, eds., *Leftist Governments in Latin America: Successes and Shortcomings* (Cambridge: Cambridge University Press, 2010); Steven Levitsky and Kenneth M. Roberts, eds., *The Resurgence of the Latin American Left* (Baltimore: Johns Hopkins University Press, 2011).

35. On institutional design, see Barbara Koremenos, Charles Lipson, and Duncan Snidal, "The Rational Design of International Institutions," *International Organization* 55, no. 4 (2001): 761–99.

1. THE PARAMETERS OF NATIONALISM AND ENERGY POLICY

1. Some scholars focus on "rent appropriation," but governments can also attempt to drive down the "normal" profit rates and thus appropriate not just "rents" or "excess profits" (the theoretical concept of rents and the issues that arise as they are generated are discussed further in the chapter). Some analysts focus on "revenue appropriation" rather than distinguish between normal and super profits. But

there is value or wealth in discovered resources that are not yet brought to market and producing revenues; governments and third parties have conflicted over who can book these reserves, indicating their value. Consequently, government policy may be focused in a particular instance on capturing significant portions of the wealth in the sector, or of the revenue being generated, or simply on the excess profits.

2. Canada has a complicated legal regime regarding subsurface rights, reflecting inducements to colonization and infrastructure development as well as which sub-soil resources were deemed valuable at the time land grants were allocated. See Global CCS Institute, "Canadian Property Rights Relating to CCS," https://hub .globalccsinstitute.com/publications/property-rights-relation-ccs/canadian-pro perty-rights-relating-ccs, accessed August 18, 2017; Prowse Chowne LLP Team, "What Are Subsurface Rights in Canada?," February 23, 2017, http://prowsechowne .com/what-are-subsurface-rights-in-canada/; University of Alberta, Alberta Land Institute, "A Guide to Property Rights in Alberta," http://propertyrightsguide.ca /subsurface-property-rights/, accessed August 18, 2017.

3. Amy Harder and Lynn Cook, "Congressional Leaders Agree to Lift 40-Year Ban on Oil Exports," *Wall Street Journal*, updated December 16, 2015.

4. "The History of Regulation," NaturalGas.org, http://naturalgas.org/regulation /history/, accessed August 18, 2017

5. "The Debate Over Natual Gas Exports," Snelson Company, accessed August 18, 2017, http://www.snelsonco.com/debate-over-natural-gas-exports/; Mary Anne Sullivan, "LNG Exports—A Rare Case of Policy Continuity from Obama to Trump," May 8, 2017, https://knect365.com/flame/article/f07241ed-4652-44b6-89c0 -21446dfd1940/lng-exports-a-rare-case-of-policy-continuity-from-obama-to -trump.

6. This is a common complaint. Cf. Francisco J. Monaldi, "The Cyclical Phenome-non of Resource Nationalism in Latin America," *Oxford Handbook of International Political Economy*, March 2020, doi:10.1093/acrefore/9780190228637.013.1523; Sam Pryke, "Explaining Resource Nationalism," *Global Policy* 8, no. 4 (November 2017); Olle Östensson, "Promoting Downstream Processing: Resource Nationalism or Industrial Policy?," *Mineral Economics* 32 (2019): 205–12, https://doi.org/10.1007 /s13563-019-00170-x.

7. I come at this issue from a comparative politics perspective, but others make a sim-ilar point from different analytic perspectives. Kadir and Murray take a human rights approach when they argue that the Indonesian Constitution should alter article 33 from "full and direct state control over natural resources to fully and directly benefitting the people," which requires a non-state-centric understand-ing of "the people." They further argue that "under the control" (of the state) does not mean ownership (which rests with the people). See M. Y. Aiyub Kadir and Alexander Murray, "Resource Nationalism in the Law and Policies of Indonesia: A Contest of State, Foreign Investors, and Indigenous Peoples," *Asian Journal of International Law* 9, no. 2 (July 2019): 322–24, 333, https://doi.org/10.1017/S204425 131900002X. For critical theorizing about resource nationalism, see Natalie Koch and Tom Perreault, "Resource Nationalism," *Progress in Human Geogra-phy*, 43, no. 4 (2019): 611–31, https://doi.org/10.1177/0309132518781497; John Childs, "Geography and Resource Nationalism: A Critical Review and Reframing," *The*

Extractive Industries and Society 3, no. 2 (April 2016): 539–46, https://doi.org/10.1016/j.exis.2016.02.006.

8. Cf. Vlado Vivoda, "Resource Nationalism, Bargaining and International Oil Companies: Challenges and Change in the New Millennium," *New Political Economy* 14, no. 4 (2009): 517–34, doi:10.1080/13563460903287322, in which he repeatedly refers to "resurgent resource nationalism" and cites many authors discussing retreat and resurgence yet never defines the concept.

9. Pryke, "Explaining Resource Nationalism," 474.

10. Kretzschmar, Gavin L., Axel Kirchner, and Liliya Sharifzyanova, "Resource Nationalism—Limits to Foreign Direct Investment," *Energy Journal* 31, no. 2 (2010): 27–52.

11. Paul Stevens, "National Oil Companies and International Oil Companies in the Middle East: Under the Shadow of Government and the Resource Nationalism Cycle," *Journal of World Energy Law & Business* 1, no. 1 (2008): 5.

12. Jeffrey D. Wilson, Understanding Resource Nationalism: Economic Dynamics and Political Institutions," *Contemporary Politics* 21, no. 4 (2015): 399–416, doi:10.1080/13569775.2015.1013293.

13. Stevens, "National Oil Companies," 5–30.

14. Mapungubwe Institute for Strategic Reflection (MISTRA) and David Maimela, eds., *Resurgent Resource Nationalism: A Study Into the Global Phenomenon* (South Africa: Real African Publishers, 2016), 7, http://ebookcentral.proquest.com/lib/ucsd/detail.action?docID=4426703.

15. Kevin A. Young, *Blood of the Earth: Resource Nationalism, Revolution, and Empire in Bolivia* (Austin: University of Texas Press, 2017), 1.

16. F. T. Cawood and O. P. Oshokoya, "Resource Nationalism in the South African Mineral Sector: Sanity Through Stability," *Journal of the Southern African Institute of Mining and Metallurgy* 113, no. 1 (2013): 45–52.

17. "CNOOC Withdraws Bid for Unocal, Citing Politics," *Oil and Gas Journal*, August 8, 2005, http://www.ogj.com/articles/print/volume-103/issue-30/general-interest/cnooc-withdraws-bid-for-unocal-citing-politics.html.

18. Ian Bremmer and Robert Johnston, "The Rise and Fall of Resource Nationalism," *Survival* 51, no. 2 (March 2009):152, doi:10.1080/00396330902860884.

19. George Joffé et al., "Expropriation of Oil and Gas Investments: Historical, Legal and Economic Perspectives in a New Age of Resource Nationalism," *Journal of World Energy Law & Business* 2, no. 1 (2009): 4.

20. Paul A. Haslam and Pablo Heidrich, *The Political Economy of Natural Resources and Development: From Neoliberalism to Resource Nationalism* (London: Routledge, 2016), 1.

21. Haslam and Heidrich, 223–35.

22. Adrián Lajous, "Mexican Oil Reform: The First Two Bidding Rounds, Farmouts and Contractual Conversions in a Lower Oil Price Environment," Center on Global Energy Policy, Columbia University, October 2015.

23. Guillermo José Garcia Sánchez, "The Fine Print of the Mexican Energy Reform," in *Mexico's New Energy Reform*, ed. Duncan Wood (Washington, D.C.: Mexico Institute, Woodrow Wilson International Center for Scholars, October 2018), 36–52.

24. Juan Carlos Moreno-Brid and Alicia Puyana, "Mexico's New Wave of Market Reforms and Its Extractive Industries," in Haslam and Heidrich, *Political*

Economy of Natural Resources, 141–57; Wood, *Mexico's New Energy Reform*; Ognen Stojanovski, "Handcuffed: An Assessment of Pemex's Performance and Strategy," in *Oil and Governance: State-Owned Enterprises and the World Energy Supply*, ed. David G. Victor, David R. Hults, and Mark Thurber (Cambridge: Cambridge University Press, 2012), 280–333.

25. "Bolivia Cancels Lithium Deal With German Firm," *AFP News*, November 4, 2019, https://www.ibtimes.com/bolivia-cancels-lithium-deal-german-firm-2859668.

26. "Sustaining Bolivias [*sic*] Natural Gas Bonanza," Business News Americas, Oil & Gas Intelligence Series, August 31, 2016, 8.

27. Ley Orgánica de Hidrocarburos Gaseosos, *Gaceta Oficial*, no. 36.793, September 23, 1999, article 2.

28. Daniel Hellinger, "Resource Nationalism and the Bolivarian Revolution in Venezuela," in Haslam and Heidrich, *Political Economy of Natural Resources*, 217. The Left in Latin America has long defended the so-called Calvo Doctrine against the use of international rather than national arbitration for dispute with the state.

29. See Eduardo Gudynas, "Si Eres Tan Progresista Por Qué Destruyes la Naturaleza? Neoetactivismo, Izquierda y Alternativas," *Ecuador Debate* 79 (2010): 61–81. The author is very tough on Correa (Ecuador), Lula (Brazil), and Morales (Bolivia) but gives Chávez (Venezuela) a free pass. Nevertheless, his argument fits the Venezuelan case well. On production sharing with private capital, see Antonio Gershenson, *El Petróleo de Meéxico: La Disputa del Futuro* (Mexico City: Random House Mondadori, 2010); Jorge Alonso, "The Energy Reform: A Great Loss and a Betrayal," *Revista Envio* (Nicaragua) 390 (January 2014), http://envio.org.ni/articulo/4807.

30. Bremmer and Johnston, "The Rise and Fall of Resource Nationalism"; see also Stefan Andreasson, "Varieties of Resource Nationalism in Sub-Saharan Africa's Energy and Minerals Markets," *The Extractive Industries and Society* 2, no. 2 (April 2015): 310–19, https://doi.org/10.1016/j.exis.2015.01.004.

31. Cf. William Ascher, *Why Governments Waste Natural Resources: Policy Failures in Developing Countries* (Baltimore: Johns Hopkins University Press, 1999); Nick Holland, "Resource Nationalism Can Mean Growth and Prosperity," *Business Day*, August 16, 2013, http://www.bdlive.co.za/opinion/2013/08/16/resource-nationalism -can-mean-growth-and-prosperity.

32. For hybrid RN, see Antulio Rosales, "Pursuing Foreign Investment for Nationalist Goals: Venezuela's Hybrid Resource Nationalism," *Business and Politics* 20, no. 3 (2018): 438–64. For subnational RN, see Minerva Chaloping-March, "The Mining Policy of the Philippines and 'Resource Nationalism' Towards Nation-Building," *Journal de la Société des Océanistes* 138–39 (2014): 93–106. For people-based RN, see Kadir and Murray, "Resource Nationalism in the Law and Policies of Indonesia."

33. "The Government's Revenues," Norwegian Petroleum, updated May 15, 2019, http://www.norskpetroleum.no/en/economy/governments-revenues/, emphasis added.

34. Economists expanded the concept of "rent" beyond the natural resource sector to capture the phenomenon of distorting competitive markets to earn greater profits. See James M. Buchanan, Robert D. Tollison, and Gordon Tullock, eds., *Toward a Theory of the Rent-Seeking Society* (College Station: Texas A&M University Press, 1980). A large literature in economics and political science now routinely focuses

on "rent-seeking" behavior to explain artificially created imperfect markets that favor powerful actors. The concept of a natural resource rent, however, is based on the inherent characteristics of natural resources and their markets and theoretically belongs to the owner of the resource.

35. The country's success was not without challenges, nor is it unmitigated. Cf. Farouk Al-Kasim, *Managing Petroleum Resources: The "Norwegian Model" in a Broad Perspective* (Oxford: Oxford Institute for Energy Studies, 2006); Dag Harald Claes, "Globalization and State Oil Companies: The Case of Statoil," *Journal of Energy and Development* 29, no. 1 (Autumn 2003): 43–64; Ole Andreas Engen, Oluf Langhelle, and Reidar Bratvold, "Is Norway Really Norway?," in *Beyond the Resource Curse*, ed. Brenda Shaffer and Taleh Ziyadov (Philadelphia: University of Pennsylvania Press, 2012), 259–79; Andrew Cumbers, "North Sea Oil, the State and Divergent Development in the United Kingdom and Norway," in *Flammable Societies: Studies on the Socio-economics of Oil and Gas*, ed. John-Andrew McNeish and Owen Logan (London: Pluto Press, 2012), 221–42.

36. "The Government's Revenues," figure on the net government cash flow from petroleum activities, 1971–2017, updated May 15, 2019, http://www.norskpetroleum.no /en/economy/governments-revenues/.

37. Ernst & Young Global Limited, *Global Oil and Gas Tax Guide*, June 2015, http:// www.ey.com/Publication/vwLUAssets/EY-2015-Global-oil-and-gas-tax-guide /$FILE/EY-2015-Global-oil-and-gas-tax-guide.pdf.

38. "Fundamental Regulatory Principles," updated January 18, 2017, http://www .norskpetroleum.no/en/framework/fundamental-regulatory-principles/.

39. "The Petroleum Tax System," updated May 2, 2019, http://www.norskpetroleum .no/en/economy/petroleum-tax/.

40. Suzhe Jia, Perrine Toledano, and Sophie Thomashasuen, "Local Content: Norway—Petroleum," Columbia Center on Sustainable Investment (CCIS), May 2016, http://ccsi.columbia.edu/files/2014/03/Local-Content-Norway-Petroleum-CCSI -May-2016.pdf; Cumbers, "North Sea Oil"; Merrie G. Klapp, "The State—Landlord or Entreprenuer?," *International Organization* 36, no. 3 (Summer 1982): 575–607.

41. Richard Dobbs et al., *Reverse the Curse: Maximizing the Potential of Resource-Driven Economies*, McKinsey Global Institute, December 2013, https://www .mckinsey.com/~/media/McKinsey/Industries/Metals%20and%20Mining /Our%20Insights/Reverse%20the%20curse%20Maximizing%20the%20poten- tial%20of%20resource%20driven%20economies/MGI_Reverse_the_curse_Full _report.ashx; Cumbers, "North Sea Oil," 232–33.

42. Dobbs et al., *Reverse the Curse*, 72–73.

43. "Directive 94/22/EC of the European Parliament and of the Council of 30 May 1994," *Official Journal of the European Communities,* L164/4, Brussels, Belgium, May 30, 1994, http://eur-lex.europa.eu/legal-content/EN/ALL/?uri=CELEX %3A31994L0022; "TRIMS & Local Content," *Bridges* 12, no. 3 (May 1, 2008), International Centre for Trade and Sustainable Development.

44. "Act of 29 November 1996 No. 72 Relating to Petroleum Activities," Norwegian Petroleum Directorate, November 29, 1996, http://www.npd.no/en/Regulations /Acts/Petroleum-activities-act/.

45. Dobbs et al., *Reverse the Curse*, 72–73; Engen, Langhelle and Bratvold, "Is Norway Really Norway?," 265–66.

46. For a discussion of the various types of contracts, see Gavin Bridge and Philippe Le Billon, *Oil* (Malden, Mass.: Polity Press, 2013), 209n.10; Daniel Johnston, *International Petroleum Fiscal Systems and Production Sharing Contracts* (Tulsa, Okla.: PennWell, 1994), 21–27, https://web.archive.org/web/20080516050159/http://www .total.com/en/corporate-social-responsibility/Ethical-Business-Principles /Financial-transparency/contractual_arrangements_13289.htm.

47. Populations that continue to believe that the country is rich despite current low prices in international markets reflect this view of intrinsic wealth. See "La Izquierda Mexicana Está Unida en la Defensa del Petróleo Nacional: Sandoval," note 3760, Fundar: Centro de Análisis e Investigación, http://www.fundar.org.mx/c_e /notas.htm, accessed September 20, 2009.

48. Society of Petroleum Engineers, "Glossary of Terms Used in Petroleum Reserves/ Resources Definitions," spe.org/en/industry/terms-used-petroleum-reserves-re source-definitions/.

49. *BP Statistical Review of World Energy*, June 2018, 12n.

50. "Mexico: Oil Depletion and Illegal U.S. Immigration," Worldpress.org, April 25, 2006, http://www.worldpress.org/Americas/2326.cfm; Justin Jacobs, "Brazil's Pre-Salt Promise," *Petroleum Economist*, November 2, 2017, https://www.petroleum -economist.com/articles/upstream/exploration-production/2017/brazils-pre-salt -promise.

51. Jim Jubak, "Is Exxon Mobil's Future Running Dry?" "Jubak's Journal," *MSN Money*, May 9, 2008, https://web.archive.org/web/20111117211618/http://articles .moneycentral.msn.com/Investing/JubaksJournal/IsExxonMobilsFutureRun ningDry.

52. Abigail Wilkinson, "The Winners and Losers in Argentina's Subsidy Story—Emilio Apud," *Business News Americas*, January 20, 2012.

53. R. H. Wessel, "A Note on Economic Rent," *American Economic Review* 57, no. 5 (1967): 1222, as cited in Paul Segal, "Resource Rents, Redistribution, and Halving Global Poverty: The Resource Dividend," *World Development* 39, 4 (2011): 475–89, doi:10.1016/j.worlddev.2010.08.013.

54. Osmel Manzano, Francisco Monaldi, and Federico Sturzenegger, "The Political Economy of Oil Production in Latin America [with Comments]," *Economía* 9, no. 1 (2008): 74.

55. On upward price mobility, see Osmel Manzano and Francisco Monaldi, "The Political Economy of Oil Contract Renegotiation in Venezuela," in *Populism and Natural Resources*, ed. William Hogan and Federico Struzenegger (Cambridge, Mass.: MIT Press 2009); for downward price volatility, see Antulio Rosales, "Structural Constraints in Times of Resource Nationalism: Oil Policy and State Capacity in Post-Neoliberal Ecuador," *Globalizations* 17, no. 1 (May 8, 2019): 77–92, doi:https ://doi.org/10.1080/14747731.2019.1614722.

56. For a discussion, see Andrew Inkpen and Michael H. Moffett, *The Global Oil & Gas Industry: Management, Strategy and Finance* (Tulsa, Okla.: PennWell, 2011), 214–55.

57. Bernard Mommer, "The New Governance of Venezuelan Oil," Oxford Institute for Energy Studies, WPM, April 23, 1998, 37; Manzano and Monaldi, "The Political Economy of Oil Contract Renegotiation."

58. Example elaborated from Manzano and Monaldi, "Political Economy of Oil Contract Renegotiation."

59. Raymond Vernon, *Sovereignty at Bay: The Multinational Spread of U.S. Enterprises* (Lebanon, Ind.: Basic Books, 1971).
60. Theodore H. Moran, *Multinational Corporations and the Politics of Dependence: Copper in Chile* (Princeton, N.J.: Princeton University Press, 1974).
61. Jason Bordoff, "The 2020 Oil Crash's Unlikely Winner: Saudi Arabia," *Foreign Policy*, May 5, 2020; Bernard Mommer, *Global Oil and the Nation State* (Oxford: Oxford University Press, 2002), 63.
62. Ravi Ramamurti, "The 'Obsolescing Bargain' Model? MNC-Host Developing Country Relations Revisited," *Journal of International Business Studies* 32, no. 1 (2001): 23–39.
63. Vivoda, "Resource Nationalism"; Vlado Vivoda, "Rise of State-Firm Bargaining in the 2000s," in Haslam and Heidrich, *Political Economy of Natural Resources*, 55.
64. Vlado Vivoda, "Bargaining Model for the International Oil Industry," *Business and Politics* 13, no. 4 (2011): 1–34, doi:10.2202/1469-3569.1384.
65. Antulio Rosales, "Structural Constraints in Times of Resource Nationalism: Oil Policy and State Capacity in Post-neoliberal Ecuador," *Globalizations* 17, no. 1 (2019): 77–92, https://doi.org/10.1080/14747731.2019.1614722. See also Moran, *Multinational Corporations and the Politics of Dependence*.
66. Merrie Gilbert Klapp, *The Sovereign Entrepreneur: Oil Policies in Advanced and Less Developed Capitalist Countries* (Ithaca, N.Y.: Cornell University Press, 1987), 76–81, 92–93.
67. For Colombia and Peru, see Gabriela Valdivia and Angus Lyall, "The Oil Complex in Latin America: Politics, Frontiers, and Habits of Oil Rule," in *Routledge Handbook of Latin American Development*, ed. Julie Cupples, Marcela Palomino-Schalscha, and Manuel Prieto (New York: Routledge, 2019), 461. Brazil, under the Workers Party administration of Luiz Inácio Lula da Silva (Lula), did not renegotiate signed contracts, even though it halted auctions for offshore fields after the massive pre-salt discoveries in 2007 and instituted a new contract regime specifically for the pre-salt areas. See Stephen Sewalk, "Brazil's Energy Policy and Regulation," *Fordham Environmental Law Review* 25, no. 3 (2015): 652–705.
68. Bernard Mommer, a highly respected oil analyst who worked in Venezuela and the Oxford Institute for Energy Studies, is a fine example of how difficult it is for business-focused oil nationalists to prevail over their statist compatriots if domestic institutions cannot constrain their desire to use oil wealth for patronage. He wound up violating his own recommendation of 1994 regarding the role of the NOC when he became vice minister of oil and a member of the PDVSA Board of Directors. See Bernard Mommer, "The Political Role of National Oil Companies in Exporting Countries: The Venezuelan Case," Oxford Institute for Energy Studies, WPM 18 (September 1994), and the discussion in chapter 8 of this book.
69. George W. Grayson, "The San José Oil Facility: South-South Cooperation," *Third World Quarterly* 7, no. 2 (1985): 390–409.
70. Brian Levy and Pablo T. Spiller, *Regulations, Institutions, and Commitment: Comparative Studies of Telecommunications* (Cambridge: Cambridge University Press, 1996).
71. J. Luis Guasch and Pablo Spiller, *Managing the Regulatory Process: Design, Concepts, Issues, and the Latin America and Caribbean Story* (Washington, D.C.: World Bank, 1999), 27–29.

72. Nancy Postero, *The Indigenous State: Race, Politics, and Performance in Plurinational Bolivia* (Oakland: University of California Press, 2017), http://doi.org/10.1525/luminos.31; Derrick Hindery, *From Enron to Evo: Pipeline Politics, Global Environmentalism, and Indigenous Rights in Bolivia* (Tucson: University of Arizona Press, 2013).

73. Jan Paulsson, "The Power of States to Make Meaningful Promises to Foreigners," *Journal of International Dispute Settlement* 1, no. 2 (2010): 341–52, doi:10.1093/jnlids/idq013.

74. Barbara Geddes, *Politician's Dilemma: Building State Capacity in Latin America* (Berkeley: University of California Press, 1996), 14.

75. Cf. Rosales, "Structural Constraints"; Haslam and Heidrich, *The Political Economy of Natural Resources and Development*, 10–11.

76. Silvana Tordo with Brandon S. Tracy and Noora Arfaa, *National Oil Companies and Value Creation*, World Bank Working Paper no. 128 (Washington, D.C.: World Bank, 2011), 28.

77. "The Changing Role of National Oil Companies in International Energy Markets," *Baker Institute Policy Report*, James A. Baker III Institute for Public Policy, Rice University, no. 35 (April 2007): 5–6; Tordo, *National Oil Companies and Value Creation*.

78. Cf. Duncan Snidal, "Public Goods, Property Rights, and Political Organizations," *International Studies Quarterly* 23, no. 4 (December 1979): 532–66; Bruce Bueno de Mesquita and Alastair Smith, "Political Succession: A Model of Coups, Revolution, Purges, and Everyday Politics," *Journal of Conflict Resolution* 61, no. 4 (April 2017): 707–43.

79. Snidal, "Public Goods," 539.

80. Klaus Desmet, Ignacio Ortuño-Ortín, and Shlomo Weber, "Peripheral Diversity: Transfers Versus Public Goods," *Social Choice and Welfare* 49, no. 3/4 (December 2017): 788, relates a country's diversity to the pursuit of language homogeneity, schooling, and the location of roads and railroads. Trey Billing, "Government Fragmentation, Administrative Capacity, and Public Goods: The Negative Consequences of Reform in Burkina Faso," *Political Research Quarterly* 72, no. 3 (September 2019): 669–85, examines nighttime light intensity. Poor relief is the subject in Masayuki Tanimoto, "Introduction," in *Public Goods Provision in the Early Modern Economy: Comparative Perspectives from Japan, China, and Europe*, ed. Masayuki Tanimoto and R. Bin Wong (Berkeley: University of California Press, 2019). United Nations Industrial Development Organization, *Public Goods for Economic Development* (Vienna, 2008) focuses on international public goods for development.

81. Michael L. Ross, "The Political Economy of the Resource Curse," *World Politics* 51, no. 2 (January 1999): 297–322.

82. Thad Dunning, *Crude Democracy: Natural Resource Wealth and Political Regimes* (New York: Cambridge University Press, 2008).

83. Guillaume R. Fréchette and John H. Kagel, "Pork Versus Public Goods: An Experimental Study of Public Good Provision Within a Legislative Bargaining Framework," *Economic Theory* 49, no. 3 (April 2012), Symposium on Political Economy, 779–800; Indridi H. Indridason, "Executive Veto Power and Credit Claiming: Comparing the Effects of the Line-Item Veto and the Package Veto," *Public Choice* 146, no. 3/4 (March 2011): 375–94.

84. Significant contribution to national development is generally recognized as a characteristic of a public good. Tanimoto and Wong, *Public Goods Provision*

85. Werner Baer, "Import Substitution and Industrialization in Latin America: Experiences and Interpretations," *Latin American Research Review* 7, no. 1 (Spring 1972): 95–122; Albert O. Hirschman, "The Turn to Authoritarianism in Latin America and the Search for Its Economic Determinants," in *The New Authoritarianism in Latin America*, ed. David Collier (Princeton, N.J.: Princeton University Press, 1979), 61–98.

86. The failure of Latin American ISI is not presented here as inherent in an ISI development strategy. The debate about national development and ISI is part of the larger debate around the role of the state, particularly that of the developmental state, and not the subject of this book. For an overview of this debate, see Stephan Haggard, *Elements in the Politics of Development* (Cambridge: Cambridge University Press, 2021).

87. For example, state-owned infrastructure companies are created as public goods. But when they fail to generate their product (e.g., electricity, telephones) at the low prices they are allowed to charge, they rely on state subsidies and the product is rationed, usually ensuring supply to partisans of the government or groups of citizens that can easily disrupt political stability. See Jaime Millan and Nils-Henrik H. von der Fehr, "Introduction," in *Keeping the Lights On: Power Sector Reform in Latin America*, ed. Millan and von der Fehr (Washington, D.C.: Inter-American Development Bank, 2003), 1–16.

88. The complexities involved in conceptualizing and implementing governance can be appreciated in the following reviews: Jo Rowlands, "Review," *Development in Practice* 18, no. 6 (November 2008): 801–4; David A. Detomasi, "Review: Mapping the Governance Terrain," *International Studies Review* 8, no. 1 (March 2006): 101–3; Liana Joseph, "Review: Challenges in Effective Governance of Natural Resources," *Conservation Biology* 26, no. 3 (June 2012): 578–79.

89. The standard reference source for this evolution is Daniel Yergin, *The Prize: The Epic Quest for Oil, Money & Power* (New York: Free Press, 2008).

90. Consider the U.S. embargo on Cuba, which includes oil and related technology. Jens Erik Gould, "Cuba Would Welcome U.S. Oil Companies If Embargo Ends (Update 2)," Bloomberg.com, April 3, 2009, www.bloomberg.com/apps/news?pid=20601103&sid=aSIKErkORLLA&refer=us#.

91. Cf. HRH Faisal Bin Turki, "Perspectives on the Saudi Arabian Energy Industry," Royal Institute of International Affairs, London, December 2, 2000, http://www.saudiembassy.net/archive/2000/speeches/page0.aspx; Jad Mouawad, "Saudi Officials Seek to Temper the Price of Oil," *New York Times*, January 28, 2007, http://www.nytimes.com/2007/01/28/business/28oil.html.

92. Riots and police and military violence in multiple Venezuelan cities in 1989, known as the Caracazo, killed hundreds and forced the president to declare a state of emergency. Moisés Naím, *Paper Tigers & Minotaurs: The Politics of Venezuela's Economic Reforms* (New York: Carnegie Endowment, 1993); Marc Wolfensberger, "Tehran Revolts Iran Rations Gasoline, Sparks Protest in Tehran (Update 3)," Bloomberg.com, June 27, 2007, http://web.archive.org/web/20140215031151/http://www.bloomberg.com/apps/news?pid=newsarchive&sid=a9HiN8aoQngM&refer=india.

217

2. THE PATHS TO DIVERSE PARTNERSHIPS

93. Eduardo Silva, *Challenging Neoliberalism in Latin America* (Cambridge: Cambridge University Press, 2009).
94. José A.Valdez, "Capitalization: Privatizing Bolivian Style," *Economic Reform Today*1 (1998).
95. David R. Mares, "Energy Cooperation and Security in the Hemisphere: Mexican Challenges and Opportunities," Task Force Policy Paper series, Center for Hemispheric Policy, University of Miami, 2009.
96. Aldo Musacchio and Sergio G. Lazzarini, *Reinventing State Capitalism: Leviathan in Business, Brazil and Beyond* (Cambridge, Mass.: Harvard University Press, 2014), 108.

2. THE PATHS TO DIVERSE PARTNERSHIPS IN THE CONTEXT OF RESOURCE NATIONALISM

1. Michael L. Ross, "What Do We Know About Natural Resources and Civil War?," *Journal of Peace Research* 41, no. 3 (2004): 337–56.
2. Author website, https://sites.google.com/ucsd.edu/david-mares/home.
3. For example, George Philip's excellent history, *Oil and Politics in Latin America: Nationalist Movements and State Companies* (Cambridge: Cambridge University Press, 1982), does not discuss subsoil ownership issues in the nineteenth or early twentieth century.
4. Stephen C. Cote, *Oil and Nation: A History of Bolivia's Petroleum Sector (Energy and Society)* (Morgantown: West Virginia University Press, 2016), 1–29; Philip, *Oil and Politics*, 26–27. Philip notes that one U.S. company repatriated from Argentina US$90 million on a $300,000 initial investment, while another turned a $100,000 investment into $2 million to bring home (p. 13, citing Mira Wilkins, *The Maturing of the Multinational Enterprise: American Business Abroad from 1914–1970* [Cambridge, Mass.: Harvard University Press, 1974], 61–62). Of course, the capture of large rents by investors within the United States also occurred.
5. Donald R. Shea, *The Calvo Clause: A Problem of Inter-American and International Law and Diplomacy* (Minneapolis: University of Minnesota Press, 1955); Noel Maurer, *The Empire Trap: The Rise and Fall of U.S. Intervention to Protect American Property Overseas* (Princeton, N.J.: Princeton University Press, 2013).
6. Jonathan C. Brown, "Jersey Standard and the Politics of Latin American Oil Production, 1911–30," in *The Oil Business in Latin America: The Early Years*, ed. John D. Wirth (Lincoln: University of Nebraska Press, 1985), 1–50.
7. Cote, *Oil and Nation*, 19.
8. Rosemary Thorp and Geoffrey Bertram, *Peru: 1890–1977* (New York: Columbia University Press, 1980), 99–100, 108–9; Dale Beck Furnish, "Peruvian Domestic Law Aspects of the La Brea Y Pariñas Controversy," *Kentucky Law Journal* 59 (1970): 351, http://ssrn.com/abstract=1428605.
9. Carl E. Solberg, "YPF: The Formative Years of Latin America's Pioneer State Oil Company, 1922–1931," in Wirth, *The Oil Business in Latin America*, 86.
10. Mariana Ardizzone, "Argentina," in *Latin American Upstream Oil and Gas: A Practical Guide to the Law and Regulation*, ed. Fernando Fresco and Eduardo G. Pereira (London: Glove Business Publishing, 2015), 15. The Patagonian territory was

not divided into provinces until 1955, so it remained as federal rather than provincial territory until then.

11. Philip, *Oil and Politics*, 404–9.

12. Ardizzone, "Argentina," 16, 20, 22.

13. Ardizzone, 24.

14. Yanko Marcius de Alencar Xavier, "Legal Models of Petroleum and Natural Gas Ownership in Brazilian Law," in *Property and the Law in Energy and Natural Resources*, ed. Aileen McHarg et al. (Oxford: Oxford University Press, 2010), 223–24.

15. Pamela Murray, "Know-How and Nationalism: Colombia's First Geological and Petroleum Experts, c. 1940–1970," *Americas* 52, no. 2 (October 1995): 212n.3; Jorge Gonzalez-Jacome, "The Assault on Classical Legal Thought in Colombia (1886–1920)," 2009, 56–60, http://works.bepress.com/jorge_gonzalez_jacome/14.

16. Mira Wilkins, "Multinational Oil Companies in South America in the 1920s: Argentina, Bolivia, Brazil, Chile, Colombia, Ecuador, and Peru," *Business History Review* 42 (Autumn 1974): 430; Arnold Wilson, "Oil Legislation in Latin America," *Foreign Affairs* 8, no. 1 (October 1929): 108–19; D. M. Phelps, "Petroleum Regulation in Temperate South America," *American Economic Review* 29, no. 1 (March 1939): 48–59; E. Taylor Parks, *Colombia and the United States 1765–1934* (Durham, N.C.: Duke University Press, 1935), 449–57.

17. Robert J. Shafer and Donald J. Mabry, *Neighbors—Mexico and the United States: Wetbacks and Oil* (Chicago: Nelson-Hall, 1981), 28–31; J. Richard Powell, *The Mexican Petroleum Industry 1938–1950* (Berkeley: University of California Press, 1956), 7–8.

18. Shafer and Mabry, *Neighbors*; Powell, *The Mexican Petroleum Industry 1938–1950*, 7–8.

19. Gavin Bridge and Philippe Le Billon, *Oil* (Malden, Mass.: Polity Press, 2013), 209n.10; Daniel Johnston, *International Petroleum Fiscal Systems and Production Sharing Contracts* (Tulsa, Okla.: PennWell, 1994), 21–27.

20. Rubén Berrios, Andrea Marak, and Scott Morgenstern, "Explaining Hydrocarbon Nationalization in Latin America: Economics and Political Ideology," *Review of International Political Economy* 18, no. 5 (December 2011): 673–97. Unfortunately, this study suffers from important misclassifications of country cases and characteristics.

21. See the pioneering studies by Stephen J. Kobrin, "Foreign Enterprise and Forced Divestment in the LDCs," *International Organization* 34, no. 1 (1980): 65–88, and "Expropriation as an Attempt to Control Foreign Firms in LDCs: Trends from 1960–1979," *International Studies Quarterly* 28 (1984): 329–48.

22. Bernard Mommer, "The New Governance of Venezuelan Oil," Oxford Institute for Energy Studies, WPM 23 (April 1998): 76–77.

23. Lucy Chernykh, "Profit or Politics? Understanding Renationalizations in Russia," *Journal of Corporate Finance* 17 (2011): 1237–53.

24. Shafer and Mabry, *Neighbors*, 28–31; Powell, *The Mexican Petroleum Industry 1938–1950*, 7–8.

25. Jonathan C. Brown, "The Structure of the Foreign-Owned Petroleum Industry in Mexico, 1880–1938," in *The Mexican Petroleum Industry in the Twentieth Century*, ed. Jonathan C. Brown and Alan Knight (Austin: University of Texas Press, 1992), 3.

26. Esperanza Durán, "Pemex: The Trajectory of a National Oil Policy," in Wirth, *The Oil Business*, 167; Jose Juan Gonzales, "The Scope and Limits of the Principles of National Property in Mexico," in McHarg et al., *Property and the Law*, 213; Philip, *Oil and Politics*, 204–5.

27. Lorenzo Meyer, "The Expropriation and Great Britain," in Brown and Knight, *Mexican Petroleum Industry*, 154–55; Durán, "Pemex," 174–75.

28. Powell, *Mexican Petroleum Industry*, 23; Philip, *Oil and Politics*, 210; Durán, "Pemex," 169–70, 172–73.

29. Gonzales, "Scope and Limits," 214–15; Isidro Morales, "The Consolidation and Expansion of Pemex, 1947–1959," in Brown and Knight, *Mexican Petroleum Industry*, 209–10.

30. Morales, "The Consolidation and Expansion of Pemex," 210.

31. Edwin Lieuwen, "The Politics of Energy in Venezuela" in Wirth, *The Oil Business*, 194; David T. Day, "Petroleum and Natural Gas," in *The Mineral Industry*, vol. 29 (1929), 519.

32. Brown, "Jersey Standard," 36.

33. Judith Ewell, *Venezuela: A Century of Change* (Stanford, Calif.: Stanford University Press, 1984), 57; Lieuwen, "Politics of Energy," 194–95.

34. Kelvin Singh, "Oil Politics in Venezuela During the Lopez Contreras Administration (1936–1941)," *Journal of Latin American Studies* 21, no. 1 (February 1989): 89–104; Ewell, *Venezuela*, 67.

35. Mona Verma Makhija, "The Determinants of Government Intervention: Political Risk in the Venezuelan Petroleum Industry," Ph.D diss., University of Wisconsin-Madison, 1989, 72–76; Juan Boué, *Venezuela: The Political Economy of Oil* (Oxford: Oxford University Press, 1993), 11–12; Lieuwen, "The Politics of Energy in Venezuela," 200; Ewell, *Venezuela*, 68.

36. Boué, *Venezuela*; Karl, *The Paradox of Plenty*.

37. Makhija, "Determinants of Government Intervention," 77–78; Lieuwen, "The Politics of Energy," 203–4.

38. Bernard Mommer, "The Political Role of National Oil Companies in Exporting Countries: The Venezuelan Case," Oxford Institute for Energy Studies, WPM 18 (September 1994): 7–8.

39. Franklin Tugwell, *The Politics of Oil in Venezuela* (Stanford, Calif.: Stanford University Press, 1975), 127–29.

40. Carl E. Solberg, *Oil and Nationalism in Argentina: A History* (Stanford, Calif.: Stanford University Press, 1979), 59–60; Solberg, "Formative Years," 58–69.

41. Solberg, *Oil and Nationalism in Argentina*, 59–60.

42. Solberg, "Formative Years," 72–73; Philip, *Oil and Politics*, 166–80.

43. Vernon Lovell Phelps, *The International Economic Position of Argentina* (Philadelphia: University of Pennsylvania Press, 1938), 50–57; Sebastián Scheimberg, "The Performance of Argentine Oil Industry Over a Century (draft for comments)," IESA, http://servicios.iesa.edu.ve/portal/CIEA/argentina_scheimberg_d1.pdf, 4, accessed February 13, 2014; Philip, *Oil and Politics*, 179; Solberg, "Formative Years," 86–90.

44. Philip, *Oil and Politics*, 180–81; Solberg, "Formative Years," 92–93.

45. Philip, *Oil and Politics*, 404–9; Carl E. Solberg, "Entrepreneurship in Public Enterprise: General Enrique Mosconi and the Argentine Petroleum Industry," *Business*

History Review 56, no. 3 (Autumn 1982): 398; Celia Szusterman, *Frondizi and the Politics of Developmentalism in Argentina, 1955–62* (Pittsburgh: University of Pittsburgh Press, 1993), 44–46.

46. Solberg, "Entrepreneurship," 398.

47. Ardizzone, "Argentina," 22.

48. Solberg, "Formative Years," 91–93.

49. Philip, *Oil and Politics*, 405.

50. Philip, 419–23.

51. Hurst Davison and Robert Mabro, *Natural Gas: Governments and Oil Companies in the Third World* (Oxford: Oxford University Press, 1988), 104.

52. Joseph Ramos, *Neoconservative Economics in the Southern Cone of Latin America, 1973–1983* (Baltimore: Johns Hopkins University Press, 1986); David R. Mares, "Natural Gas Pipelines in the Southern Cone," in *Natural Gas and Geopolitics: From 1970–2040*, ed. David G. Victor, Amy M. Jaffe, and Mark H. Hayes (Cambridge: Cambridge University Press, 2006), 169–201.

53. Carlos M. Bechelli, "Gas del Estado," in *Petróleo y Gas '88: Argentina, País Para Inversiones Petroleras*, Centro Internacional de Información Empresaria (Buenos Aires: Ediciones CIEE, 1989), 27–33.

54. Muller & Associates, *Estadísticas socioeconómicas*, cited in Augusto Vargas Salguiero, *YPFB entre nacionalistas y liberales* (La Paz: Editorial "Los Amigos del Libro," 1996); Mares, "Natural Gas Pipelines," 171–76.

55. Wilkins, "Multinational Oil Companies in South America," 42, 430; Arnold Wilson, "Oil Legislation in Latin America," *Foreign Affairs* 8, no. 1 (October 1929): 108–19; D. M. Phelps, "Petroleum Regulation in Temperate South America," *American Economic Review* 29, no. 1 (March 1939): 48–59; E. Taylor Parks, *Colombia and the United States 1765–1934* (Durham, N.C.: Duke University Press, 1935), 449–57; Brown, "Jersey Standard," 28.

56. Brown, "Jersey Standard," 28–29.

57. Telegrams between the United States and Colombia, University of Wisconsin-Madison Library, http://images.library.wisc.edu/FRUS/EFacs/1928v02/reference /frus.frus1928v02.i0008.pdf; "U.S. Rebukes Colombia in Oil Argument," *Pittsburgh Press*, September 23, 1928, https://news.google.com/newspapers?nid=1144& dat=19280923&id=DO8aAAAAIBAJ&sjid=OEoEAAAAIBAJ&pg=6389,4437555 &hl=en.

58. Parks, *Colombia and the United* States, 476; Wilkins, "Multinational Oil Companies," 441–42.

59. Parks, *Colombia and the United States*, 468ff; Marcelo Bucheli, "Multinational Oil Companies in Colombia and Mexico: Corporate Strategy, Nationalism, and Local Politics, 1900–1951," paper presented at the International Economic History Conference, Helsinki, 2006, 13.

60. Parks, *Colombia and the United* States, 475.

61. Ewell E. Murphy, Jr., "Oil Operations in Latin America: The Scope for Private Enterprise," *International Lawyer* 2, no. 3 (April 1968): 463; Philip, *Oil and Politics*, 69; Ecopetrol, "Our History," updated November 10, 2014, https://www .ecopetrol.com.co/wps/portal/web_es/ecopetrol-web/our-company/about-us /ecopetrol-about/our-history; Hydrocarbons Technology, "Refineria de Cartagena (Reficar) Refinery Expansion," accessed April 1, 2018, https://www.hydrocarbons

-technology.com/projects/refineria-de-cartagena-reficar-refinery-expansion/. In 1974 Ecopetrol also bought the Cartagena refinery that had been constructed by Intercol in 1956, http://www.ecopetrol.com.co/contenido.aspx?catID=32&conID =36271, accessed October 24, 2009.

62. Murphy, "Oil Operations in Latin America," 463; David Arce Rojas, "Colombia Towards a New Petroleum Contractual Regime," *Revista Colombiana de Derecho Internacional*, no. 3 (June 2004): 255–56; Raymond F. Mikesell, *Petroleum Company Operations and Agreements in the Developing Countries* (New York: Resources for the Future, 1984; Routledge, 2015), 110. Mikesell citations refer to the Routledge edition.

63. World Bank, *Comparative Study on the Distribution of Oil Rents in Bolivia, Colombia, Ecuador and Peru (English)*, Energy Sector Management Assistance Program (ESMAP) Working Paper series (Washington, D.C.: World Bank), 16, http:// documents.worldbank.org/curated/en/465991468770681995/Comparative-study -on-the-distribution-of-oil-rents-in-Bolivia-Colombia-Ecuador-and-Peru; Juan Carlos Palau, "Transactional, Social, and Legal Aspects of Oil Exploration and Extraction in Colombia," *Northwestern Journal of International Law & Business* 22 (2001): 35; Arce Rojas, "Colombia Towards a New Petroleum Contractual Regime," 256–57.

64. Federal Research Division, Library of Congress, *Colombia: A Country Study*, http:// www.country-data.com/cgi-bin/query/r-3059.html. From 1997 to 2003 a small private refinery accounted for 4.2 percent of total Colombian capacity. "El proyecto de la refinería privada," *Semana*, November 24, 2003, http://www.semana.com /nacion/recuadro/el-proyecto-refineria-privada/127485-3.

65. Mikesell, *Petroleum Country Operations and Agreements*, 111.

66. Philip, *Oil and Politics*, 482.

67. Philip, 243. See also Wilkins, "Multinational Oil Companies," 436–39; Thorp and Bertram *Peru*, 98–111, 165–66.

68. Thorp and Bertram, *Peru*, 99–100, 108–9; Furnish, "Peruvian Domestic Law Aspects of the La Brea Y Pariñas Controversy," 351.

69. Wilkins, "Multinational Oil Companies," 436–39; Thorp and Bertram, *Peru*, 98–111, 165–66.

70. Thorp and Bertram, *Peru*, 166.

71. Humberto Campodónico, *La Política Petrolera 1970–1987: El Estado, las contratistas y PetroPeru* (Lima: Peru, Centro de Estudios y Promoción del Desarrollo, 1986), 74–76; Thorp and Betram, *Peru*, 163–69, 221–29; Philip, *Oil and Politics*, 243–49.

72. Philip, *Oil and Politics*, 249–57; PetroPeru, "Historia," accessed February 13, 2014, https://www.petroperu.com.pe/acerca-de-petroperu-s-a-/historia/; Defensa de PetroPeru, "Historia," accessed February 13, 2014, http://defensadepetroperu.blog spot.com/p/resena-historica.html.

73. John D. Martz, *Politics and Petroleum in Ecuador* (New Brunswick, N.J.: Transaction, 1987), 45–48.

74. Wilkins, "Multinational Oil Companies," 431; Day, "Petroleum and Natural Gas," 517; Martz, *Politics and Petroleum*, 47.

75. Enrique Sierra C., *Ecuador, Ecuador: Tu Petróleo! Tu Gente!* (Quito: Ediciones Cultura y Didática, 1995), 30–31; Henry Llanes, *Ecuador: La subasta del petróleo* (Quito: RG grafistas, 2016), 41.

76. M. S. Steyn, "Oil Politics in Ecuador and Nigeria: A Perspective from Environmental History on the Struggles Between Ethnic Minority Groups, Multinational Oil Companies and National Governments," Ph.D. diss., University of the Free State, 2003," 167.
77. Enrique Sierra Castro. *Ecuador, Ecuador: Tu Petróleo! Tu Gente!* (Quito: Ediciones Cultura y Didáctica, 1995), 31.
78. Steyn, "Oil Politics in Ecuador and Nigeria," 169–70.
79. Martz, *Politics and Petroleum in Ecuador*, 27, 607; Christopher Brogan, "The Retreat from Oil Nationalism in Ecuador 1976–1983," Working Paper 13, Institute of Latin American Studies, University of London, 1984, http://sas-space.sas.ac.uk/3401/1 /B51_-_The_Retreat_from_Oil_Nationalism_in_Ecuador_1976-1983.pdf.; Llanes, *Ecuador*, 50.
80. Luis Alberto Araúz, *Derecho Petrolero Ecuatoriano* (Quito: Comité de Empresa de los Trabajadores de Petroproduccion, 2009), cited in Llanes, *Ecuador*, 49.
81. Sierra Castro, *Ecuador, Ecuador*, 38–40, 46–47.
82. Llanes, *Ecuador*, 68–69.
83. Antulio Rosales, "Structural Constraints in Times of Resource Nationalism: Oil Policy and State Capacity in Post-Neoliberal Ecuador, *Globalizations* 17, no. 1 (May 8, 2019): 80–88.
84. Maria Luise Wagner, "The Liberal Party and the Rise of Tin," in *Bolivia: A Country Side*, ed. Rex A. Hudson and Dennis M. Hanratty (Washington, D.C.: GPO for the Library of Congress, 1989); Frederick B. Pike, *The United States and the Andean Republics: Peru, Bolivia, and Ecuador* (Cambridge, Mass.: Harvard University Press, 1977), 164–65.
85. Day, "Petroleum and Natural Gas," 514–15; Wilkins, "Multinational Oil Companies," 431.
86. Wilkins, "Multinational Oil Companies," 432, 440, 442.
87. Philip, *Oil and Politics*, 194–95.
88. Wilkins, "Multinational Oil Companies," 443.
89. Philip, *Oil and Politics*, 228–31.
90. de Alencar Xavier, "Legal Models of Petroleum and Gas Ownership," 224.
91. Solberg, "Formative Years," 95.
92. de Alencar Xavier, "Legal Models of Petroleum and Gas Ownership," 224–25.
93. Alan Knight, "The Politics of the Expropriation," in Brown and Knight, *Mexican Petroleum Industry*, 90–128.
94. Oliver Stuenkel, "The Brazil-Bolivia Dispute, a Decade On," July 10, 2016, https:// www.postwesternworld.com/2016/07/10/bolivia-dispute-decade/.
95. In 1978 the government gave Ecopetrol a monopoly over oil exports, requiring all domestic production to be sold to the NOC. Mikesell, *Petroleum Company Operations and Agreements*, 111.
96. "Privatizaciones en la Argentina. Marcos regulatorios tarifarios y evolución de los precios relativos durante la convertibilidad," Proyecto "Privatización y Regulación en la Economía Argentina," Working Paper no. 4 (Buenos Aires: FLACSO, May 1998).
97. "Enarsa: un joven funcionario de Alicia Kirchner encabezará la empresa con la que De Vido manejó millones," *La Nación*, March 3, 2020.
98. "Argentina to Pay Repsol for YPF Nationalization," *Americas Quarterly*, April 25, 2014.

99. Philip, *Oil and Politics*, 227–41; John D. Wirth, "Setting the Brazilian Agenda, 1936–1953," in Wirth, *The Oil Business in Latin America* 103, 123.
100. Meyer, "The Expropriation and Great Britain," 154–55; Durán, "Pemex," 174–75.
101. Gustavo Coronel, *The Nationalization of the Venezuelan Oil Industry: From Technocratic Success to Political Failure* (Lexington, Mass.: Lexington Books, 1983.)
102. Marius S. Vassiliou, *The A to Z of the Petroleum Industry* (Plymouth, UK: Scarecrow Press, 2009), 141.
103. Thorp and Bertram, *Peru*, 166–67, 301; Campodónico, *La Política Petrolera*, 76–77.
104. Philip, *Oil and Politics*, 266, 454–60; Peter DeShazo, "Bolivia," in *Energy Cooperation in the Western Hemisphere: Benefits and Impediments*, ed. Sidney Weintraub (Washington, D.C.: CSIS, 2007), 341.
105. Merrie Gilbert Klapp, *The Sovereign Entrepreneur: Oil Policies in Advanced and Less Developed Capitalist Countries* (Ithaca, N.Y.: Cornell University Press, 1987), 20.
106. Though Chile is not an oil or gas producer and thus is not included in this study, it represents a very interesting case. Chile nationalized the importation, distribution, and sale of petroleum products in 1932, eighteen years before it created its NOC (Empresa Nacional del Petróleo, ENAP), preferring to rely on general government agencies to implement the regulations.
107. Thorp and Bertram, *Peru*, 166.
108. Solberg, "Entrepreneurship" 392
109. Vassiliou, *The A to Z of the Petroleum Industry*, 141.
110. "'Bonos ciudadanos' la Alternativa para Pemex" *El Economista*, May 11, 2011, https://www.eleconomista.com.mx/economia/Bonos-ciudadanos-la-alternativa-para-Pemex-20110511-0096.html.
111. Andrea Goldstein, "The Emergence of Multilatinas: The Petrobras Experience," *Universia Business Review*, first quarter (2010): 101–2.
112. There is a large literature on just what those conditions are. See Organización Latinoamericana de Energía (OLADE), *Regulatory Frameworks: Efficient State-Owned Oil and Gas Enterprises* January 2009; Silvana Tordo with Brandon S. Tracy and Noora Arfaa, *National Oil Companies and Value Creation*, Working Paper no. 218 (Washington, D.C.: World Bank, 2011); Miranda Ferrell Wainberg et al, "Commercial Frameworks for National Oil Companies," CEE-UT, University of Texas, Austin, March 2007, https://www.beg.utexas.edu/files/cee/legacy/CEE%20National_Oil_Company_Mar%2007.pdf; Kenneth Medlock and John Hartley, "The Changing Role of National Oil Companies in International Energy Markets," James A. Baker III Institute for Public Policy, April 2007, https://www.bakerinstitute.org/media/files/Research/5be0c5c4/BI_PolicyReport_35.pdf.

3. EXPLAINING OIL AND GAS POLICY

1. EIA, "Oil and Natural Gas Resource Categories Reflect Varying Degrees of Certainty," July 17, 2014, https://www.eia.gov/todayinenergy/detail.php?id=17151.
2. Bruce Bueno de Mesquita et al., *The Logic of Political Survival* (Cambridge, Mass.: MIT Press, 2003), https://doi.org/10.7551/mitpress/4292.001.0001.

3. Carter Dougherty, "Global Trade Talks Collapse Over Agricultural Subsidies," *New York Times*, June 21, 2007, http://www.nytimes.com/2007/06/21/business /worldbusiness/21iht-wto.4.6264066.html.

4. Selwyn Parker, "Weighing Bolivia's Gas Export Options," *Petroleum Economist*, August 9, 2018, https://www.petroleum-economist.com/articles/midstream-down stream/pipelines/2018/weighing-bolivias-gas-export-options.

5. Luigi Manzetti, "Political Manipulations and Market Reforms Failures," *World Politics* 55, no. 3 (April 2003): 315–60.

6. See Angelo Bonfiglioli, "Empowering the Poor," United Nations Capital Development Fund, 2003, esp. 41–58, http://unpan1.un.org/intradoc/groups/public/docu ments/un/unpano10168.pdf.

7. Anibal Pérez-Liñan, *Presidential Impeachment and the New Political Instability in Latin America* (Cambridge: Cambridge University Press, 2007), 27, 183; Kenneth J. Mijeski and Scott H. Beck, *Pachakutik and the Rise and Decline of the Ecuadorian Indigenous Movement* (Columbus: Ohio University Press, 2011), 100.

8. David Pion-Berlin and Harold Trinkunas, "Civilian Praetorianism and Military Shirking During Constitutional Crises in Latin America," *Comparative Politics* 42, no. 4 (July 2010): 404; Jeffrey R. Weber, "Carlos Mesa, Evo Morales, and a Divided Bolivia (2003–2005)," *Latin American Perspectives* 37, no. 3 (May 2010): 51–70.

9. Pion-Berlin and Trinkunas, "Civilian Praetorianism," 402.

10. I differ on this from those who define inclusion by whether a government acts in ways that, at least in the short term, can be considered to be reflections of what a social group advocates. Cf. Federico M. Rossi, "The Second Wave of Incorporation in Latin America: A Conceptualization of the Quest for Inclusion Applied to Argentina," *Latin American Politics and Society* 57, no. 1 (Spring 2015): 1–28.

11. Consequently, the concept of a "selectorate" used by Bueno de Mesquita and his collaborators is broader than my category of the included since "in modern mass democracies, the selectorate is the electorate." See Bruce Bueno de Mesquita et al., "Political Institutions, Policy Choice and the Survival of Leaders," *British Journal of Political Science* 32, no. 4 (October 2002): 561. My inclusiveness variable fits in Dryzek's category of "authentic political inclusion." See John S. Dryzek, "Political Inclusion and the Dynamics of Democratization," *American Political Science Review* 90, no. 1 (September 1996): 475–87.

12. Susan C. Stokes, *Mandates and Democracies: Neoliberalism by Surprise in Latin America* (Cambridge: Cambridge University Press, 2001).

13. Social mobilization determines which groups demand a seat at the table, but their impact on policy depends on the ruling coalition or an alternate one poised to take power including those interests in their platform. Because my goal is to explain the impact on policy of having included and excluded groups rather than to explain their mobilization, a theory of social mobilization is not necessary.

14. *Bulletin of Latin American Research* 19 (2000), issue devoted to "old" and "new" populism; Kurt Weyland, "Clarifying a Contested Concept: Populism in the Study of Latin American Politics," *Comparative Politics* 34, no. 1 (October 2001): 1–22.

15. Kurt Weyland, "Neoliberal Populism in Latin America and Eastern Europe," *Comparative Politics* 31, no. 4 (July 1999): 379–401.

16. Aaron M. Mihaly, "Por qué se ha caído Goni? Explicando la renuncia forzada del Presidente Sánchez de Lozada en octubre de 2003," in *Conflictos politicos y*

movimientos sociales en Bolivia, ed. Nicholas A Robins (La Paz: Plural, 2006), 95–120; Willem Assies, "David Versus Goliath in Cochabamba: Water Rights, Neoliberalism, and the Revival of Social Protest in Bolivia," *Latin American Perspectives* 30, no. 3 (2003): 14–36.

17. Manzetti, "Political Manipulations and Market Reforms Failures."

18. Benjamin A. Olken, "Direct Democracy and Local Public Goods: Evidence from a Field Experiment in Indonesia," *American Political Science Review* 104, no. 2 (May 2010): 243–67.

19. Marxist critiques of this problem in leftist governments see the roots of it in the inability to make a clear break from the international capitalist system. Cf. Derrick Hindery, *From Evo to Enron: Pipeline Politics, Global Environmentalism, and Indigenous Rights in Bolivia* (Tucson: University of Arizona Press, 2013); Jeffrey R. Webber, "Carlos Mesa, Evo Morales, and a Divided Bolivia (2003–2005)," *Latin American Perspectives* 37, no. 3 (May 2010): 51–70. Liberals and progressives disagree about the causes but see the weaknesses in inclusiveness, transparency, and accountability. Enrique Krause, *Por una democracia sin adjetivos* (Mexico City: Joaquín Mortiz/Planeta, 1986); David Collier and Steve Levitsky, "Democracy with Adjectives: Conceptual Innovation in Comparative Research," *World Politics* 49, no. 3 (April 1997): 430–51; J. Mark Payne and Juan Cruz Perusia, "Reforming the Rules of the Game: Political Reform," in *The State of State Reform in Latin America*, ed. Eduardo Lora (Washington, D.C.: Inter-American Development Bank, 2007), 57–86. Although Latin Americanist scholars tend to see Costa Rica, Uruguay, and Chile as longstanding democracies, Polity IV post-1995 analysis classifies Costa Rica as only in the upper levels of the −10 to 10 scale (democracy begins at 6) across the entire period (10 for the entire period); Uruguay does not achieve a 9 ranking until 1986, Chile until 2007.

20. See Scott Mainwaring, Ana María Bejarano, and Eduardo Pizarro Leongómez, eds., *The Crisis of Democratic Representation in the Andes* (Stanford, Calif.: Stanford University Press, 2006).

21. Cf. Miriam Kornblith and Daniel H. Levine, "Venezuela: The Life and Times of the Party System," in *Building Democratic Institutions: Party Systems in Latin America*, ed. Scott Mainwaring and Timothy R. Scully (Stanford, Calif.: Stanford University Press, 1995), 37–71; Martin Tanaka, "From Crisis to Collapse of the Party Systems and Dilemmas of Democratic Representation: Peru and Venezuela," in Mainwaring, Bejarano, and Leongómez, *The Crisis of Democratic Representation*, 47–77; Noam Lupu, "Brand Dilution and the Breakdown of Political Parties in Latin America," *World Politics* 66, no. 4 (October 2014): 561–602.

22. See the discussion of political institutions, inequity, and development in World Bank, *World Development Report 2006: Equity and Development* (Washington, D.C.; World Bank, 2006); Ian Gary and Terry Lynn Karl, *Bottom of the Barrel: Africa's Oil Boom and the Poor* (Catholic Relief Services, June 2003), http://www.puaf .umd.edu/faculty/rosencranz/Week1/oil_report_full.pdf; and the review of the economic and political science literature in Michael L. Ross, "The Political Economy of the Resource Curse," *World Politics* 51, no. 2 (1999): 297–322.

23. Scott Pegg, "Can Policy Intervention Beat the Resource Curse? Evidence from the Chad-Cameroon Pipeline Project," *African Affairs* 105/418 (December 2005): 1–25.

24. Other critiques of efforts to align FDI interests with transparency and accountability of governments include James Van Alstine, "Transparency in Energy Governance: The Extractive Industries Transparency Initiative and Publish What You Pay Campaign," in *Transparency in Global Envirnmental Governance: Critical Perspectives*, ed. Aarti Gupta and Michael Mason (Cambridge, Mass.: MIT Press, 2014), 249–70; Glen Whelan, "The Political Perspective of Corporate Social Responsibility: A Critical Research Agenda," *Business Ethics Quarterly* 22, no. 4 (October 2012): 709–37.

25. Daniel Kaufmann, Aart Kraay, and Massimo Mastruzzi, *The Worldwide Governance Indicators: Methodology and Analytical Issues*, Policy Research Working Papers 5430, World Bank, Development Research Group, Macroeconomics and Growth Team, September 2010.

26. "Component Variables: Political Competition and Opposition (vars. 3.5 and 3.6) (see also var. 3.9and Addendum C: Political Competition Concepts). A third general authority trait of polities is participation. As Eckstein and Gurr defined it, participation involves the following: "Subordinates need not be merely Passive recipients of direction, and they seldom are. Some of them generally attempt to influence the directive activities of supers. Acts by which subs attempt to wield such influence are acts of participation." (Harry Eckstein and Ted Robert Gurr, *Patterns of Authority: A Structural Basis for Political Inquiry* [New York: Wiley 1975], 60.) The operational question is the extent to which the political system enables nonelites to influence political elites in regular ways. The Polity IV dataset measures this concept in two ways: (1) by the degree of institutionalization or "regulation" of political participation, and (2) by the extent of government restriction on political competition (p. 25). In summary, while PARREG measures the degree of organization and institutionalization of participation, PARCOMP measures the degree to which this political participation is free from government control (p. 67). See Monty G. Marshall, Ted Robert Gurr, and Keith Jaggers, "POLITY™ IV PROJECT, Political Regime Characteristics and Transitions, 1800-2016. Dataset Users' Manual," Center for Systemic Peace, 2017, http://www.systemicpeace.org.

27. Barry Ames, *Political Survival: Politicians and Public Policy in Latin America* (Berkeley: University of California Press, 1990); see also Bueno de Mesquita et al., "Political Survival, Policy Choice."

28. Barbara Geddes, *Politician's Dilemma: Building State Capacity in Latin America* (Berkeley: University of California Press, 1994).

29. See the discussion by Alfred Stepan, "Paths Toward Redemocratization: Theoretical and Comparative Considerations," in *Transitions from Authoritarian Rule*, ed. Guillermo O'Donnell, Philippe C. Schmitter, and Laurence Whitehead (Baltimore: Johns Hopkins University Press, 1986), 64–84.

30. Ames, *Political Survival*; Geddes, *Politician's Dilemma*; Bueno de Mesquita et al., "Political Institutions, Policy Choice"; Pablo T. Spiller, Ernesto Stein, and Mariano Tommas, *Political Institutions, Policymaking Processes, and Policy Outcome: An Intertemporal Transactions Framework* (Washington, D.C.: InterAmerican Development Bank, April 2003).

31. Note that the Competitiveness variable is different from the notion of regulation of competition in the Inclusiveness variable. In the latter variable, Polity is

concerned with the ability to compete, but here I am focused on the competition among those who are permitted to compete. Hence we can have very restricted ability to compete for office, but competition among those who do contest the elections.

32. Geddes, *Politician's Dilemma*.
33. Alejandro Bonvecchi and Emilia Simison, "Legislative Institutions and Performance in Authoritarian Regimes," *Comparative Politics* 49, no. 4 (July 2017): 521–39.
34. Merilee S. Grindle and John W. Thomas, *Public Choices and Policy Change: The Political Economy of Reform in Developing Countries* (Baltimore: Johns Hopkins University Press, 1991).
35. Albert O. Hirschman, *Journeys Toward Progress* (New York: Norton, 1973); Martha Finnemore and Kathryn Sikkink, "International Norm Dynamics and Political Change," *International Organization* 52, no. 4 (Autumn 1998): 887–917.

4. VENEZUELA'S POLITICAL ECONOMY, 1989-2016

1. Cf. Terry Lynn Karl, "The Paradox of Plenty: Oil Booms and Petro-States," *Journal of International Affairs* 53, no. 1 (Fall 1999): 31–48; Moisés Naím, *Paper Tigers and Minotaurs: The Politics of Venezuela's Economic Reforms* (New York: Carnegie Endowment for International Peace, 1993).
2. Brian F. Crisp, "Lessons from Economic Reform in the Venezuelan Democracy," *Latin American Research Review* 33, no. 1 (1998): 24; John D. Martz and David J. Myers, "Technological Elites and Political Parties: The Venezuelan Professional Community" *Latin American Research Review* 29, no. 1 (1994): 7–27.
3. The thrust of the plan was announced by Pérez's chief economic advisor before the election. See the interview with Miguel Rodríguez by Pedro Palma on Radio Caracas Televisión, November 13, 1988, http://www.pedroapalma.com/miguel-rodriguez-ad/.
4. Miriam Kornblith, *Venezuela en los 90: La crisis de la democracia* (Caracas: Ediciones IESA, 1998), 153.
5. "Venezuelan Reforms Favor Oil Work," *Oil and Gas Journal*, March 19, 1990, https://www.ogj.com/articles/print/volume-88/issue-12/in-this-issue/general-interest/venezuelan-reforms-favor-oil-work.html.
6. Naím, *Paper Tigers & Minotaurs*, 60.
7. Margarita López Maya, "The Venezuelan *Caracazo* of 1989: Popular Protest and Institutional Weakness," *Journal of Latin American Studies* 35, no. 1 (2003): 117–37.
8. Naím, *Paper Tigers & Minotaurs*, 60–84.
9. Brian F. Crisp and Daniel H. Levine, "Democratizing the Democracy? Crisis and Reform in Venezuela," *Journal of InterAmerican and World Affairs* 40, no. 2 (Summer 1998): 27–61; Juan Carlos Rey, "Corruption and Political Illegitimacy in Venezuelan Democracy," in *Reinventing Legitimacy: Democracy and Political Change in Venezuela*, ed. Damarys Canache and Michael R. Kulisheck (Westport, Conn.: Greenwood, 1998).
10. Alberto Garrido, *De la guerrilla al militarismo: Revelaciones del Comandante Arias Cárdenas*. Mérida, Venezuela: Producciones Karol, 2000.

11. Javier Corrales, *Presidents Without Parties: The Politics of Economic Reform in Argentina and Venezuela in the 1990s* (College Park: Pennsylvania State University Press, 2002), 62; Naím, *Paper Tigers & Minotaurs*, 102.
12. Deborah Norden, "Democracy in Uniform," in *Venezuelan Politics in the Chávez Era*, ed. Steve Ellner and Daniel Hellinger, (Boulder, Colo.: Lynne Rienner, 2003); Harold A. Trinkunas, *Crafting Civilian Control of the Military in Venezuela: A Comparative Perspective* (Durham: University of North Carolina Press, 2005).
13. Rickard Lalander, "The Impeachment of Carlos Andrés Pérez and the Collapse of Venezuelan Partyarchy," in *Presidential Breakdowns in Latin America: Causes and Outcomes of Instability in Developing Countries*, ed. Mariana Lavos and Leiv Marsteintredit (New York: Palgrave McMillan, 2009), 139–40.
14. Trinkunas, *Crafting Civilian Control*, 199–200.
15. Crisp, "Lessons from Economic Reform."
16. Ruth de Krivoy, "The Venezuelan Banking Crisis—Epilogue," 7, Toronto Centre, accessed January 13, 2019, http://siteresources.worldbank.org/EXTFINANCIAL SECTOR/Resources/282884-1239831335682/6028531-1239831365859/K2_Toronto _Center_Venezuela_Bkg_Epil.pdf.
17. James Brooke, "Venezuela Proposes Opening Oil Industry to Private Investment," *New York Times*, April 28, 1994.
18. Francisco Monaldi and Michael J. Penfold, "Institutional Collapse: The Rise and Breakdown of Democratic Governance in Venezuela," in *Venezuela Before Chávez: Anatomy of an Economic Collapse*, ed. Ricardo Hausmann and Francisco R. Rodriguez (University Park: Pennsylvania State University Press, 2014), 304 and overall.
19. Nestor Rojas, "Venezuela's Deepening Economic Crisis Frustrated President Rafael Caldera's Defiant," *UPI Archives*, December 22, 1995, https://www.upi.com/Arch ives/1995/12/22/Venezuelas-deepening-economic-crisis-frustrated-President -Rafael-Calderas-defiant/9756819608400/.
20. Paul Lewis, "Venezuela Gets Big I.M.F. Credit, Backing Market Reforms," *UPI Archives*, July 13, 1996.
21. Jorge Salazar-Carrillo and Bernadette West, *Oil and Development in Venezuela during the 20th Century* (Praeger: Westport, Conn., 2004), 238–40.
22. J. R. D. Ramirez, "Was the Apertura Petrolera in Venezuela Beneficial from the Economical Perspective?," *Oil, Gas & Energy Law* OGEL, archive issue, www.ogel .org/article.asp?key=856.
23. Kenneth Roberts, "Social Polarization and the Populist Resurgence in Venezuela," in Ellner and Hellinger, *Venezuelan Politics in the Chávez Era*, 59.
24. See the analysis of the constitution in Allan R. Brewer-Carias, *Dismantling Democracy in Venezuela: The Chávez Authoritarian Experiment* (New York: Cambridge University Press, 2010).
25. Paul Westervelt, "Venezuela's New Constitution Gives Rise to New Legal Issues on Oil, Gas Investment," *Oil and Gas Journal*, April 10, 2000.
26. Cf. Daniel H. Levine, "The Decline and Fall of Democracy in Venezuela: Ten Theses," *Bulletin of Latin American Research* 21, no. 2 (April 2002): 248–69; Andean Group Report, "Chávez Makes Conciliatory Noises After Lightning Coup and Counter-coup," *Latin American Regional Reports*, May 14, 2002; "ChevronTexaco Plans Another Facility to Process Extra-heavy Crude in Venezuela," *Oil and Gas Journal*, August 9, 2004.

229

27. Steve Striffler, "Something Left in Latin America: Venezuela and the Struggle for Twenty-First Century Socialism," in *Rethinking Revolution: Socialist Register 2017*, ed. Leo Panitch and Albo Greg (New York: New York University Press, 2016), 207–29, doi:10.2307/j.ctt1bpmbn2.13.

28. Transcript of Aló Presidente program, Sistema Bolivariana de Comunicación e Información of the Ministerio del Poder Popular para la Comunicación y la Información No. 156 from the Miraflores Palace with Rafael Ramirez, Alí Rodríguez Araque, Jorge Giordani, and Nelson Nuñez, July 13, 2003, *Aporrea*, July 14, 2003, https://www.aporrea.org/actualidad/a3852.html.

29. Cristiana Marcano and Alberto Barrera Tyszka, *Hugo Chávez: The Definitive Biography of Venezuela's Controversial President* (New York: Random House, 2007). After consolidating control, Chávez returned to his favored education policy in 2007.

30. Steve Ellner, "Organized Labor and the Challenge of *Chavismo*," in Ellner and Hellinger, *Venezuelan Politics in the Chávez Era*, 161–78. In 2003 three factors came together to facilitate a successful challenge by the *chavistas* against the CTV: the failed coup in 2002, CTV's funding by the U.S. National Endowment for Democracy, and rising oil prices.

31. Anthony Man, "After Making South Florida Home, Venezuelans Turning to Politics," *Sun Sentinel* (Florida), July 2, 2015; Peter Baker and Edward Wong, "On Venezuela, Rubio Assumes U.S. Role of Ouster in Chief," *New York Times*, January 26, 2019.

32. The "Enabling Law" had been significantly expanded under the Constitution of 1999, providing a presidential administration with significantly greater ability to influence not only the economy but also politics and society. Mario J. García-Serra, "The 'Enabling Law': The Demise of the Separation of Powers in Hugo Chavez's Venezuela," *University of Miami Inter-American Law Review* 32, no. 2 (Spring–Summer 2001): 265–93.

33. See the discussion in David R. Mares and Nelson Altamirano, "Venezuela's PDVSA and World Energy Markets," James A. Baker III Institute for Public Policy, Rice University, 2007.

34. Berry Cannon, "Venezuela, April 2002: Coup or Popular Rebellion? The Myth of a United Venezuela," *Bulletin of Latin American Research* 23, no. 3 (2004): 285–302.

35. "OPEC to Name New Venezuelan Chief After Caracas Coup," *Agence France Presse*, June 26, 2002; "Venezuela's Chávez Appoints PDVSA Saviour," *Latin America Regional Reports: Andean Group*, May 14, 2002.

36. "Ali Rodríguez: 'I Am Not Neutral,' " BBC Mundo, April 23, 2002.

37. "Venezuela Totals Losses from 2002–2003 Oil Strike," *Globe & Mail* (Toronto), July 27, 2005.

38. Thad Dunning, *Crude Democracy: Natural Resource Wealth and Political Regimes* (Cambridge: Cambridge University Press, 2008), 185–86.

39. Carter Center, "Feature: The Carter Center and the 2004 Venezuela Elections," September 15, 2004.

40. "Politizaciín de PDVSA (Discurso de Ramírez) Buen Sonido!," Youtube Video, 9:57, "Avila79," November 3, 2006, https://www.youtube.com/watch?v=2I925uJ9U48.

41. In 2009 the reelection proposal returned in simpler form and Chávez was not singled out. The referendum covered five constitutional articles, with reelection for president, national deputy, governor, state legislator, and mayor. Rory Carroll,

"Hugo Chávez Wins Referendum Allowing Indefinite Re-election," *Guardian*, February 16, 2009.

42. James Suggett, "Chávez Signs 26 Law-Decrees on Final Day of Enabling Law Power," *Venezuelanalysis*, August 5, 2008, https://venezuelanalysis.com/news/3691.

43. Rory Carroll, "Chávez Party Dominates in Venezuela Regional Elections," *Guardian*, November 24, 2008; "Top Court in Venezuela Upholds Ban on Chávez Foe," CNN, October 17, 2011; Thor Halvorssen and Larry Diamond, "Venezuela's Upcoming Election Won't Be Any Fairer than the Last One," *New Republic*, April 11, 2013.

44. World Bank, "GDP Growth," https://data.worldbank.org/indicator/NY.GDP .MKTP.KD.ZG?end=2014&locations=VE&start=2002&view=chart.

45. BP, *Statistical Review of World Energy*, June 2012, 3.

46. Brian Ellsworth and Marianna Parraga, "Venezuela Expands China Oil-for-Loan Deal to $8 Billion," *Reuters*, May 22, 2012.

47. Carter Center, *Study Mission to the October 7, 2012, Presidential Election in Venezuela: Final Report*, October 2012, 17.

48. Virginia López and Jonathan Watts, "Nicolás Maduro Narrowly Wins Venezuelan Presidential Election," *Guardian*, April 15, 2013.

49. World Bank, "Inflation, Consumer Prices (Annual %)," https://data.worldbank.org /indicator/FP.CPI.TOTL.ZG?locations=VE. Hyperinflation began in 2017 and would surpass one million in 2019.

50. Cf. Brian Ellsworth, "Former Venezuela Supreme Court Judge Flees to U.S., Denounces Maduro," *Reuters*, January 6, 2019; Rachelle Krygier, "Chávez Yes, Maduro No. The Growing Split in Venezuela," *Americas Quarterly*, September 14, 2016; Jorge Rueda and Joshua Goodman, "Venezuela Arrests Top Oil Officials in Corruption Probe," *Associated Press*, November 30, 2017, http://abcnews.go.com /International/wireStory/venezuela-arrests-top-oil-officials-corruption-probe -51485922; Bryan Bowman, "Confidante of 'Tyrants': An Interview with Former Chavez Advisor Eva Golinger," *Globe Post*, January 30, 2019, https://theglobepost .com/2019/01/30/eva-golinger-interview-venezuela/.

51. In 2017, after our period of study, Maduro held a referendum for a new constitution and a Constituent Assembly was elected, which formally replaced the National Assembly. The voting rules and the opposition's ambivalence about participating gave the government a supermajority in the new legislature.

52. "Venezuela's Maduro Talks of Shutdown of Opposition-Controlled Congress," *Associated Press*, July 8, 2016.

5. SCORING THE VARIABLES

1. The caveats about investment and price are provided in chapter 2.

2. Richard A. Haggerty, ed., *Venezuela: A Country Study* (Washington, D.C.: GPO for the Library of Congress, 1990), http://countrystudies.us/venezuela/30.htm.

3. See Juan Carlos Boué's very pessimistic conclusion to his book *Venezuela: The Political Economy of Oil* (Oxford: Oxford University Press, 1993), 197–207.

4. These were not yet commercially viable flows, but they did prove the concept. L. R. Aalund, "Technology, Money Unlocking Vast Orinoco Reserves," *Oil and Gas Journal*, October 19, 1998, https://www.ogj.com/articles/print/volume-96/issue-42

/in-this-issue/general-interest/technology-money-unlocking-vast-orinoco
-reserves.html.

5. BP, *BP Statistical Review of World Energy*, 2002, 4.

6. BP, *BP Statistical Review of World Energy*, 2003, calculated from Excel spreadsheet
from Mazama Science, https://mazamascience.com/OilExport/BP_2003.xls.

7. BP, *BP Statistical Review of World Energy*, 2018, 12; OPEC, *OPEC Bulletin*, 8–9/12,
51, https://www.opec.org/opec_web/flipbook/OB08092012/OB08092012/assets
/basic-html/page1.html; Larry B. Pascal, "Developments in the Venezuelan Hydrocarbon Sector," *Law and Business Review of the Americas* 15, 531 (2009): 554.

8. World Energy Council, "Gas in Venezuela," 2014 figures, https://www.worldenergy
.org/data/resources/country/venezuela/gas/.

9. Turnout for the 2009 constitutional reform, presidential, and parliamentary elections in 2010, 2012, 2013, and 2015 rose significantly, despite the evidence from now
numerous surveys that voice and accountability had deteriorated significantly. The
government's insistence on recipients of public benefits such as government jobs
and the opposition's expectation that international pressure was necessary to force
the government to level the playing field and recognize opposition victories probably explain the contrast between survey results and voter turnout in this latter
period.

10. Center for Systemic Peace, *Polity IV: Regime Authority Characteristics and Transitions Datasets*, Polity IV Annual Time-Series, 1800–2016, 2017: 25, http://www
.systemicpeace.org/inscrdata.html.

11. The interaction and resulting polcomp scoring is found in addendum C of the Polity IV Manual, 2016.

12. *Polity IV* description of this classification. Center for Systemic Peace, *Polity IV*, 74.

13. Steve Ellner, "Social and Political Diversity and the Democratic Road to Change
in Venezuela," *Latin American Perspectives* 40, no. 3 (May 2013): 63–82.

14. Given the crackdown on protests that escalated in 2016, when the opposition now
had a supermajority in the National Assembly, and subsequent arrests of opposition leaders, I suspect that when the next version of Polity appears, the values for
2016 will be lower. Certainly, they will have to be lower for 2017, when the National
Assembly was completely ignored by the executive and judicial branches of government and the constitution is effectively suspended while a new Constituent
Assembly purportedly works on drafts of another, more authoritarian constitution. Cf. Paul Dobson, "How Long Does It Take To Write A New Constitution?"
Venezuela Analysis, April 25, 2019, http://venezuelanalysis.com/analysis/14444.

15. Refer to chapter 2 for details on categories.

16. See https://sites.google.com/ucsd.edu/david-mares/home.

6. EXPLAINING ENERGY POLICY UNDER
A COLLAPSING PUNTO FIJO

1. Octavio Lepage and Ramón José Velázquez, the interim presidents between
Pérez's forced resignation and Caldera's second presidential term, were in office
for a combined period of less than a year and undertook no major energy
policies.

2. Miguel Tinker-Salas, "Fueling Concern: The Role of Oil in Venezuela," *Harvard International Review* 26, no. 4 (2005): 53, reports that in 1999 *Time*'s Latin America edition contained an eight-page special advertising section on PDVSA that included the statement that privatization was "almost inevitable."

3. The tension between NOC management strategies and government development strategies is a common one and can be understood within the context of a principal-agent model. Many observers critical of NOC autonomy have accused various NOCs of acting as a "state within a state." Stevens notes that "state within a state" is widely known as "the Pemex syndrome" and that Pertamina of Indonesia, as well as PDVSA, had been so labeled. See Paul Stevens, "National Oil Companies and International Oil Companies in the Middle East: Under the Shadow of Government and the Resource Nationalism Cycle," *Journal of World Energy Law & Business* 1, no. 1 (2008): 5.

4. José Enrique Arrioja, *Clientes negros: Petróleos de Venezuela bajo la generación de Shell* (Caracas: Los Libros de El Nacional, 1998). The book advances an explanation of the Apertura as developing out of staff meetings of the NOC and PDVSA president Giusti as the policy maker behind Caldera's oil and gas policies.

5. Latin American regional reports: Andean Group, November 10, 1988, 6; "Surprising about face by Pérez on oil," as cited in Mark Cupolo, "Oil and Politics in Mexico and Venezuela (1976–1992)," Ph.D. diss., University of Connecticut, 1994, 246–47; César E. Baena, *The Policy Process in a Petro-State* (Farnham, UK: Ashgate, 1999), 162.

6. Baena, *The Policy Process in a Petro-State*, 205. The author notes that a less aggressive internationalization policy benefited NOC corporate strategy, but he neither demonstrates nor claims that PDVSA moved in this direction before Pérez's pronouncements.

7. "Venezuelan Reforms Favor Oil Work," *Oil and Gas Journal*, March 19, 1990 https://www.ogj.com/articles/print/volume-88/issue-12/in-this-issue/general-interest/venezuelan-reforms-favor-oil-work.html.

8. "Venezuelan Government Actions Cloud Pdvsa's Outlook," *Oil and Gas Journal*, March 12, 1990.

9. G. Philip, "When Oil Prices Were Low: Petróleos de Venezuela (PdVSA) and Economic Policy-Making in Venezuela Since 1989," *Bulletin of Latin American Research* 18, no. 3 (July 1999): 361–76; José Enrique Arrioja, *Clientes negros: Petróleos de Venezuela Bajo la generación Shell* (Caracas: Los Libros de El Nacional, 1998), 11–80; Luisa Mercedes Palacios, "Explaining Policy Choice in the Oil Industry: A Look at Rentier Institutions in Mexico and Venezuela (1988–1999)" (Ph.D. diss., Johns Hopkins University, 2001); David R. Hults, Petróleos de Venezuela, S.A. (PDVSA): From Independence to Subservience," in *Oil and Governance: State-owned Enterprises and the World Energy Supply*, ed. David G. Victor (Cambridge University Press, 2012).

10. Their impressive biographies can be found online.

11. CORDIPLAN, *VIII Plan de la Nación*, Caracas, presented to Congress January 1990, http://cir.unet.edu.ve/files/Documentos/0020.pdf, 35–37.

12. CORDIPLAN, 35–37.

13. Baena, *The Policy Process in a Petro-State*, 210.

14. Baena, 211.

15. Juan Carlos Boué, *Venezuela: The Political Economy of Oil* (Oxford: Oxford University Press, 1993), 85.
16. Andrés Sosa Pietri, *Petróleo y Poder* (Caracas: Editorial Planeta Venezolana, 1993), 81–85.
17. Boué, *Venezuela*, 23–26; Baena, *The Policy Process in a Petro-State*, 238. Palacios, "Explaining Policy Choice in the Oil Industry," 146, is less emphatic but does note that regarding the OSAs, the president, the minister, and PDVSA all agreed and acted together.
18. Arrioja, *Clientes negros*, 87–90.
19. Arrioja, 41. Tinker-Salas, "Fueling Concern," 53, interprets Caldera's reversal to indicate the growing autonomy of PDVSA. But since Arrieta, Petkoff, and La Silvia were not PDVSA employees and Roosen had support on the PDVSA board, Giusti's appointment responds more to the role that these three Caldera advisors wanted the NOC to assume than to a plan of the NOC itself.
20. Manuel Bermúdez Romero, *PDVSA en carne Propia: Testimonio del derrumbe de la primera empresa Venezolana* (Caracas: OME Estudios de Mercado y Comunicación, 2004), 44–69. This is a standard accusation analysts hurl when an administration disagrees with the NOC—Coronel made it in 1981, Chacín in 1989.
21. Arrioja, *Clientes negros*, 48–49; Daniel Hellinger, "Resource Nationalism and the Bolivarian Revolution in Venezuela," in *The Political Economy of Natural Resources and Development: From Neoliberalism to Resource Nationalism*, ed. Paul A. Haslam and Pablo Heidrich (London: Routledge, 2016), 204–19. Hults, "Petróleos de Venezuela," 429, claims it was an NOC idea. Giusti dates the Apertura from his ascension to the NOC presidency. Luis E. Giusti, "La Apertura: The Opening of Venezuela's Oil Industry," *Journal of International Affairs* 53, no. 1 (Fall 1999): 117–28.
22. Arrioja, *Clientes negros*, 56–57, 138–39; on being a Caldera advisor, 85.
23. Arrioja, 25–28.
24. Arrioja, 53–56.
25. Arrioja, 99–100, 102.
26. Bernard Mommer, "The New Governance of Venezuelan Oil," Oxford Institute for Energy Studies, *WPM* 23 (April 1998): 28–35.
27. Baena, *The Policy Process in a Petro-State*, 158–61, 168–71, 209–10; Boué, *Venezuela*, 29.
28. Baena, *The Policy Process in a Petro-State*, 222.
29. Boué, *Venezuela*, 87; Bernard Mommer, *El mito de la Orimulsion: la valorización del crudo extrapesado de la faja petrolífera del Orinoco* (Caracas: Ministerio de Energía y Minas, 2004). Crude from these projects would not be commercial for almost a decade, so the impact of this decision was nil. By the time these crudes entered the market in the early 2000s the oil market had recovered and Venezuelan overproduction was no longer an issue.
30. Baena, *The Policy Process in a Petro-State*, 225.
31. Anne Reifenberg, "OPEC Members Boldly Violate Quotas, but See End to Limits," *Wall Street Journal*, updated April 25, 1996; Pavel Molchanov, "A Statistical Analysis of OPEC Quota Violations," Duke University, Durham, N.C., April 2003 https://sites.duke.edu/djepapers/files/2016/08/paveldje.pdf.

32. "Venezuelan Government Actions Cloud Pdvsa's Outlook," *Oil and Gas Journal,* March 12, 1990. The Chávez administration also announced at its beginning that CITGO would be sold but did not do so.

33. Arrioja, *Clientes negros,* chap. 4.

34. "New Government Rules Cloud Pdvsa Outlook," *Oil and Gas Journal,* September 2, 1991.

35. Buoé, *Venezuela,* 162–64.

36. Baena, *The Policy Process in a Petro-State,* 221.

37. CORDIPLAN, 35: "Minimizer el riesgo de colocación de los crudos y productos de menor calidad . . . mediante estratégias adecuadas de comercialización"; "Venezuelan Government Actions Cloud Pdvsa's Outlook."

38. Baena, *The Policy Process in a Petro-State,* 223–24.

39. Uisdean R. Vass and Rubén Eduardo Lujan, "Venezuela Hatching Big Plans for Jump-Starting Natural Gas Sector," *Oil and Gas Journal,* August 8, 1999, https://www.ogj.com/articles/print/volume-97/issue-32/special-report/venezuela-hatching-big-plans-for-jump-starting-natural-gas-sectorl.html.

40. CORDIPLAN, *Plan de la Nación,* 68.

41. Palacios, "Explaining Policy Choice in the Oil Industry," 158.

42. Arrioja, *Clientes negros,* 63.

43. Miriam Kornblith, *Venezuela en los 90. La crisis de la democracia* (Caracas: Ediciones IESA, 1998), 142.

44. Kornblith, *Venezuela en los 90,* 134, 145.

45. Boué, *Venezuela,* 56–58; Arrioja, *Clientes negros,* 134ff.

46. Palacios, "Explaining Policy Choice in the Oil Industry," 159.

47. Buoé, *Venezuela,* 56–58; Arrioja, *Clientes negros,* 63.

48. CORDIPLAN, *Plan de la Nación.*

49. Boué, *Venezuela,* 103–9. Boué uses the term "ordered" many times when referring to government policy for the NOC.

50. Arrioja, *Clientes negros,* 63–80.

51. "PDVSA to Choose LNG Project Partners Soon," *Oil and Gas Journal,* June 25, 1990.

52. Arrioja, *Clientes negros,* 76; Boué, *Venezuela,* 99–109; Knight-Ridder Financial, "EXXON Joins Venezuelan LNG Project," *Journal of Commerce Online,* March 10, 1991, https://www.joc.com/exxon-joins-venezuelan-lng-project_19910310.html.

53. Arrioja, *Clientes negros,* chap. 3, 65–67. It would be resurrected a decade later during the Chávez administration as the Mariscal Sucre project; see chap. 7.

54. Boué, *Venezuela,* 75–87.

55. Arrioja, *Clientes negros,* 49–50; Boué, *Venezuela,* 203–5.

56. Osmel Manzano and Francisco Monaldi, "The Political Economy of Oil Contract Renegotiation in Venezuela," in *The Natural Resources Trap: Private Investment Without Public Commitment,* ed. William Hogan and Federico Struzenegger (Cambridge, Mass.: MIT Press 2010), 439.

57. Arrioja, *Clientes negros,* 52–56.

58. "Arrieta: Private Investment in Tune with the Times," *Daily Journal* (October 1994), as cited in *Contemporary Issues in International Arbitration and Mediation: The Fordham Papers 2013,* ed. Arthur W. Rovine (Leiden: Brill/Nijhoff, 2015), 223.

59. PDVSA, *Modalidades de aperture: Empresas Mixtas*, 1995, http://www.pdvsa.com /espanol/apertura_empresas_es.html, as cited in Jose Rafael Duque Ramírez, "Was the Apertura Petrolera in Venezuela Beneficial from the Economical Perspective?," *Oil, Gas & Energy Law Intelligence*, 2003, OGEL Archive, 6.

60. Arrioja, *Clientes negros*, 102–4.

61. Arrioja, 110, 144–46.

62. Manzano and Monaldi, "Political Economy of Oil Contract Renegotiation," 23.

63. Arrioja, *Clientes negros*, 143–44; Hults, "Petroleos de Venezuela," 430, is incorrect in writing that PDVSA sold stock in PEQUIVEN in 1997. With the Chávez victory at the end of 1998, neither of these openings led to actual foreign investment.

64. Hults, "Petroleos de Venezuela," 431; Mommer, "New Governance," 70–71.

65. Index Mundi, "Venezuela Crude Oil Production by Year," using United States Energy Information Administration data, accessed January 12, 2019, https://web .archive.org/web/20190801164824/https://www.indexmundi.com/energy/?countr y=ve&product=oil&graph=production; "Venezuela: Recent Economic Developments," IMF Staff Country Report no. 98/117, October 1998, preliminary figures for 1997.

66. Manzano and Monaldi, "Political Economy of Oil Contract Renegotiation," 441.

67. "Sosa: Government Tax Burden Has Pdvsa Facing Cash Crisis," *Oil and Gas Journal*, August 26, 1991.

68. Baena, *The Policy Process in a Petro-State*, 211.

69. Bernard Mommer and Ramón Espinasa, "Venezuelan Oil Policy in the Long Run," *Energy*, East-West Center, Hawaii, 1991, 123; Manzano and Monaldi, "Political Economy of Oil Contract Renegotiation," 440–41.

70. Manzano and Monaldi, "Political Economy of Oil Contract Renegotiation," 23.

71. Mommer, "New Governance," 48.

72. Arrioja, *Clientes negros*, 122ff, 145ff.

73. Bernard Mommer, "The Political Role of National Oil Companies in Exporting Countries: The Venezuelan Case," Oxford Institute for Energy Studies, *WPM* 18 (September 1994); Manzano and Monaldi, "Political Economy of Oil Contract Renegotiation," 458.

74. Manzano and Monaldi, "Political Economy of Oil Contract Renegotiation," 445.

75. Arrioja, *Clientes negros*, 117; Manzano and Monaldi, "Political Economy of Oil Contract Renegotiation," 459.

76. Arrioja, *Clientes negros*, 145; "Venezuelan Reforms Favor Oil Work," *Oil and Gas Journal*, March 19, 1990, https://www.ogj.com/articles/print/volume-88/issue-12/in -this-issue/general-interest/venezuelan-reforms-favor-oil-work.html.

77. Mommer, Subversive Oil," in *Venezuelan Politics in the Chávez Era: Polarization and Social Conflict*, ed. Steve Ellner and Daniel Hellinger (London: Lynne Rienner, 2002), 137.

78. Ramírez, "Was the Apertura Petrolera," 14, also makes this point.

79. José Piñeda and Francisco Rodríguez, "Public Investment and Productivity Growth in the Venezuelan Manufacturing Sector," in *Venezuela Before Chávez: Anatomy of an Economic Collapse*, ed. Ricardo Hausmann and Francisco R. Rodríguez (University Park: Pennsylvania State University Press, 2014), 92. They also note that in 1993 just after Pérez's impeachment, Congress created the Intergovernmental Decentralization Fund (FIDES), funded by the Pérez value-added tax,

which required that 15 percent of these revenues go to state governments for public investment programs and projects that would be vetted by the fund's management (94). While this is not attributable to the Pérez administration, it is the same Congress and supports the hypothesis that the competitive characteristics of the decision-making unit would promote public goods.

80. As noted in table 6.1, Venezuela ceased providing the information that would permit the World Bank to calculate a Gini Index after 2006.

81. Gasoline subsidies are regressive and not public goods. See Paul Segal, "'El Petróleo Es Nuestro': La Distribución De Los Ingresos Provenientes Del Petróleo En México," James A. Baker Institute for Public Policy, Rice University April 29, 2011, 21.

82. "Chaos in Caracas," *Economist*, April 10, 1997.

83. World Bank, "GDP Growth (annual %) Venezuela," https://data.worldbank.org /indicator/NY.GDP.MKTP.KD.ZG?locations=VE; International Monetary Fund, "IMF DataMapper: Inflation Rate, Average Consumer Prices: Venezuela," https:// www.imf.org/external/datamapper/PCPIPCH@WEO/WEOWORLD/VEN.

84. Piñeda and Rodríguez, "Public Investment and Productivity Growth," 92.

7. ENERGY POLICY IN THE BOLIVARIAN REVOLUTION

1. Alí Rodríguez Araque, *Antes de que se me olivde: Conversación con Rosa Miriam Elizalde* (Havana: Editora Política, 2014), http://www.editpolitica.cu; Tim Padgett, "The Latin Oil Czar," *El Furrial*, July 18, 2004, http://content.time.com/time /magazine/article/0,9171,665069,00.html; Susie Cruz, "Venezuela Gets New Oil Minister," *Oil & Gas Journal*, December 28, 2000, https://www.ogj.com/articles /2000/12/venezuela-gets-new-oil-minister.html; Faisal Islam, "Opec Boss Tries to Pour Oil on Troubled Waters," *Guardian*, October 25, 2003; Riitta-Ilona Koivu-maeki, "Evading the Constraints of Globalization: Oil and Gas Nationalization in Venezuela and Bolivia," *Comparative Politics* 48, no. 1 (2015): 107–25, http://www .jstor.org/stable/43664172, 114; Bernard Mommer, "Subversive Oil," in *Venezuelan Politics in the Chávez Era: Polarization and Social Conflict*, ed. Steve Ellner and Daniel Hellinger (London: Lynne Rienner, 2002), 141.

2. Thomas T. Vogel Jr., "Exodus at Petroleos de Venezuela Creates Worries on Firm's Health," *Wall Street Journal*, September 3, 1999; Luis A. Pacheco, "11 de abril 2002: Como lo Recuerdo," Petroleumworld, April 19, 2009, https://vdebate.blogspot.com /2009/04/11-de-abril-como-lo-recuerdo-luis.html; Rafael Quiroz Serrano, *Meritocracia Petrolera: ¿mito o realidad?* (Caracas: Panapo, 2003), 119–20; Héctor Ciavaldini, interview, "Héctor Ciavaldini, expresidentes de Pdvsa," Intelego, June 7, 2015, http://intelego-latam.blogspot.com/2015/06/hector-ciavaldini-expres identes-de-pdvsa.html.

3. General Lameda (brigadier general, Venezuelan Army), YouTube interview, April 2002, https://www.youtube.com/watch?v=5LsL3HM-x10.

4. Christian Parenti, "Venezuela's Revolution and the Oil Company Inside," *NACLA*, September 25, 2007, https://nacla.org/article/venezuelas-revolution-and-the-oil-comp any-inside.

5. Javier Corrales and Michael Penfold, *Dragon in the Tropics: Venezuela and the Legacy of Hugo Chávez* (Washington, D.C.: Brookings Institution Press, 2015), 80.

6. PDVSA, *The New PDVSA*, http://www.pdvsa.com/, accessed August 2, 2017.

7. "Storm Over Venezuela Oil Speech," BBC News, November 4, 2006, http://news
.bbc.co.uk/2/hi/americas/6114682.stm; "Politizacion de PDVSA (Discurso de
Ramirez) Buen Sonido!," Youtube video.

8. Paul Crowney, "Ali Rodríguez of Petroleos de Venezuela: Starting Over," *Institutional Investor*, May 1, 2003, https://www.institutionalinvestor.com/article
/b151360hqtmcoq/ali-rodriguez-of-petroleos-de-venezuela-starting-over.

9. Bernard Mommer, "The Political Role of National Oil Companies in Exporting
Countries: The Case of Venezuela," *WPM* 18 (September 1994), Oxford Institute
for Energy Studies.

10. *Aló Presidente*, episode 156, aired July 13, 2003.

11. Andy Webb-Vidal, "Venezuela Buys Russia Oil to Avoid Defaulting on Deals,"
Financial Times, April 28, 2006.

12. Plan Siembra Petrolera 2005–2030 was announced in 2005 but adopted in 2006,
so it officially became Plan Siembra Petrolera 2006–2030. The PDVSA website no
longer carries the plan, but it can be reviewed in PowerPoint slides at Nelson Her-
nandez, "Plan siembra petrolera 2006–2012 (PDVSA)," *Linkedin Slideshare*,
https://es.slideshare.net/energia/plan-siembra-petrolera-20062012-pdvsa; and a
discussion is at "Plan Siembra Petrolera 2005–2030," *Rocío Ramírez un blog
petrolero*, August 20, 2014, https://rocioramirezproyectandotupetroleo.wordpress
.com/2014/08/20/plan-siembra-petrolera-2005-2030/.

13. "PDVSA Planes Estratégicos," Acto Inaugural, Hotel Caracas Hilton, Caracas,
August 18, 2005, PDVSA website, "Planes Estratégicos" tab.

14. Mommer, "Subversive Oil," 144.

15. Julián Cárdenas García, "Rebalancing Oil Contracts in Venezuela," *Cornell Law
School Inter-University Graduate Student Conference Papers*, paper 55, 2001, http://
scholarship.law.cornell.edu/lps_clacp/55 fn. 55. "Preliminary analysis shows that
by placing a cap on the royalty and export tax, the reform reduces the revenues
paid to the Venezuelan Central Bank that should be transferred to the National
Budget controlled by the Legislative. Instead, it increases payments to the
National Development Fund (FONDEN), an off-budget spending vehicle under
exclusive control of the Executive. Thus, the new redistribution seems to agree
more with government strategy seeking cash flow for the presidential elections of
2012, rather than a new balance of revenues distribution between the Government and IOCs."

16. Corrales and Penfold, *Dragon in the Tropics*, 85.

17. Business News Americas, *PDVSA: A Need for Change*, Intelligence Series, January 2014, 3, 6; Business News Americas, *Oil in Venezuela: A New Pragmatism?*,
Intelligence Series, March 2017, 5, 11, 7.

18. IESA, *Venezuela—Energy in Figures 2012: The Oil and Gas Sector*, 2012. Production figures in Venezuela are controversial, but the fact of decline has become
obvious.

19. "Presidente de Pdvsa Eulogio Del Pino Pone su Cargo a la Orden por Diferencias
con Área de Finanzas," infovzla, April 14, 2015, http://infovzla.net/nacionales
/presidente-de-pdvsa-eulogio-del-pino-pone-su-cargo-a-la-orden-por-diferen
cias-con-area-de-finanzas/. Del Pino exchanged positions with Oil Minister Nelson Martínez in August 2017, then both were arrested in November 2017. In

December 2018 Martínez died in custody. As of February 2021, Del Pino remained in jail, awaiting trial: "Jailed Ex-Venezuela Oil Minister Nelson Martinez Dies," "Confirman el juicio del exministro de Petróleo de Venezuela Eulogio del Pino" Agencia EFE, 10 de febrero de 2021 https://es-us.finanzas.yahoo.com /noticias/confirman-juicio-exministro-petr%C3%B3leo-venezuela-212803451 .html. Maduro turned in 2017 (after our study period) to National Guard general Manuel Quevedo (an active officer, unlike retired general Lameda) to run the NOC as a militarized organization to make it productive without increasing its budget or paying its workers a decent wage. See Alexandra Ulmer and Marianna Parraga, "Special Report: Oil Output Goes AWOL in Venezuela as Soldiers Run PDVSA," *Reuters*, December 26, 2018.

20. Mommer, "Subversive Oil," 140.

21. BP, *Statistical Review of World Energy*, June 2002, 6.

22. Mommer, "Subversive Oil," 136.

23. "Global Market Brief: Venezuela: Selling Citgo Assets to Hedge U.S. Influence," Stratfor, February 7, 2005, https://worldview.stratfor.com/article/global-market -brief-venezuela-selling-citgo-assets-hedge-us-influence; "Ramírez: Citgo es un pésimo negocio," *El Universal*, October 27, 2010; Mike Stone, "Venezuela Taps Lazard to Sell Citgo Petroleum—Sources," *Reuters*, August 12, 2014; "PDVSA Seeking Offers for CITGO," *CSP Daily News*, September 10, 2014, https://www .cspdailynews.com/mergers-acquisitions/pdvsa-seeking-offers-citgo.

24. "PDVSA en el mundo," PDVSA, http://www.pdvsa.com/index.php?option=com _content&view=article&id=6516&Itemid=579&lang=es.

25. Julian Dowling, "PDVSA, Enarsa to buy Rhasa distributor for US$92mn," *Business News Americas*, September 30, 2005, http://www.bnamericas.com/en/news /oilandgas/PDVSA,_Enarsa_to_buy_Rhasa_distributor_for_US*92mn.

26. The fifteen countries in Petrocaribe are Antigua and Barbuda, Bahamas, Belize, Cuba, Dominica, Grenada, Guyana, Haiti, Jamaica, Domincan Republica, Saint Christopher and Nieves, Santa Lucía, Saint Vincent and the Grenadines, Surinam, and Venezuela. Haiti was incorporated in November 2005, and Cuba maintains credit conditions that do not follow Petrocaribe rules. Cuba started barter agreements in 2000.

27. Daniel Hellinger, "Resource Nationalism and the Bolivarian Revolution in Venezuela," in *The Political Economy of Natural Resources: From Neoliberalism to Resource Nationalism*, ed. Paul A. Haslam and Pablo Heidrich (London: Routledge, 2016), 214–16.

28. "Venezuela Suspends Oil Delivery to Antigua and Barbuda and Others," *Daily Observer* (Antigua), June 12, 2018, https://antiguaobserver.com/venezuela-suspends -oil-delivery-to-antigua-and-barbuda-and-others/; "Fin para el sueño chavista en la Argentina: a la filial local de PDVSA le quedan pocas estaciones y está en rojo financiero," *Infobae*, June 5, 2019, https://www.infobae.com/economia/2019/06/05 /fin-para-el-sueno-chavista-en-la-argentina-a-la-filial-local-de-pdvsa-le-quedan -pocas-estaciones-y-esta-en-rojo-financiero/.

29. Marianna Párraga and Jeanne Liendo, "Exclusive: As Venezuelans Suffer, Maduro Buys Foreign Oil to Subsidize Cuba," *Reuters*, May 15, 2018, https://www.reuters .com/article/us-venezuela-oil-imports-exclusive/exclusive-as-venezuelans-suffer -maduro-buys-foreign-oil-to-subsidize-cuba-idUSKCN1IG1TO.

30. IEA, *South American Gas: Daring to Tap the Bounty* (Paris: OECD Publishing, 2003), 191, https://doi.org/10.1787/9789264195820-en.

31. Benedict Mander, "Fears Over Chávez Threaten Oil Auction," *Financial Times*, August 30, 2009. Carlos Camacho, "PDVSA Seeks Deltana Block 1 Partner, Sees Early Output at 200Mf3/d," *Business News Americas*, May 31, 2006. The auctions for three blocks in the Carabobo area were finally held in 2010 after three postponements, but only two blocks were awarded.

32. EIA, "Country Analysis Briefs-Venezuela," March 2011, http://www.eia.gov/cabs/venezuela/NaturalGas.html.

33. Energy Intelligence Service, "Venezuela's Gas Potential Entices Investors," *Business News Americas*, July 2011; "The Chavez Gas Revolution Is Still Pending," *Free Library*, November 23, 2009, https://www.thefreelibrary.com/The+Chavez+Gas+Revolution+Is+Still+Pending.-a0212699229.

34. Nathan Crooks, "LNG Investments to Hit US$19.6bn, JVs Include Chevron, Gazprom, and Eni," *Business News Americas*, September 19, 2008.

35. "Venezuela Signs Perla Gas Deal with Eni and Repsol," *LNG World News*, December 25, 2011, http://www.lngworldnews.com/venezuela-signs-perla-gas-deal-with-eni-and-repsol/.

36. EIA, "Country Analysis Brief: Venezuela," June 2018; Nathan Crooks, "Analysis: Natural Gas Mega Fields Could Take Years to Develop," *Business News Americas*, September 15, 2009.

37. EIA, "Country Analysis Brief: Venezuela," June 2018.

38. Reuters Caracas, "Gas: Venezuela prepara una ley para estatizar la extracción," December 24, 2010, *El Cronista Comercial* FACTIVE Document SABICR002010 1224e6c00000m.

39. Constitución de la República Bolivariana de Venezuela, articles 12, 302, 303, http://pdba.georgetown.edu/Parties/Venezuela/Leyes/constitucion.pdf. Translation my own.

40. "PDVSA Privatization of Subsidiary Motivated by Capital Needs—Analyst," *Business News Americas*, March 1, 2012.

41. "Venezuela Sells Oil Stake to China's Citic," *Latin Finance*, February 29, 2012, https://www.latinfinance.com/daily-briefs/2012/2/29/venezuela-sells-oil-stake-to-chinas-citic.

42. Hellinger, "Resource Nationalism," 204, 213.

43. Decree with Rank and Force of Organic Law of Gaseous Hydrocarbons, *Gaceta Oficial*, no. 36.793, September 23, 1999. Uisdean R. Vass and Rubén Eduardo Lujan, "Venezuela Hatching Big Plans for Jump-Starting Natural Gas Sector." *Oil and Gas Journal*, August 8, 1999. Mommer, "Subversive Oil," 141, attributes the gas law to Alí Rodríguez Araque.

44. The Gas Law defines natural gas and gaseous hydrocarbons differently: gaseous hydrocarbons are defined as "hydrocarbons that, under standard pressure and temperature conditions, are found in gaseous state and come either from reservoirs or from any of the transformation processes of such hydrocarbons"; natural gas is defined as "a gaseous hydrocarbon mix coming from natural hydrocarbon reservoirs, the production of which may or may not be associated to the production of crude petroleum, condensates, or other fossils." Adriana Lezcano Huncal and Gabriela Rachadell de Delgado, "The Impact of the Organic Hydrocarbons

Law on the Venezuelan Natural Gas Industry," OGEL 2 (2008), www.ogel.org /article.asp?key=2756, 3, n. 5.

45. Lezcano Huncal and Rachadell de Delgado, 4–5, 9.

46. "Venezuela Hatching Big Plans for Jump-Starting Natural Gas Sector," *Oil & Gas Journal*, August 9, 1999.

47. "Decree with Rank and Force of Organic Law of Hydrocarbons," *Gaceta Oficial*, no. 37.323, November 13, 2001.

48. Mommer, "Subversive Oil," 141, says Silva Calderon consulted; Coronel Gustavo Coronel, "Re Venezuela: A Letter to Time Padgett, a TIME Journalist," Venezuela in Crisis blog, July 21, 2004, attributes the Hydrocarbon Law to both Silva Calderon and Rodríguez.

49. Alberto F. Ravell, "A Brief Overview of Venezuela's Oil Policies" *Lex Petrolera*, fourth quarter (2011), King and Spaulding LLP, https://s3.amazonaws.com /documents.lexology.com/55dc1112-a8aa-48da-82aa-73290c805b3f.pdf, 9–11; Mommer, writing from Oxford, also noted that year that "in Venezuela new Hydrocarbon Laws are not retroactive." Bernard Mommer, "Venezuelan Oil Policy at the Crossroads," Oxford Institute for Energy Studies, 2001, https://www.oxfordenergy .org/publications/venezuelan-oil-politics-at-the-crossroads/.

50. La Asamblea Nacional de la República Bolivariana de Venezuela, "Acuerdo mediante el cual se autoriza la celebración del Convenio de Asociación para la producción de Bitumen, diseño, construcción y operación de un módulo de producción y emulsificación de Bitumen natural para la elaboración de Orimulsión, entre las empresas Bitúmenes Orinoco, S.A. (BITOR) y la empresa China National Oil and Gas Exploration and Development Corporation (CNODC)." *Gaceta Oficial* de la República Bolivariana de Venezuela, no. 37.347 (December 17, 2001), 10. http:// historico.tsj.gob.ve/gaceta/diciembre/171201/171201-37347-10.html.

51. John Keffer and María Victoria Vargas, "Venezuela: Migrating Away from the Apertura Petrolera," *Oil, Gas & Energy Law Intelligence* 6, no. 2 (April 2008).

52. República Bolivariana de Venezuela, Asamblea Nacional, "Informe que presenta ante la Asamblea Nacional, La Comisión Especial para Investigar las Irregularidades Detectadas por el Ministero de Energia y Petróleo, Cometidas en la Formulación, Celebración y Ejecución de los Convenios Operativos, Asociaciones Estratégicas y Negocios de Internacionalización," March 29, 2006.

53. Rafael Ramírez, "Discurso de Rafael Ramírez, Presidente de PDVSA y Ministro de Energía y Petróleo, ante la Asamblea Nacional," May 25, 2005, www.aporrea.org /energia/a14338.html.

54. República Bolivariana de Venezuela, Asamblea Nacional, "Informe que presenta ante la Asamblea Nacional," March 29, 2006.

55. Osmel Manzano and Francisco Monaldi, "Political Economy of Oil Contract Renegotiation in Venezuela," in *The Natural Resources Trap: Private Investment Without Public Commitment*, ed. William Hogan and Federico Sturzenegger (Cambridge, Mass.: MIT Press 2010), 443; Justin Dargin, "Investor-State Relations in the Chavez Age: The Nature of Resource Nationalism in the 21st Century," Harvard University, John F. Kennedy School of Government, May 2010, 22–27.

56. Dargin, "Investor-State Relations in the Chavez Age," 17.

57. Venezolana de Televisión, *Aló Presidente*, "PDVSA Strategic Planning: Opening Ceremony," Caracas, Hotel Caracas Hilton, August 18, 2002, 21, www.alopresidente .gob.ve.

58. "Empresa estatal Petrolera busca empresas mixtas," *Associated Press*, April 22, 2006 https://oklahoman.com/article/1823858/empresa-estatal-petrolera-venezol ana-busca-empresas-mixtas?

59. Bernard Mommer, "ExxonMobil Is Isolated," *En Confianza*, interview by Ernesto Villegas, Venezolana de Television (VTV), Caracas, February 12, 2008, http://www .pdvsa.com/index.php?tpl=interface.sp/design/readmenu.tpl.html&newsid_obj _id=5532&newsid_temas=80.

60. Riitta-Ilona Koivumaeki, "Evading the Constraints of Globalization: Oil and Gas Nationalization in Venezuela and Bolivia" *Comparative Politics* 48, no. 1 (October 2015): 114.

61. Corina Rodríguez Pons, "Este año PDVSA será socio mayoritario en empresas de la Faja del Orinoco," *El Nacional*, August 30, 2006.

62. "Decree With Rank, Value and Force of Law of Migration to Mixed Companies of the Association Agreements of the Orinoco Oil Belt, as Well as the Risk and Profit Sharing Exploration Agreements," Decree no. 5,200, *Gaceta Oficial*, no. 38,632, February 26, 2007.

63. Manzano and Monaldi, "Political Economy of Oil Contract Renegotiation," 443–44.

64. Ministerio del Poder Popular para la Energía y Petróleo, "El 1º de mayo PDVSA recupera soberanía total en la Faja Petrolífera del Orinoco," *Contacto con la nueva PDVSA: Boletín informativo sobre la industria petrolera venezolana*, no. 11 (February 2007): 10.

65. Añez Jhonny et al., "Mercado Interno de los Hidrocarburos en Venezuela," Universidad Santa Maria, Caracas, November 22, 2013, https://usmpetrolero.wordpress .com/2012/06/20/mercado-interno-venezolano-grupo-4/.

66. "Decreto No. 356, Decreto con Rango y Fuerza de Ley de Promoción y Protección de Inversiones," *Gaceta Oficial*, no. 5,390 (Extraordinario), October 22, 1999.

67. Manzano and Monaldi, "Political Economy of Oil Contract Renegotiation," 442.

68. Manzano and Monaldi, "Political Economy of Oil Contract Renegotiation."

69. Peter Wilson, "Chávez Sees a Gusher in a Windfall Tax," *Business Week*, February. 21, 2008, as cited in Dargin, "Investor-State Relations in the Chávez Age," 20.

70. Grant Hanessian et al, "Investment-State Disputes in the Oil and Gas Sector in Bolivia, Ecuador and Venezuela," *The Global Oil and Gas Report*, Baker and McKenzie (February 2009), as cited in Dargin, "Investor-State Relations in the Chavez Age," 19.

71. Manzano and Monaldi, "Political Economy of Oil Contract Renegotiation," 442–43.

72. Mayela Armas H. and Marianna Parraga, "AN aprobó reforma de ISLR para sector petrolero," *El Universal*, August 30, 2006.

73. Manzano and Monaldi, draft version of "Political Economy of Oil Contract Renegotiation," 27. This fact was left out of the published version.

74. Carlos Bellorín, "Venezuela's Petroleum Fiscal and Contractual Regime Flexibility Provisions: 10 Years of the 2001 Hydrocarbons Organic Law: A View of the

Current State of Affairs," *International Association for Energy Economics*, third quarter (2011): 41.

75. Cárdenas García, "Rebalancing Oil Contracts in Venezuela."

76. Manzano and Monaldi, "Political Economy of Oil Contract Renegotiation in Venezuela," 445.

77. Staff reporters, "PDVSA Privatization of Subsidiary Motivated by Capital Needs—Analyst," *Business News Americas*, March 1, 2012; "Venezuela Sells Oil Stake to China's Citic."

78. In 2017 the NOC offered Rosneft the same deal. Alexandra Ulmer and Marianna Parraga, "Exclusive: Venezuela's Cash-Strapped PDVSA Offers Rosneft oil stake—sources," *Reuters*, March 16, 2017.

79. Benedict Mander, "Venezuela Secures $80bn Oil Investment," *Financial Times*, February 16, 2010, cited in Dargin, "Investor-State Relations in the Chavez Age," 33–35.

80. Riitta-Ilona Koivumaeki, "Evading the Constraints of Globalization: Oil and Gas Nationalization in Venezuela and Bolivia," *Comparative Politics* 48, no. 1 (October 2015): 114, 115.

81. Bellorín, "Venezuela's Petroleum Fiscal and Contractual Regime."

82. Vass and Lujan, "Venezuela Hatching Big Plans"; IEA, *South American Gas*.

83. IEA, *South American Gas*, 191.

84. Marianna Párraga, "Cuatro firmas participarán en licitación proyecto gas Venezuela," *Reuters*, February 15, 2011.

85. Tamara Pearson, "Venezuelan Government Expropriates Petroleum Related Activities," *Venezuelanalysis.com*, May 9, 2009, https://venezuelanalysis.com/news /4434; Nathan Crooks, "Ensco on Track with Chevron Rig Mobilization," *Business News Americas*, February 4, 2009.

86. Nathan Crooks, "Reports: Ramírez Calls for Probe Into Chevron Award," *Business News Americas*, June 24, 2009. After failing to get Chevron to accept questionable purchase orders, the Maduro administration in 2017–2018 temporarily arrested local management on charges later dropped. Alexandra Ulmer, Marianna Párraga, Ernest Scheyder, "Chevron Evacuates Venezuela Executives Following Staff Arrests," *Reuters*, April 25, 2018, https://www.reuters.com/article/us-venezuela -oil-chevron-insight/chevron-evacuates-venezuela-executives-following-staff -arrests-idUSKBN1HW2BD.

87. IESA, *Venezuela—Energy in Figures 2012: The Oil and Gas Sector*, 2012, 11–12, https://www.yumpu.com/en/document/view/53560497/venezuela-energy-in -figures-servicios-iesa.

88. W. Neuman, "Venezuela, in Quiet Shift, Gives Foreign Partners More Control in Oil Ventures," *New York Times*, October 9, 2014, as cited in Hellinger, "Resource Nationalism," 216.

89. Juan Cristobal Nagel, "One Man's 'Acuerdo' Is Another Man's 'Privatización,'" *Caracas Chronicles*, May 27, 2013, https://www.caracaschronicles.com/2013/05/27 /one-mans-acuerdo-is-another-mans-privatizacion/.

90. Juan Cristobal Nagel, "The Small Print," *Caracas Chronicles*, June 12, 2013, https:// www.caracaschronicles.com/2013/06/12/the-small-print/; Francisco Toro, "The End of a Long Debate," *Caracas Chronicles*, June 13, 2013, http://caracaschronicles .com/2013/06/13/the-end-of-a-long-debate/.

91. Deisy Buitrago, "Update 1-Schlumberger Extends Venezuela's PDVSA $1 bln Credit Line," *Reuters*, May 24, 2013.

92. Julián de Cárdenas García, "The New Integrated Oil Service Contracts in a Venezuela in Dire Straits," *Journal of Energy & Natural Resources Law* 35, no. 4 (2017): 417–31, https://doi.org/10.1080/02646811.2017.1371412.

93. Mark Weisbrot and Luis Sándoval, "The Venezuelan Economy in the Chávez Years," Center for Economic and Policy Research, July 2007, https://cepr.net /documents/publications/venezuela_2007_07.pdf.

94. Transcript of *Aló Presidente* program, Sistema Bolivariana de Comunicación e Información of the Ministerio del Poder Popular para la Comunicación y la Información No. 156 from the Miraflores Palace with Rafael Ramírez, Alí Rodríguez Araque, Jorge Giordani, and Nelson Nuñez, July 13, 2003, *Aporrea*, https://www .aporrea.org/actualidad/a3852.html.

95. Data on the missions are hard to collect, thereby reinforcing the notion that they are private, not public, goods. For evidence of discriminatory practices and general opaqueness of how decisions regarding missions are made, see Matthew Rhodes-Purdy, "Participatory Populism: Theory and Evidence from Bolivarian Venezuela," *Political Research Quarterly* 68, no. 3 (September 2015): 415–27.

96. A group of sympathetic economists proposed an adjustment plan to Maduro, but he rejected it. The program is discussed in Mark Weisbrot, "Venezuela's Economic Crisis: Does It Mean That the Left Has Failed?," *Truthout*, October 23, 2016, https:// truthout.org/articles/venezuela-s-economic-crisis-does-it-mean-that-the-left -has-failed/.

CONCLUSIONS

1. Argus Media reported that "49.9pc of the PdV Holding shares is pledged to Rosneft for a $1.5bn oil-backed loan," in "PdV Gasoline Imports, DCO Exports Soar in Sept," October 19, 2018, https://www.argusmedia.com/en/news/1776557-pdv-gaso line-imports-dco-exports-soar-in-sept; also, "PdV Signs Offtake Deals with Delaware Firm," *Argus Media*, January 2, 2019, https://www.argusmedia.com/en/news /1820607-pdv-signs-offtake-deals-with-delaware-firm; Corina Ponds, "Exclusive: Venezuela Signs Oil Deals Similar to Ones Rolled Back Under Chávez—Document," *Reuters*, September 10, 2018, https://www.reuters.com/article/us-venezuela-oil-excl usive/exclusive-venezuela-signs-oil-deals-similar-to-ones-rolled-back-under-cha vez-document.

2. George Philip, "When Oil Prices Were Low: Petróleos De Venezuela (PdVSA) and Economic Policy-Making in Venezuela Since 1989," *Bulletin of Latin American Research* 18, no. 3 (1999): 361–76, https://doi.org/10.1111/j.1470-9856.1999 .tb00140.x; Hults, "Petróleos de Venezuela, S.A.: From Independence to Subservience," in *Oil and Governance: State-owned Enterprises and the World Energy Supply*, ed. David G. Victor et al. (Cambridge: Cambridge University Press, 2012), 450.

3. Dargent claims that technocratic autonomy, present in Colombia since the 1960s, explains the shift toward pro-market nationalism in the 2000s. But clearly

technocratic autonomy did not stop the shift in the 1980s and 1990s toward stat-ist nationalism, so its explanatory power is weak. Eduardo Dargent, "Agents or Actors? Assessing the Autonomy of Economic Technocrats in Colombia and Peru," *Comparative Politics* 43, no. 3 (April 2011): 318–19.

4. Carolina A. Fornos, Timothy J. Power, and James C. Garland, "Explaining Voter Turnout in Latin America, 1980 to 2000," *Comparative Political Studies* 37, no. 8 (2004): 909–40; Evaristo Tomás Acuña, "Colombia entre la crisis de la representatividad y la democracia directa," paper presented at the International Conference on Direct Democracy in Latin America, *Research Center on Direct Democracy*, Buenos Aires, March 14–15, 2006, as cited in Anita Breuer, "Policy-making by Referendum in Presidential Systems: Evidence from the Bolivian and Colombian Cases," *Latin American Politics and Society* 50, no. 4 (Winter 2008): 77.

5. For 2002, Registraduria Nacional de Colombia, "National Summary of Votes and Seats," Legislative elections of March 10, 2002, http://psephos.adam-carr.net /countries/c/colombia/colombia20022.txt; for 2006; "National Summary," Legis-lative elections of March 12, 2006, http://psephos.adam-carr.net/countries/c /colombia/colombia2006pres.txt.

6. Registraduria Nacional de Colombia, "Changes in Congressional Representation 1998–2002," legislative elections of March 10, 2002, http://psephos.adam-carr.net /countries/c/colombia/colombia20023.txt.

7. Registraduria Nacional de Colombia, http://psephos.adam-carr.net/countries/c /colombia/colombia2006.txt.

8. Luz María Sierra, "Álvaro Uribe: Un presidente de Teflón la estrategia de opin-ión pública que lo hizo inmune a las crisis," in *De Uribe, Santos y otras especies políticas: Comunicación de gobierno en Colombia, Argentina y Brasil*, ed. Omar Rincón and Catalina Uribe (Bogota: Universidad de Los Andes, Colombia, 2015), 67.

9. Polity IV, *Country Report 2010: Colombia*, 3–4, http://www.systemicpeace.org /polity/Colombia2010.pdf.

10. "Uribe Starts with Congress Behind Him; Liberals Seek to Reclaim Him, No Real Opposition," *Latin American Weekly Report*, June 11, 2002, as cited in Breuer, "Pol-icymaking by Referendum," 78.

11. Breuer, "Policymaking by Referendum," 79–80; Laura Gamboa, "Opposition at the Margins: Strategies Against the Erosion of Democracy in Colombia and Venezu-ela," *Comparative Politics* 49, no. 4 (July 2017): 457–77.

12. Polity IV, *Country Report 2010: Colombia*, 2–3.

13. See my website, https://sites.google.com/ucsd.edu/david-mares/home.

14. José V. Zapata Lugo and Claro M. Cotes Ricciulli, "Colombia," in *Oil and Gas Law Review* (October 2008): 78.

15. Ecopetrol, http://www.ecopetrol.com.co/english/documentos/41462_Ley_1118 _de_2006.pdf.

16. Presidencia de la República, "Gobierno Uribe tiene un impacto favorable en la reducción de la pobreza," September 29, 2006, https://web.archive.org/web /20070929132215/http://noticias.presidencia.gov.co/sne/2005/febrero/12/03122005 .htm.

17. Povcal Net, the online tool for poverty measurement developed by the Development Research Group of the World Bank, http://iresearch.worldbank.org/Pov calNet/home.aspx.
18. Povcal Net.
19. See the discussion in chapter 2.

BIBLIOGRAPHY

Aalund, L. R. "Technology, Money Unlocking Vast Orinoco Reserves." *Oil and Gas Journal*, October 19, 1998. https://www.ogj.com/articles/print/volume-96/issue-42/in-this-issue/general-interest/technology-money-unlocking-vast-orinoco-reserves.html

Abbott, Jared, Hillel Soifer, and Matthias Vom Hau. "Transforming the Nation? The Bolivarian Education Reform in Venezuela." *Journal of Latin American Studies* 49, no. 4 (2017): 885–916. doi: 10.1017/S0022216X17000402.

AFP News. "Bolivia Cancels Lithium Deal with German Firm," November 4, 2019. https://www.ibtimes.com/bolivia-cancels-lithium-deal-german-firm-2859668.

Agence France Presse. "OPEC to Name New Venezuelan Chief After Caracas Coup," June 26, 2002.

Agencia Venezolana de Noticias (AVN). "Safe Homeland Plan Reduced Murders by 55% in Caracas Parish," May 20, 2013. http://www.avn.info.ve/node/173225.

Al Jazeera. "Jailed ex-Venezuela Oil Minister Nelson Martínez Dies." December 12, 2018. https://www.aljazeera.com/news/2018/12/13/jailed-ex-venezuela-oil-minister-nelson-martinez-dies.

Al-Kasim, Farouk. *Managing Petroleum Resources: The "Norwegian Model" in a Broad Perspective*. Oxford: Oxford Institute for Energy Studies, 2006.

Aló Presidente. "Episode 156." Aired July 13, 2003. Transcription available at https://www.aporrea.org/actualidad/a3852.html.

Alonso, Jorge. "The Energy Reform: A Great Loss and a Betrayal." *Revista Envio* 390 (January 2014). http://envio.org.ni/articulo/4807.

Alvarez, Angel E. "Comité de Organización Política Electoral Independiente (COPEI)." In *Partidos Políticos de América Latina: Países Andinos*, ed. Manuel Alcántara and Flavia Feidenberg, 510–13. Mexico City: Fondo de Cultura Económica, 2003.

Americas Quarterly. "Argentina to Pay Repsol for YPF Nationalization," April 25, 2014.

Ames, Barry. *Political Survival: Politicians and Public Policy in Latin America*. Berkeley: University of California Press, 1990.

Andean Group. "Chávez Makes Conciliatory Noises After Lightning Coup and Counter-Coup." *Latin American Regional Reports*, May 14, 2002.

——. "Venezuela's Chávez Appoints PDVSA Saviour." *Latin America Regional Reports*, May 14, 2002.

Anderson, Kym. "Introduction." In *Finishing Global Farm Trade Reform: Implications for Developing Countries*, 1–5. South Australia: University of Adelaide Press, 2017. http://www.jstor.org/stable/10.20851/j.ctt1sq5wc5.8.

Andreasson, Stefan. "Varieties of Resource Nationalism in Sub-Saharan Africa's Energy and Minerals Markets," *The Extractive Industries and Society* 2, no. 2 (April 2015): 310–19. https://doi.org/10.1016/j.exis.2015.01.004.

Añez, Jhonny, et al. "Mercado Interno de los Hidrocarburos en Venezuela." *Usmpetrolero y estadístico*, November 22, 2013. https://usmpetrolero.wordpress.com/2012/06/20/mercado-interno-venezolano-grupo-4/.

Aranzazu García García, Maria. "Alianza Bolivariana para los Pueblos de Nuestra América (ALBA)." *InterNaciones* 6, no. 19 (July–December 2020): 221–47.

Arce Rojas, David. "Colombia Towards a New Petroleum Contractual Regime." *Revista Colombiana de Derecho Internacional*, no. 3 (June 2004): 252–74.

Ardizzone, Mariana. "Argentina." In *Latin American Upstream Oil and Gas: A Practical Guide to the Law and Regulation*, ed. Fernando Fresco and Eduardo G. Pereira, 15–24. London: Glove Business Publishing, 2015.

Argus Media. "PdV Gasoline Imports, DCO Exports Soar in Sept," October 19, 2018. https://www.argusmedia.com/en/news/1776557-pdv-gasoline-imports-dco-exports-soar-in-sept.

——. "PdV Signs Offtake Deals with Delaware Firm," January 2, 2019. https://www.argusmedia.com/en/news/1820607-pdv-signs-offtake-deals-with-delaware-firm.

Armas, Mayela, and Marianna Párraga. "AN aprobó reforma de ISLR para sector petrolero." *El Universal*, August 30, 2006.

Arrioja, José Enrique. *Clientes negros: Petróleos de Venezuela Bajo la generación Shell*. Caracas: Los Libros de El Nacional, 1998.

Ascher, William. *Why Governments Waste Natural Resources: Policy Failures in Developing Countries*. Baltimore: Johns Hopkins University Press, 1999.

Assies, Willem. "David Versus Goliath in Cochabamba: Water Rights, Neoliberalism, and the Revival of Social Protest in Bolivia." *Latin American Perspectives* 30, no. 3 (2003): 14–36.

Associated Press. "Empresa Estatal Petrolera Busca Empresas Mixtas." April 22, 2006 https://oklahoman.com/article/1823858/empresa-estatal-petrolera-venezolana-busca-empresas-mixtas?

——. "Venezuela's Maduro Talks of Shutdown of Opposition-Controlled Congress." July 8, 2016.

Axton, Matilda F., Rogers P. Churchill, Francis C. Prescott, John G. Reid, NoO. Sappington, Louis E. Gates, and Shirely L. Phillips. *Foreign Relations of the United States, 1939*. Vol. 5: *The American Republics*. Washington, D.C.: United States Government Printing Office, 1957).

Baena, César E. *The Policy Process in a Petro-State: An Analysis of Pdvsa's (Petroleos de Venezuela SA's) Internationalism Strategy*. Farnham, UK: Ashgate, 1999

Baer, Werner. "Import Substitution and Industrialization in Latin America: Experiences and Interpretations." *Latin American Research Review* 7, no. 1 (Spring 1972): 95–122.

Baker, Peter, and Edward Wong. "On Venezuela, Rubio Assumes U.S. Role of Ouster in Chief." *New York Times*, January 26, 2019.

BBC News. "Storm Over Venezuela Oil Speech." November 4, 2006. http://news.bbc .co.uk/2/hi/americas/6114682.stm.

——. "Venezuela's Maduro Breaks Diplomatic Links with Panama." March 6, 2014.

BBD Mundo. "Ali Rodríguez: 'I Am Not Neutral.'" April 23, 2002.

Bechelli, Carlos M. "Gas del Estado." In *Petróleo y Gas '88: Argentina, País Para Inversiones Petroleras*, Centro Internacional de Información Empresaria, 27–33. Buenos Aires: Ediciones CIEE, 1989.

Beck Furnish, Dale. "Peruvian Domestic Law Aspects of the La Brea Y Pariñas Controversy." *Kentucky Law Journal* 59 (1970): 351. http://ssrn.com/abstract=1428605.

Bellorín, Carlos. "Venezuela's Petroleum Fiscal and Contractual Regime Flexibility Provisions: 10 Years of the 2001 Hydrocarbons Organic Law: A View of the Current State of Affairs." *International Association for Energy Economics* (third quarter, 2011).

Berrios, Rubén, Andrea Marak, and Scott Morgenstern. "Explaining Hydrocarbon Nationalization in Latin America: Economics and Political Ideology." *Review of International Political Economy* 18, no. 5 (December 2011): 673–97.

Billing, Trey. "Government Fragmentation, Administrative Capacity, and Public Goods: The Negative Consequences of Reform in Burkina Faso." *Political Research Quarterly* 72, no. 3 (September 2019): 669–85.

Bin Turki Bin Faisal Al Saud, Faisal, His Royal Highness Prince of Saudi Arabia. "Perspectives on the Saudi Arabian Energy Industry." Speech at Royal Institute of International Affairs in London, UK, December 2, 2000. http://www.saudiembassy.net /archive/2000/speeches/page0.aspx.

Bonfiglioli, Angelo. "Empowering the Poor." United Nations Capital Development Fund, 2003. http://unpan1.un.org/intradoc/groups/public/documents/un/unpan010168.pdf

Bonvecchi, Alejandro, and Emilia Simison. "Legislative Institutions and Performance in Authoritarian Regimes." *Comparative Politics* 49, no. 4 (July 2017): 521–39.

Bordoff, Jason. "The 2020 Oil Crash's Unlikely Winner: Saudi Arabia." *Foreign Policy*. May 5, 2020.

Boué, Juan Carlos. *Venezuela: The Political Economy of Oil*. Oxford: Oxford University Press, 1993.

Bowman, Bryan. "Confidante of 'Tyrants': An Interview with Former Chavez Advisor Eva Golinger." *Globe Post*, January 30, 2019. https://theglobepost.com/2019/01/30/eva -golinger-interview-venezuela/.

BP. *BP Statistical Review of World Energy*. June 2002.

——. *BP Statistical Review of World Energy*. June 2012.

——. *BP Statistical Review of World Energy*. June 2018.

Bremmer, Ian, and Robert Johnston. "The Rise and Fall of Resource Nationalism." *Survival* 51, no. 2 (March 2009): 152. doi:10.1080/00396330902860884.

Breuer, Anita. "Policymaking by Referendum in Presidential Systems: Evidence from the Bolivian and Colombian Cases." *Latin American Politics and Society* 50, no. 4 (2008): 59–89. https://doi.org/10.1111/j.1548-2456.2008.00030.x.

Brewer-Carias, Allan R. *Dismantling Democracy in Venezuela: The Chavez Authoritarian Experiment*. New York: Cambridge University Press, 2010.

Bridge, Gavin, and Philippe Le Billon. *Oil.* Malden, Mass.: Polity Press, 2013.

Bridges. "TRIMS & Local Content" 12, no. 3 (May 1, 2008). International Centre for Trade and Sustainable Development. https://www.ictsd.org/bridges-news/bridges /news/trims-local-content.

Brogan, Christopher. "The Retreat from Oil Nationalism in Ecuador 1976–1983." Working Papers 13, Institute of Latin American Studies, University of London, 1984. http://sas-space.sas.ac.uk/3401/1/B51_-_The_Retreat_from_Oil_Nationalism_in _Ecuador_1976-1983.pdf.

Brooke, James. "Venezuela Proposes Opening Oil Industry to Private Investment." *New York Times*, April 28, 1994.

Brown, Jonathan C. "Jersey Standard and the Politics of Latin American Oil Production, 1911–30." In *The Oil Business in Latin America: The Early Years*, ed. John D. Wirth, 1–50. Lincoln: University of Nebraska Press, 1985.

——. "The Structure of the Foreign-Owned Petroleum Industry in Mexico, 1880–1938." In *The Mexican Petroleum Industry in the Twentieth Century*, ed. Jonathan C. Brown and Alan Knight, 3. Austin: University of Texas Press 1992.

Buchanan, James M., Robert D. Tollison, and GordonTullock. *Toward a Theory of the Rent-Seeking Society.* College Station: Texas A&M University Press, 1980.

Bucheli, Marcelo. "Multinational Oil Companies in Colombia and Mexico: Corporate Strategy, Nationalism, and Local Politics, 1900–1951." Paper presented at the International Economic History Conference, Helsinki, 2006.

Bueno de Mesquita, Bruce, James D. Morrow, Randolph M. Siverson, and Alastair Smith. "Political Institutions, Policy Choice and the Survival of Leaders." *British Journal of Political Science*, 32, no. 4 (October 2002): 561.

Bueno de Mesquita, Bruce, and Alastair Smith. "Political Succession: A Model of Coups, Revolution, Purges, and Everyday Politics." *Journal of Conflict Resolution* 61, no. 4 (April 2017): 707–43.

Bueno de Mesquita, Bruce, Alastair Smith, Randolph M. Siverson, and James D. Morrow. *The Logic of Political Survival.* Cambridge, Mass.: MIT Press, 2003. doi:https:// doi.org/10.7551/mitpress/4292.001.0001

Buitrago, Deisy. "UPDATE 1-Schlumberger Extends Venezuela's PDVSA $1 Bln Credit Line." *Reuters,* May 24, 2013. https://www.reuters.com/article/venezuela-schlumb erger/update-1-schlumberger-extends-venezuelas-pdvsa-1-bln-credit-line-idUSL 2N0E51MA20130524.

Bulletin of Latin American Research. "Special Issue: Old and New Populism in Latin America." 19, no. 2 (2000).

Business News Americas. "Oil in Venezuela: A New Pragmatism?" Intelligence Series. March 2017.

——. "PDVSA: A Need for Change." Intelligence Series. January 2014.

——. "PDVSA Privatization of Subsidiary Motivated by Capital Needs—Analyst," March 1, 2012.

——. "Sustaining Bolivias [*sic*] Natural Gas Bonanza." Oil & Gas Intelligence Series, August 31, 2016.

Calvert, Peter. "Venezuela: The FALN/FLN." In *Democracy and Counterterrorism: Lessons from the Past*, ed. Robert J. Art and Louise Richardson, 167–94. Washington, D.C.: U.S. Institute of Peace, 2007.

Camacho, Carlos. "PDVSA Seeks Deltana Block 1 Partner, Sees Early Output at 200Mf3/d." *Business News Americas*, May 31, 2006.

Campodónico, Humberto. *La Política Petrolera 1970–1985: El Estado, Las Contratistas y PetroPeru*. Lima: Centro de Estudios y Promoción del Desarrollo, 1986.

Cannon, Berry. "Venezuela, April 2002: Coup or Popular Rebellion? The Myth of a United Venezuela." *Bulletin of Latin American Research* 23, no. 3 (2004): 285–302.

Cárdenas García, Julián. "The New Integrated Oil Service Contracts in a Venezuela in Dire Straits." *Journal of Energy & Natural Resources Law* 35, no. 4 (2017): 417–31. https://doi.org/10.1080/02646811.2017.1371412.

——. "Rebalancing Oil Contracts in Venezuela." *Cornell Law School Inter-University Graduate Student Conference Papers* 55. 2011. https://scholarship.law.cornell.edu/lps_clacp/55.

Carroll, Rory. "Chávez Party Dominates in Venezuela Regional Elections." *Guardian*, November 24, 2008.

——. "Hugo Chávez Wins Referendum Allowing Indefinite Re-Election." *Guardian*, February 16, 2009.

Carruthers, David, and Patricia Rodríguez. "Mapuche Protest, Environmental Conflict and Social Movement Linkage in Chile." *Third World Quarterly* 30, no. 4 (2009): 743–60.

Carter Center. "Feature: The Carter Center and the 2004 Venezuela Elections." September 15, 2004.

——. *Study Mission to the October 7, 2012, Presidential Election in Venezuela: Final Report*. October 2012.

Cawood, F. T., and O. P. Oshokoya. "Resource Nationalism in the South African Mineral Sector: Sanity Through Stability." *Journal of the Southern African Institute of Mining and Metallurgy* 113, no. 1 (2013): 45–52.

Center for Systemic Peace. "Country Report 2010: Colombia." *Polity IV*. http://www.systemicpeace.org/polity/Colombia2010.pdf.

——. *Polity IV: Regime Authority Characteristics and Transitions Datasets*. Polity IV Annual Time-Series, 1800–2016. http://www.systemicpeace.org/inscrdata.html.

Chaloping-March, Minerva. "The Mining Policy of the Philippines and 'Resource Nationalism' Towards Nation-Building." *Journal de la Société des Océanistes* 138–39 (2014): 93–106.

Chávez, Hugo. "Aló Presidente Program." By Rafael Ramírez, Alí Rodríguez Araque, Jorge Giordani, and Nelson Nuñez. *Sistema Bolivariana de Comunicación e Información of the Ministerio del Poder Popular para la Comunicación y la Información*, no. 156, from the Miraflores Palace (July 13, 2003). Transcript published July 14, 2003 by Aporrea. https://www.aporrea.org/actualidad/a3852.html.

Chernykh, Lucy. "Profit or Politics? Understanding Renationalizations in Russia." *Journal of Corporate Finance* 17 (2011): 1237–53.

Childs, John. "Geography and Resource Nationalism: A Critical Review and Reframing." *The Extractive Industries and Society* 3, no. 2 (April 2016): 539–46. https://doi.org/10.1016/j.exis.2016.02.006.

CIDOB. "Carlos Andrés Pérez Rodríguez." (Barcelona, Spain) n.d. https://www.cidob.org/es/content/pdf/1795, accessed March 17, 2021.

Claes, Dag Harald. "Globalization and State Oil Companies: The Case of Statoil." *Journal of Energy and Development* 29, no. 1 (Autumn 2003): 43–64.

CNN. "Top Court in Venezuela Upholds Ban on Chávez Foe," October 17, 2011.

Collier, David, and Steve Levitsky. "Democracy with Adjectives: Conceptual Innovation in Comparative Research." *World Politics* 49, no. 3 (April 1997): 430–45.

Congreso de Colombia, "Ley 1118 de 2006," December 27, 2006. https://www.funcion publica.gov.co/eva/gestornormativo/norma.php?i=68321

Consejo Supremo Electoral: Secretaria General. "Elecciones Presidenciales Cuadro Comparativo 1958–2000 (Voto Grande)." *Consejo Nacional Electoral.* http://www .cne.gob.ve/web/documentos/estadisticas/e006.pdf.

Coppedge, Michael. *Strong Parties and Lame Ducks: Presidential Partyarchy and Factionalism in Venezuela.* Stanford, Calif.: Stanford University Press, 1997.

——. "Venezuela: Conservative Representation Without Conservative Parties." Working Paper no. 268. Notre Dame, Ind.: Kellogg Institute for International Studies, June 1999.

——. "Venezuela: Democratic Despite Presidentialism." In *The Crisis of Presidential Democracy,* ed. Juan Linz and Arturo Valenzuela. Baltimore: Johns Hopkins University Press, 1994.

Coronel, Gustavo. *The Nationalization of the Venezuelan Oil Industry: From Technocratic Success to Political Failure.* Lexington, Mass.: Lexington Books, 1983.

——. "Re Venezuela: A Letter to Tim Padgett, a TIME Journalist." *Venezuela in Crisis* blog, July 21, 2004. http://www.vcrisis.com/index.php?content=letters/200407221142.

Corporación Latinobarómetro. "Informe Latinobarómetro 2007" and "Informe 2008." https://www.latinobarometro.org/lat.jsp.

Corrales, Javier. *Presidents Without Parties: The Politics of Economic Reform in Argentina and Venezuela in the 1990s.* College Park: Pennsylvania State University Press, 2002.

Corrales, Javier, and Michael Penfold. *Dragon in the Tropics: Venezuela and the Legacy of Hugo Chávez.* Washington, D.C.: Brookings Institution Press, 2015.

Cote, Stephen C. *Oil and Nation: A History of Bolivia's Petroleum Sector (Energy and Society).* Morgantown: West Virginia University Press, 2016.

Crisp, Brian F. *Democratic Institutional Design: The Powers and Incentives of Venezuelan Politicians and Interest Groups.* Stanford, Calif.: Stanford University Press, 2000.

——. "Lessons from Economic Reform in the Venezuelan Democracy." *Latin American Research Review* 33, no. 1 (1998): 7–41.

Crisp, Brian F., and Daniel H. Levine. "Democratizing the Democracy? Crisis and Reform in Venezuela." *Journal of InterAmerican and World Affairs* 40, no. 2 (Summer 1998): 27–61.

Crooks, Nathan. "Analysis: Natural Gas Mega Fields Could Take Years to Develop." *Business News Americas,* September 15, 2009.

——. "Ensco on Track with Chevron Rig Mobilization." *Business News Americas,* February 4, 2009.

——. "LNG Investments to Hit US$19.6 Bn, JVs Include Chevron, Gazprom, and Eni." *Business News Americas,* September 19, 2008.

——. "Reports: Ramírez Calls for Probe Into Chevron Award." *Business News Americas,* June 24, 2009.

Crowney, Paul. "Ali Rodríguez of Petróleos de Venezuela: Starting Over." *Institutional Investor*, May 1, 2003. https://www.institutionalinvestor.com/article/b15136ohqtmcoq /ali-rodriguez-of-petroleos-de-venezuela-starting-over.

Cruz, Susie. "VenezuelaGets New Oil Minister." *Oil & Gas Journal*, December 28, 2000. https://www.ogj.com/articles/2000/12/venezuela-gets-new-oil-minister.html.

CSP Daily News. "PDVSA Seeking Offers for CITGO," September 10, 2014. https://www .cspdailynews.com/mergers-acquisitions/pdvsa-seeking-offers-citgo.

Cumbers, Andrew. "North Sea Oil, the State and Divergent Development in the United Kingdom and Norway." In *Flammable Societies: Studies on the Socio-economics of Oil and Gas*, ed. McNeish John-Andrew and Logan Owen, 221–42. London: Pluto Press, 2012.

Cummings, Peter M. M. "Democracy and Student Discontent: Chilean Student Protest in the Post Pinochet Era." *Journal of Politics in Latin America* 7, no. 3 (2015): 49–84.

Cupolo, Mark. "Oil and Politics in Mexico and Venezuela (1976–1992)." Ph.D. diss., University of Connecticut, 1994.

Daily Observer. "Venezuela Suspends Oil Delivery to Antigua and Barbuda and Others." June 12, 2018. https://antiguaobserver.com/venezuela-suspends-oil-delivery-to -antigua-and-barbuda-and-others/.

Dargent, Eduardo. "Agents or Actors? Assessing the Autonomy of Economic Technocrats in Colombia and Peru." *Comparative Politics* 43, no. 3 (April 2011): 318–19. https://doi.org/10.5129/001041511795274913.

Dargin, Justin. "Investor-State Relations in the Chávez Age: The Nature of Resource Nationalism in the 21st Century." John F. Kennedy School of Government, Harvard University, May 2010.

Davison, Ann, Chris Hurst, and Robert Mabro. *Natural Gas: Governments and Oil Companies in the Third World*. Oxford: Oxford University Press, 1988.

Day, David T. "Petroleum and Natural Gas." In *The Mineral Industry*, vol. 29 (1929), 514–19.

de Alencar Xavier, Yanko Marcius. "Legal Models of Petroleum and Natural Gas Ownership in Brazilian Law." In *Property and the Law in Energy and Natural Resources*, ed. Aileen McHarg, Barry Barton, Adrian Bradbrook, and Lee Godden, 223–26. Oxford: Oxford University Press, 2010.

de Krivoy, Ruth. *Collapse: The Venezuelan Banking Crisis of '94*. Washington, D.C.: Group of 30, 2000.

——. "The Venezuelan Banking Crisis—Epilogue." Toronto Centre. Accessed January 13, 2019. http://siteresources.worldbank.org/EXTFINANCIALSECTOR/Resou rces/282884-1239831335682/6028531-1239831365859/K2_Toronto_Center_Venezu ela_Bkg_Epil.pdf.

Defensa de PetroPerú. "Historia." Accessed February 13, 2014. http://defensadepetroperu .blogspot.com/p/resena-historica.html.

DeShazo, Peter. "Bolivia." In *Energy Cooperation in the Western Hemisphere: Benefits and Impediments*, ed. Sidney Weintraub, 341. Washington, D.C.: CSIS, 2007.

Desmet, Klaus, Ignacio Ortuño-Ortín, and Shlomo Weber. "Peripheral Diversity: Transfers Versus Public Goods." *Social Choice and Welfare* 49, no. 3/4 (December 2017): 788.

Detomasi, David A. "Review: Mapping the Governance Terrain." *International Studies Review* 8, no. 1 (March 2006): 101–3.

Dittrick, Patrick. "CNOOC Withdraws Bid for Unocal, Citing Politics." *Oil and Gas Journal*, August 2, 2005. http://www.ogj.com/articles/print/volume-103/issue-30 /general-interest/cnooc-withdraws-bid-for-unocal-citing-politics.html.

Dobbs, Richard, Jeremy Oppenheim, Adam Kendall, Fraser Thompson, Martin Bratt, and Fransje van der Marel. *Reverse the Curse: Maximizing the Potential of Resource-Driven Economies.* McKinsey Global Institute, December 2013. https:// www.mckinsey.com/~/media/McKinsey/Industries/Metals%20and%20Mining /Our%20Insights/Reverse%20the%20curse%20Maximizing%20the%20poten tial%20of%20resource%20driven%20economies/MGI_Reverse_the_curse_Full _report.ashx.

Dobson, Paul. "How Long Does It Take to Write a New Constitution?" *Venezuelan Analysis*, April 25, 2019. https://venezuelanalysis.com/analysis/14444.

Dowling, Julian. "PDVSA, Enarsa to Buy Rhasa Distributor for US$92mn." *Business News Americas*, September 30, 2005. http://www.bnamericas.com/en/news/oila ndgas/PDVSA,_Enarsa_to_buy_Rhasa_distributor_for_US*92mn

Dryzek, John S. "Political Inclusion and the Dynamics of Democratization." *American Political Science Review* 90, no. 1 (September 1996): 475–87.

Dunning, Thad. *Crude Democracy: Natural Resource Wealth and Political Regimes.* Cambridge: Cambridge University Press, 2008.

Durán, Esperanza. "Pemex: The Trajectory of a National Oil Policy." In *The Oil Business in Latin America: The Early Years*, ed. John D. Wirth, 167–75. Philadelphia: Beard Books, 2001.

Ecopetrol. "Our History." Updated November 10, 2014. https://www.ecopetrol.com.co /wps/portal/web_es/ecopetrol-web/our-company/about-us/ecopetrol-about/our -history.

EIA. "Country Analysis Brief: Venezuela." Updated June 21, 2018. https://www.eia.gov /international/content/analysis/countries_long/Venezuela/archive/pdf/venezu ela_2018.pdf.

——. "Oil and Natural Gas Resource Categories Reflect Varying Degrees of Certainty." July 17, 2014. https://www.eia.gov/todayinenergy/detail.php?id=17151.

El Economista. "'Bonos Ciudadanos' la Alternativa para Pemex." May 11, 2011. https:// www.eleconomista.com.mx/economia/Bonos-ciudadanos-la-alternativa-para -Pemex-20110511-0096.html.

El Universal. "Ramírez: Citgo es un pésimo negocio." October 27, 2010.

Ellner, Steve. "Organized Labor and the Challenge of Chavismo." In *Venezuelan Politics in the Chávez Era: Class, Polarization, and Conflict*, ed. Steve Ellner and Daniel Hellinger, 161–78. Boulder, Colo.: Lynne Rienner, 2003.

——. "Social and Political Diversity and the Democratic Road to Change in Venezuela." *Latin American Perspectives* 40, no. 3 (2013): 63–82. https://doi.org/10.1177 /0094582x13476002.

Ellsworth, Brian. "Former Venezuela Supreme Court Judge Flees to U.S., Denounces Maduro." *Reuters*, January 6, 2019.

Ellsworth, Brian, and Marianna Párraga. "Venezuela Expands China Oil-for-Loan Deal to $8 Billion." *Reuters*, May 22, 2012.

Energy Intelligence Service. "Venezuela's Gas Potential Entices Investors." *Business News Americas*, July 2011.

Engen, Ole Andreas, Oluf Langhelle, and Reidar Bratvold. "Is Norway Really Norway?" In *Beyond the Resource Curse*, ed. Shaffer Brenda and Ziyadov Taleh, 259–80. Philadelphia: University of Pennsylvania Press, 2012.

Ernst & Young Global Limited. *Global Oil and Gas Tax Guide*. June 2015. http://www .ey.com/Publication/vwLUAssets/EY-2015-Global-oil-and-gas-tax-guide/$FILE /EY-2015-Global-oil-and-gas-tax-guide.pdf.

European Commission. "Directive 94/22/EC of the European Parliament and of the Council of 30 May 1994." *Official Journal of the European Communities*. L164/4. Brussels, Belgium, May 30, 1994. http://eur-lex.europa.eu/legal-content/EN/ALL /?uri=CELEX%3A31994L0022.

Ewell, Judith. *Venezuela: A Century of Change*. Stanford, Calif.: Stanford University Press, 1984.

Farthing, Linda. "An Opportunity Squandered? Elites, Social Movements, and the Government of Evo Morales." *Latin American Perspectives* 46, no. 1 (January 2019): 212–229. doi:10.1177/0094582X18798797.

Federal Research Division, Library of Congress. *Colombia: A Country Study*. http:// www.country-data.com/cgi-bin/query/r-3059.html.

Ferrell Wainberg, Miranda, Michelle Michot Foss, Mariano Gurfinkel, and Gürcan Gülen. "Commercial Frameworks for National Oil Companies." Working paper, CEE-UT, University of Texas, Austin, March 2007. https://www.beg.utexas.edu/files /cee/legacy/CEE%20National_Oil_Company_Mar%2007.pdf.

Finnemore, Martha, and Kathryn Sikkink. "International Norm Dynamics and Political Change." *International Organization* 52, no. 4 (Autumn 1998): 887–917.

Fornos, Carolina A., Timothy J. Power, and James C. Garand. "Explaining Voter Turnout in Latin America, 1980 to 2000." *Comparative Political Studies* 37, no. 8 (2004): 909–40.

Fréchette, Guillaume R., and John H. Kagel. "Pork Versus Public Goods: An Experimental Study of Public Good Provision Within a Legislative Bargaining Framework." *Economic Theory* 49, no. 3, Symposium on Political Economy (April 2012): 779–800.

Free Library. "The Chávez Gas Revolution Is Still Pending." November 23, 2009. https:// www.thefreelibrary.com/The+Chavez+Gas+Revolution+Is+Still+Pending.-a02126 99229.

Fundar: Centro de Análisis e Investigación. "La izquierda mexicana está unida en la defensa del petróleo nacional: Sandoval." Note 3760. Accessed September 20, 2009. http://www.fundar.org.mx/c_e/notas.htm.

Gamboa, Laura. "Opposition at the Margins: Strategies Against the Erosion of Democracy in Colombia and Venezuela." *Comparative Politics* 49, no. 4 (July 2017): 457–77. https://doi.org/10.5129/001041517821273044.

García Sánchez, Guillermo José. "The Fine Print of the Mexican Energy Reform." In *Mexico's New Energy Reform*, ed. Duncan Wood, 36–52. Washington, D.C.: Mexico Institute, Woodrow Wilson International Center for Scholars, October 2018.

García-Serra, Mario J. "The "Enabling Law': The Demise of the Separation of Powers in Hugo Chávez's Venezuela." *University of Miami Inter-American Law Review* 32, no. 2 (Spring–Summer 2001): 265–93.

Garrido, Alberto. *De la Guerrilla al Militarismo: Revelaciones del Comandante Arias Cárdenas*. Mérida, Venezuela: Producciones Karol, 2000.

Gary, Ian, and Terry Lynn Karl. *Bottom of the Barrel: Africa's Oil Boom and the Poor.* Catholic Relief Services, June 2003. http://www.puaf.umd.edu/faculty/rosencranz/Week1/oil_report_full.pdf.

Geddes, Barbara. *Politician's Dilemma: Building State Capacity in Latin America.* Berkeley: University of California Press, 1994.

Gershenson, Antonio. *El Petróleo de México: La Disputa del Futuro.* Mexico City: Random House Mondadori, 2010.

Giusti, Luis E. "La Apertura: The Opening of Venezuela's Oil Industry." *Journal of International Affairs* 53, no. 1 (1999): 117–28. http://www.jstor.org/stable/24357788.

Global CCS Institute. "Canadian Property Rights Relating to CCS." Accessed August 18, 2017.

Globe & Mail (Toronto). "Venezuela Totals Losses from 2002–2003 Oil Strike." July 27, 2005.

Gobierno Bolivariano de Venezuela. "Decree with Rank and Force of Organic Law of Gaseous Hydrocarbons." No. 36.793. *Gaceta Oficial,* September 23, 1999.

——. "Decree with Rank and Force of Organic Law of Hydrocarbons." No. 37.323. *Gaceta Oficial,* November 13, 2001.

——. "Decree with Rank, Value and Force of Law of Migration to Mixed Companies of the Association Agreements of the Orinoco Oil Belt, as Well as the Risk and Profit Sharing Exploration Agreements." No. 38.632. *Gaceta Oficial,* February 26, 2007.

——. "Decreto No. 356, Decreto con Rango y Fuerza de Ley de Promoción y Protección de Inversiones." No. 5.390 (Extraordinario). *Gaceta Oficial,* October 22, 1999.

——. Ministerio de Poder Popular de Petróleo. PDVSA website. http://www.pdvsa.com/.

Goldstein, Andrea. "The Emergence of Multilatinas: The Petrobras Experience." *Universia Business Review,* first quarter (2010): 98–111.

Gonzales, José Juan. "The Scope and Limits of the Principles of National Property in Mexico." In *Property and the Law in Energy and Natural Resources,* ed. Aileen McHarg, Barry Barton, Adrian Bradbrook, and Lee Godden, 210–21. Oxford: Oxford University Press, 2010.

González-Jacome, Jorge. "The Assault on Classical Legal Thought in Colombia (1886–1920)." Ms., 2009. http://works.bepress.com/jorge_gonzalez_jacome/14.

González Vargas, José. "Luisa Ortega Díaz: The Venezuelan Opposition's Unlikely Ally." *Americas Quarterly,* August 23, 2017.

Gould, Jens Erik. "Cuba Would Welcome U.S. Oil Companies if Embargo Ends (Update 2)." Bloomberg.com, April 3, 2009. www.bloomberg.com/apps/news?pid=20601103&sid=aSIKErkORLLA&refer=us#.

Grayson, George W. "The San José Oil Facility: South-South Cooperation." *Third World Quarterly* 7, no. 2 (1985): 390–409.

Grindle Merilee S., and John W. Thomas. *Public Choices and Policy Change: The Political Economy of Reform in Developing Countries.* Baltimore: Johns Hopkins University Press, 1991.

Guasch, J. Luís, and Pablo Spiller. *Managing the Regulatory Process: Design, Concepts, Issues, and the Latin America and Caribbean Story.* Washington, D.C.: World Bank, 1999.

Gudynas, Eduardo. "Si Eres Tan Progresista ¿Por Qué Destruyes la Naturaleza? Neoextractivismo, Izquierda y Alternativas." *Ecuador Debate* 79 (2010): 61–81.

Haggard, Stephan. *Elements in the Politics of Development*. Cambridge: Cambridge University Press, 2021.

Haggerty, Richard A., Howard I Blutstein, and Library of Congress. *Venezuela: A Country Study*. Washington, D.C.: Federal Research Division, Library of Congress: 1993. https://www.loc.gov/item/92010376/ for pdf. http://countrystudies.us/venezuela/24.htm.

Halvorssen, Thor, and Larry Diamond. "Venezuela's Upcoming Election Won't Be Any Fairer than the Last One." *New Republic*, April 11, 2013.

Hanessian, Grant, et al. "Investment-State Disputes in the Oil and Gas Sector in Bolivia, Ecuador and Venezuela." *Global Oil and Gas Report*. Baker and McKenzie, February 2009

Harder, Amy, and Lynn Cook. "Congressional Leaders Agree to Lift 40-Year Ban on Oil Exports." *Wall Street Journal*, updated December 16, 2015.

Haslam, Paul A., and Pablo Heidrich, *The Political Economy of Natural Resources and Development: From Neoliberalism to Resource Nationalism*. London: Routledge, 2016.

Hellinger, Daniel. "Resource Nationalism and the Bolivarian Revolution in Venezuela." In *The Political Economy of Natural Resources: From Neoliberalism to Resource Nationalism*, ed. Paul A. Haslam and Pablo Heidrich, 204–19. London: Routledge, 2016.

Hernández, Nelson. "Plan siembra petrolera 2006–2012 (PDVSA)." PowerPoint presentation, March 2006. *Linkedin Slideshare*. https://es.slideshare.net/energia/plan-siembra-petrolera-20062012-pdvsa.

Hindery, Derrick. *From Enron to Evo: Pipeline Politics, Global Environmentalism, and Indigenous Rights in Bolivia*. Tucson: University of Arizona Press, 2013.

Hirschman, Albert O. "The Turn to Authoritarianism in Latin America and the Search for Its Economic Determinants." In *The New Authoritarianism in Latin America*, ed. David Collier, 61–98. Princeton, N.J.: Princeton University Press, 1979.

Hirschman, Albert O. *Journeys Toward Progress*. New York: Norton, 1973.

Hirst, Joel D. "A Guide to ALBA." *Americas Quarterly*, n.d. Accessed March 15, 2021. https://www.americasquarterly.org/a-guide-to-alba/.

Holland, Nick. "Resource Nationalism Can Mean Growth and Prosperity." *Business Day*, August 16, 2013. http://www.bdlive.co.za/opinion/2013/08/16/resource-nationalism-can-mean-growth-and-prosperity.

Hults, David R. "Petróleos de Venezuela, S.A. (PDVSA): From Independence to Subservience." In *Oil and Governance: State-owned Enterprises and the World Energy Supply*, ed. David G. Victor et al. Cambridge: Cambridge University Press, 2012.

Huncal Lezcano, Adriana, and Gabriela Rachadell de Delgado. "The Impact of the Organic Hydrocarbons Law on the Venezuelan Natural Gas Industry." *OGEL* 2 (2008). www.ogel.org/article.asp?key=2756.

Hydrocarbons Technology. "Refinería de Cartagena (Reficar) Refinery Expansion." Accessed April 1, 2018. https://www.hydrocarbons-technology.com/projects/refineria-de-cartagena-reficar-refinery-expansion/.

IEA. *South American Gas: Daring to Tap the Bounty*. Paris: OECD Publishing, 2003. https://doi.org/10.1787/9789264195820-en.

IESA. *Venezuela—Energy in Figures 2012: The Oil and Gas Sector*. 2012. https://www.yumpu.com/en/document/view/53560497/venezuela-energy-in-figures-servicios-iesa.

Index Mundi. "Venezuela Crude Oil Production by Year (Thousand Barrels per Day). Accessed January 12, 2019. https://web.archive.org/web/20190801164824/https://www.indexmundi.com/energy/?country=ve&product=oil&graph=production.

Indridason, Indridi H. "Executive Veto Power and Credit Claiming: Comparing the Effects of the Line-Item Veto and the Package Veto." *Public Choice* 146, no. 3/4 (March 2011): 375–94.

Infobae. "Fin para el sueño chavista en la Argentina: a la filial local de PDVSA le quedan pocas estaciones y está en rojo financiero." June 5, 2019. https://www.infobae.com/economia/2019/06/05/fin-para-el-sueno-chavista-en-la-argentina-a-la-filial-local-de-pdvsa-le-quedan-pocas-estaciones-y-esta-en-rojo-financiero/.

Inkpen, Andrew, and Michael H. Moffett. *The Global Oil & Gas Industry: Management, Strategy and Finance.* Tulsa, Okla.: PennWell, 2011.

Intelego. "Héctor Ciavaldini, Expresidentes de Pdvsa." June 7, 2015. http://intelego-latam.blogspot.com/2015/06/hector-ciavaldini-expresidentes-de-pdvsa.html

International Monetary Fund. "IMF DataMapper: Inflation Rate, Average Consumer Prices: Venezuela." https://www.imf.org/external/datamapper/PCPIPCH@WEO/WEOWORLD/VEN. 1.

——. "Venezuela: Recent Economic Developments." Staff Country Report No. 98/117. Washington, D.C.: IMF, 1998.

Internet Archive. "Gobierno Uribe tiene un impacto favorable en la reducción de la pobreza." https://web.archive.org/web/20070929132215/http://noticias.presidencia.gov.co/sne/2005/febrero/12/03122005.htm.

Islam, Faisal. "Opec Boss Tries to Pour Oil on Troubled Waters." *Guardian*, October 26, 2003. https://www.theguardian.com/business/2003/oct/26/oilandpetrol.venezuela.

Jacobs, Justin. "Brazil's Pre-salt Promise." *Petroleum Economist*, November 2, 2017. https://www.petroleum-economist.com/articles/upstream/exploration-production/2017/brazils-pre-salt-promise.

James A. Baker III Institute for Public Policy. *The Changing Role of National Oil Companies in International Energy Markets.* Baker Institute Policy Report 35, Rice University, April 2007.

Jastreblansky, Maia. "Enarsa: Un joven funcionario de Alicia Kirchner Encabezará la Empresa con la que de vido manejó millones." *La Nación*, March 3, 2020.

Jia, Suzhe, Perrine Toledano, and Sophie Thomashauseen. "Local Content: Norway—Petroleum." Columbia Center on Sustainable Investment (CCIS). May 2016. http://ccsi.columbia.edu/files/2014/03/Local-Content-Norway-Petroleum-CCSI-May-2016.pdf.

Joc.com. "Exxon Joins Venezuelan LNG Project." March 10, 1991. https://www.joc.com/exxon-joins-venezuelan-lng-project_19910310.html

Joffé, George, Paul Stevens, Tony George, Jonathan Lux, and Carol Searle. "Expropriation of Oil and Gas Investments: Historical, Legal and Economic Perspectives in a New Age of Resource Nationalism." *Journal of World Energy Law & Business* 2, no. 1 (2009): 4.

Johnston, Daniel. *International Petroleum Fiscal Systems and Production Sharing Contracts.* Tulsa, Okla.: PennWell, 1994. https://web.archive.org/web/20080516050159/http://www.total.com/en/corporate-social-responsibility/Ethical-Business-Principles/Financial-transparency/contractual_arrangements_13289.htm.

Joseph, Liana. "Review: Challenges in Effective Governance of Natural Resources." *Conservation Biology* 26, no. 3 (June 2012): 578–79.

Jubak, Jim. "Is Exxon Mobil's Future Running Dry?" "Jubak's Journal," *MSN Money*, May 9, 2008. https://web.archive.org/web/20111117211618/http://articles.moneycentral.msn.com/Investing/JubaksJournal/IsExxonMobilsFutureRunningDry.

Kadir, M. Y. Aiyub, and Alexander Murray. "Resource Nationalism in the Law and Policies of Indonesia: A Contest of State, Foreign Investors, and Indigenous Peoples." *Asian Journal of International Law* 9, no. 2 (July 2019): 298–333. https://doi.org/10.1017/S204425131900002X.

Kaese, Fynn, and Jonas Wolff. "Piqueteros After the Hype: Unemployed Movements in Argentina, 2008–2015." *European Review of Latin American and Caribbean Studies* 102 (October 2016): 47–68. http://doi.org/10.18352/erlacs.10112.

Kaiman, Jonathan. "China Agrees to Invest $20bn in Venezuela to Help Offset Effects of Oil Price Slump." *Guardian*, January 8, 2015.

Karl, Terry Lynn. "The Paradox of Plenty: Oil Booms and Petro-States." *Journal of International Affairs* 53, no. 1 (Fall 1999): 31–48.

Kaufmann, Daniel, Aart Kraay, and Massimo Mastruzzi. "The Worldwide Governance Indicators: Methodology and Analytical Issues." Policy Research Working Papers 5430, World Bank, Development Research Group, Macroeconomics and Growth Team, September 2010.

Keffer, J. L., and M. V. Vargas. "Venezuela: Migrating Away from the Apertura Petrolera." Oil, Gas & Energy Law Intelligence, *OGEL* 2 (2008). https://www.ogel.org/article.asp?key=2755.

Klapp, Merrie Gilbert. *The Sovereign Entrepreneur: Oil Policies in Advanced and Less Developed Capitalist Countries*. Ithaca, N.Y.: Cornell University Press, 1987.

——. "The State—Landlord or Entrepreneur?" *International Organization* 36, no. 3 (Summer 1982): 575–607.

Knight, Alan. "The Politics of the Expropriation." In *Mexican Petroleum Industry in the Twentieth Century*, ed. Jonathan C. Brown and Alan Knight, 90–128. Austin: University of Texas Press, 1993.

Kobrin, Stephen J. "Expropriation as an Attempt to Control Foreign Firms in LDCs: Trends from 1960–1979." *International Studies Quarterly* 28, no. 3 (September 1984): 329–48.

——. "Foreign Enterprise and Forced Divestment in the LDCs." *International Organization* 34, no. 1 (Winter 1980): 65–88.

Koch, Natalie, and Tom Perreault. "Resource Nationalism." *Progress in Human Geography* 43, no. 4 (2019): 611–31. https://doi.org/10.1177/0309132518781497.

Koivumaeki, Riitta-Ilona. "Evading the Constraints of Globalization: Oil and Gas Nationalization in Venezuela and Bolivia." *Comparative Politics* 48, no. 1 (2015): 107–25. http://www.jstor.org/stable/43664172.

Kornblith, Miriam. *Venezuela en los 90: La crisis de la democracia*. Caracas: Ediciones IESA, 1998.

Kornblith, Miriam, and Daniel H. Levine. "Venezuela: The Life and Times of the Party System." In *Building Democratic Institutions: Party Systems in Latin America*, ed. Scott Mainwaring and Timothy R. Scully, 37–71. Stanford, Calif.: Stanford University Press, 1995.

Krause, Enrique. *Por una democracia sin adjetivos*. Mexico City: Joaquín Mortiz/Planeta, 1986.

Kretzschmar, Gavin L., Axel Kirchner, and Liliya Sharifzyanova. "Resource Nationalism—Limits to Foreign Direct Investment." *Energy Journal* 31, no. 2 (2010): 27–52.

Krygier, Rachelle. "Chávez Yes, Maduro No. The Growing Split in Venezuela." *Americas Quarterly* (September 14, 2016). https://www.americasquarterly.org/article/chavez-yes-maduro-no-the-growing-split-in-venezuela/.

La Asamblea Nacional de la República Bolivariana de Venezuela. "Acuerdo mediante el cual se autoriza la celebración del Convenio de Asociación para la producción de Bitumen, diseño, construcción y operación de un módulo de producción y emulsificación de Bitumen natural para la elaboración de Orimulsión, entre las empresas Bitúmenes Orinoco, S.A. (BITOR) y la empresa China National Oil and Gas Exploration and Development Corporation (CNODC)." *Gaceta Oficial* de la República Bolivariana de Venezuela, no. 37.347 (December 17, 2001): 10. http://historico.tsj.gob.ve/gaceta/diciembre/171201/171201-37347-10.html.

Lajous, Adrián. "Mexican Oil Reform: The First Two Bidding Rounds, Farmouts and Contractual Conversions in a Lower Oil Price Environment." Center on Global Energy Policy, Columbia University, October 2015.

Lalander, Rickard. "The Impeachment of Carlos Andrés Pérez and the Collapse of Venezuelan Partyarchy." In *Presidential Breakdowns in Latin America: Causes and Outcomes of Instability in Developing Countries*, ed. Mariana Lavos and Leiv Marsteintredit, 139–40. New York: Palgrave Macmillan, 2009.

Lameda, Guaicaipuro. "Guaicaipuro Lameda habla de PDVSA abril 2002." YouTube video, April 2002, 10:57. https://www.youtube.com/watch?v=5LsL3HM-x1o.

Lansberg-Rodríguez, Daniel. "Nicolás Maduro's Excellent Adventure." *Foreign Policy*, January 15, 2015.

Latin American Weekly Report. "Uribe Starts with Congress Behind Him; Liberals Seek to Reclaim Him, No Real Opposition." June 11, 2002. London.

Latin Finance. "Venezuela Sells Oil Stake to China's Citic." February 29, 2012. https://www.latinfinance.com/daily-briefs/2012/2/29/venezuela-sells-oil-stake-to-chinas-citic.

Levine, Daniel H. "The Decline and Fall of Democracy in Venezuela: Ten Theses." *Bulletin of Latin American Research* 21, no. 2 (April 2002): 248–69.

Levy, Brian, and Pablo T. Spiller. *Regulations, Institutions, and Commitment: Comparative Studies of Telecommunications*. Cambridge: Cambridge University Press, 1996.

Lewis, Paul. "Venezuela Gets Big I.M.F. Credit, Backing Market Reforms." *UPI*, July 13, 1996.

Ley Orgánica de Hidrocarburos Gaseosos. *Gaceta Oficial*, no. 36.793. Venezuela. 1999.

Lieuwen, Edwin. "Politics of Energy in Venezuela." In *The Oil Business in Latin America: The Early Years*, ed. John D. Wirth, 194–204. Philadelphia: Beard Books, 2001.

Llanes, Henry. *Ecuador: La Subasta del Petróleo*. Quito: RG Grafistas, 2016.

López Maya, Margarita. "The Venezuelan *Caracazo* of 1989: Popular Protest and Institutional Weakness." *Journal of Latin American Studies* 35, no. 1 (2003): 117–37.

López, Virginia, and Jonathan Watts. "Nicolás Maduro Narrowly Wins Venezuelan Presidential Election." *Guardian*, April 15, 2013.

Lugo, José V. Zapata, and Claro M. Cotes Ricciulli. "Colombia." In *The Oil and Gas Law Review* (October 2008): 77–89.

Lupu, Noam. "Brand Dilution and the Breakdown of Political Parties in Latin America." *World Politics* 66, no. 4 (October 2014): 561–602.

Mainwaring, Scott, Ana María Bejarano, and Eduardo Pizarro Leongómez. *The Crisis of Democratic Representation in the Andes.* Stanford, Calif.: Stanford University Press, 2006.

Makhija, Mona Verma. "Determinants of Government Intervention: Political Risk in the Venezuelan Petroleum Industry." Ph.D. diss., University of Wisconsin, 1989.

Man, Anthony. "After Making South Florida Home, Venezuelans Turning to Politics." *Sun Sentinel* (Florida), July 2, 2015.

Mander, Benedict. "Fears Over Chávez Threaten Oil Auction." *Financial Times,* August 30, 2009. https://www.ft.com/content/3cf4416a-9585-11de-90e0-00144fe abdco.

——. "Venezuela Secures $80bn Oil Investment." *Financial Times,* February 16, 2010. https://www.ft.com/content/ab888ca2-1b1e-11df-953f-00144feab49a.

Manzano, Osmel, and Francisco Monaldi. "The Political Economy of Oil Contract Renegotiation in Venezuela." In *The Natural Resources Trap: Private Investment Without Public Commitment,* ed. William Hogan and Federico Sturzenegger, 409–66. Cambridge, Mass.: MIT Press 2010.

Manzano, Osmel, Francisco Monaldi, and Federico Sturzenegger. "The Political Economy of Oil Production in Latin America [with Comments]." *Economía* 9, no. 1 (2008): 59–103.

Manzetti, Luigi. "Political Manipulations and Market Reforms Failures." *World Politics* 55, no. 3 (April 2003): 315–60.

Mapungubwe Institute for Strategic Reflection (MISTRA) and David Maimela, eds. *Resurgent Resource Nationalism: A Study Into the Global Phenomenon.* South Africa: Real African Publishers, 2016. http://ebookcentral.proquest.com/lib/ucsd/detail .action?docID=4426703.

Marcano, Cristiana, and Alberto Barrera Tyszka. *Hugo Chávez: The Definitive Biography of Venezuela's Controversial President.* New York: Random House, 2007.

Mares, David R. "Energy Cooperation and Security in the Hemisphere: Mexican Challenges and Opportunities." Task Force Policy Paper series, Center for Hemispheric Policy, University of Miami, 2009.

——. "Natural Gas Pipelines in the Southern Cone." In *Natural Gas and Geopolitics: From 1970–2040,* ed. David G. Victor, Amy M. Jaffe, and Mark H. Hayes, 169–201. Cambridge: Cambridge University Press, 2006.

Mares, David R., and Nelson Altamirano. "Venezuela's PDVSA and World Energy Markets." James A. Baker III Institute for Public Policy, Rice University, 2007.

Martz, John D. *Politics and Petroleum in Ecuador.* New Brunswick, N.J.: Transaction, 1987.

Martz, John D., and David J. Meyers. "Technological Elites and Political Parties: The Venezuelan Professional Community." *Latin American Research Review* 29, no. 1 (1994): 7–27.

——. *Venezuela: The Democratic Experience.* Westport, Conn.: Praeger, 1986.

Maurer, Noel. *The Empire Trap: The Rise and Fall of U.S. Intervention to Protect American Property Overseas.* Princeton. N.J.: Princeton University Press, 2013.

Medlock, Kenneth, and John Hartley. "The Changing Role of National Oil Companies in International Energy Markets." James A. Baker III Institute for Public Policy, Rice University, April 2007. https://www.bakerinstitute.org/media/files/Research /5beoc5c4/BI_PolicyReport_35.pdf.

Meyer, Lorenzo. "The Expropriation and Great Britain." In *The Mexican Petroleum Industry in the Twentieth Century*, ed. Jonathan Brown and Alan Knight, 154–55. Austin: University of Texas Press, 1992.

Mihaly, Aaron M. "Por qué se ha caído Goni? Explicando la renuncia forzada del Presidente Sánchez de Lozada en Octubre de 2003." in *Conflictos politicos y movimientos sociales en Bolivia*, ed. Nicholas A Robins, 95–120. La Paz: Plural, 2006.

Mijeski, Kenneth J., and Scott H. Beck. *Pachakutik and the Rise and Decline of the Ecuadorian Indigenous Movement*. Athens: Ohio University Press, 2011.

Mikesell, Raymond F. *Petroleum Company Operations and Agreements in the Developing Countries*. New York: Resources for the Future, 1984; Routledge, 2015.

Millan, Jaime, and Nils-Henrik H. von der Fehr. "Introduction." In *Keeping the Lights On: Power Sector Reform in Latin America*, ed. Jaime Millan and Nils-Henrik H. von der Fehr, 1–16. Washington, D.C: Inter-American Development Bank, 2003.

Molchanov, Pavel. "A Statistical Analysis of OPEC Quota Violations." Duke University, Durham, N.C., April 2003. https://sites.duke.edu/djepapers/files/2016/08/pa veldje.pdf.

Molina, José E. Molina. "Venezuela." In *Partidos políticos de América Latina: Países Andinos*, ed. Manuel Alcántara and Flavia Feidenberg, 487. Mexico City: Fondo de Cultura Económica, 2003.

Mommer, Bernard. *El mito de la orimulsión: la valorización del crudo extrapesado de la faja petrolífera del Orinoco*. Caracas: Ministerio de Energía y Minas, 2004.

——. "ExxonMobil Is isolated." *En Confianza*. Interview by Ernesto Villegas, Venezolana de Televisión (VTV), Caracas, February 12, 2008.

——. *Global Oil and the Nation State*. Oxford: Oxford University Press, 2002.

——. "The New Governance of Venezuelan Oil." Oxford Institute for Energy Studies, *WPM* 23 (April 1998).

——. "The Political Role of National Oil Companies in Exporting Countries: The Venezuelan Case." Oxford Institute for Energy Studies, WPM 18 (September 1994).

——. "Subversive Oil." In *Venezuelan Politics in the Chávez Era: Polarization and Social Conflict*, ed. Steve Ellner and Daniel Hellinger. London: Lynne Rienner, 2002.

——. "Venezuelan Oil Policy at the Crossroads." Oxford Institute for Energy Studies, 2001. https://www.oxfordenergy.org/publications/venezuelan-oil-politics-at-the -crossroads/

Mommer, Bernard, and Ramón Espinasa. "Venezuelan Oil Policy in the Long Run." *Energy*, East-West Center, Hawaii, 1991.

Monaldi, Francisco J. "The Cyclical Phenomenon of Resource Nationalism in Latin America." *Oxford Handbook of International Political Economy*, March 2020. doi:10 .1093/acrefore/9780190228637.013.1523.

Monaldi, Francisco, and Michael J. Penfold. "Institutional Collapse: The Rise and Breakdown of Democratic Governance in Venezuela." In *Venezuela Before Chávez: Anatomy of an Economic Collapse*, ed. Ricardo Hausmann and Francisco R. Rodríguez, 285–320. University Park: Pennsylvania State University Press, 2014.

Morales, Isidro. "The Consolidation and Expansion of Pemex, 1947–1959." In *The Mexican Petroleum Industry in the Twentieth Century,* ed. Jonathan Brown and Alan Knight, 209–10. Austin: University of Texas Press, 1992.

Morales Manzur, Juan Carlos, and Lucrecia Morales García. "Origen y naturaleza de la Alternativa Bolivariana para las Américas." *Polis* (México) 3, no. 1 (2007): 55–85.

Moran, Theodore H. *Multinational Corporations and the Politics of Dependence: Copper in Chile.* Princeton, N.J.: Princeton University Press, 1974.

Moreno-Brid, Juan Carlos, and Alicia Puyana. "Mexico's New Wave of Market Reforms and Its Extractive Industries." In *Political Economy of Natural Resources,* ed. Paul A. Haslam and Pablo Heidrich, 141–57. London: Routledge, 2016.

Mouawad, Jad. "Saudi Officials Seek to Temper the Price of Oil." *New York Times,* January 28, 2007. http://www.nytimes.com/2007/01/28/business/28oil.html.

Murphy, Jr., Ewell E. "Oil Operations in Latin America: The Scope for Private Enterprise." *International Lawyer* 2, no. 3 (April 1968): 463.

Murray, Pamela. "Know-How and Nationalism: Colombia's First Geological and Petroleum Experts, c. 1940–1970." *Americas* 52, no. 2 (October 1995): 211–26.

Musacchio, Aldo, and Sergio G. Lazzarini. *Reinventing State Capitalism: Leviathan in Business, Brazil and Beyond.* Cambridge, Mass.: Harvard University Press, 2014.

Nagel, Juan Cristóbal. "One Man's 'Acuerdo' Is Another Man's 'Privatización.'" *Caracas* Chronicles, May 27, 2013. https://www.caracaschronicles.com/2013/05/27/one -mans-acuerdo-is-another-mans-privatizacion/.

——. "The Small Print." *Caracas Chronicles,* June 12, 2013. https://www.caracaschronicles .com/2013/06/12/the-small-print/.

Naím, Moisés. *Paper Tigers & Minotaurs: The Politics of Venezuela's Economic Reforms.* New York: Carnegie Endowment for International Peace, 1993.

National Public Radio. "Venezuelan Assembly Grants President Maduro Emergency Powers." March 16, 2015. https://www.npr.org/2015/03/16/393403183/venezuelan -assembly-grants-president-maduro-emergency-powers.

NaturalGas.org. "The History of Regulation." Accessed August 18, 2017. http://naturalgas .org/regulation/history/.

Neuman, W. "Venezuela, in Quiet Shift, Gives Foreign Partners More Control in Oil Ventures." *New York Times,* October 9, 2014. https://www.nytimes.com/2014/10/10 /world/venezuela-in-a-quiet-shift-gives-foreign-partners-more-control-in-oil -ventures.html.

Norden, Deborah. "Democracy in Uniform." In *Venezuelan Politics in the Chávez Era: Class, Polarization, and Conflict,* ed. Steve Ellner and Daniel Hellinger, 93–112. Boulder, Colo.: Lynne Rienner, 2003.

Norwegian Petroleum. "Fundamental Regulatory Principles." Updated January 18, 2017. http://www.norskpetroleum.no/en/framework/fundamental-regulatory-principles/

——. "The Government's Revenues." Updated May 15, 2019. http://www.norskpetroleum .no/en/economy/governments-revenues/.

——. "The Petroleum Tax System." Updated May 2, 2019. http://www.norskpetroleum .no/en/economy/petroleum-tax/.

Norwegian Petroleum Directorate. "Act of 29 November 1996 No. 72 Relating to Petroleum Activities." November 29, 1996. http://www.npd.no/en/Regulations/Acts /Petroleum-activities-act/.

Offshore Energy. "Venezuela Signs Perla Gas Deal with Eni and Repsol," *LNG World News*, December 25, 2011. http://www.lngworldnews.com/venezuela-signs-perla-gas -deal-with-eni-and-repsol/.

Oil and Gas Journal. "Chevron Texaco Plans Another Facility to Process Extra-Heavy Crude in Venezuela." August 9, 2004.

——. "New Government Rules Cloud PDVSA Outlook." September 2, 1991. https://www .ogj.com/home/article/17237717/new-government-rules-cloud-pdvsa-outlook.

——. "PDVSA to Choose LNG Project Partners Soon." June 25, 1990. https://www.ogj .com/pipelines-transportation/lng/article/17214472/pdvsa-to-choose-lng-project -partners-soon.

——. "Sosa: Government Tax Burden Has Pdvsa Facing Cash Crisis."August 26, 1991. https://www.ogj.com/home/article/17238322/sosa-government-tax-burden-has -pdvsa-facing-cash-crisis.

——. "Venezuelan Government Actions Cloud PDVSA's Outlook." March 12, 1990. https://www.ogj.com/general-interest/companies/article/17213405/venezuelan -government-actions-cloud-pdvsa39s-outlook.

——. "Venezuelan Reforms Favor Oil Work." March 19, 1990. https://www.ogj.com /articles/print/volume-88/issue-12/in-this-issue/general-interest/venezuelan -reforms-favor-oil-work.html.

Olken, Benjamin A. "Direct Democracy and Local Public Goods: Evidence from a Field Experiment in Indonesia." *American Political Science Review* 104, no. 2 (May 2010): 243–67.

OPEC. *OPEC Bulletin* 43, no. 6 (August–September 2012): 51. https://www.opec.org /opec_web/flipbook/OB08092012/OB08092012/assets/basic-html/page1.html.

Organización Latinoamericana de Energía (OLADE). *Regulatory Frameworks: Efficient State-Owned Oil and Gas Enterprises*. January 2009.

Östensson, Olle. "Promoting Downstream Processing: Resource Nationalism or Indus-trial Policy?" *Mineral Economics* 32 (2019): 205–12. https://doi.org/10.1007/s13563 -019-00170-x.

Pacheco, Luis A. "11 de abril 2002: Como lo Recuerdo." *Petroleumworld*, April 19, 2009. http://www.petroleumworldve.com/pv09041201.htm, now available at https:// vdebate.blogspot.com/2009/04/11-de-abril-como-lo-recuerdo-luis.html.

Padgett, Tim. "The Latin Oil Czar." *Time*, July 18, 2004. http://content.time.com/time /magazine/article/0,9171,665069,00.html.

Palacios, Luisa Mercedes. "Explaining Policy Choice in the Oil Industry: A Look at Rentier Institutions in Mexico and Venezuela (1988–1999)." Ph.D. diss., Johns Hop-kins University, 2001.

Palau, Juan Carlos. "Transactional, Social, and Legal Aspects of Oil Exploration and Extraction in Colombia." *Northwestern Journal of International Law & Business* 22 (2001): 35.

Parenti, Christian. "Venezuela's Revolution and the Oil Company Inside." *NACLA*, Sep-tember 25, 2007. https://nacla.org/article/venezuelas-revolution-and-oil-company -inside.

Parker, Selwyn. "Weighing Bolivia's Gas Export Options." *Petroleum Economist* 9 (August 2018). https://www.petroleum-economist.com/articles/midstream-down stream/pipelines/2018/weighing-bolivias-gas-export-options.

Parks, E. Taylor. *Colombia and the United States 1765–1934.* Durham, N.C.: Duke University Press, 1935.

Párraga, Marianna. "Cuatro firmas participarán en licitación proyecto gas Venezuela." *Reuters,* February, 15, 2011. https://www.reuters.com/article/latinoamerica-gas -venezuela-mariscalsucr-idLTASIE71E13520110215.

Párraga, Marianna, and Jeanne Liendo. "Exclusive: As Venezuelans Suffer, Maduro Buys Foreign Oil to Subsidize Cuba." *Reuters,* May 15, 2018. https://www.reuters.com /article/us-venezuela-oil-imports-exclusive/exclusive-as-venezuelans-suffer -maduro-buys-foreign-oil-to-subsidize-cuba-idUSKCN1IG1TO.

Pascal, Larry B. "Developments in the Venezuelan Hydrocarbon Sector." *Law and Business Review of the Americas* 15, 531, no. 3-4 (2009). https://scholar.smu.edu/lbra /vol15/iss3/4.

Paulsson, Jan. "The Power of States to Make Meaningful Promises to Foreigners." *Journal of International Dispute Settlement* 1, no. 2 (2010): 341–52. doi:10.1093/jnlids /idq013.

Payne, J. Mark, and Juan Cruz Perusia. "Reforming the Rules of the Game: Political Reform." In *The State of State Reform in Latin America,* ed. Eduardo Lora, 57–86. Washington, D.C.: Inter-American Development Bank, 2007.

PDVSA. "Gestión y resultados 2007." http://uniondelsur.menpet.gob.ve/images/pdf /RELACION%20CON%20INVERSIONISTAS/Informes%20Anuales/informe%20 de%20gestion/2007/GESTIO%CC%81N%20Y%20RESULTADOS%202007.pdf.

——. "Memoria y cuenta de Petróleos de Venezuela, S.A.," 2007, 5. http://www.pdvsa .com.

——. *Modalidades de apertura: Empresas mixtas* 1995. http://www.pdvsa.com/espanol /apertura_empresas_es.html.

——. "PDVSA en el mundo." http://www.pdvsa.com/index.php?option=com_content &view=article&id=6516&Itemid=579&lang=es.

——. "PDVSA planes estratégicos." Acto Inaugural, Hotel Caracas Hilton, Caracas. August 18, 2005.

Pearson, Tamara. "Venezuelan Government Expropriates Petroleum Related Activities." *Venezuelanalysis,* May 9, 2009. https://venezuelanalysis.com/news/4434.

——. "Venezuela's Law of Fair Prices Goes Into Effect." *Venezuelanalysis,* November 23, 2011. https://venezuelanalysis.com/news/6649.

Pegg, Scott. "Can Policy Intervention Beat the Resource Curse? Evidence from the Chad-Cameroon Pipeline Project." *African Affairs* 105, no. 418 (December 2005): 1–25.

Pérez-Liñan, Aníbal. *Presidential Impeachment and the New Political Instability in Latin America.* Cambridge: Cambridge University Press, 2007.

Petkoff, Teodoro. *Hugo Chávez, tal cual.* Madrid: Los Libros de la Catarata, 2002.

Petroleum Economist. "Brazil's Pre-Salt Promise," November 2, 2017. https:// pemedianetwork.com/petroleum-economist/articles/upstream/2017/brazils-pre -salt-promise.

PetroPerú. "Historia." Accessed February 13, 2014. https://www.petroperu.com.pe /acerca-de-petroperu-s-a-/historia/.

Phelps, D. M. "Petroleum Regulation in Temperate South America." *American Economic Review* 29, no. 1 (March 1939): 48–59.

Phelps, Vernon Lovell. *The International Economic Position of Argentina*. Philadelphia: University of Pennsylvania Press, 1938.

Philip, George. *Oil and Politics in Latin America: Nationalist Movements and State Companies*. Cambridge: Cambridge University Press, 1982.

——. "When Oil Prices Were Low: Petroleos De Venezuela (PdVSA) and Economic Policy-Making in Venezuela Since 1989." *Bulletin of Latin American Research* 18, no. 3 (1999): 361–76. https://doi.org/10.1111/j.1470-9856.1999.tb00140.x.

Pike, Frederick B. *The United States and the Andean Republics: Peru, Bolivia, and Ecuador*. Cambridge, Mass.: Harvard University Press, 1977.

Piñeda, José, and Francisco Rodríguez. "Public Investment and Productivity Growth in the Venezuelan Manufacturing Industry." In *Venezuela Before Chávez: Anatomy of an Economic Collapse*, ed. Ricardo Hausmann and Francisco R. Rodríguez, 91–114. University Park: Pennsylvania State University Press, 2014. doi:10.5325/j.ctv14gp2r6.7.

Pion-Berlin, David, and Harold Trinkunas. "Civilian Praetorianism and Military Shirking During Constitutional Crises in Latin America." *Comparative Politics* 42, no. 4 (July 2010): 402–4.

Pittsburgh Press. "U.S. Rebukes Colombia in Oil Argument." September 23, 1928. https://news.google.com/newspapers?nid=1144&dat=19280923&id=DO8aAAAAIBAJ&sjid=OEoEAAAAIBAJ&pg=6389,4437555&hl=en.

Pons, Corina Rodríguez. "Este año PDVSA será socio mayoritario en empresas de la Faja del Orinoco." *El Nacional*, August 30, 2006.

——. "Exclusive: Venezuela Signs Oil Deals Similar to Ones Rolled Back Under Chávez—Document." *Reuters*, September 10, 2018. https://www.reuters.com/article/us-venezuela-oil-exclusive/exclusive-venezuela-signs-oil-deals-similar-to-ones-rolled-back-under-chavez-document-idUSKCN1LQ2FQ.

Postero, Nancy. *The Indigenous State: Race, Politics, and Performance in Plurinational Bolivia*. Oakland: University of California Press, 2017. http://doi.org/10.1525/luminos.31.

Powell, J. Richard. *The Mexican Petroleum Industry 1938–1950*. Berkeley: University of California Press, 1956.

Presidencia de la República de Venezuela, Oficina Central de Coordinación y Planificación, CORDIPLAN. *El gran viraje: lineamientos generales del VIII Plan de la Nación*. Caracas. Presented to Congress January 1990.

Prowse Chowne LLP Team. "What Are Subsurface Rights in Canada?" February 23, 2017. http://prowsechowne.com/what-are-subsurface-rights-in-canada/.

Proyecto Privatización y Regulación en la Economía Argentina. "Privatizaciones en la Argentina. Marcos regulatorios Tarifarios y Evolución de los Precios Relativos Durante la Convertibilidad." Working Paper no. 4. Buenos Aires: FLACSO, May 1998.

Pryke, Sam. "Explaining Resource Nationalism." *Global Policy* 8, no. 4 (November 2017).

Ramamurti, Ravi. "The Obsolescing 'Bargain Model'? MNC-Host Developing Country Relations Revisited." *Journal of International Business Studies* 32, no. 1 (2001): 23–39.

Ramírez, J. R. D. "Was the Apertura Petrolera in Venezuela Beneficial from the Economical Perspective?" *Oil, Gas & Energy Law*. OGEL. Archive issue. http://www.ogel.org/article.asp?key=856.

Ramírez, Rafael. "Discurso de Rafael Ramírez, presidente de PDVSA y Ministro de Energía y Petróleo, ante la Asamblea Nacional." *Aporrea*. May 25, 2005. http://www.aporrea.org/energia/a14338.html.

——. "Politizacion de PDVSA (discurso de Ramirez) buen sonido!" YouTube video, 9:57. "Avila79." November 3, 2006. https://www.youtube.com/watch?v=2I925uJ9U48.

Ramírez, Rocío. "Plan Siembra Petrolera 2005–2030." August 20, 2014. https://rociora mirezproyectandotupetroleo.wordpress.com/2014/08/20/plan-siembra-petrolera -2005-2030/.

Ramonet, D. "Caldera Orders Expropriation of Venezuelan 'Banking Mafia.'" *EIR Economics* 21, no. 30, July 29, 1994. http://www.larouchepub.com/eiw/public/1994/eirv21n 30-19940729/eirv21n30-19940729_004-caldera_orders_expropriation_of.pdf.

Ramos, Joseph. *Neoconservative Economics in the Southern Cone of Latin America, 1973–1983.* Baltimore: Johns Hopkins University Press, 1986.

Ravell F., Alberto. "A Brief Overview of Venezuela's Oil Policies." *Lex Petrolera* 4 (2011), King and Spaulding LLP. https://s3.amazonaws.com/documents.lexology.com/55 dc1112-a8aa-48da-82aa-73290c805b3f.pdf.

Registraduria Nacional de Colombia. "Changes in Congressional Representation 1998–2002." Legislative elections of March 10, 2002. http://psephos.adam-carr.net/cou ntries/c/colombia/colombia20023.txt.

——. "National Summary." Legislative elections of March 12, 2006. http://psephos.adam -carr.net/countries/c/colombia/colombia2006.txt.

——. "National Summary of Votes and Seats." Legislative elections of March 10, 2002. http://psephos.adam-carr.net/countries/c/colombia/colombia20022.txt.

Registraduria Nacional de Estado Civil. "National Summary." Presidential election of May 28, 2006. http://psephos.adam-carr.net/countries/c/colombia/colombia2006pres.txt.

Reifenberg, Anne. "OPEC Members Boldly Violate Quotas, but See End to Limits." *Wall Street Journal,* April 25, 1996. https://www.wsj.com/articles/SB830395173370706000.

República Bolivariana de Venezuela, Asamblea Nacional. "Informe que presenta ante la Asamblea Nacional, La Comisión Especial para Investigar las Irregularidades Detectadas por el Ministero de Energía y Petróleo, Cometidas en la Formulación, Celebración y Ejecución de los Convenios Operativos, Asociaciones Estratégicas y Negocios de Internacionalización." March 29, 2006.

Reuters Caracas. "Gas: Venezuela prepara una ley para estatizar la extracción." *El Cronista,* December 24, 2010, https://www.cronista.com/impresa-general/Gas-Venezue la-prepara-una-ley-para-estatizar-la-extraccion-20101224-0089.html.

Rey, Juan Carlos. "Corruption and Political Illegitimacy in Venezuelan Democracy." In *Reinventing Legitimacy: Democracy and Political Change in Venezuela,* ed. Damarys Canache and Michael R. Kulisheck, 113–24. Westport, Conn.: Greenwood, 1998.

Rhodes-Purdy, Matthew. "Participatory Populism: Theory and Evidence from Bolivarian Venezuela." *Political Research Quarterly* 68, no. 3 (September 2015): 415–27. https://doi.org/10.1177/1065912915592183.

Roberts, Kenneth. "Social Polarization and the Populist Resurgence in Venezuela." In *Venezuelan Politics in the Chaves Era: Class, Polarization, and Conflict,* ed. Steve Ellner and Daniel Hellinger, 161–78. Boulder, Colo.: Lynne Rienner, 2003.

Robertson, Ewan. "Venezuelan Government Applies Law Limiting Costs, Prices and Profits." *Venezuelanalysis.com.* February 10, 2014. https://venezuelanalysis.com /news/10343.

Rodríguez, Miguel. "Interview with Miguel Rodriguez," by Pedro Palma. *Enfoque.* Radio Caracas Televisión, November 13, 1988. http://www.pedroapalma.com/miguel -rodriguez-ad/.

Rodríguez Araque, Alí. *Antes De Que Se Me Olvide: Conversación con Rosa Miriam Elizalde*. Havana: Editora Política, 2014.

Rojas, Nestor. "Venezuela's Deepening Economic Crisis Frustrated President Rafael Caldera's Defiant." *UPI Archives*, December 22, 1995. https://www.upi.com/Archives /1995/12/22/Venezuelas-deepening-economic-crisis-frustrated-President-Rafael -Calderas-defiant/9756819608400/.

Romero, Manuel Bermudez. *PDVSA En Carne Propia: Testimonio Del Derrumbe De La Primera Empresa Venezolana*. Caracas: OME Estudios de Mercado y Comunicación, 2004.

Rosales, Antulio. "Pursuing Foreign Investment for Nationalist Goals: Venezuela's Hybrid Resource Nationalism." *Business and Politics* 20, no. 3 (2018): 438–64.

——. "Structural Constraints in Times of Resource Nationalism: Oil Policy and State Capacity in Post-Neoliberal Ecuador." *Globalizations* 17, no. 1 (May 8, 2019): 77–92. https://doi.org/10.1080/14747731.2019.1614722.

Ross, Michael L. "The Political Economy of the Resource Curse." *World Politics* 51, no. 2 (January 1999): 297–322.

——. "What Do We Know About Natural Resources and Civil War?" *Journal of Peace Research* 41, no. 3 (2004): 337–56.

Rossi, Federico M. "The Second Wave of Incorporation in Latin America: A Conceptualization of the Quest for Inclusion Applied to Argentina." *Latin American Politics and Society* 57, no. 1 (December 29, 2014): 1–28.

Rovine, Arthur W., ed. *Contemporary Issues in International Arbitration and Mediation: The Fordham Papers (2013)*. Leiden, Netherlands: Brill/Nijhoff, 2014). https:// doi.org/10.1163/9789004274945.

Rowlands, Jo. "Review." *Development in Practice* 18, no. 6 (November 2008): 801–4.

Rueda, Jorge, and Joshua Goodman. "Venezuela Arrests Top Oil Officials in Corruption Probe." *Associated Press*, November 30, 2017. http://abcnews.go.com/Intern ational/wireStory/venezuela-arrests-top-oil-officials-corruption-probe-51485922.

Runrun.es. "Presidente de Pdvsa Eulogio Del Pino Pone su Cargo a la Orden por Diferencias con Área de Finanzas." April 14, 2015. https://runrun.es/la-economia/oil _energy/197706/las-10-noticias-petroleras-mas-importantes-de-hoy-15a/.

Salazar-Carrillo, Jorge, and Bernadette West. *Oil and Development in Venezuela During the 20th Century*. Westport, Conn.: Praeger, 2004.

Scheimberg, Sebastián. "The Performance of Argentine Oil Industry over a Century (draft for comments)." IESA. Accessed February 13, 2014. http://servicios.iesa.edu .ve/portal/CIEA/argentina_scheimberg_d1.pdf.

Seawright, Jason. *Party-System Collapse: The Roots of Crisis in Peru and Venezuela*. Stanford, Calif.: Stanford University Press, 2012.

Segal, Paul. "El Petróleo Es Nuestro: La Distribución de los Ingresos Petroleros en México," in *El Futuro del Sector Petrolero en México* (Oxford: Oxford University Press, 2011).

——. "Resource Rents, Redistribution, and Halving Global Poverty: The Resource Dividend." *World Development* 39, no. 4 (2011): 475–89. doi:10.1016/j.worlddev.2010.08.013.

Semana. "El Proyecto de la Refinería Privada." November 24, 2003. http://www.semana .com/nacion/recuadro/el-proyecto-refineria-privada/127485-3.

Serrano, Rafael Quiroz. *Meritocracia petrolera, ¿Mito o realidad?* Caracas: Editorial Panapo, 2003.

Sewalk, Stephen. "Brazil's Energy Policy and Regulation." *Fordham Environmental Law Review* 25, no. 3 (2015): 652–705.

Shafer, Robert J., and Donald J. Mabry. *Neighbors—Mexico and the United States: Wetbacks and Oil.* Chicago: Nelson-Hall, 1981. http://historicaltextarchive.com/sections.php?op=viewarticle&artid=371.

Shea, Donald R. *The Calvo Clause: A Problem of Inter-American and International Law and Diplomacy.* Minneapolis: University of Minnesota Press, 1955.

Sierra, Luz María. "Álvaro Uribe: Un presidente de Teflón la estrategia de opinión pública que lo izo inmune a las crisis." In *De Uribe, Santos y otras especies políticas: Comunicación de gobierno en Colombia, Argentina y Brasil,* ed. Omar Rincón and Catalina Uribe, 65–100. Bogota: Universidad de los Andes, Colombia, 2015. doi:10.7440/j.ctt1bd6k61.6.

Sierra Castro, Enrique. *Ecuador, Ecuador: Tu petróleo! Tu gente!* Quito: Ediciones Cultura y Didáctica, 1995.

Silva, Eduardo. *Challenging Neoliberalism in Latin America.* Cambridge: Cambridge University Press, 2009.

Singh, Kelvin "Oil Politics in Venezuela During the Lopez Contreras Administration (1936–1941)." *Journal of Latin American Studies* 21, no. 1. (February 1989): 89–104.

Snelson Companies. "The Debate Over Natural Gas Exports." Accessed August 18, 2017. http://www.snelsonco.com/debate-over-natural-gas-exports/.

Snidal, Duncan. "Public Goods, Property Rights, and Political Organizations." *International Studies Quarterly* 23, no. 4 (December 1979): 532–66.

Society of Petroleum Engineers. "Glossary of Terms Used in Petroleum Reserves/Resources Definitions." http://spe.org/en/industry/terms-used-petroleum-reserves-resource-definitions/.

Solberg, Carl E. "Entrepreneurship in Public Enterprise: General Enrique Mosconi and the Argentine Petroleum Industry." *Business History Review* 56, no. 3 (Autumn 1982): 392–98.

——. *Oil and Nationalism in Argentina: A History.* Stanford, Calif.: Stanford University Press, 1979.

——. "YPF: The Formative Years of Latin America's Pioneer State Oil Company, 1922–1931." In *The Oil Business in Latin America: The Early Years,* ed. John D. Wirth, 58–95. Philadelphia: Beard Books, 2001.

Sosa Pietri, Andrés. *Petróleo y poder.* Caracas: Editorial Planeta Venezolana, 1993.

Spiller, Pablo T., Ernesto Stein, and Mariano Tommas. *Political Institutions, Policymaking Processes, and Policy Outcome: An Intertemporal Transactions Framework.* Washington, D.C.: InterAmerican Development Bank, April 2003.

Stambouli, Andrés. "An Evaluation of the First Year of Government of Carlos Andrés Pérez." In *Venezuela in the Wake of Radical Reform,* ed. Joseph S. Tulchin with Gary Bland, 119–24. Washington, D.C.: Woodrow Wilson Center, 1993.

Stepan, Alfred. "Paths Toward Redemocratization: Theoretical and Comparative Considerations." In *Transitions from Authoritarian Rule,* ed. Guillermo O'Donnell, Philippe C. Schmitter, and Laurence Whitehead, 64–84. Baltimore: Johns Hopkins University Press, 1986.

Stevens, Paul. "National Oil Companies and International Oil Companies in the Middle East: Under the Shadow of Government and the Resource Nationalism Cycle." *Journal of World Energy Law & Business* 1, no. 1 (2008): 5.

Steyn, M. S. "Oil Politics in Ecuador and Nigeria: A Perspective from Environmental History on The Struggles Between Ethnic Minority Groups, Multinational Oil Companies and National Governments." Ph.D. diss., University of the Free State, 2003.

Stojanovski, Ognen. "Handcuffed: An Assessment of Pemex's Performance and Strategy." In *Oil and Governance: State-Owned Enterprises and the World Energy Supply*, ed. David G. Victor, David R. Hults, and Mark Thurber, 280–333. Cambridge: Cambridge University Press, 2012.

Stokes, Susan C. *Mandates and Democracies: Neoliberalism by Surprise in Latin America*. Cambridge: Cambridge University Press, 2001.

Stone, Mike. "Venezuela Taps Lazard to Sell Citgo Petroleum—Sources." *Reuters*, August 12, 2014. https://www.reuters.com/article/idUSL2N0QH1YZ20140812.

Stratfor. "Global Market Brief: Venezuela: Selling Citgo Assets to Hedge U.S. Influence." February 7, 2005. https://worldview.stratfor.com/article/global-market-brief -venezuela-selling-citgo-assets-hedge-us-influence.

Striffler, Steve. "Something Left in Latin America: Venezuela and the Struggle for Twenty-First Century Socialism." In *Rethinking Revolution: Socialist Register 2017*, ed. Leo Panitch and Albo Greg, 207–29. New York: New York University Press, 2016. doi:10.2307/j.ctt1bpmbn2.13.

Stuenkel, Oliver. "The Brazil-Bolivia Dispute, a Decade On." July 10, 2016. https://www .postwesternworld.com/2016/07/10/bolivia-dispute-decade/.

Suggett, James. "Chávez Signs 26 Law-Decrees on Final Day of Enabling Law Power." *Venezuelanalysis.com*, August 5, 2008. https://venezuelanalysis.com/news/3691.

Sullivan, Mark P. "Venezuela: Issues for Congress." Washington, D.C.: Congressional Research Service, March 29, 2012.

——. "Venezuela's December 2, 2007 Constitutional Reform." Washington, D.C.: Congressional Research Service, December 18, 2007.

Sullivan, Mary Anne. "LNG Exports—A Rare Case of Policy Continuity from Obama to Trump." May 8, 2017. https://knect365.com/flame/article/f07241ed-4652-44b6-89c0-21 446dfd1940/lng-exports-a-rare-case-of-policy-continuity-from-obama-to-trump.

Szusterman, Celia. *Frondizi and the Politics of Developmentalism in Argentina, 1955– 62*. Pittsburgh: University of Pittsburgh Press, 1993.

Tanaka, Martin. "From Crisis to Collapse of the Party Systems and Dilemmas of Democratic Representation: Peru and Venezuela." In *The Crisis of Democratic Representation*, ed. Scott Mainwaring, Ana María Bejarano, and Eduardo Pizarro Leongómez, 47–77. Stanford, Calif.: Stanford University Press, 2006.

Tanimoto, Masayuki, and R. Bin Wong. *Public Goods Provision in the Early Modern Economy: Comparative Perspectives from Japan, China, and Europe*. Berkeley: University of California Press, 2019.

Thomas Acuña, Evaristo. "Colombia entre la crisis de la representatividad y la democracia directa." Paper presented at the International Conference on Direct Democracy in Latin America. *Research Center on Direct Democracy*, Buenos Aires, March 14–15, 2006.

Thorp, Rosemary, and Geoffrey Bertram. *Peru: 1890–1977*. New York: Columbia University Press, 1980.

Tinker-Salas, Miguel. "Fueling Concern: The Role of Oil in Venezuela." *Harvard International Review* 26 (2005): 50.

Tordo, Silvana, with Brandon S. Tracy and Noora Arfaa. "National Oil Companies and Value Creation." Working Paper no. 128. Washington, D.C.: World Bank, 2011.

Toro, Francisco. "The End of a Long Debate." *Caracas Chronicles*, June 13, 2013. http:// caracaschronicles.com/2013/06/13/the-end-of-a-long-debate/.

Total. "The Main Types of Oil and Gas Contractual Arrangements." https://web.archive .org/web/20080516050159/http://www.total.com/en/corporate-social-responsibi lity/Ethical-Business-Principles/Financial-transparency/contractual_arrangements _13289.htm.

Trinkunas, Harold A. *Crafting Civilian Control of the Military in Venezuela: A Comparative Perspective.* Durham, N.C.: University of North Carolina Press, 2005.

——. "Three Things to Know About the Venezuelan Election Results." Washington, D.C.: Brookings Institution, December 8, 2015. https://www.brookings.edu/blog /order-from-chaos/2015/12/08/three-things-to-know-about-the-venezuelan-electi on-results/.

Tugwell, Franklin. *The Politics of Oil in Venezuela.* Stanford, Calif.: Stanford University Press, 1975.

Ullán de la Rosa, Francisco Javier. "La Alianza Bolivariana para las Américas-Tratado de Comercio de los Pueblos (ALBA-TCP): análisis de un proyecto de integración regional latinoamericana con una fuerte dimensión altermundista." *Estudios políticos* (México), no. 25 (January/April 2012): 131–70.

Ulmer, Alexandra, and Marianna Párraga. "Special Report: Oil Output Goes AWOL in Venezuela as Soldiers Run PDVSA." *Reuters*, December 26, 2018. https://www .reuters.com/article/us-venezuela-pdvsa-military-specialrepor-idUSKCN1OP0RZ.

Ulmer, Alexandra, Marianna Párraga, and Ernest Scheyder. "Chevron Evacuates Venezuela Executives Following Staff Arrests." *Reuters*, April 25, 2018. https://www .reuters.com/article/us-venezuela-oil-chevron-insight/chevron-evacuates-venez uela-executives-following-staff-arrests-idUSKBN1HW2BD.

United Nations Industrial Development Organization. *Public Goods for Economic Development.* Vienna, 2008.

United States Energy Information Administration. "Country Analysis—Venezuela." October 3, 2012. https://www.eia.gov/international/content/analysis/countries_long /Venezuela/archive/pdf/venezuela_2012.pdf.

University of Alberta, Alberta Land Institute. "A Guide to Property Rights in Alberta." Accessed August 18, 2017. http://propertyrightsguide.ca/subsurface-property-rights/.

Valdez, José A. "Capitalization: Privatizing Bolivian Style." *Economic Reform Today* 1 (1998).

Valdivia, Gabriela, and Angus Lyall. "The Oil Complex in Latin America: Politics, Frontiers and Habits of Oil Rule." In *Routledge Handbook of Latin American Development*, ed. Julie Cupples, Marcela Palomino-Schalscha, and Manuel Prieto, 461. New York: Routledge, 2019.

Van Alstine, James. "Transparency in Energy Governance: The Extractive Industries Transparency Initiative and Publish What You Pay Campaign." In *Transparency in Global Environmental Governance: Critical Perspectives*, ed. Aarti Gupta and Michael Mason, 249–70. Cambridge, Mass.: MIT Press, 2014.

Vass, Uisdean R., and Rubén Eduardo Lujan. "Venezuela Hatching Big Plans for Jump-Starting Natural Gas Sector." *Oil and Gas Journal*, August 8, 1999. https://www.ogj

.com/articles/print/volume-97/issue-32/special-report/venezuela-hatching-big
-plans-for-jump-starting-natural-gas-sectorl.html.

Vassiliou, Marius S. *The A to Z of the Petroleum Industry*. Plymouth, UK: Scarecrow
Press, 2009.

Venezolana de Televisión. *Aló Presidente*, "PDVSA Strategic Planning: Opening Ceremony." Caracas, August 18, 2002, 21. http://www.alopresidente.gob.ve.

Venezuela. Constitución de la República Bolivariana de Venezuela, Articles 12, 302, 303.
http://pdba.georgetown.edu/Parties/Venezuela/Leyes/constitucion.pdf.

Venezuelan Solidarity Campaign. "Q & A: The National Constituent Assembly in Venezuela." *Venezuelanalysis.com*. July 24, 2017. https://venezuelanalysis.com/analysis
/13260m.

Vernon, Raymond. *Sovereignty at Bay: The Multinational Spread of U.S. Enterprises*.
Lebanon, Ind.: Basic Books, 1971.

Vivoda, Vlado. "Bargaining Model for the International Oil Industry." *Business and
Politics* 13, no. 4 (2011): 1–34. doi:10.2202/1469-3569.1384.

——. "Resource Nationalism, Bargaining and International Oil Companies: Challenges
and Change in the New Millennium." *New Political Economy* 14, no. 4 (2009): 517–
34. doi:10.1080/13563460903287322.

——. "Rise of State-Firm Bargaining in the 2000s." In *The Political Economy of Natural Resources and Development*, ed. Paul A. Haslam and Pablo Heidrich, 55–69. London: Routledge, 2016.

Vogel, Thomas T. "Exodus at Petróleos De Venezuela Creates Worries on Firm's Health."
Wall Street Journal, September 3, 1999. https://www.wsj.com/articles/SB9363110
9288317752.

Wagner, Maria Luise. "The Liberal Party and the Rise of Tin." In *Bolivia: A Country
Side*, ed. Rex A. Hudson and Dennis M. Hanratty, 25–27. Washington, D.C.: GPO
for the Library of Congress, 1989.

Webb-Vidal, Andy. "Venezuela Buys Russia Oil to Avoid Defaulting on Deals." *Financial Times*. April 28, 2006. https://www.ft.com/content/212f6658-d63e-11da-8b3a
-0000779e2340

Webber, Jeffrey R. "Carlos Mesa, Evo Morales, and a Divided Bolivia (2003–2005)."
Latin American Perspectives 37, no. 3 (May 2010): 51–70.

Weisbrot, Mark. "Venezuela's Economic Crisis: Does It Mean That the Left Has Failed?"
Truthout, October 23, 2016. https://truthout.org/articles/venezuela-s-economic
-crisis-does-it-mean-that-the-left-has-failed/.

Weisbrot, Mark, and Luis Sandoval. "The Venezuelan Economy in the Chávez Years."
Center for Economic and Policy Research. July 2007. https://cepr.net/documents
/publications/venezuela_2007_07.pdf.

Wessel, R. H. 1967. "A Note on Economic Rent." *American Economic Review* 57, no. 5
(1967): 1222.

Westervelt, Paul. "Venezuela's New Constitution Gives Rise to New Legal Issues on Oil,
Gas Investment." *Oil and Gas Journal*, April 10, 2000.

Weyland, Kurt. "Clarifying a Contested Concept: Populism in the Study of Latin American Politics." *Comparative Politics* 34, no. 1 (October 2001): 1–22.

——. "Neoliberal Populism in Latin America and Eastern Europe." *Comparative Politics* 31, no. 4 (July 1999): 379–401.

Whelan, Glen. "The Political Perspective of Corporate Social Responsibility: A Critical Research Agenda." *Business Ethics Quarterly* 22, no. 4 (October 2012): 709–37.

Wilkins, Mira. *The Maturing of the Multinational Enterprise: American Business Abroad from 1914–1970.* Cambridge, Mass.: Harvard University Press, 1974.

——. "Multinational Oil Companies in South America in the 1920s: Argentina, Bolivia, Brazil, Chile, Colombia, Ecuador, and Peru." *Business History Review* 48, no. 3 (Autumn 1974): 414–46.

Wilkinson, Abigail. "The Winners and Losers in Argentina's Subsidy Story—Emilio Apud." *Business News Americas,* January 20, 2012.

Wilson, Arnold. "Oil Legislation in Latin America." *Foreign Affairs* 8, no. 1 (October 1929): 108–19.

Wilson, Jeffrey D. "Understanding Resource Nationalism: Economic Dynamics and Political Institutions." *Contemporary Politics* 21, no. 4 (2015): 399–416. doi:10.1080 /13569775.2015.1013293.

Wilson, Peter. "Chávez Sees a Gusher in a Windfall Tax." *Business Week,* February 21, 2008

Wirth, John D. "Setting the Brazilian Agenda, 1936–1953." In *The Oil Business in Latin America: The Early Years,* ed. John D. Wirth, 103–23. Philadelphia: Beard Books, 2001.

Wolfensberger, Marc. "Tehran Revolts Iran Rations Gasoline, Sparks Protest in Tehran (Update3)." *Bloomberg,* June 27, 2007. http://web.archive.org/web/20140215031151 /http://www.bloomberg.com/apps/news?pid=newsarchive&sid=a9HiN8aoQngM &refer=india.

Wood, Duncan, ed. *Mexico's New Energy Reform.* Washington, D.C.: Mexico Institute, Woodrow Wilson International Center for Scholars, 2018.

World Bank. "Comparative Study on the Distribution of Oil Rents in Bolivia, Colombia, Ecuador and Peru." Energy Sector Management Assistance Program (ESMAP) working paper series. Washington, D.C.: World Bank, 2005. http://documents .worldbank.org/curated/en/465991468770681995/Comparative-study-on-the -distribution-of-oil-rents-in-Bolivia-Colombia-Ecuador-and-Peru.

——. "GDP Growth (Annual %)—Venezuela, RB." https://data.worldbank.org/indicator /NY.GDP.MKTP.KD.ZG?locations=VE.

——. "Inflation, Consumer Prices (Annual %)—Venezuela RB." https://data.worldbank .org/indicator/FP.CPI.TOTL.ZG?locations=E.

——. "PovcalNet: An Online Analysis Tool for Global Poverty Monitoring." http:// iresearch.worldbank.org/PovcalNet/home.aspx.

——. *World Development Report 2006: Equity and Development.* Washington, D.C.: World Bank, 2006.

World Energy Council. "Gas in Venezuela." 2014 figures. https://www.worldenergy.org /data/resources/country/venezuela/gas/.

Worldpress. "Mexico: Oil Depletion and Illegal U.S. Immigration." April 25, 2006. http://www.worldpress.org/Americas/2326.cfm.

Yergin, Daniel. *The Prize: The Epic Quest for Oil, Money & Power.* New York: Free Press, 2008.

Young, Kevin A. *Blood of the Earth: Resource Nationalism, Revolution, and Empire in Bolivia.* Austin: University of Texas Press, 2017.

INDEX

Note: page numbers followed by *f* and *t* refer to figures and tables respectively.

access to natural resources in Venezuela, 1989–1998, 151–52

access to natural resources in Venezuela, under Bolivarian Revolution, 176–81; and Apertura contracts, altering of terms for, 179–80, 196–97; under Constitution of 1999, 176–77, 188; under Gaseous Hydrocarbons Law of 1999, 177–78, 180, 185, 188, 239–40n44; nationalizations and, 179–81; and natural gas, separation from national ownership requirements, 177–78; under Organic Hydrocarbon Law of 2001, 178–79

accountability, inclusiveness and, 77–78

Administración General del Petróleo (Mexico), 67

Agencia Nacional de Hidrocarburos (ANH) [Colombia], 201–2

Agenda Venezuela (Caldera), 98–100, 143, 146, 155, 162; economic decline under, 99; initial opposition to Pérez's IMF reforms, 143–46; opening of oil sector to foreign investment, 99, 155

Allred, C. Stephen, 206n1

Ames, Barry, 79

Arab oil embargo, energy security measures in response to, 41

Argentina: Alfonsín government as high inclusiveness, high competitiveness regime with innovative and risk-averse leader, 89; and Bolivian-Argentine pipeline, 56; domestic oil market, regulation of, 55; early struggle over ownership of subsurface resources, 49–50; energy subsidies, cost of, 28; extreme swings in oil and gas policies, 6; Gas del Estado, creation of, 66; large-scale demonstrations (2001), 74; Menem government as low inclusiveness, low competitiveness regime with innovative and risk-acceptant leader, 88–89; nationalizations in, 54–55, 62–66, 63t; Oil Law of 1935, 55; refusal to allow Bolivian pipeline to sea, 61–62; reliance on market to set

oil and gas supply and demand in 1990s, 16

Argentina, oil and gas production in: mining code of 1887 and, 49–50; oil production in early twentieth century, 51; policies starving gas sector of capital, 55–56; and provincial vs. national ownership of subsoil resources, 49–50; shale oil, as technical challenge, 28; and tight markets of 2003–2014, inability to attract E&P investments in, 9

Argentina, regulation of access to hydrocarbon sector in, 54–56; banning of private companies in some areas, 54; division of domestic market between foreigners and Argentines, 55; dramatic swings in, 55; efforts to end IOCs' monopoly on oil imports, 55; and IOCs' refusal to enter market, 55; provincial leniency vs. federal government, 54–55

Argentina's national oil company. See Energía Argentina, Sociedad Anónima (ENARSA) [Argentina]; Yacimientos Petrolíferos Fiscales (YPF)

Arias Cardenas, Francisco: and election of 2000, 102; and military coups against Pérez, 97

Armas, Celestino, 140, 146, 150, 152

Arrieta, Erwin, 143–45, 154

Arrioja, José Enrique, 139, 152, 232n3

Article 5. See Venezuela, article 5 of nationalization legislation

Ascher, William, 206n10

Baena, César E., 147

Banzer, Hugo, 75

Baptista, Asdrúbal, 144

Barco, Virgilio, 56

bargain between resource owner (government) and resource extractor: determining influences on, as goal of this book, 31; fair/legitimate, as distinct from resource nationalism per se, 3; and government take,

contract renegotiation, factors causing, 31
Convergencia party (Venezuela), 97–98
CORDIPLAN development plan under
  Pérez, 140–41, 149; heavy crude oils
  and, 152; natural gas sector and,
  140–41, 149
Corporación Estatal Petrolera
  Ecuatoriana (CEPE): creation of, 66t,
  67, 68; and Ecuador's nationalizations,
  66t, 67; land gifted to, 60; legal right to
  purchase up to 25 percent of any oil or
  gas business, 60
Corporación Venezolana de Petróleo
  (CVP) [Venezuela]: creation of,
  43–44, 54, 66t; LNG export
  monopoly, 54; and Venezuela's
  nationalizations, 66t, 88
Correa Delgado, Rafael Vicente, 64
credibility: of government, effect of
  institutions on, 33–34, 35; low, of
  Venezuelan government, impact of,
  132, 133, 156, 184, 187; as necessary for
  inclusiveness of political system,
  76, 77
CVP. See Corporación Venezolana de
  Petróleo
CVT. See Confederación de Trabajadores
  de Venezuela

Dargent, Eduardo, 243–44n3
Del Pino, Eulogio, 172, 180, 237–38n19
democracy, direct, 89; current pressure
  for, from newly incorporated groups,
  76
demonstrations, large-scale, as
  empowerment from outside the
  system, 74
Department of Energy (U.S.), regulation
  of liquified natural gas (LNG)
  exports, 16
Díaz, Porfirio, and energy policy, 52–53
direct state control of oil and gas sector,
  24, 24t. See also statist resource
  nationalists
distribution of oil and gas revenue:
  determining by oil and gas policies,
  15, 16–17; as indication of resource

nationalism levels, in common
  understanding, 16–17
domestic oil and gas production: and
  energy security, 41–42; opportunity
  costs of, 41
downstream component of oil and gas
  value chain, 22, 23f
Dutch Disease, resource curse and, 8

E&P. See exploration and production
Eckstein, Harry, 225n19
Ecopetrol [Colombia]: and Colombia's
  nationalizations, 66t, 67, 68; creation
  of, 57, 66t, 67, 68; ending of
  monopoly, 197; as independent
  shareholding company, 201, 202;
  monopoly over refining and exports,
  57–58; and private investors, 69, 69t;
  role in energy policy, 200–201
Ecuador: early policies on ownership of
  subsurface resources, 49; large-scale
  demonstrations (1997), 74; Law of
  Hydrocarbons of 1971, 60; left-wing
  governments' hard line with oil
  companies, 60; minor oil production,
  1920s–60s, 60; nationalizations in,
  63t, 64, 65; oil companies caution
  toward production in, 51; oil
  companies flight from, in 1970s, 60;
  oil law of 1957, 60; Petroleum
  Department, 68; petroleum law of
  1921, 51; taxes on oil producers, 60–61
Ecuador, regulation of access to
  hydrocarbon sector, 59–61; Amazon
  concessions, 60; changes in, with
  economic environment, 60–61;
  production requirements, 51, 60;
  required levels of investment, 60;
  requirements for hiring Equadorian
  staff, 60; short-term profits from,
  60–61; tightening of fees and
  restrictions in 1970s, 60
Ecuador's national oil company. See
  Corporación Estatal Petrolera
  Ecuatoriana (CEPE); Petroecuador
efficient depletion of resources, vs.
  sustainable development, 4

Orinoco *(continued)*
  foreign investors, 6, 68, 187;
  nationalization of projects in (2007),
  68, 180; and need for foreign
  expertise, 197; oil from, delays in
  bringing to market, 233n29; and oil
  law, 196; and OPEC quotas, 147;
  Pérez's call for development of, 140;
  promising prospects for, 111; raising
  of royalty rates by Chávez, 182;
  technology needed to capitalize on,
  127, 138; and Venezuelan
  nationalizations, 179–80
ownership of subsurface resources:
  competing claims of state and
  resource extractor, 39–40; countries'
  ownership of, in Latin America, 26;
  as key concept, 26; legal structures
  allowing others access to resources,
  26; resource nationalism as dominant
  legal reality for, 4–5; by surface
  property owners, in U.S. and parts of
  Canada, 4–5, 15, 16
ownership of subsurface resources in
  Latin America, 48–50

Paraguay, and Chaco War, 62
Parra Luzardo, Gastón, 166
Partido Socialista Unido de Venezuela
  (PSUV): Chávez's merging of
  multiple parties into, 105; founding
  of, 105
PDVSA (Petroleos de Venezuela,
  Sociedad Anónima) [Venezuela]:
  appointment of Sosa Pietri as
  president of, 140; and Caldera's
  opening of oil sector to outside
  investors, 99; Chávez's efforts to
  control, 102, 103; creation of, 66t; and
  preference for privatization, 138; and
  debt repayment, 137–38; experiences
  as both pinnacle and nadir of oil
  company status, 136; joint venture
  with Chevron, 19; and Mexican
  nationalizations, 66t; OPEC quotas
  and prices and, 146–47; and opening
  of midstream and downstream to

investors, 148–49; opening to outside
  investors, 147, 149–55; operational
  decisions, political determinants of,
  137; partnerships with Chinese and
  Russian national oil companies
  (2010), 184; Pérez's call for
  internalization of, 139–40, 147;
  Pérez's call for opening to outside
  investors, 140, 141, 145, 148, 149;
  Pérez's interest in petrochemical
  development, 140; Pérez's opposition
  to privatization of, 141;
  petrochemical subsidiary, sale of
  stock, 155; presidential appointment
  of PDVSA president, 139; purchases
  of international companies under
  Pérez, 147–48; role in oil and gas
  policy, 139–46; as state within a state,
  136–37, 139; strikes of 2002–2003,
  102–3; strong-arming of voters in
  support of Chávez, 104; subsidiaries
  of, as privatizable, 177; successful
  weathering of oil market bust, 9; and
  swings in Venezuela's energy policy,
  5–6; taxes on, 155–56, 158
PDVSA and Orimulsion: deal with
  China on, 178–79; and need for
  foreign partners, 152; OPEC quotas
  and, 172; plans to develop, 141, 142,
  152
PDVSA internationalization in
  Bolivarian Revolution, 172–74;
  development of natural gas sector,
  174–76; exports to poor allies at low
  price, 169, 173–74; Maduro's
  continuation of policies, 173; overseas
  PDVSA subsidiaries and, 172–73;
  partnerships with foreign refineries,
  173; Petrocaribe, Petrosur, and
  Petroandina initiatives, 173
PDVSA internationalization under Pérez
  and Caldera, 137, 146–47; Pérez's
  efforts to limit, 146–47; purchase of
  asphalt refineries, 147; purchases of
  international companies, 146–47
PDVSA role in oil and gas policy in
  Bolivarian Revolution, 165–72;

subsidies for consumers, as private gain from national resource rents, 32
sustainable development: vs. efficient depletion, 4; as goal for pro-market nationalists, 32; government's ability to work effectively with markets as key to, 80; investment of resource wealth in future means of generating wealth as goal of, 4; of oil and gas value chain, as key to national wealth and development, 22–23; as standard for legitimate political use of resources, 4, 194, 206n10
Syncrude, and OPEC quotas, 172

taxes: on oil producers, as point of contention, 52; on oil producers in Colombia, 56–57; on oil producers in Bolivia, 61; on oil producers in Ecuador, 60–61; and regulation, control through, 24–26, 24t, 52; resource rent tax in Norway, 25; use to capture rents, problems with, 29
taxes in Venezuela: Caldera's lowering of VAT tax, 98; on oil producers, 155–58; on PDVSA, 155–56, 158, 170
Texaco-Gulf, in Ecuador, 60, 67
Total, and Venezuelan nationalization under Chávez, 181
transparency, inclusiveness and, 76, 77–78
Trinkunas, Julius, 143
Tropical Oil Company, 56

Union Oil Company (UNOCAL), CNOOC takeover attempt, 18
Union Oil of California, joint venture with Venezuela (UNO-VEN), 147
United Kingdom: reliance of market to set oil and gas supply and demand, 16; renegotiation of oil contracts with price increase, 36
United States: energy security measures, 41; market controls on oil and gas sector, 16; private ownership of subsurface resources, 4–5, 15–16; and resource nationalism, 18, 206n1;

subsurface resources of government lands, responsibility to use in public interest, 16
UNOCAL. See Union Oil Company
upstream component of oil and gas value chain, 22, 23f; in Norway, through tax and regulation, 24–26
Uribe, Alvaro: characteristics as leader, 200; and election of 2002, 198, 199; popularity of, 198; provision of public goods, 203; reform of Colombia's oil and gas sector, 197

value chain, oil and gas, 22, 23f; level of government intervention, variation across each component, 24, 24t; nationalizations of different parts of, 65
Vargas, Getúlio, 62, 67
Velázquez, Ramón J., 95–97, 231n1
Venezuela: and Bolivarian Revolution, 19–20, 95; Chávez Natural Gas Law, 19; creation of national oil company, 43–44; drop in oil prices and, 93; early policies on ownership of subsurface resources, 49; economic collapse, misuse of oil and gas revenues as cause of, 175–76; efforts to attract foreign direct investment, 20; and expropriations of private investments, 64; extra-heavy oil, as technical challenge, 28; extreme swings in oil and gas policies, 5–6; Fondespa program, PDVSA funding of, 170; and gasoline subsidies, riots in response to reduction of, 42; gas reserves, as seventh largest in world, 5; Intergovernmental Decentralization Fund (FIDES), 235–36n79; leaders' characteristics, 126, 127t; nationalizations in, 53, 63t, 64–66, 66t, 93; natural gas reserves, 1989–2016, 112–13, 113t; oil company influence in, 53; oil exports in early twentieth century, 51; oil production, 1989–2016, 111, 112t; oil reserves, 5, 110–12, 111f; Organic Hydrocarbon

GPSR Authorized Representative: Easy Access System Europe, Mustamäe tee
50, 10621 Tallinn, Estonia, gpsr.requests@easproject.com

www.ingramcontent.com/pod-product-compliance
Lightning Source LLC
Chambersburg PA
CBHW032116020426
42334CB00016B/975